HTML5 Data and Services Cookbook

Over one hundred website building recipes utilizing all the modern HTML5 features and techniques!

Gorgi Kosev

Mite Mitreski

[PACKT]
PUBLISHING

BIRMINGHAM - MUMBAI

HTML5 Data and Services Cookbook

First published: August 2013

Production Reference: 2270813

Published by Packt Publishing Ltd.
Livery Place
35 Livery Street
Birmingham B3 2PB, UK.

ISBN 978-1-78355-928-2

www.packtpub.com

Cover Image by Jarosław Blaminsky (milak6@wp.pl)

Credits

Authors

Gorgi Kosev

Mite Mitreski

Reviewers

Rade Despodovski

Santiago Martín-Cleto

Kevin Roast

Ljubomir Zivanovic

Acquisition Editor

Mary Nadar

Lead Technical Editor

Anila Vincent

Technical Editors

Dipika Gaonkar

Kapil Hemnani

Krishnaveni Haridas

Dennis John

Anita Nayak

Project Coordinator

Hardik Patel

Proofreader

Clyde Jenkins

Indexer

Rekha Nair

Graphics

Sheetal Aute

Production Coordinator

Arvindkumar Gupta

Cover Work

Arvindkumar Gupta

About the Authors

Gorgi Kosev is the lead software engineer at CreationPal, where he currently works on development of mobile and desktop HTML5 applications, as well as cloud solutions based on Node.js. He is also responsible for the selection and development of the technology stack used in CreationPal products, such as SportyPal and Appzer for Google Docs.

He completed his graduation in Electrical Engineering from University of Ss. Cyril and Methodius in 2008, and his Masters in Intelligent Information Systems in 2011. His research interests includes collaborative computer systems and machine learning.

In his spare time, he enjoys sharing code and hardware hacks with members of the local hack lab and playing the piano.

I would like to thank Svetle for her patience, support, and understanding during the restless nights and weekends spent writing this book.

Mite Mitreski works on custom enterprise application development with primary focus on Java and JVM-based solutions. He has worked as a programming course trainer in the past. He is deeply involved in activities surrounding development groups in Macedonia, where he is currently the JUG Leader of Java User Group, Macedonia. Mite has a great passion for free and open source software, open data formats, and the open web. Occasionally, he writes at his blog at `http://blog.mitemitreski.com` and can be reached on Twitter, his Twitter handle being `@mitemitreski`.

I would first like to thank my brother Stojan, who has been my inspiration throughout the years and was always someone to look up to. Thanks also to my great parents who raised me up to the person I'm today. I would also like to thank my girlfriend Marija and all the friends and colleagues at Netcetera who had to put up with me while I was away or half present. Thanks to all the reviewers, as well as the team at Packt Publishing who made the book happen. And last but not the least, thanks to W3C, the Mozilla team, Apache Software Foundation, and all of you who work on open technologies and make or keep the Internet free and open so the rest of us can enjoy it each day.

About the Reviewers

Rade Despodovski graduated from the Faculty of Electrical Engineering and Information Technologies in Skopje, Macedonia, in the year 2011 as a software engineer. He has been developing and using Microsoft technologies for eight years. In the last two years, his professional efforts have been concentrated on web technologies, in particular, using HTML5 and JavaScript. At present, his biggest interests lay in the development of multiplatform applications based on open-source technologies. Contact Rade at `rade.despodovski@gmail.com`.

Santiago Martín-Cleto started his career as a web designer for an outstanding Spanish media group in 1999. Passionate about design and code, he considers himself as a web standards and open source advocate. He has been involved in huge projects for mass media and financial corporations as a contributor to launch start-ups. As a front-end developer, he is specialized in high traffic websites performance issues.

He has also reviewed *HTML5 Enterprise Application Development*, published by Packt Publishing.

Kevin Roast is a front-end software developer with 15 years professional experience and a lifelong interest in computer science and computer graphics. He has developed software for several companies and is a founding developer at Alfresco Software Ltd. He is very excited by the prospect of the HTML5 standardization of the web and the progress of web-browser software in recent years. He was also the co-author of a book *Professional Alfresco: Practical Solutions for Enterprise Content Management, Wrox* and has been a technical reviewer on several HTML5 and software development related books.

> I would like to thank my wife for putting up with me tapping away in the evenings reviewing book chapters and to my three lovely kids Ben, Alex, and Izzy.

Ljubomir Zivanovic is a senior software developer at Netcetera and lead of Microsoft Competence Center within the company. He has over a decade of experience in the software industry, mainly focused on web stack and front-end technologies that affect UX in every way. One of the founders of the Macedonian .NET User Group, devoted husband and father, and a passionate amateur photographer.

I would like to thank both the authors of this book for giving me the opportunity to work on this book as a reviewer; it was an extraordinary experience for me. I would also like to express my gratitude to my beloved wife for giving me the support and understanding what every passionate developer can only think of.

www.PacktPub.com

Support files, eBooks, discount offers and more

You might want to visit www.PacktPub.com for support files and downloads related to your book.

Did you know that Packt offers eBook versions of every book published, with PDF and ePub files available? You can upgrade to the eBook version at www.PacktPub.com and as a print book customer, you are entitled to a discount on the eBook copy. Get in touch with us at service@packtpub.com for more details.

At www.PacktPub.com, you can also read a collection of free technical articles, sign up for a range of free newsletters and receive exclusive discounts and offers on Packt books and eBooks.

http://PacktLib.PacktPub.com

Do you need instant solutions to your IT questions? PacktLib is Packt's online digital book library. Here, you can access, read and search across Packt's entire library of books.

Why Subscribe?

- ▶ Fully searchable across every book published by Packt
- ▶ Copy and paste, print and bookmark content
- ▶ On demand and accessible via web browser

Free Access for Packt account holders

If you have an account with Packt at www.PacktPub.com, you can use this to access PacktLib today and view nine entirely free books. Simply use your login credentials for immediate access.

Table of Contents

Preface

HTML5 is everywhere, from PCs to tablets, smartphones, and even modern TV sets. The web is the most ubiquitous application platform and information medium. More recently, HTML5 has become a first-class citizen in established operating systems such as Microsoft Windows 8, Firefox OS, and Google Chrome OS.

Openness is one of the important aspects of the web. HTML5 is one of the primary ways to oppose private and proprietary solutions that force the usage of certain technologies. There is a true revolution happening in the past few years. JavaScript has risen to the lead position in web application development for both server side and client side.

In the past, it was very common to get half done scripts and poorly written JavaScript, thus the language formed a bad reputation. HTML5 features are already available and widely underused. There is a huge deal of web applications that reinvent the wheel, when there is already a feature in HTML5 that they need.

This book will get you on the fast track to learning modern HTML5 features. By the end of the book, you should have a solid understanding of JavaScript in the browser and server. On top of that, you will end up creating cool, little applications using new HTML5 technologies, and learn how to adapt your existing applications to use these great new features.

What this book covers

Chapter 1, *Display of Textual Data*, covers what you need to know about displaying text in HTML5. This includes formatting numbers, displaying math formulas, and measurements. Additionally, there are sections on displaying tabular data and rendering Markdown that show some of the everyday development functionality.

Chapter 2, *Display of Graphical Data*, begins by covering the creation of charts using the Flot chart library, as well as the more modern data-driven D3.js. Displaying maps with routes and markers is also covered in this chapter.

Chapter 3, *Animated Data Display*, explores the creation of animated and interactive visualizations. Most of the chapter visualization are based on `D3.js`, but there are also examples that start from scratch or use technology such as the notifications API.

Chapter 4, *Using HTML5 Input Components*, begins by covering the use of simple text input elements, and moves to the new input types that are added by HTML5. It also covers the use of the new attributes, as well as making more advanced input that uses geolocation or drag-and-drop areas.

Chapter 5, *Custom Input Components*, continues with the topics from the preceding chapter, with the main focus shifting to the creation of custom controls that add new functionality, or mimic components available in the desktop applications. This chapter explains how to create controls, such as menus, dialogs, list selection, and rich-text input.

Chapter 6, *Data Validation*, introduces the HTML5 way of handling form validation. The chapter will cover validation of text and numbers, built-in validations for e-mail and numbers. Furthermore, it also covers server-side validation with Node.js, and shows how to combine client and server-side validation.

Chapter 7, *Data Serialization*, provides an in-depth look into the creation of JSON, base64, and XML from client-side JavaScript, as well as the reverse process of making the JavaScript objects from the formats.

Chapter 8, *Communicating with Servers*, gets you started with Node.js and the creation of REST API's. The chapter also contains detailed information on how to make HTTP calls from pure JavaScript, how to handle binary files, as well as communication security.

Chapter 9, *Client-side Templates*, introduces the use of the popular client-side template languages Handlebars, EJS, and Jade. It covers and compares the basic uses of these languages, as well as their more advanced features, such as partials, filters, and mixins.

Chapter 10, *Data Binding Frameworks*, gets you started with two different types of web frameworks. On the one hand we have Angular, a powerful representative of the many different client-side MVC frameworks, and on the other hand we have Meteor, a reactive framework that cuts down the development time in certain domains.

Chapter 11, *Data Storage*, explores the new client-side storage APIs available in HTML5, as well as the new APIs for working with files. These new features enable us to persist data beyond page refresh, and save client-side information that will not be transferred back and forth on each request.

Chapter 12, *Multimedia*, covers some of the ways for playing video and audio files in the browser, something that was done by external plugins in the past.

Appendix A, Installing Node.js and Using npm, gives a simple introduction on installing Node.js and using its package manager npm.

Appendix B, Community and Resources, contains a short history and references to the main organizations that empower the development of HTML5.

What you need for this book

All you need to get started is a modern browser, such as Firefox, Chrome, Safari, Opera, or Internet Explorer 9, a simple text editor such as Notepad++, Emacs, or Vim, and an Internet connection.

In *Chapter 7, Data Serialization* and later chapters, you will also need to install Node.js to try out some of the recipes. The installation process is covered in *Appendix A, Installing Node.js and Using npm*.

Who this book is for

This book is for programmers who already have used JavaScript in one way or the other. It's for people who work with a lot of backend code, and want to get up to speed with the world of HTML5 and JavaScript. It's for people who have used copy/paste to patch up a part of a page and want to know more about how things work in the background. It's for JavaScript developers who would like to update their knowledge with new techniques and capabilities made possible with HTML5.

The book is for both beginners and seasoned developers, assuming that you will have some experience in HTML, JavaScript, and jQuery already, but not necessary an in-depth knowledge.

Conventions

In this book, you will find a number of styles of text that distinguish among different kinds of information. Here are some examples of these styles, and an explanation of their meaning.

Code words in text are shown as follows: "The `d3.behavior.zoom()` method enables us to add automatic zoom functionality to our `projection` type with the given scale and range of zoom in `scaleExtent`."

A block of code is set as follows:

```
<!DOCTYPE HTML>
<html>
  <head>
    <title>Chart example</title>
  </head>
  <body>
    <div id="chart" style="height:200px;
      width:800px;"></div>
```

```html
  <script src="http://ajax.googleapis.com/ajax/libs/
    jquery/1.8.2/jquery.min.js"></script>
  <script src="flot/jquery.flot.js"></script>
  <script src="flot/jquery.flot.navigate.js"></script>
  <script type="text/javascript" src=
    "example.js"></script>
</body>
</html>
```

When we wish to draw your attention to a particular part of a code block, the relevant lines or items are set in bold:

```css
#carousel {
  perspective: 500px;
  -webkit-perspective: 500px;
  position:relative; display:inline-block;
  overflow:hidden;
}
```

Any command-line input or output is written as follows:

```
Object:
  color: "#00cc00"
  data: Array[50]
  name: "one"
```

New terms and **important words** are shown in bold. Words that you see on the screen, in menus or dialog boxes for example, appear in the text like this: "Also we can add an attribute data-placeholder that will contain default text, such as **Occupation** in our example. If this is not specified, it will default to **Select Some Option** for single select."

[📝   Warnings or important notes appear in a box like this.]

[💡   Tips and tricks appear like this.]

Reader feedback

Feedback from our readers is always welcome. Let us know what you think about this book—what you liked or may have disliked. Reader feedback is important for us to develop titles that you really find useful.

To send us general feedback, simply send an e-mail to feedback@packtpub.com, and mention the book title via the subject of your message.

If there is a topic in which you have expertise, and you are interested in either writing or contributing to a book, see our author guide on www.packtpub.com/authors.

Customer support

Now that you are the proud owner of a Packt book, we have a number of things to help you to get the most from your purchase.

Downloading the example code

You can download the example code files for all Packt books you have purchased from your account at http://www.packtpub.com. If you purchased this book elsewhere, you can visit http://www.packtpub.com/support and register to have the files e-mailed directly to you.

Errata

Although we have taken every care to ensure the accuracy of our content, mistakes do happen. If you find a mistake in one of our books—maybe a mistake in the text or the code—we would be grateful if you would report this to us. By doing so, you can save other readers from frustration, and help us improve subsequent versions of this book. If you find any errata, please report them by visiting http://www.packtpub.com/submit-errata, selecting your book, clicking on the **errata submission form** link, and entering the details of your errata. Once your errata are verified, your submission will be accepted and the errata will be uploaded on our website, or added to any list of existing errata, under the Errata section of that title. Any existing errata can be viewed by selecting your title from http://www.packtpub.com/support.

Piracy

Piracy of copyright material on the Internet is an ongoing problem across all media. At Packt, we take the protection of our copyright and licenses very seriously. If you come across any illegal copies of our works, in any form, on the Internet, please provide us with the location address or website name immediately so that we can pursue a remedy.

Please contact us at copyright@packtpub.com with a link to the suspected pirated material.

We appreciate your help in protecting our authors, and our ability to bring you valuable content.

Questions

You can contact us at questions@packtpub.com if you are having a problem with any aspect of the book, and we will do our best to address it.

1
Display of Textual Data

In this chapter, we're going to cover the following topics:

- ► Rounding numbers for display
- ► Padding numbers
- ► Displaying metric and imperial measurements
- ► Displaying formatted dates in the user's time zone
- ► Displaying the dynamic time that has elapsed
- ► Displaying Math
- ► Creating an endless scrolling list
- ► Creating a sortable paginated table
- ► Creating multiple-choice filters
- ► Creating range filters
- ► Creating combined complex filters
- ► Displaying code in HTML
- ► Rendering Markdown
- ► Autoupdating fields

Introduction

The most common task related to web application development is the displaying of text. This chapter will cover some of the issues programmers face when displaying data in browsers, and will explain how to tackle the problems in a simple yet effective way, giving several different options for the programmer from which to choose. These examples will contain the rendering of markup or the conversion of other datatypes into plain text.

Rounding numbers for display

The second, most common datatype used in applications after text is numbers. There are many different ways of working with numbers, and we will take a look at some of these ways when a given precision is required. The first obvious option is to use the JavaScript `Number` object wrapper to work with numerical values.

Getting ready

The `Number` object contains the `toFixed([digits])` method that can be used to display numbers; here the `digits` parameter can have a value between 0 and 20. The number will either get rounded automatically if needed, or the number will get padded with additional zeros if necessary. Ok, so let's see it in action.

How to do it...

Perform the following steps do demonstrate working with the `Number` object:

1. First, we'll create a list of numbers; note that the numbers have been picked intentionally to illustrate some of the characteristics of the functions:

```
var listOfNumbers=
        [1.551, 1.556, 1.5444, 1.5454, 1.5464, 1.615, 1.616, 1.4,
1.446,1.45];
```

2. Iterate the list and display numbers using the `.toFixed()` method with the `digits` parameter's values 0, 1, and 2 accordingly:

```
for (var i = 0; i < listOfNumbers.length; i++) {
        var number = listOfNumbers[i];
            // iterate over all of the numbers and write to output
all the value
        document.write(number + "---"
                    + number.toFixed(2) + "---"
                    + number.toFixed(1) + "---"
                    + number.toFixed() + "<br />");
    };
```

How it works...

The result retrieved from executing the code will print out the numbers with their respective `toFixed` representation, which should be straightforward.

Let's take a look at some of the characteristic values:

- `1.616.toFixed(2)` will return `1.62`
- `1.4.toFixed(2)` will return `1.40` as expected, adding a trailing zero
- `1.5454.toFixed()` will return `2`, because the default value for `toFixed()` is `0`; this means that no decimal points, and additionally the `0.5` segment is rounded to `1` so the ceiling value is used here
- `1.615.toFixed(2)` will either return `1.61`, ignoring the `0.005` segment, or the floor value will be used

The `toFixed()` method works mostly as expected so long as we don't need the higher precision or are only using it to display numbers where the type of rounding is not mission critical.

Additionally, we cannot rely on `toFixed()` when we need rounding in cases where we have numbers such as **1.446** and others that fall in the same category; calling `1.446.toFixed(1)` would result in inconsistent and unpredictable results.

There's more...

There are various ways to solve this. The quick and dirty solution would be to redefine the `Number.prototype.toFixed()` function, but we encourage you to not do so, as doing this may have side effects that are not apparent. Any redefinition of the functions from the built-in objects is considered an anti-pattern if it is not absolutely essential. The problem arises if another library or a piece of code is using the same function. The other library might expect our redefined function to work a certain way. These types of redefinitions are hard to track; even if we are to add a function instead of redefining it, someone else might do the same thing. For example, say we decided to add some function to the `Number` object:

```
Number.prototype.theFunction = function(arg1,arg2){}
```

There are no guarantees that someone else has not already added `theFunction` to the `Number` object. We could do additional checks to verify if the function already exists, but we cannot be sure if it does what we want it to do.

Instead, using a utility function for achieving consistent data would be a better option.

One way of tackling the problem is to first multiply the number with `10 ^ digits` and then call the `Math.round(number)` method on the result, or you can call `Math.ceil(number)`. For example, if you need to have the value rounded upwards to the nearest integer, use the following:

```
function round(number, digits) {
    if(typeof digits === "undefined" || digits < 0){
      digits = 0;
    }
    var power = Math.pow(10, digits),
```

```
        fixed = (Math.round(number * power) / power).toString();
        return fixed;
    };
```

Now, as the number gets multiplied with `10 ^ digits` and then gets rounded, we do not observe the problems with `toFixed()`. Note that this method has a different behavior from `toFixed()` not just in the way of how rounding is being handled, but also the addition of trailing zeroes.

A different option would be to use an arbitrary precision library such as Big.js if precision is crucial (`https://github.com/MikeMcl/big.js`).

Padding numbers

We are sometimes faced with the need to pad numbers to a certain range. For example, suppose we want to display a number in five possible digits, such as `00042`. One obvious solution would be to use the iterative approach and prepend characters, but there are a few cleaner solutions.

Getting ready

First, we need to take a look at some of the functions that we are going to use. Let's take a look at the `Array.join(separator)` method that can be applied to create joined text from a list of elements:

```
new Array('life','is','life').join('*')
```

This will result in `"life*is*life"` that shows fairly simple elements that are joined with a given separator. Another method that is of interest is `Array.slice(begin[, end])` that returns a copy of a portion of an array. For our use, we are only interested in the `begin` parameter that can have both positive and negative values. If we use a positive value, it means that this will be the starting index for the slice using zero-based indexing; for example, consider the following line of code:

```
new Array('a','b','c','d','e','f','g').slice(4);
```

The preceding line of code will return an array with the elements `'e'`, `'f'`, and `'g'`.

If, on the other hand, using a negative value for the `begin` element indicates an offset from the end of the array, consider the same example using a negative value as follows:

```
new Array('a','b','c','d','e','f','g').slice(-3);
```

The result would be `'e'`, `'f'`, `'g'`, as we are slicing from the end.

How to do it...

Let's get back to our problem: how do we create a clean solution for prepending zeros to a number? For an iterative solution, we create a method that accepts the number, the size of the formatted result, and the character that will be used for padding; let's take `'0'` for example:

```
function iterativeSolution(number,size,character) {
    var strNumber = number.toString(),
     len = strNumber.length,

     prefix = '';
    for (var i=size-len;i>0;i--) {
       prefix += character;
    }
  return prefix + strNumber;
}
```

Here we converted the number to a string in order to get the length of its representation; afterwards, we simply create `prefix` that will have the `size-len` characters of the `character` variable, and just return the resulting `prefix + strNumber` that is the string representation for that number.

You may notice that in the case where `size` is smaller than `len`, the original number is returned, and this should probably be changed in order to have the function working for that corner case.

Another way would be to use the `Array.slice()` method to achieve similar results:

```
function sliceExample(number,prefix){
    return (prefix+number).slice(-prefix.length);
}
sliceExample(42,"00000");
```

This will just prepend a prefix to a number and slice off the extra `'0'` counting from the end, making the solution a lot cleaner and, additionally, enabling us to be more flexible around what will be part of the prefix. The downside of this is that we are manually constructing the prefix that will be part of the method call `sliceExample(42,"00000")`. In order to make this process automatic, we can make use of `Array.join`:

```
function padNumber(number,size,character){
    var prefix = new Array(1 + size).join(character);
```

We create an array of the expected `size + 1` as on joining, we'll get the total array `size-1` `joined elements`. This will construct the prefix with the expected size, and the other part will remain the same:

```
    return (prefix + number).slice(-prefix.length);
  }
```

A sample method call will be `padNumber(42,5,'0');` this will not have the flexibility of the previous method, but it will be a lot simpler to use in larger numbers.

How it works...

The recipe is fairly straightforward, but an important thing to note is the functional approach. If there is one thing to take with you from this recipe, it is that the iterative solution is not always the best. When it comes to JavaScript, there are usually a few other ways to complete the task that you have; they are not always *that* straightforward and sometimes not even faster, but they can be much cleaner.

There's more...

If, for some reason, we are padding numbers very often, it might make sense to add the function into the `Number` object and remove the `input` parameter number with the `this` keyword:

```
Number.prototype.pad=function(size,character){
    //same functionality here
}
```

As the function is now part of every `Number` object, we can use it directly from any number; let's take the following example:

```
3.4.pad(5,'#');
```

Additionally, if the `'.'` character should not be included in the calculation of the padding, we could add an additional check that would reduce the size of the prefix.

> Note that in the *Rounding numbers for display* recipe, we explained why adding functions to a standard object is a hack that can backfire at us.

Displaying metric and imperial measurements

Websites that deal with calculations and measurements often need to solve the problem of using both metric and imperial units of measurement. This recipe will demonstrate a data-driven approach to dealing with unit conversions. As this is an HTML5 book, the solution will be implemented on the client side rather than on the server side.

We're going to implement a client-side, "ideal weight" calculator that supports metric and imperial measurements. This time, we're going to create a more general and elegant data-driven solution that utilizes modern HTML5 capabilities, such as data attributes. The goal is to abstract away the messy and error-prone conversion as much as possible.

Getting ready

The formula for calculating the body mass index (BMI) is as follows:

BMI = (Weight in kilograms / (height in meters x height in meters))

We're going to use BMI = 22 to calculate the "ideal weight".

How to do it...

1. Create the following HTML page:

```
<!DOCTYPE HTML>
<html>
    <head>
        <title>BMI Units</title>
    </head>
    <body>
        <label>Unit system</label>
        <select id="unit">
            <option selected value="height=m,cm 0;weight=kg
1;distance=km 1">Metric</option>
            <option value="height=ft,inch 0;weight=lbs
0;distance=mi 1">Imperial</option>
        </select><br>

        <label>Height</label>
        <span data-measurement="height" id="height">
            <input data-value-display type="text" id="height"
class="calc">
            <span data-unit-display></span>
            <input data-value-display type="text" id="height"
class="calc">
            <span data-unit-display></span>
        </span>
        <br>
        <label>Ideal Weight</label>
        <span data-measurement="weight" id="weight">
            <span data-value-display type="text">0</span>
            <span data-unit-display></span>
```

```
        </span> <br>

        <script src="http://ajax.googleapis.com/ajax/libs/
jquery/1.8.2/jquery.min.js"></script>
            <script type="text/javascript" src="unitval.js"></script>
            <script type="text/javascript" src="example.js"></script>
            </script>
        </body>
</html>
```

This page looks very much like the regular page we would make for a BMI-based ideal weight calculator. The main differences are as follows:

- We have an imperial/metric selection input
- We also have additional custom data attributes to give special meanings to the HTML fields
- We use `data-measurement` to denote the kind of measurement that the element will display (for example, either the weight or the height)
- We use `data-display-unit` and `data-display-value` to denote fields that display unit strings and values of the measurement respectively

2. Create a file named `example.js` with the following code:

```
(function() {
    // Setup unitval
    $.unitval({
        weight: {
            "lbs": 0.453592, // kg
            "kg" : 1 // kg
        },
        height: {
            "ft"  : 0.3048, // m
            "inch": 0.0254, // m
            "m"   : 1, // m
            "cm"  : 0.01, // m
        }
    });
    $("#unit").change(function() {
        var measurementUnits = $(this).val().split(';').
map(function(u) {
            var type_unitround = u.split('='),
                unitround = type_unitround[1].split(' ');
            return {
                type: type_unitround[0],
                units: unitround[0].split(','),
```

```
                 round: unitround[1]
           };
      });
      // Setup units for measurements.
      $('body').unitval(measurementUnits);
   });

   $("#unit").trigger("change");

   $('#height').on('keyup change',function() {
      var height = $('#height').unitval(), bmi = 22;
      var idealWeight = bmi * height * height;
      $("#weight").unitval(idealWeight);
   })`;


}
```

The first part of the code configures a jQuery plugin called `unitval`, with the conversion factors for the measurements and units that we are going to use (weight and height).

The second part sets the measurement units for the document by reading the specification from the `select` field. It specifies an array of measurements, each having the following:

- A type string, for example `"height"`
- A list of units, for example `["ft", "inch"]`
- The number of decimals to use for the last unit

The third part is a regular calculator that is written almost exactly as it would be written if there were no unit conversions. The only exception is that values are taken from the elements that have the `data-measurement` attribute using the jQuery plugin named `$.unitval`.

3. We're going to write a generic unit converter. It will need two functions: one that will convert user-displayed (input) data to standard international (SI) measurement units, and another to convert it back from SI units to user-friendly display units. Our converter will support using multiple units at the same time. When converting from input, the first argument is the measurement type (for example, distance), the second is an array of value-unit pairs (for example, `[[5, 'km'], [300,'m']]`), a single pair (for example `[5,'km']`), or simply the value (for example `5`).

4. If the second parameter is a simple value, we're going to accept a third one containing the unit (for example `'km'`). The output is always a simple SI value.

    When converting a value to the desired output units, we specify the units as an array, for example, as either `['km', 'm']` or as a single unit. We also specify rounding decimals for the last unit. Our output is an array of converted values.

Conversion is done using the values in the `Factors` object. This object contains a property for every measurement name that we're going to use. Each such property is an object with the available units for that measurement as properties, and their SI factors as values. Look in the following in `example.js` for an example.

5. The source code of the jQuery plugin, `unitval.js`, is as follows:

```
(function() {
    var Factors = {};
    var Convert = window.Convert = {
        fromInput: function(measurement, valunits, unit) {
            valunits = unit ? [[valunits, unit]] // 3 arguments
                : valunits instanceof Array && valunits[0]
instanceof Array ? valunits
                : [valunits]; // [val, unit] array

            var sivalues = valunits.map(function(valunit) { //
convert each to SI
                return valunit[0] * Factors[measurement]
[valunit[1]];
            });
            // sivalues.sum():
            return sivalues.reduce(function(a, e) { return a + e;
});
        },
        toOutput: function(measurement, val, units, round) {
            units = units instanceof Array ? units : [units];
            var reduced = val;
            return units.map(function(unit, index) {
                var isLast = index == units.length - 1,
                    factor = Factors[measurement][unit];
                var showValue = reduced / factor;
                if (isLast && (typeof(round) != 'undefined'))
                    showValue = showValue.toFixed(round) - 0;
                else if (!isLast) showValue = Math.
floor(showValue);
                reduced -= showValue * factor;
                return showValue;
            });
        }
    };
    $.unitval = function(fac) {
        Factors = fac;
    }
    // Uses .val() in input/textarea and .text() in other fields.
    var uval = function() {
```

```
        return ['input','textarea'].indexOf(this[0].tagName.
toLowerCase()) < 0 ?
                this.text.apply(this, arguments) : this.val.
apply(this, arguments);
    }
```

6. Our generic convertor is useful, but not very convenient or user friendly; we still have to do all the conversions manually. To avoid this, we're going to put data attributes on our elements, denoting the measurements that they display. Inside them, we're going to put separate elements for displaying the value(s) and unit(s). When we set the measurement units, the function `setMeasurementUnits` will set them on every element that has this data attribute. Furthermore, it will also adjust the inner value and unit elements accordingly:

```
// Sets the measurement units within a specific element.
// @param measurements An array in the format
[{type:"measurement", units: ["unit", ...], round:N}]
// for example [{type:"height", units:["ft","inch"], round:0}]
    var setMeasurementUnits = function(measurements) {
        var $this = this;
        measurements.forEach(function(measurement) {
            var holders = $this.find('[data-
measurement="'+measurement.type+'"]');
            var unconverted = holders.map(function() { return
$(this).unitval(); })
            holders.attr('data-round', measurement.round);
            holders.find('[data-value-display]').
each(function(index) {
                if (index < measurement.units.length)
                    $(this).show().attr('data-unit', measurement.
units[index]);
                else $(this).hide();
            });
            holders.find('[data-unit-display]').
each(function(index) {
                if (index < measurement.units.length)
                    $(this).show().html(measurement.units[index]);
                else $(this).hide();
            });

            holders.each(function(index) { $(this).
unitval(unconverted[index]); });
        });
    };
```

7. As every element knows its measurement and units, we can now simply put SI values inside them and have them display converted values. To do this, we'll write `unitval`. It allows us to set and get "united" values, or set unit options on elements that have the `data-measurement` property:

```
$.fn.unitval = function(value) {
    if (value instanceof Array) {
        setMeasurementUnits.apply(this, arguments);
    }
    else if (typeof(value) == 'undefined') {
        // Read value from element
        var first       = this.eq(0),
            measurement = first.attr('data-measurement'),
            displays    = first.find('[data-value-
display]:visible'),
            // Get units of visible holders.
            valunits = displays.toArray().map(function(el) {
                return [uval.call($(el)), $(el).attr('data-
unit')] });
        // Convert them from input
        return Convert.fromInput(measurement, valunits);
    }
    else if (!isNaN(value)) {
        // Write value to elements
        this.each(function() {
            var measurement   = $(this).attr('data-
measurement'),
                round         = $(this).attr('data-round'),
                displays      = $(this).find('[data-value-
display]:visible'),
                units         = displays.map(function() {
                    return $(this).attr('data-unit');
}).toArray();
    var values = Convert.toOutput(measurement, value, units, round);
            displays.each(function(index) { uval.call($(this),
values[index]); });
        });
    }
}());
```

This plugin will be explained in the next section.

How it works...

HTML elements have no notion of measurement units. To support unit conversion, we added our own data attributes. These allow us to give a special meaning to certain elements—the specifics of which are then decided by our own code.

Our convention is that an element with a `data-measurement` attribute will be used to display values and units for the specified measurement. For example, a field with the `data-measurement="weight"` attribute will be used to display weight.

This element contains two types of subelements. The first type has a `data-display-value` attribute, and displays the value of the measurement (always a number). The second type has a `data-display-unit` attribute, and displays the unit of the measurement (for example, `"kg"`). For measurements expressed in multiple units (for example, height can be expressed in the form of "5 ft 3 inch"), we can use multiple fields of both types.

When we change our unit system, `setMeasurementUnits` adds additional data attributes to the following elements:

- ▶ `data-round` attributes are attached to `data-measurement` elements
- ▶ `data-unit attributes` containing the appropriate unit is added to the `data-display-value` elements
- ▶ `data-display-unit` elements are filled with the appropriate units

As a result, `$.unitval()` knows both the values and units displayed on every measurement element on our page. The function reads and converts the measurement to SI before returning it. We do all our calculations using the SI units. Finally, when calling `$.unitval(si_value)`, our value is automatically converted to the appropriate units before display.

This system minimizes the amount of error-prone unit conversion code by recognizing that conversions are only really needed when reading user input and displaying output. Additionally, the data-driven approach allows us to omit conversions entirely from our code and focus on our application logic.

Displaying formatted dates in the user's time zone

In this recipe, we will learn how to format the user's date in their local time zone and display it; additionally, we are going to see how dates are used and represented in JavaScript. The best way to do this is to have the user pick the time zone in which they would like the dates to be displayed, but unfortunately, this is rarely an option.

Getting ready

Just like most programming languages, JavaScript uses Unix time. This is actually a system for representing a given instance of time, for how many seconds or, in JavaScript's case, milliseconds have passed since midnight January 1, 1970 in Universal Coordinated Time, commonly known as UTC.

> Some fun trivia regarding UTC: the abbreviation is a compromise between the French version Temps Universel Coordonné, which would be TUC, and the English version Coordinated Universal Time, which would be CUT (http://en.wikipedia.org/wiki/Coordinated_Universal_Time#Abbreviation).

This number is actually not fully compliant with UTC, nor does it account for the various atypical situations such as leap seconds, but this is acceptable in most cases.

In JavaScript, we have the Date object that can be constructed in different ways:

```
new Date() // uses local time
new Date(someNumber) //create date with milliseconds since epoch
new Date(dateString) // create date from input string representation
new Date(year, month, day [, hour, minute, second, millisecond])
```

> Note that creating a date from a string representation can have different behaviors in various browsers, and that the same thing applies for the Date.parse method that parses a string into a date.

During construction, if you supply some of the arguments and leave out the optional ones, they get defaulted to zero. And one other thing to note is that months in JavaScript are zero based while days are not.

> Using the JavaScript Date object as a function rather than as a constructor, with new Date(...), will result in your getting a string representation of that date and not getting the Date object, like you would expect in most of the other JavaScript objects.

How to do it...

1. The first thing you need to do is to create the Date object:

   ```
   var endOfTheWorld= new Date(1355270400000);
   ```

2. Then, just use the localized date and time representation:

```
document.writeln(endOfTheWorld.toLocaleDateString());
document.writeln(endOfTheWorld.toLocaleTimeString());
```

3. If you need to know the offset in hours in the user's time zone from UTC, you can use the following code:

```
var offset = - new Date().getTimezoneOffset()/60;
```

4. This offset variable represents the number of hours from the local user's time zone to UTC. The minus sign here reverts the logic for the date; this means that the difference will be from date to UTC instead of the original from UTC to date.

How it works...

What we can usually do is return the millisecond representation from the server side and have the number formatted in the local time zone. So let's say that our API returned us the milliseconds `1355270400000` that is actually **12.12.2012**, which is also known as the end-of-the-world date.

The creation of the date is as follows:

```
var endOfTheWorld= new Date(1355270400000);
```

When printing in the local string, there are few available options; one of them is `toLocaleDateString`:

```
endOfTheWorld.toLocaleDateString()
```

This method uses the underlying operation system to get the formatting convention. For example, in the U.S. the format is month/day/year while in other countries it is day/month/year. For our case, the end of the world is on "Wednesday, December 12, 2012". You could also manually construct the printed date using the appropriate `getX` methods.

There is also a method of printing out the local time called `toLocaleTimeString` that can be used on our end-of-the-world date. Because this method also uses the operating system's local time for us, it is 01:00:00, because we are in the UTC+1 time zone. For us, this means that we have one extra hour to live; or maybe not?

In order to get the offset for the local user, there is a method in the `Date` object called `getTimezoneOffset()` that returns the time zone offset from the date to UTC in minutes. The problem is that there is no such method for hours and, additionally, it is contraintuitive as we usually want to know the difference from UTC to the given date.

There's more...

If working with dates is something common that you need for your application, it makes sense to use a library, such as **Moment.js** (http://momentjs.com/).

Moment.js provides support for internationalization and the more advanced manipulation of dates. For example, removing 10 days from the current date can simply be accomplished with the following code:

```
moment().subtract('days', 10).calendar();
```

For getting the time from today's start of day, use the following code:

```
moment().startOf('day').fromNow();
```

Displaying the dynamic time that has elapsed

It is very common on every major site to have these great counters that display timestamps on various elements on the page. For example, this would be "you opened this page 3 hours ago" or "commented 2 minutes ago". That is why, this feature, besides the name "dynamic time elapsed", is also known as "time ago".

Getting ready

We are going to use a jQuery plugin called **timeago** that has especially been designed for this purpose that can be retrieved from http://timeago.yarp.com/.

How to do it...

We will create a simple page where we will display the passed time by performing the following steps:

1. Because `timeago` is a jQuery plugin, we first need to include jQuery and then add the `timeago` plugin:

   ```
   <script src="http://ajax.googleapis.com/ajax/libs/jquery/1.8.2/
   jquery.min.js">
   </script>
   <script src="jquery.timeago.js" type="text/javascript"></script>
   ```

2. Just as an example, add the following HTML:

```
        <p> Debian was first announced <abbr class='timeago'
title="1993-08-16T00:00:00Z">16 August 1993</abbr>
        </p>
        <p> You opened this page <span class='page-opened' /> </
p>
        <p> This is done use the time element
            <time datetime="2012-12-12 20:09-0700">8:09pm on
December 12th, 2012</time>
        </p>
```

3. This will enable us to get an overview of the basic features provided by the `timeago` plugin. Afterwards, let's add the following JavaScript:

```
$(document).ready(function() {
        jQuery.timeago.settings.allowFuture = true;
        var now= new Date();
        $(".timeago").timeago();
        $(".page-opened").text( $.timeago(now));
        $("time").timeago();
        //$("some-future-date") $.timeago(new
Date(999999999999));
    });
```

And that is it; you now have a fully working time example that will calculate the time since a given date and update it, and additionally, the second part selected with `page-opened` will be autoupdated as the user spends more time on the page.

How it works...

The first thing you might be wondering is about the `abbr` and `time` tags. The first one, in actuality, is a representation of "abbreviation" and optionally provides a full description for it. If the full description is present, the `title` attribute must contain this full description and nothing else. The full description is usually presented as a tool tip in the browsers, but this is a noting standard. Why have we picked the `abbr` tag to display time? Well, there is the new HTML5 time element named `time` that had some controversies surrounding it, as it was pulled from the spec but then gotten back. This element is more semantically correct and, additionally, represents the date in a machine-readable format that can be used by browsers to enable something like the "add to calendar" feature. The rationale for the use of the `abbr` element is only supported for older browsers, but this becomes more and more irrelevant as time passes. Currently, most modern browsers for desktops and mobiles provide support for the semantically correct `time` element—even IE 9+ has support for it.

The rest of the HTML consists of standard, well-known tags and a few markers, such as different CSS classes added in order to later select those elements.

Let's take a look at the JavaScript; first we use the standard jQuery document-ready function:

```
$(document).ready(function() {
```

Afterwards, we set the setting for `allowFuture` to `true` to enable the `timeago` plugin to work with future dates, as this has not been set by default:

```
jQuery.timeago.settings.allowFuture = true;
```

If `timeago` is applied directly on the selected `abbr` or `time` elements, there is no need for us to do anything else as the calculations are done automatically:

```
$(".timeago").timeago();
$("time").timeago();
```

You can also notice that we can get the text for a given date directly from JavaScript, and work with it in whatever way we see fit:

```
$(".page-opened").text( $.timeago(now) );
```

There's more...

There are a few questions that come in mind when working on internationalized and localized applications. One of them is time zone support that `timeago` handles automatically. The only thing we need to make sure of is that our timestamps follow the **ISO 8601** (http://en.wikipedia.org/wiki/ISO_8601) time format and have a full time zone designator (http://en.wikipedia.org/wiki/ISO_8601#Time_zone_designators). The other issue that often comes up is language support, but we are mostly covered in that area as there are localized versions of the plugin for many languages, and you can even create your own version and contribute it to the community. To do this, you can use the code hosted on https://github.com/rmm5t/jquery-timeago/tree/master/locales.

There are a few other implementations that perform a similar job, like for example, *pretty date* by *John Resig* available at his blog at http://ejohn.org/blog/javascript-pretty-date/.

Displaying Math

When it comes to technical writing, we often want to display mathematical formulas inside the page. In the past, this was done by creating an image on the server from some kind of markup, or even manually creating an image with an external program. Since the introduction of MathML, this is no longer needed; this thereby saves us time, which was otherwise spent on sorting out layout issues, and enables native support from the browsers for the display of equations. At the time of writing this book, not all of the major browsers support MathML, even though the spec for most of the features has been available for a few years now.

$$\pi = 3 + \cfrac{1}{7 + \cfrac{1}{15 + \cfrac{1}{1 + \cfrac{1}{292 + \cfrac{1}{1 + \cfrac{1}{1 + \cfrac{1}{1 + \cfrac{1}{1 + \ddots}}}}}}}}$$

Getting ready

Mathematical Markup Language (**MathML**) is a standardized way for an application to describe a formula, and is intended not only to enable integration for the Web, but also to be used in other applications.

There is a list of software that uses MathML maintained by the W3C; it can be found at `http://www.w3.org/Math/Software/`. Few revisions of the specification are done from the working group (`http://www.w3.org/Math/`), with the latest being number 3 (`http://www.w3.org/TR/MathML3/`).

HTML5 adds the support for embedding MathML documents inside HTML.

What we are going to do in this recipe is describe a formula, as shown in the previous continued fraction of Pi, with MathML where we have an example of a different representation of the number π.

How to do it...

1. We will be using a library called `MathJax` that can either be retrieved from the author's CDN or downloaded separately and included in the project.

```
<script type="text/javascript"
      src="http://cdn.mathjax.org/mathjax/latest/MathJax.
js?config=TeX-AMS-MML_HTMLorMML">
 </script>
```

2. We can proceed by adding the MathML example as follows:

```
<math xmlns="http://www.w3.org/1998/Math/MathML">
      <mrow>
          <mi>π</mi>
      <mo>=</mo>
      <mfrac>
         <mstyle scriptlevel="0">
           <mn>3</mn>
         </mstyle>
         <mstyle scriptlevel="0">
```

```
            <mrow>
              <mn>7</mn>
              <mo>+</mo>
              <mfrac numalign="left">
                <mstyle scriptlevel="0">
                  <msup><mn>1</mn></msup>
                </mstyle>
              </mfrac>
            </mrow>
          </mstyle>
        </mfrac>
      </mrow>
    </math>
```

The basics on what the elements mean will be explained later, but you can notice that the example becomes really big after very few nesting levels and is hard to read. This is because MathML was never intended to be created manually, but to be used instead as a format by some application.

3. So what are the real simple options for us if we want to enable human-editable markup? Well, the simplest possible option is something called ASCIIMath; in order to enable it, we need to change the config parameter in the request:

```
<script type="text/javascript" src="http://cdn.mathjax.org/
mathjax/latest/MathJax.js?config=AM_HTMLorMML-full"> </script>
```

We generally use the version with all the possible input formats and rendering options, but that way we would have a problem with the size of the JavaScript file.

So how much simpler is the use of ASCIIMath? Well, the expression we explained previously can be displayed with a single line:

```
<p>
        `π = 3+1/(7+1/(15+1/(1+1/...)))`
</p>
```

Note that the the expression is encompassed in a ` character, which is also known as the Grave accent.

How it works...

The use of raw MathML without the `MathJax` library will not work on most browsers, but with the library, the output is automatically rendered either as an SVG or as a standard image. In the MathML example, we use XML nesting to designate where the elements will be contained, and elements such as `mrow` and `mfrac` are all defined in the MathML namespace (`http://www.w3.org/1998/Math/MathML`) with a root element called `math`. Although the concept is very simple, in practice it is extremely hard to create expressions like this one without the help of external software.

An additional downside to MathML is the fact that it is not fully supported in all browsers.

`ASCIIMath`, on the other hand, is very simple to use and very intuitive; basically, anything enclosed in "`" or the Grave accent character will get rendered to HTML and CSS or any other rendering method that has been configured.

There's more...

The `ASCIIMath` method is very simple and extremely popular with major websites such as Khan Academy (`https://www.khanacademy.org/`) and Math StackExchange (`http://math.stackexchange.com/`). If you are interested to get more details on how `ASCIIMath` can be used, you can get more info on its official web page at `http://www1.chapman.edu/~jipsen/mathml/asciimath.html`. Using `MathJax` you can also render other markup format languages such as Tex and Latex.

> Tex is a typesetting format made by *Donald Knuth* for the purpose of helping him with the writing of his famous books. Latex, on the other hand, is a document markup that uses Tex as the typesetting format. More information on them can be found at `http://en.wikipedia.org/wiki/TeX` and `http://www.latex-project.org/`.

Creating an endless scrolling list

Endless scrolling lists were popularized by social networking websites, such as Facebook and Twitter. Their goal is to create the illusion that the entire available content has already been loaded. Additionally, with this technique, interruptions to the normal scrolling that are caused by the user trying to find the button for the next page are avoided.

At the same time, we would also want to avoid unnecessary waste of bandwidth; this means that loading the whole set of data at once is not an option.

The solution is to monitor the user's scrolling and detect the approach at the bottom of the page. When the user is sufficiently close to the bottom, we can automatically load the next page of content by appending it to the end of the currently shown content.

Getting ready

You must already have a service that provides the content on a page-by-page basis. This example works without such a service by default, but to make it fully functional, an actual HTTP server is needed in order for the Ajax requests for the next page to work.

How to do it...

Let's write the HTML page, CSS style, and JavaScript code.

1. Create a file named `index.html` that will contain the full HTML, CSS, and JavaScript code of our example. We need to insert a DOCTYPE into our HTML document; otherwise, the browser will operate in "quirks mode" and the height measurement function `$(window).height()` will not work.

   ```
   <!DOCTYPE HTML>
   ```

   We'll add a content placeholder element in the page:

   ```
   <div id="content"></div>
   ```

2. For demonstration purposes, we'll add the following CSS code to make the pages visible. Feel free to skip this CSS:

   ```
   div.page {
       min-height: 1200px;
       width: 800px;
       background-color:#f1f1f1;
       margin:0.3em;
       font-size: 3em;
   }
   div.error {
       color:#f00;
   }
   ```

3. Finally, we add the JavaScript code. First we load jQuery:

   ```
   <script src="http://ajax.googleapis.com/ajax/libs/jquery/1.8.2/
   jquery.min.js">
   </script>
   ```

   Then we can add our script:

   ```
   <script type="text/javascript">
   (function() {
   ```

Our page getter calls the callback with a null error argument and a simple string containing the page number as the content (for example, `Page 1`), but it can also perform an Ajax request. See the following code for more info on how to modify it to make an Ajax request.

This function is artificially limited to 10 pages of content. After the tenth page, the callback function is called with an error, indicating that there are no more pages available:

```
var page = 1;
function getPage(callback) {
    if (page <= 10)
        callback(null, 'Page ' + page);
    else
        callback("No more pages");
    page += 1;
};
```

4. We use `triggerPxFromBottom` to specify when to start loading the next page. When only `triggerPxFromBottom` pixels remain to be scrolled, the loading of the next page will begin. Its value is set to `0`; this means that the user must reach the end of the currently visible page to trigger the loading process:

```
var currentlyLoading = false;
var triggerPxFromBottom = 0;
```

5. `loadNext` appends the next page into the `#content` div. However, if the callback function is called with an error, it will display `No more content` below the last part of the page. After an error event, no more pages will be loaded. This means that when `getPage` returns an error, our code will stop loading new pages. This is the desired behavior:

```
function loadNext() {
    currentlyLoading = true;
    getPage(function(err, html) {
        if (err) {
            $("<div />")
                .addClass('error')
                .html("No more content")
                .appendTo("#content");
        } else {
            $("<div />")
                .addClass('page')
                .html(html).appendTo("#content");
            currentlyLoading = false;
        }
    });
}
```

6. This event handler is called when the page is scrolled in any way. It calculates the number of pixels of scrolling that remain below. If the number of the pixels is small enough and the code is not currently loading a page, it calls the page-loading function:

```
$(window).on('scroll', function() {
    var remainingPx = $(document).height()
        - $(window).scrollTop()
        - $(window).height();
    if (remainingPx <= triggerPxFromBottom
        && !currentlyLoading)
        loadNext();
});
```

7. Finally, we call `loadNext()` for the first time to load the first page:

```
loadNext();
}());
</script>
```

How it works...

The visible area of the browser (also called the viewport) has its own dimensions that can be fetched by calling jQuery's `$.fn.height()` function on the `$(window)` object. On the other hand, `$(document).height()` provides us with the height of the entire content of the page. Finally, `$(window).scrollTop()` gives us the scroll offset.

Using these functions, we can calculate the remaining pixels to be scrolled. Then we recalculate and check this value every time the user scrolls the page. If the value is sufficiently small, we call our loading function. At the same time, we make sure to stop loading new pages until the current loading process is finished. (Otherwise, the user's scrolling actions might load a couple of more pages while they wait for the content to load.)

There's more...

Here is a possible Ajax implementation of the `getPage` function. This function sends Ajax requests to a request handler hosted on the same domain at the path /pages/<number> to retrieve the HTML contents of the next page:

```
function getPage(cb) {
    $.get('/pages/' + page)
        .success(function(html) { cb(null, html); })
        .error(function() { cb("Error"); }
    page += 1;
}
```

To make this version work, you will need to implement the request handler in your server-side code.

Your server-side code can return an error, such as 404, to indicate that there is no more content available. As a result, jQuery will never call our success callback, and our code will stop loading new pages.

The endless scrolling list recipe provides great user experience, but it has one significant drawback. We must make sure that we don't have any important page content below the `contents` element. This means that page elements placed at the bottom (usually the footer links and copyright messages) might become unreachable.

Creating a sortable paginated table

One of the most common tasks we encounter when creating websites is displaying lists and tables. Most techniques focus on server-side sorting, paging, and the rendering of data. Our solution will be completely on the client side, suitable for small to medium amounts of data. The main benefit of a client-side solution is speed; sorting and switching pages will be nearly instantaneous.

In this recipe, we're going to create a client-side, sortable paginated table.

Getting ready

We assume that a service provides the data in a JSON object, containing a `data` property that is an array of arrays:

```
{data:[["object1col1", "object1col2"], ["object2col1", "object2col2"],
…]}
```

In our example, we're going to display a list of people near us. Every person in the table will have their own ID number, name, age, distance from us, and transportation method.

We're going to display the distance in km, and would like to be able to sort the list of people by their last names.

As table display problems quickly grow beyond the original simple problem, we're not going to build our own solution. Instead, we're going to use the excellent jQuery DataTables plugin available at `http://datatables.net/`.

How to do it...

Let's write the HTML page, CSS style, and JavaScript code.

1. First, we're going to create an HTML page containing an empty table. We're also going to add some CSS to import a basic DataTables style for the table. The stylesheets are normally available with the DataTables distribution. Our `index.html` file is as follows:

```
<!DOCTYPE HTML>
<html>
    <head>
        <title>Sortable paged table</title>
        <style type="text/css">
            @import "http://live.datatables.net/media/css/demo_
page.css";
            @import "http://live.datatables.net/media/css/demo_
table.css";
            #demo, #container {
                width:700px;
            }
            #demo td {
                padding: 0.2em 2em;
            }
            #demo_info {
                width:690px;
                height:auto;
            }
        </style>
    </head>
    <body>
        <div id="container">
            <table id="demo">
                <thead>
                    <tr>
                        <th>Id</th><th>Name</th><th>Age</
th><th>Distance</th><th>Transportation</th>
                    </tr>
                </thead>
                <tbody>
                </tbody>
            </table>
        </div>
        <script src="http://ajax.googleapis.com/ajax/libs/
jquery/1.8.2/jquery.min.js"></script>
```

```
        <script type="text/javascript" src="http://datatables.net/
download/build/jquery.dataTables.min.js"></script>
        <script type="text/javascript" src="example.js"></script>
    </body>
</html>
```

The example includes a link to the minified version of DataTables hosted on the official website.

The DataTables plugin appends the `pager` and `info` elements below the table. Because of this, we need to wrap our table inside a `container` element.

2. And the `example.js` file is as follows:

```
(function() {
    $.extend($.fn.dataTableExt.oSort, {
        "lastname-sort-pre": function (a) {
            return a.split(' ').reverse().join(' ');
        },
        "lastname-sort-asc": function(a, b) { return a < b ? -1 :
a > b ? 1 : 0; },
        "lastname-sort-desc": function(a, b) { return a > b ? -1 :
a < b ? 1 : 0; },
        "unitnumber-pre": function(a) { return new Number(a.
split(' ')[0]); },
        "unitnumber-asc": function(a, b) { return a - b; },
        "unitnumber-desc": function(a, b) { return b - a; }
    } )
    var fetchData = function(callback) {
        var data = [
            [1,'Louis Garland', 12, 32, 'Walking'],
            [2,'Misty Lamar',32, 42, 'Bus'],
            [3,'Steve Ernest',32, 12, 'Cycling'],
            [4,'Marcia Reinhart',42, 180, 'Bus'],
            [5,'Lydia Rouse',35, 31, 'Driving'],
            [6,'Sean Kasten',80,42, 'Driving'],
            [7,'Patrick Sharkey',65,43, 'Cycling'],
            [8,'Becky Rashid',63, 51, 'Bus'],
            [9,'Michael Fort',34, 23, 'Walking'],
            [10,'Genevieve Blaine',55, 11, 'Walking'],
            [11,'Victoria Fry',58, 14, 'Walking'],
            [12,'Donald Mcgary',34, 15, 'Cycling'],
            [13,'Daniel Dreher',16, 23, 'Walking'],
            [14,'Valerie Santacruz',43, 35, 'Driving'],
            [15,'Jodi Bee',23, 13, 'Walking'],
            [16,'Jo Montana',14, 31, 'Cycling'],
            [17,'Stephanie Keegan',53, 24, 'Driving'],
```

```
                    [18,'Philip Dewey',12, 29, 'Cycling'],
                    [19,'Jack Clemons',11, 44, 'Walking'],
                    [20,'Steve Serna',14, 60, 'Cycling']
                ];
            callback({data:data});
        };
        window.myTable = {};
        var table = window.myTable.table = $("#demo").dataTable({
            'bLengthChange': false, 'bFilter': false,
            'iDisplayLength': 10,
            'aoColumnDefs':[{
                aTargets: [3], // distance
                mRender: function(data) { return data + ' km'; },
                sType: 'unitnumber'
            }, {
                aTargets: [1],
                sType: 'lastname-sort'
            }]
        });
        var setData = window.myTable.setData = function(data) {
            table.fnClearTable();
            table.fnAddData(data);
            table.fnDraw();
        };

        fetchData(function(result) {
            window.myTable.data = result.data;
            setData(result.data);
        });

    }());
```

The implementation of `fetchData` in the example provides hardcoded example data. You can easily replace it with a request to your service. The `setData` function is a convenient function to change the table data—we're going to use the same script, which will call this function to set its own data, for multiple recipes. Finally, the rest of the code is specific to DataTables and will be explained in the next section.

How it works...

The following image shows the resulting table:

Id ▲	Name	Age	Distance	Transportation
1	Louis Garland	12	32 km	Walking
2	Misty Lamar	32	42 km	Bus
3	Steve Ernest	32	12 km	Cycling
4	Marcia Reinhart	42	180 km	Bus
5	Lydia Rouse	35	31 km	Driving
6	Sean Kasten	80	42 km	Driving
7	Patrick Sharkey	65	43 km	Cycling
8	Becky Rashid	63	51 km	Bus
9	Michael Fort	34	23 km	Walking
10	Genevieve Blaine	55	11 km	Walking

Showing 1 to 10 of 20 entries

◀ Previous Next ▶

To initialize the table we use the `dataTable` initialization function. We can pass multiple options to the function. For example, we can specify that we want 10 items per page by setting the value of the `iDisplayLength` property to `10`.

Because we're going to render the **Distance** column (column 3) slightly differently than just displaying it, we add an item to the `aoColumnDefs` option for target column 3 that sets a custom rendering function for that column. This is a function that simply appends the `km` string to our number; but we could also use a more elaborate function (involving custom date formatting, unit conversions, and so on).

Paging works automatically with DataTables—the plugin appends a pager control that provides access to the previous/next page. Sorting also mostly works automatically. However, in our particular example, we need special sorting for the **Name** column (by last name) even though it's displayed in the format "firstname lastname". To do this, we specify a custom sort type for that column called `lastname-sort`. We also specify a special sort type for the **Distance** column called `unitnumber`.

DataTables allows us to define custom sort types as plugins. Custom sorters have the following properties:

- A preprocessing function that pre-processes the column value before passing it to the sorter
- An ascending sorting function that returns a value depending on the value of the two arguments that are passed: -1 if the first value is smaller, 0 if they are equal, or 1 if the first value is larger
- A descending order sorting function that works similarly to the ascending sorting function

These properties allow us to implement sorting by last name for the **Name** column, as well as by number for the **Distance** column.

There's more...

Here is a simple Ajax replacement of the `fetchData` function, sending an Ajax request to a request handler hosted on the same domain at the path `/people` to retrieve the array data:

```
function fetchData(cb) {
    $.get('/people/').success(cb);
}
```

Note that this solution doesn't work very well for large datasets. While modern clients have the performance to manipulate a lot of data, bandwidth is also a consideration. A careful consideration of bandwidth requirements and the target clients (desktop or mobile) should be exercised before using this solution.

Creating multiple-choice filters

One common task when displaying tables is to filter the data in the table to a subset that satisfies a certain criteria. Multiple-choice table filters work on columns with a finite number of values. For example, if we had a table containing data of some people where one column is the transportation method used by the person, the filter used on this column would be a multiple-choice filter. The user should be able to select one or more transportation methods, and the table view would display all the people that are using the selected methods.

Getting ready

We're going to assume that we're using the code and data from the previous recipe. We have a list of people with their transportation methods displayed in a sortable, paginated table using the DataTables jQuery plugin. We will copy the files from the previous recipe, and then add to them.

The data that we need to filter is already available in the `tableData` global variable; we can filter this data and then use the global `tableSetData` function to display the filtered table.

The filter is going to work on the **Transportation** field.

How to do it...

Let's modify the previous code to add multiple-choice filters to our table:

1. In the `index.html` file from the previous recipe, add a multiple-choice select list after the opening `<body>` tag:

    ```
    <select id="list" style="width:100px;"  multiple>
    </select>
    ```

2. Add a script element for `filter.js` before the closing `</body>` tag:

    ```
    <script type="text/javascript" src="filter.js"></script>
    ```

3. We're also going to modify the `fetchData` call at the end of `example.js` to trigger a custom event notifying any observers that the data has been fetched and set:

    ```
    $(function() {
        fetchData(function(result) {
            window.myTable.data = result.data;
            setData(result.data);
            $("#demo").trigger("table:data");
        });
    });
    ```

    The code is wrapped to be executed after the page is loaded in order for event triggering to work. Before the page load, no events can be triggered.

4. Create a file named `filter.js` and add the following code:

    ```
    (function() {
        function getUnique(data, column) {
            var unique = [];
            data.forEach(function(row) {
                if (unique.indexOf(row[column]) < 0) unique.
    push(row[column]); });
            return unique;
        }

        function choiceFilter(valueList, col) {
            return function filter(el) {
                return valueList.indexOf(el[col]) >= 0;
            }
        }
    ```

```
    $("#demo").on('table:data', function() {
        getUnique(window.myTable.data, 4).forEach(function(item) {
            $("<option />").attr('value', item).html(item).
appendTo("#list");
        });
    })
    $("#list").change(function() {
        var filtered = window.myTable.data.filter(
            choiceFilter($("#list").val(), 4));
        window.myTable.setData(filtered);
    });
}());
```

How it works...

The easiest way to implement a user interface for a multiple-choice filter is to use a multiple-choice select element.

We also need to populate the element when the data becomes available. To do this, we trigger our new custom event `table:data` after fetching the data (either from our server or otherwise). The listener extracts the unique values from the **Transportation** column of the data and populates the select list with options for the values.

When the selection changes, we extract the selected values (as an array) and create a new filter function using `choiceFilter`, a higher-order function. The higher-order function returns a new filtering function. This filtering function takes a table row argument and returns `true` if the value of the fourth column of that row is contained within the specified list.

The filtering function is passed to `Array.filter`; it applies this function to every row and returns an array containing only the rows for which the filtering function returns `true`. The filtered data is then displayed instead of the original data.

Creating range filters

Tables can also be filtered by their numerical columns. For example, given a table where each row is a person and one of the columns contain data about the person's age, we might need to filter this table by specifying the age range. To do this, we use range filters.

Getting ready

We're going to assume that we're using the code and data from the *Creating a sortable paginated table* recipe. We have a list of people with their age displayed in a sortable, paginated table using the DataTables jQuery plugin. We will copy the files from the recipe and then add some extra filtering code.

The data that we need to filter is already available in the `tableData` global variable; we can filter this data and then use the `tableSetData` global function to display the filtered table.

The filter is going to work on the **Age** field.

How to do it...

Let's modify the previous code to add range filters to our table:

1. In the `index.html` file from the previous recipe, add two input elements after the opening `<body>` tag:

    ```
    Age: <input id="range1" type="text">
    to <input id="range2" type="text"> <br>
    ```

2. Add a script element for `filter.js` before the closing `</body>` tag:

    ```
    <script type="text/javascript" src="filter.js"></script>
    ```

3. Finally, we create our `filter.js` script:

    ```javascript
    (function() {
        function number(n, def) {
            if (n == '') return def;
            n = new Number(n);
            if (isNaN(n)) return def;
            return n;
        }
        function rangeFilter(start, end, col) {
            var start = number(start, -Infinity),
                end = number(end, Infinity);
            return function filter(el) {
                return start < el[col] && el[col] < end;
            }
        }
        $("#range1,#range2").on('change keyup', function() {
            var filtered = window.myTable.data.filter(
                rangeFilter($("#range1").val(), $("#range2").val(),
    2));
            window.myTable.setData(filtered);
        });
    }());
    ```

How it works...

The easiest way to filter array data is to use JavaScript's built-in `Array.filter` function. This is a higher-order function; its first argument is a function that takes a row argument and returns `true` if the row is to be added to the filtered array or `false` if the row is to be left out.

To provide such a function, we create our own higher-order function. It takes the start and end ranges and the specified column. The return result is a function that filters every row.

To ignore empty or invalid values from the input, we use the number function. If the input field is empty or contains non-number data, a default value is provided (`-Infinity` for the start of the range and `+Infinity` for the end). This also enables us to do one-sided range filtering.

The `Array.filter` function returns an array of all the elements that pass the filter. We display this array in our table.

Creating combined complex filters

When displaying tables, we sometimes want to filter table elements using multiple criteria involving multiple columns. For example, given a table of people that contains information such as their name, age, and transportation method, we might only want to view the people older than 30 that use a bus for transportation. We might also want to filter people by name. To do this, we have to apply multiple filters, such as an age range filter, a multiple-choice filter, and a text filter, to the data at the same time. The easiest way to do this is to make a filter combination function.

Getting ready

We're going to assume that we're using the code from the *Creating a sortable paginated table* recipe, and we're going to add our filters as described in the previous two recipes. This time we're going to allow for the combination of filters.

How to do it...

Let's modify the previous code to add multiple filters to our table:

1. We're going to add filter-related inputs to our page after the opening `<body>` tag:

    ```
    <select id="list" style="width:100px;"  multiple>
    </select>
    Age: <input id="range1" type="text">
    to <input id="range2" type="text">,
    Name: <input type="text" id="name"> <br>
    ```

2. Add the `filter.js` script before the closing `</body>` tag:

```
<script type="text/javascript" src="filter.js"></script>
```

3. We're going to modify `example.js` to fetch data after the page is loaded and trigger a `table:data` event after displaying the data:

```
$(function() {
    fetchData(function(data) {
        window.myTable.data = data;
        setData(data);
        $("#demo").trigger("table:data");
    });
});
```

4. Then we can create `filter.js` by combining the code from the previous two recipes:

```
(function() {
    function getUnique(data, column) {
        var unique = [];
        data.forEach(function(row) {
            if (unique.indexOf(row[column]) < 0)
                unique.push(row[column]);
        });
        return unique;
    }
    function choiceFilter(valueList, col) {
        return function filter(el) {
            return valueList.indexOf(el[col]) >= 0;
        }
    }
    function number(n, def) {
        if (n == '') return def;
        n = new Number(n);
        if (isNaN(n)) return def;
        return n;
    }
    function rangeFilter(start, end, col) {
        var start = number(start, -Infinity),
            end = number(end, Infinity);
        return function filter(el) {
            return start < el[col] && el[col] < end;
        };
    }
    function textFilter(txt, col) {
        return function filter(el) {
            return el[col].indexOf(txt) >= 0;
```

```
        };
    }
    $("#demo").on('table:data', function() {
        getUnique(window.myTable.data, 4)
        .forEach(function(item) {
            $("<option />").attr('value', item)
                .html(item).appendTo("#list");
        });
    });
    var filters = [null, null, null];
    $("#list").change(function() {
        filters[0] = choiceFilter($("#list").val(), 4);
        filterAndShow();
    });
    $("#range1,#range2").on('change keyup', function() {
        filters[1] = rangeFilter($("#range1").val(),
            $("#range2").val(), 2);
        filterAndShow();
    });
    $("#name").on('change keyup', function() {
        filters[2] = textFilter($("#name").val(), 1);
filterAndShow();
    });
    function filterAndShow() {
        var filtered = window.myTable.data;
        filters.forEach(function(filter) {
            if (filter) filtered = filtered.filter(filter);
        });
        window.myTable.setData(filtered);
    };
}());
```

How it works...

Like in the previous recipes, we use the `Array.filter` function to filter the table. This time we apply multiple filters in succession. We store all of the filter functions in an array.

Whenever there is a change in the inputs, we update the appropriate filter function and rerun `filterAndShow()` to display the filtered data.

There's more...

DataTables is a highly flexible table library with many options and a rich API. More information and examples can be found on the official website at `http://www.datatables.net/`.

Displaying code in HTML

There is a common need to display code in HTML or even to display HTML code inside HTML, especially in technical documentation or blogs. This has been done far too many times by taking an image from a piece of formatted code and making it part of the page. The code in the image will probably not get picked up by search engines. Additionally, it can limit us to a specific page layout or even screen size, and with today's mobile revolution, that is just not an option.

Getting ready

The only requirement for this recipe is that the data that will be displayed needs to be properly escaped; this means that `<p>awesome </p>` needs to be translated into `&lt;p&gt;awesome &lt;/p&gt;`. This can be done either on the server side or escaped before saving.

How to do it...

1. We will be using **Google code prettify** because, at the time of speaking, this library is not available completely on any of the CDN's; you can get it from `http://code.google.com/p/google-code-prettify/`.

2. Afterwards, we can add the escaped code in the `<pre />` `<code />` block:

```
<body onload="prettyPrint()">
    <div>
        <pre class="prettyprint">
          <code>
            SELECT *
            FROM Book
            WHERE price &lt; 100.00
            ORDER BY name;
          </code>
        </pre>
    </div>
</body>
```

3. Either one of these two tags has to include the `prettyprint` CSS class. In addition to that, we need to include the `onload="prettyPrint()"` attribute.

4. There is also the option to call the `prettyPrint` function from other event listeners added in JavaScript:

```
<script>
    window.addEventListener('load', function (e){
        prettyPrint();
    }, false);
</script>
```

How it works...

The `prettyprint` class automatically selects all the blocks marked with the appropriate CSS class, and autodetects the programming language used, and does the highlighting afterwards.

The lexer should work on most languages; in the common languages there are custom scripts for specific languages, for example, for the lisp-based ones.

There's more...

Because `prettyprint` automatically detects the source language, we could additionally specify it ourselves if we want to get better results. For example, if we wanted to display XML, the code would be as follows:

```
<pre class="prettyprint"><code class="language-xml">...</code></pre>
```

There are CSS classes for most of the common languages.

`prettyprint` is one of the older scripts available, and there are few alternatives that can offer many more customization options and better JavaScript APIs.

Some of them, such as **SyntaxHighliger** (`http://alexgorbatchev.com/SyntaxHighlighter/`), **Rainbow** (`http://craig.is/making/rainbows`), and **Highlight.js** (`http://softwaremaniacs.org/soft/highlight/en/`), are commonly found on most of the sites.

Rendering Markdown

Markdown is a popular, lightweight markup language. The language is similar to Wiki markup (used on Wikipedia), with an emphasis on simplicity. Its main purpose is to enable users to write plain text and get stylized, formatted HTML output. As such, it is used by popular websites, such as Reddit, Stack Overflow, GitHub, as well as various forums as a replacement of the less intuitive BBCode format.

Markdown is the fastest way to enable formatted text input for our users without embedding a full-fledged HTML editor into the page. There are multiple libraries to render markdown; in this recipe, we're going to use the simple `markdown-js` script to render markdown in real time.

How to do it...

Rendering markdown is very simple. A minimal example is as follows:

```
<!DOCTYPE HTML>
<html>
    <head>
```

```
            <title>Render markdown</title>
            <style type="text/css">
                #markdown, #render { width: 48%; min-height:320px; }
                #markdown { float: left; }
                #render { float: right; }
            </style>
        </head>
        <body>
            <textarea id="markdown">
# Markdown example.
This is an example of markdown text. We can link to [Google](http://
www.google.com)
or insert Google's logo:
![Google Logo](https://www.google.com/images/srpr/logo3w.png)

## Text formatting
We can use *emphasis* or **strong** text,
> insert a quote
etc.</textarea>
            <div id="render"></div>
            <script src="http://ajax.googleapis.com/ajax/libs/
jquery/1.8.2/jquery.min.js"></script>
            <script src="https://raw.github.com/spion/markdown-js/master/
lib/markdown.js"></script>
            <script type="text/javascript">
                function rendermd(val) { $("#render").html(markdown.
toHTML($("#markdown").val())); }
                $("#markdown").on('keyup', rendermd); $(rendermd);
            </script>
        </body>
</html>
```

How it works...

When the page is loaded, the markdown text in the `textarea` element is rendered into the `#render` element on the right-hand side. Every key press will also cause the script to update the rendered element.

There's more...

Find out more about the markdown format from its official website at http://daringfireball.net/projects/markdown/.

Autoupdating fields

These days, it is common to have an autoupdate on fields where one section is either the result of given choices or it displays a given image or text block. One example of this is having a password strength calculation; for example, searching for "currency converter" on Google will result in a box where you can do currency conversion between USD and EUR. Linking fields in this way makes sense when we have two or more that are logically linked, or when one is a result form of the other.

To demonstrate this, we will create a converter for temperature where updating one of the fields will result in changes in the other, as the values are linked.

Getting ready

For this recipe, we only need a basic knowledge of jQuery and a simple formula to convert the temperatures between Celsius and Fahrenheit and vice versa:

```
Celsius = (Fahrenheit -32) x (5/9)
```

Or:

```
Fahrenheit = Celsius  x(9/5) +32
```

How to do it...

1. First, we are going to create the HTML part and create two input fields that will get autoupdated and add the appropriate labels:

```
<div>
<label for='celsius'>C&deg;</label>
<input id='celsius' type='text' /> =
<label for='fahrenheit'>F&deg;</label>
<input id='fahrenheit' type='text' />
</div>
```

2. Afterwards, we have to make sure that we have included jQuery:

```
<script src="http://ajax.googleapis.com/ajax/libs/jquery/1.8.2/
jquery.min.js"> </script>
```

3. Following this, we can add the script that will handle the binding between the fields:

```
$(document).ready(function() {
  $('#celsius').keyup(function(data) {
  var celsius = new Number(data.currentTarget.value);
  var farenheit =celsius *(9/5) + 32;
```

```
    $('#farenheit').val(farenheit);
    });
$('#farenheit').keyup(function(data) {
    var farenheit = new Number(data.currentTarget.value);
    var celsius = (farenheit-32)*(5/9);
    $('#celsius').val(celsius);
    });
        });
```

This will connect and automatically calculate the temperature back and forward.

How it works...

Let's first take a look at the display part where there is nothing specific; here we use a simple input type text and add the appropriate labels for each field. Furthermore, we can use the escaped character ° that will show the degree character.

If we take a look at the jQuery `keyup` event, we can see that it's executed when a user releases a key on the keyboard on a given element. This event can be attached on any HTML element, but it will only work when the element is in focus; so it mostly makes sense to use it on input elements. As the `keyup` event has an option to execute a function that will accept the event object, so for our case, it is as follows:

```
$('#celsius').keyup(function(event) {
```

In the `event` object, we can access the element that fired the event and access its value:

```
event.currentTarget.value
```

After that, we can do the calculation (*celsius *(9/5) + 32*) and set the result as a value to the other element that displays it in Fahrenheit:

```
$('#fahrenheit').val(fahrenheit);
```

As we wanted the binding to work both ways, we can do the same on the input field for Fahrenheit:

```
$('#farenheit').keyup(function(event) {
```

And of course, you need to use the appropriate formula (*fahrenheit-32)*(5/9)*) for returning back to Celsius.

There's more...

While this recipe shows a simple use of jQuery `event` to make an instant update on input text, it can also be applied for creating autocomplete boxes or features, such as Google's instant search. The idea here is that we can and should use one- or two-way binding for various HTML elements, especially when we are talking about derived data or data that is a representation of the same source.

2
Display of Graphical Data

In this chapter, we are going to cover many common graphical tasks, such as the following:

- ▶ Creating a line chart
- ▶ Creating a bar chart
- ▶ Creating a pie chart
- ▶ Creating an area chart
- ▶ Displaying combined charts
- ▶ Creating a bubble chart
- ▶ Showing a map with a marked location
- ▶ Showing a map with a path
- ▶ Displaying gauges
- ▶ Displaying a tree
- ▶ LED scoreboard using web fonts

Introduction

In this chapter, we will take a look at displaying graphical data using various JavaScript libraries that are based on modern HTML5 standards. The main idea is to get you interested into various visual parts ranging from 2D graphics with canvas and SVG data-driven documents, with the help of problem-solving examples.

Creating a line chart

Line charts are the most basic type of charts. They display a series of data points connected together by lines. Line charts are often used to visualize time series data.

There are various libraries that implement this charting functionality, both paid and free. We're going to use the **Flot** chart library. It's free, simple, and easy to use and it has been in active development for the past 4 years. It also aims to produce aesthetically pleasing charts.

In this recipe, we're going to make a time series chart that displays the outside temperature history for the past 24 hours.

Getting ready

We'll need to download Flot from the official website at `http://www.flotcharts.org/`, and extract the contents to a separate folder named `flot`.

How to do it...

Let's write the HTML and JavaScript code.

1. Create a basic HTML page with a placeholder for our chart. We're also going to include jQuery (needed by Flot) and Flot itself. Flot needs to draw the chart canvas a placeholder div, so we're going to provide one. The chart placeholder needs to have its width and height specified, otherwise Flot will be unable to draw correctly:

```
<!DOCTYPE HTML>
<html>
    <head>
        <title>Chart example</title>
    </head>
    <body>
        <div id="chart" style="height:200px; width:800px;"></div>
        <script src="http://ajax.googleapis.com/ajax/libs/
jquery/1.8.2/jquery.min.js"></script>
        <script src="flot/jquery.flot.js"></script>
        <script type="text/javascript" src="example.js"></script>
    </body>
</html>
```

2. Add the code that draws our chart in `example.js`. The `getData` function generates some convincing-looking random data—you can easily replace it with a function that fetches data from the server. The data needs to be returned as an array of two-element arrays. The first (x axis) value in the pair is a standard UNIX timestamp in milliseconds as commonly used in JavaScript, while the second (y axis) value is the temperature.

3. Drawing the chart is very simple. The `$.plot` function draws the chart in the specified placeholder containing the specified series with the specified chart options:

```
$(function() {
    function getData(cb) {
        var now   = Date.now();
        var hour = 60 * 60 * 1000;
        var temperatures = [];
        for (var k = 24; k > 0; --k)
            temperatures.push([now - k*hour,
                Math.random()*2 + 10*Math.pow((k-12)/12,2)]);
        cb({data:temperatures});
    }
    getData(function(data) {
        $.plot("#chart", [data], {xaxis: {mode: 'time'}});
    });
});
```

That's it! The following is how the end result looks like:

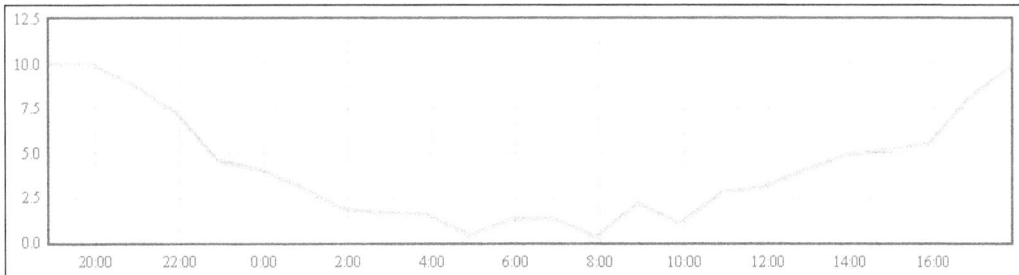

How it works...

The $.plot function takes three arguments:

- ▶ The placeholder selector. This is where Flot will draw the chart.

- ▶ The array of series to draw. Flot can simultaneously draw multiple series on the same chart. Every series is an object that must at least contain the data property. This property is an array of two-element arrays that are the x and y values of the series. Additional properties allow us to control the way the particular series is drawn—those will be explored in more detail in the next recipes. By default, Flot draws a regular line chart with a preset color.

- ▶ An options object that contains extensive chart drawing options for the chart labels, axes, legend, and grid. These options will also be explored in the next recipes.

In this recipe we've specified the "time" mode for the x axis. This causes Flot to appropriately label the hours, days, months, or years on our axis (depending on the timespan of the data).

There's more...

The following is a simple Ajax replacement of the getData function, sending an Ajax request to a request handler hosted on the same domain at the path /chart to retrieve the chart data:

```
function getData(cb) {
    $.get('/chart').success(cb);
}
```

Creating a bar chart

In contrast to a line chart, which is usually used to display averages or momentary values, bar charts are used to visualize data that belongs to discrete groups. Examples include daily, monthly, and weekly sales (the groups are days, months, and weeks respectively), page visits per user, fuel consumption for each car, and so on.

The Flot chart library can also draw bar charts. In this example, we're going to visualize the number of daily sales for the past seven days. We're also going to show the sales from separate products separately, stacked on top of each other.

Getting ready

We'll need to download Flot from the official website at http://www.flotcharts.org/ and extract the contents to a separate folder named flot.

How to do it...

Let's modify the line chart code to make it draw our bar charts.

1. First, we're going to copy the same HTML page from the previous line chart recipe, but we'll make some changes. In order to draw stacking bars, we're going to need the stacking plugin, which is located in the `jquery.flot.stack.js` file. The height of the chart placeholder is increased to get a better overview of the individual stacking bars:

```
<!DOCTYPE HTML>
<html>
    <head>
        <title>Chart example</title>
    </head>
    <body>
        <div id="chart" style="height:300px; width:800px;"></div>
        <script src="http://ajax.googleapis.com/ajax/libs/
jquery/1.8.2/jquery.min.js"></script>
        <script src="flot/jquery.flot.js"></script>
        <script src="flot/jquery.flot.stack.js"></script>
        <script type="text/javascript" src="example.js"></script>
    </body>
</html>
```

2. Then we will create the `example.js` script:

```
$(function() {
    var day = 24 * 60 * 60 * 1000;
    function getData(cb) {
        var now  = new Date();
        now = new Date(now.getYear(), now.getMonth(), now.
getDate()).getTime();
        var products = [];
        for (var product = 1; product < 4; ++product) {
            var sales = { label: "Product " + product, data: [] };
            for (var k = 7; k > 0; --k)
                sales.data.push([now - k*day, Math.round(Math.
random()*10)]);
            products.push(sales);
        }
        cb({series:products});
    }

    getData(function(data) {
        $.plot("#chart", data.series, {
            series: {
```

```
                    stack: true, lines: { show: false },
                    bars: { show: true, barWidth: 0.8 * day,
         align:'center' }
                  }, xaxis: {mode: 'time'}
             });
          });
       });
```

The code is explained in the next section. The following is how the resulting chart appears:

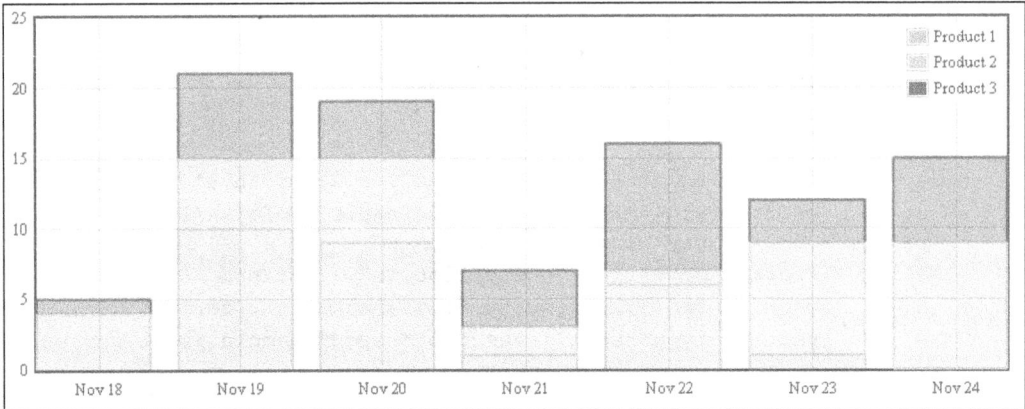

How it works...

Like in the previous recipe, the `$.plot` function takes three arguments. The first argument is the chart placeholder, the second is data, and the third is an object containing the chart options.

The following is a scheme of our input data:

```
[
  {label: "Product 1", data:[
    [timestamp, value],
    [timestamp, value], ...]},
  {label: "Product 2", data: [...]},
  {label: "Product 3", data: [...]}
]
```

The input data is an array of series. Each series represents the sales for a product. The series object has a `label` property denoting the product, and a `data` property, which is an array of data points. Every data point is a two-dimensional array. The first element of this array is the date represented as a UNIX timestamp in milliseconds—the exact beginning of the day. The second is the number of sales for that day.

To manipulate the dates more easily, we define a variable representing the number of milliseconds in a day. Later, we use this variable to define the width of the bars in the chart.

Flot automatically picks the series colors for us from a predefined list (however, it's also possible to specify the colors we need, as we will see in the following recipes).

There are several series options specified in the code. We tell Flot to stack our series by setting the value of the `stack` property to `true`. We also make sure to hide the lines that would otherwise be shown by default.

To get the bar centers to align with the x-axis ticks for the day, we set the value of the `align` property in the `bar` object to `center`.

Each series in our input data has a label. As a result, Flot automatically generates a legend placed in the upper-right corner.

The boundaries of the axes are automatically picked by Flot, but it's possible to control them using the `options` object.

Creating a pie chart

When visualizing proportions or percentages as a whole, we usually use pie charts. Pie charts are simple enough to draw on our own; however, to get more flexibility and aesthetically pleasing results, we're going to use the Flot charting library with its pie plugin.

Flot's pie plugin can show a pie with or without a legend, and has extensive options for controlling the position of the labels. It's also capable of rendering tilted pies and donuts. Support for interactive pies is also included.

In this recipe, we're going to make a pie chart of our visitor's browsers.

Getting ready

We'll need to download Flot from the official website at `http://www.flotcharts.org/` and extract the contents to a separate folder named `flot`.

How to do it...

Let's write the HTML and JavaScript code.

1. Create the following HTML page in `index.html`:

```
<!DOCTYPE HTML>
<html>
    <head>
        <title>Chart example</title>
```

```
        </head>
        <body>
            <div id="chart" style="height:600px; width:600px;"></div>
            <script src="http://ajax.googleapis.com/ajax/libs/
    jquery/1.8.2/jquery.min.js"></script>
            <script src="flot/jquery.flot.js"></script>
            <script src="flot/jquery.flot.pie.js"></script>
            <script type="text/javascript" src="example.js"></script>
        </body>
    </html>
```

The page has a placeholder element for our chart.

Flot depends on the jQuery library that is included. To draw pie charts, we need to add Flot's pie plugin.

2. Create the example.js script:

```
$(function() {
    var day = 24 * 60 * 60 * 1000;
    function getData(cb) {
        var browsers = [
            {label: 'IE', data: 35.5, color:"#369"},
            {label: 'Firefox', data: 24.5, color: "#639"},
            {label: 'Chrome', data: 32.1, color: "#963"},
            {label: 'Other', data: 7.9, color: "#396"}
        ];
        cb(browsers);
    }

    getData(function(data) {
        $.plot("#chart", data, {
        series: {
            pie: {
                show: true,
                radius: 0.9,
                label: {
                    show: true,
                    radius: 0.6,
                },
                tilt: 0.5
            }
        },
        legend: { show: false }
        });
    });
});
```

It produces the following pie chart:

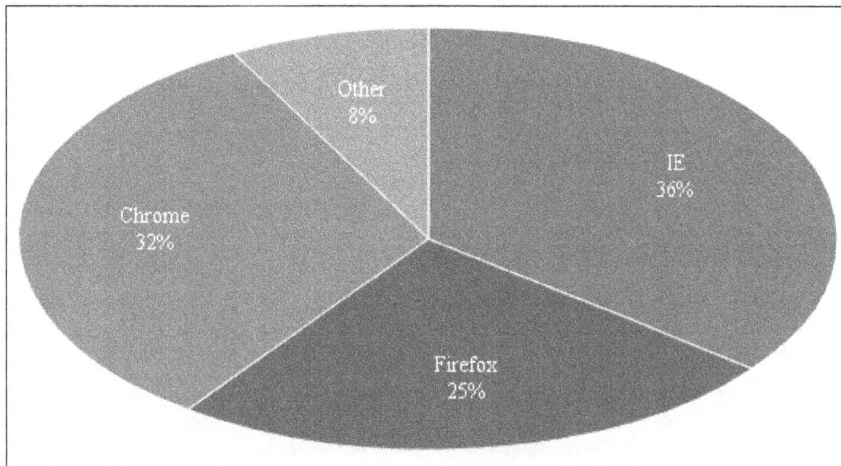

How it works...

Flot requires that the pie slices data are provided as an array of objects. Every object contains the following two properties:

- ▶ `label`: This is the label of the slice
- ▶ `data`: This is the number of the slice—a number which can be any value (doesn't need to be a percentage)

When calling `$.plot`, the first argument is the placeholder element for the pie, the second is the array of pie slices, and the third contains the pie options.

In order to show a pie, a minimum `options` object is as follows:

```
{pie: {show: true}}
```

To customize the default pie, we use the following additions to the `pie` property:

- ▶ `radius`: This specifies the size of the pie as a percentage of the canvas.
- ▶ `label`: The `show` (Boolean) property is set to `true` to show the pie labels, and the `radius` property controls the distance of the labels from the center of the pie.
- ▶ `tilt`: This performs a 3D tilt of the pie. If omitted, Flot will render an untitled circle-shaped pie.

There's more...

There are more options available, such as the following:

- `innerRadius`: This is set to a value such as `0.5` to create a donut chart.
- `combine`: This property is used to combine smaller slices into a single slice. It's an object containing the following properties:
    - `threshold`: This is set to a percentage of the whole, for example, `0.1`
    - `color`: This is the color to use to render the "other" slice, for example, `#888`

For more details, see the pie examples at `http://people.iola.dk/olau/flot/examples/pie.html`.

Creating an area chart

Area charts are usually used in place of line charts when we want to stack multiple results on top of each other. They can also be used to enhance the visual appeal of the chart in certain circumstances.

This recipe will present an example where the area chart is used for an enhanced visual appeal: displaying altitude data.

Let's say we need to visualize the altitude of a 8-km downhill hike succeeded by 12 km of flat walking. We would also like to mark the "mountain" portion of the chart. Finally, we would like the area below the altitude line to be filled in a way reminiscent of color relief maps with the color green for low, yellow for medium, and white for high-altitude.

Getting ready

We'll also use the Flot chart library in this example, so we will need to download Flot from the official website ta `http://www.flotcharts.org/` and extract the content to a separate folder named `flot`.

How to do it...

1. Our HTML file needs a chart placeholder element and the necessary scripts included. The following is the content:

```
<!DOCTYPE HTML>
<html>
    <head>
        <title>Chart example</title>
        <style type="text/css">
            #chart { font-family: Verdana; }
```

```
            </style>
        </head>
        <body>
            <div id="chart" style="height:200px; width:800px;"></div>
            <script src="http://ajax.googleapis.com/ajax/libs/
jquery/1.8.2/jquery.min.js"></script>
            <script src="flot/jquery.flot.js"></script>
            <script type="text/javascript" src="example.js"></script>
        </body>
    </html>
```

2. We're going to draw the chart in our `example.js` script that contains the
    following code:

```javascript
$(function() {
    function getData(cb) {
        var altitudes = [];
        // Generate random but convincing-looking data.
        for (var k = 0; k < 20; k += 0.5)
            altitudes.push([k, Math.random()*50 + 1000*Math.
pow((k-15)/15,2)]);
        cb(altitudes);
    }

    getData(function(data) {
        $.plot("#chart", [{data: data}], {
            xaxis: {
                tickFormatter: function(km) { return km + ' km'; }
            },
            lines: {
                fill: true,
                fillColor: {colors: ["#393", "#990", "#cc7",
"#eee"] }
            },
            grid: {
                markings: [{ xaxis: { from: 0, to: 8 }, color:
"#eef" }]
            }
        });
    });
});
```

And the following is how our result looks like:

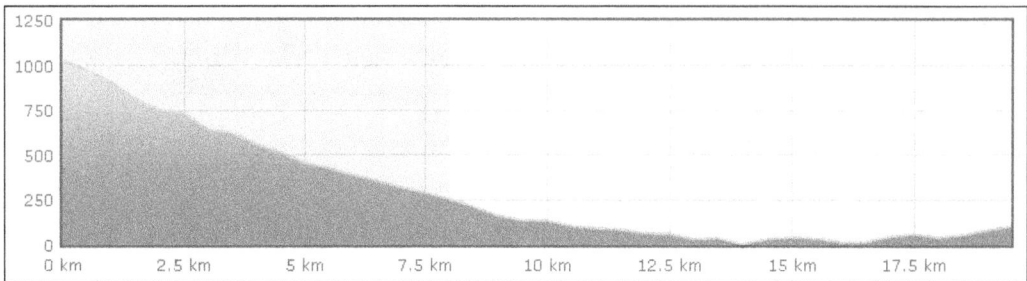

The area below the altitude line is filled in a way reminiscent of color relief. The mountain section is marked with a blue area, created by the `markings` object.

How it works...

As in all of our examples, the `getData` function in `example.js` generates random data, and then calls the provided callback function with the data. We can easily write a replacement that fetches the data from a server instead, using jQuery.

A single call to `$.plot` will draw the area chart. The first argument is the target container. The second argument is an array of series to draw—in this case just one.

The third argument is more complex. It consists of the following parts:

- The `xaxis` property specifies the behavior of our x axis. We override the default tick labels by providing our own tick formatter. This formatter adds the `"km"` string after the tick value.

- The `lines` property specifies that we'll be using a filled line chart. We want a mountain-like gradient fill effect, so we specify a gradient object that contains an array of CSS color strings, that is, `{color: [array of colors]}`.

- The `grid` property is used to mark the mountain segment on our chart. We specify that it should contain a marking of the x axis segment spanning in the range 0 to 8 km and having a light blue color.

There's more...

Flot has more area chart options—they can be found in the API documentation that is included with the distribution.

To use this recipe, we would need to provide our own data array from the server. The following is a simple Ajax replacement of the `getData` function, sending an Ajax request to a request handler hosted on the same domain at the path `/areachart` to retrieve the chart data. It is very simple:

```
function getData(cb) {
    $.get('/areachart').success(cb);
}
```

Displaying combined charts

Combined charts are charts that have more than one x or y axis, and may have multiple types of series (lines, bars, and areas). Sometimes, we may want to present multiple heterogeneous types of data on a single chart, usually to visualize its correlation.

In this recipe, we're going to try and visualize a mountain hike by presenting both temperature and altitude on a single chart. The altitude series will be an area chart with gradient colors reminiscent of relief maps, but the temperature series will be a line chart, which we would like to be red if above 19 degrees Celsius and blue if below that.

In order to do this, we're going to need a charting library that can handle two y axes. We're going to use the Flot charting library because it is capable of displaying charts with two or more x or y axes.

Getting ready

Like in the previous recipes, we need to download Flot from the official website at `http://www.flotcharts.org/` and extract the contents to a separate folder named `flot`.

How to do it...

Let's write the HTML and JavaScript code.

1. Our HTML file needs a chart placeholder, jQuery, Flot, and our example script. This time we're also going to need the `threshold` plugin in order to have two temperature colors. The following is the content:

```
<!DOCTYPE HTML>
<html>
    <head>
        <title>Chart example</title>
        <style type="text/css">
            #chart { font-family: Verdana; }
        </style>
```

```
        </head>
        <body>
            <div id="chart" style="height:200px; width:800px;"></div>
            <script src="http://ajax.googleapis.com/ajax/libs/
    jquery/1.8.2/jquery.min.js"></script>
            <script src="flot/jquery.flot.js"></script>
            <script src="flot/jquery.flot.threshold.js"></script>
            <script type="text/javascript" src="example.js"></script>
        </body>
    </html>
```

2. Our chart is drawn in `example.js` using the following code:

```
$(function() {
    function getData(cb) {
        var altitudes = [], temperatures = [];
        // Generate random but convincing-looking data.
        for (var k = 0; k < 20; k += 0.5) {
            altitudes.push([k, Math.random()*50 + 1000*Math.
pow((k-15)/15,2)]);
            temperatures.push([k, Math.random()*0.5 + k/4 + 15]);
        }
        cb({alt:altitudes, temp:temperatures});
    }

    getData(function(data) {
        $.plot("#chart", [
            {
              data: data.alt, yaxis:1,
              lines: {fill:true, fillColor: {
              colors: ["#393", "#990", "#cc7", "#eee"] } }
                },
            {
              data: data.temp, yaxis:2, color: "rgb(200, 20, 30)",
              threshold: { below: 19, color: "rgb(20, 100, 200)" }
                }
            ], {
            yaxes: [ { }, { position: "right"}],
            xaxis: {
                tickFormatter: function(km) { return km + ' km'; }
            },
            grid: {
                markings: [{ xaxis: { from: 0, to: 8 }, color:
"#eef" }]
            }
        });
    });
});
```

The following screenshot shows the end result:

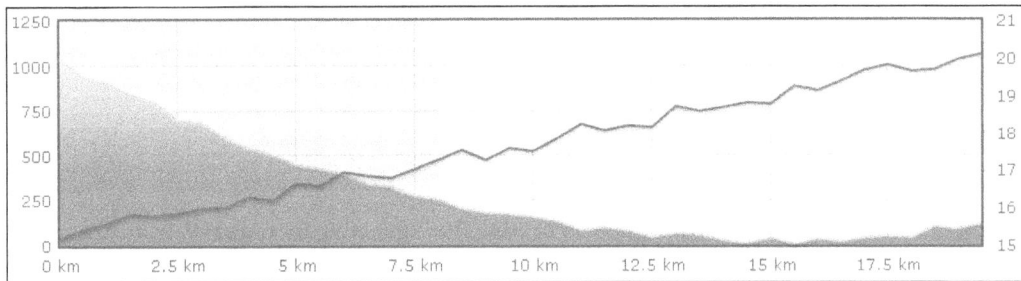

How it works...

With the `getData` function, we generate two series for the plot, one containing temperature and the other containing altitude.

When drawing the plot, we call the `getData` function first. In the provided callback, we take the data and pass it to the `$.plot` function, which takes the target container element, an array of series, and plot options.

The first series in the array contains altitude data. We have two y axes so we need to declare the y axis we're going to use for this series—the first y axis. The rest of the parameters declare the fill gradient; for more information see the *Creating an area chart* recipe.

The second series uses the second y axis. What is new here is the `threshold` property. It specifies that for values below 19 degrees, the color of the line should be different (blue rather than red).

We're going to configure the second y axis in the `options` object by specifying the `yaxes` property (note the plural in the name). This property is an array containing y axis options. We're going to use the defaults for the first axis, hence the empty object. We will place the second axis on the right-hand side.

The unit of the x axis is kilometers and therefore our `tickformatter` function adds the string " km" to the number.

Finally, we mark the "mountain part" (from 0 to 8 km) in blue with the grid markings option.

There's more...

Here is a simple Ajax replacement of the `getData` function, sending an Ajax request to a request handler hosted on the same domain at the `/charts` path to retrieve the chart data. This handler should return an object in the following format:

```
{alt: data1, temp: data2}
```

Where `data1` and `data2` are two-dimensional arrays containing the data.

```
function getData(cb) {
    $.get('/charts').success(cb);
}
```

Creating a bubble chart

Bubble charts can display sets of values as circles. They're usable for datasets with sizes in the range 10 through 100. They're particularly useful for visualizing values that differ by orders of magnitude and can replace pie charts in those situations.

As bubble charts are more complex and slightly less common, we're going to need a flexible library to draw them. The excellent D3 library (`http://d3js.org/`) is a great fit; it provides a set of tools, (the core data-driven DOM API plus the "pack" data layout) that enables the creation of bubble charts.

We're going to draw a bubble chart displaying the numbers of visitors coming to our website from referring websites.

How to do it...

Let's write the HTML and JavaScript code.

1. We're going to create an HTML page containing our chart placeholder. We're going to include the chart library D3, and the code that will draw the bubble chart from our `example.js` file:

```
<!DOCTYPE HTML>
<html>
    <head>
        <title>Chart example</title>
        <style type="text/css">
            #chart text { font-family: Verdana; font-size:10px; }
        </style>
    </head>
    <body>
        <div id="chart"></div>
        <script src="http://mbostock.github.com/d3/d3.v2.
js?2.9.5"></script>
        <script type="text/javascript" src="example.js"></script>
    </body>
</html>
```

2. Then we're going to add the following code in `example.js`:

```
(function() {
var getData = function(cb) {
    cb({children: [
        {domain: 'google.com', value: 6413},
        {domain: 'yahoo.com', value: 831},
        {domain: 'bing.com', value: 1855},
        {domain: 'news.ycombinator.com', value: 5341},
        {domain: 'reddit.com', value: 511},
        {domain: 'blog.someone.com', value: 131},
        {domain: 'blog.another.com', value: 23},
        {domain: 'slashdot.org', value: 288},
        {domain: 'twitter.com', value: 327},
        {domain: 'review-website.com', value: 231}
    ]});
}


// r is the dimension of the bubble chart
var r = 640,
    fill = d3.scale.category20c();

// create the visualization placeholder
var vis = d3.select("#chart").append("svg")
    .attr("width", r)
    .attr("height", r)
    .attr("class", "bubble");

// create a pack layout for the bubbles
var bubble = window.bubble = d3.layout.pack()
    .sort(null)
    .size([r, r])
    .padding(1.5);

    getData(function(json) {
        // Process the data with the pack layout
        var data = bubble.nodes(json);
        // Create a node for every leaf data element
        var selection = vis.selectAll("g.node")
            .data(data.filter(function(d) { return !d.children;
})));
        var node = selection.enter().append("g");

        node.attr("class", "node");
        node.append("title")
```

```
                  .text(function(d) { return d.domain });
           node.attr("transform", function(d) { return "translate(" +
      d.x + "," + d.y + ")"; });
           node.append("circle")
                .attr("r", function(d) { return d.r; })
                .style("fill", function(d) { return fill(d.domain);
       });
           node.append("text")
                .attr("text-anchor", "middle")
                .attr("dy", ".3em")
                .text(function(d) { return d.domain.substring(0, d.r /
      3); });
          });
      }());
```

In the following section, we're going to explain how D3 works and how we're using it to create a bubble chart:

How it works...

Unlike most other chart libraries, D3 doesn't have any predefined chart types that it is capable of drawing. Instead, it comes with a set of modular tools that you can freely mix and match to create any kind of data-driven documents.

However, D3 contains some very visualization-specific tools.

For example, `d3.scale.category20c` creates an ordinal scale. An ordinal scale maps input values to a discrete set of output values. In this case, the discrete set of values is a set of 20 predefined output colors. The scale is a function—it maps the input values to the output. We can specify explicitly which input values map to which outputs, but if we don't, it's inferred from usage. In our case, it means that the first domain name will be mapped to the first color, the second to the second, and so on.

Other tools include jQuery-like DOM selection tools, which, in our recipe, we use to add the SVG element to our chart placeholder.

Another example are D3 layouts. To draw a bubble chart we need a pack layout. Layouts map a set of objects with values to a set of output coordinates based on certain rules and constrains. A popular example is a **force layout**, which is a graph layout that arranges the objects by iteratively applying virtual forces between graph nodes.

We're using the pack layout that produces hierarchical packing of objects into circles. Our data is flat, therefore the pack layout is only used to arrange our circles automatically. A pack layout is created and assigned to the `bubble` variable.

The pack layout works by applying the `bubble.nodes` function to the input data. This function looks for the `value` property in each of the objects in the input data. Based on this property (which it treats as a relative radius) and the size of the layout, it adds the following properties into our data: x, y, and r and returns the resulting array of objects.

At this point we have most of the data needed for our bubble chart: we have the positions and dimensions of our bubbles. All we need to do now is to turn them into the appropriate SVG elements. The tool we use to do this is D3's `selectAll` function.

Unlike jQuery selectors, D3's `selectAll` can be used to maintain a two-way mapping between the document and a data object. We specify the data array mapped to our selection by using the selection's `.data` function.

After we declare this mapping, we can decide what happens when an element is added to our data array using the `.enter` function. In our recipe, we declare that a new SVG graphic element is added to the SVG canvas, and assign that declaration to the `node` variable.

It's important to note that our node variable is not holding the SVG element; rather, it's a selection of every graphics SVG element in the set of nodes that will be created in the future, whenever a new data element "enters" the selection. Therefore, operations on the node specify the operations that will be executed on every added SVG element.

We specify that every node will have a `title` attribute (which will appear on mouse over). The inner text of this title is dependent on the specific element in the data array. To describe this, we pass a function as the argument to the `.text()` call. The first argument of the passed function will be the data element of the particular node, and the returned value should be the text that will be set as the title.

Similarly, we move our bubbles to the position calculated by the pack layout. Afterwards, we add the circle with a radius calculated by the pack layout for the circle and the colors scale to generate colors for the circle.

Finally, a text node is appended in the same way.

The following is how the result looks like:

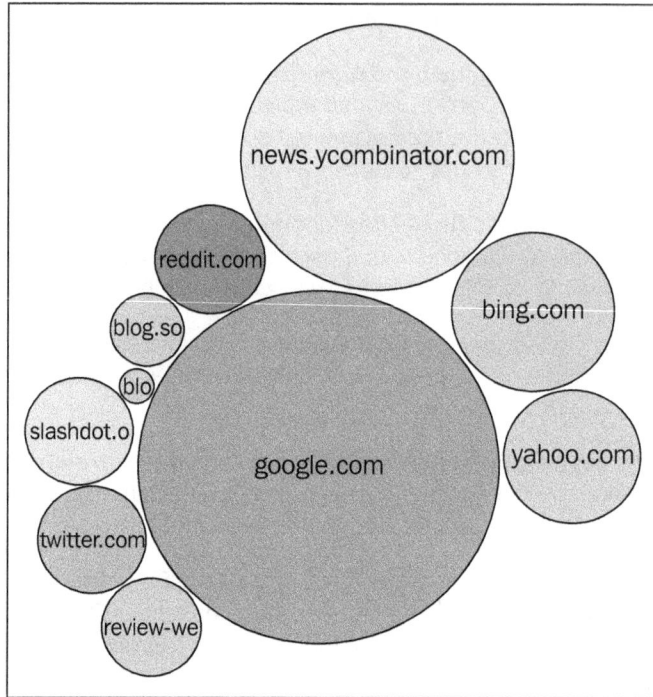

There's more...

This example used SVG (scalable vector graphics) markup to render the visualization. Most modern browsers support SVG, but Internet Explorer versions prior to IE9 don't. However, D3 isn't limited to SVG—it is also able to generate HTML elements that could be used as a replacement in older versions of IE.

Showing a map with a marked location

The rise of Google Maps and their excellent API popularized the embedding of maps on websites. Embedded maps have a variety of uses: displaying places that users have been to, displaying locations of events, displaying locations of stores owned by a business, and many others. Maps can be displayed along with every textual address displayed on our websites.

In this recipe we're going to make a simple map with a single location marked on it. To do this, we're going to use the **Leaflet** library (`http://leafletjs.com/`), which is a well known and widely library used by Flickr, FourSquare, Craigslist, Wikimedia, and other popular sites.

We're going to display an **OpenStreetMap** map layer. OpenStreetMap (`http://www.openstreetmap.org/`) is a free Wikipedia-like collaboratively created street map with great coverage.

We're also going to add a description balloon, which would be displayed when the placemark is clicked.

How to do it...

Let's write the HTML and JavaScript code.

1. Add Leaflet's stylesheet in our HTML file, along with a conditional extra CSS required for IE8 and older:

   ```
   <link rel="stylesheet" href="http://cdn.leafletjs.com/leaflet-0.4/
   leaflet.css" />
    <!--[if lte IE 8]>
        <link rel="stylesheet" href="http://cdn.leafletjs.com/
   leaflet-0.4/leaflet.ie.css" />
   <![endif]-->
   ```

2. Include the Leaflet library JS file in our scripts:

   ```
   <script src="http://cdn.leafletjs.com/leaflet-0.4/leaflet.js"></
   script>
   ```

3. Put a placeholder for the map on our page. We must also specify its height, otherwise Leaflet will not work properly:

   ```
   <div id="map" style="height:200px;"></div>
   ```

4. Add our JS code by adding `example.js`:

   ```
   <script src="example.js"></script>
   ```

5. Finally, add the code to create the map in `example.js`:

```
var map = L.map('map').setView([51.505, -0.09], 13);

L.tileLayer('http://{s}.tile.openstreetmap.org/{z}/{x}/{y}.png',{
        attribution:'Copyright (C) OpenStreetMap.org',
        maxZoom:18
        }).addTo(map);

var marker = L.marker([51.5, -0.09]).addTo(map);
marker.bindPopup("<b>Hello world!</b><br>I am a popup.").
openPopup();
```

How it works...

Most map libraries draw their maps by using a tile image layer. Tile image layers are grids of images with a predefined, fixed size. The images are sliced parts of the map, which has been pre-rendered and hosted on the tile servers.

The map uses discrete points of zoom called **zoom levels**. Different tile images are used at different zoom levels.

In some cases, especially at high zoom levels, the server renders the tiles on the fly as the space needed to cache the images exceeds reasonable storage space sizes. For example, OpenStreetMap uses 19 zoom levels. The first level uses a single tile, the second splits this tile into four tiles, the third uses 16, and so on. At the 19th zoom level, there are 48 billion tiles—assuming an average tile size of 10 KB, that would take 480 terabytes of storage.

When the user scrolls the map, tiles of previously unloaded areas are loaded on the fly and shown in the container. When the user changes a zoom level, tiles for the old zoom level are removed and new tiles are added.

In our `example.js` file, we use Leaflet's functions (found in the `L` namespace object) to create the map. The map is initialized with a center placed in London with the help of as array representing a `[latitude, longitude]` pair. The other parameter is the zoom level, which is set at `13`.

Afterwards a tile layer is added. We specify the tile server pattern that OpenStreetMap uses as follows:

```
http://{s}.tile.openstreetmap.org/{z}/{x}/{y}.png
```

Where `s` is the server letter (`a`, `b`, or `c`), `z` is the zoom level and `x` and `y` are the discrete coordinates of the tile. For example, at zoom level 1, each of `x` and `y` can be either `1` or `2`, while at zoom level 2 they can be in the range 1 to 4 and so on. We also specify the maximum zoom level available.

We add our own marker to the map. The initialization parameter is a `[latitude, longitude]` pair. Afterwards, we can add a pop up inside the marker showing text and/or arbitrary HTML. We open the pop up immediately.

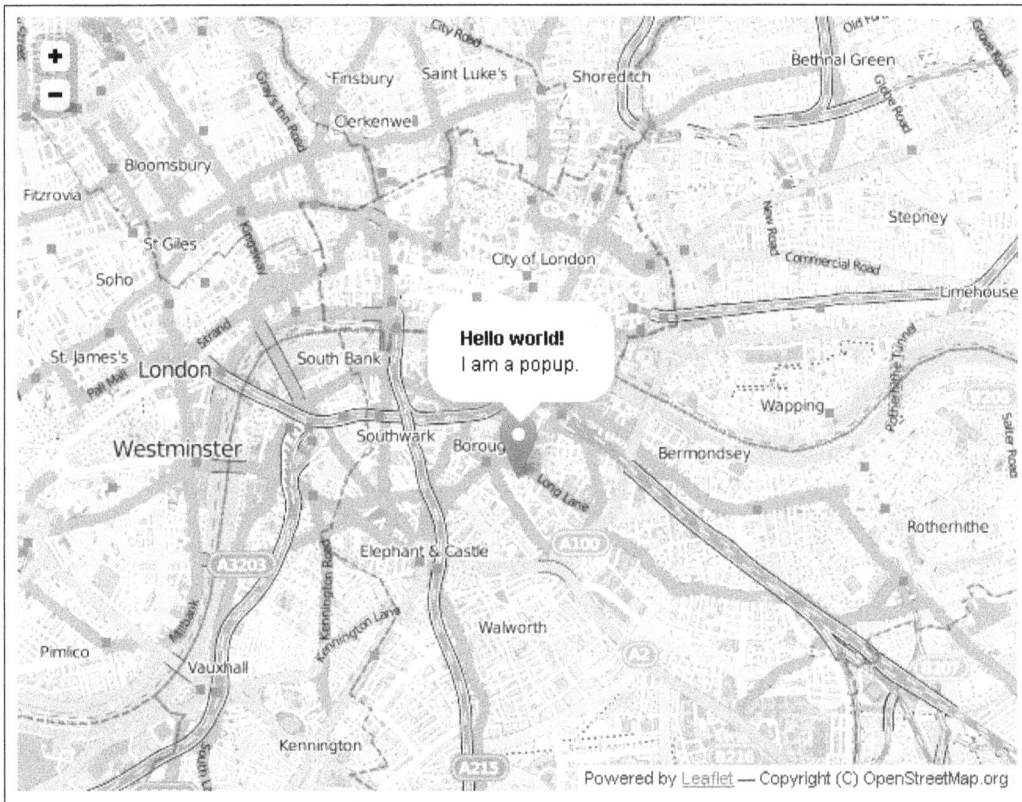

Map drawn with Leaflet

Showing a map with a path

When displaying maps, sometimes we may want to show more than just locations. Besides markers, the other most common map overlays are paths and areas.

In this recipe, we're going to create a map showing a path and an area.

How to do it...

Let's write the HTML and JavaScript code.

1. Like in the *Showing a map with a marked location* recipe, we'll need to include the appropriate CSS and scripts. The following is an example HTML file:

```
<!DOCTYPE HTML>
<html>
    <head>
        <title>Map example</title>
        <link rel="stylesheet" href="http://cdn.leafletjs.com/
leaflet-0.4/leaflet.css" />
        <!--[if lte IE 8]>
        <link rel="stylesheet" href="http://cdn.leafletjs.com/
leaflet-0.4/leaflet.ie.css" />
        <![endif]-->
    </head>
    <body>
        <div id="map" style="height:480px; width:640px;"></div>
        <script src="http://ajax.googleapis.com/ajax/libs/
jquery/1.8.2/jquery.min.js"></script>
        <script src="http://cdn.leafletjs.com/leaflet-0.4/leaflet.
js"></script>
        <script type="text/javascript" src="example.js"></script>
    </body>
</html>
```

2. Then we can add our code to example.js:

```
var map = L.map('map').setView([52.513, -0.06], 14)

L.tileLayer('http://{s}.tile.openstreetmap.org/{z}/{x}/{y}.png',{
    attribution:'Copyright (C) OpenStreetMap.org',
    maxZoom:18
}).addTo(map);

var polyline = L.polyline([
    [52.519, -0.08],
    [52.513, -0.06],
    [52.52, -0.047]
]).addTo(map);


var polygon = L.polygon([
    [52.509, -0.08],
```

```
        [52.503, -0.06],
        [52.51, -0.047]
    ], {
        color:"#f5f",
        stroke: false,
        fillOpacity:0.5
    }).addTo(map);
```

How it works...

We create our map using the `L.map` function and set the map's position using `setView` at the specified `[latitude, longitude]` array and the zoom level. We also add the standard OpenStreetMap tile layer.

First we create and add a standard polyline. As we don't specify any options, Leaflet uses reasonable defaults for colors, opacity, borders, and so on. The polyline constructor takes an array of `[latitude, longitude]` pairs and draws a line with vertices that go through them.

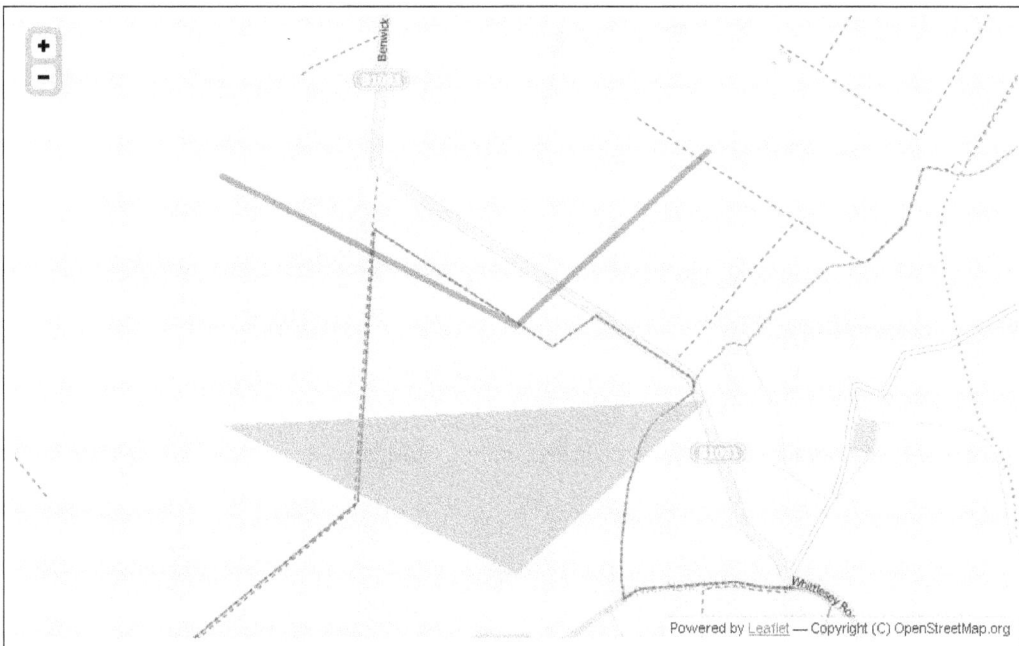

Afterwards, we create a slightly customized polygon. Like the polyline constructor, the polygon also takes an array of `[latitude, longitude]` pairs. Additionally, we customize the background color, remove the polygon's border, and specify the polygon's opacity to be 50 percent.

Displaying gauges

Analog gauges are useful for visualizing data with values bound between predefined minimums and maximums, which undergo changes over time. Examples include amount of fuel, current speed, disk space, process and memory usage, and so on.

In this recipe, we're going to make a very flexible, data-driven gauge plugin for jQuery. Then we're going to use this plugin to display an analog car speedometer. The following is how the speedometer will look:

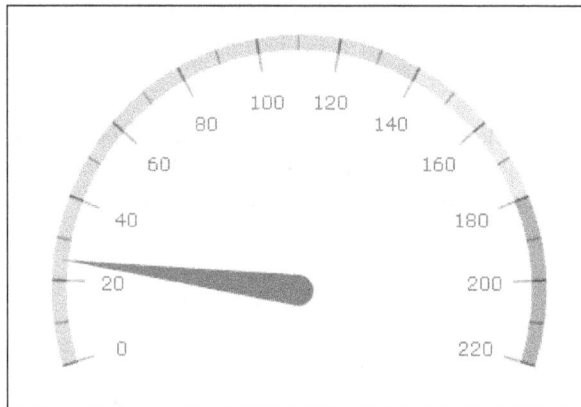

The recipe makes extensive use of HTML5's canvas.

How to do it...

Let's write the HTML code for our example, the gauge plugin and the code that ties them together.

1. Make a simple HTML file with a canvas for our gauge:

```
<!DOCTYPE HTML>
<html>
    <head>
        <title>Gauge example</title>
    </head>
    <body>
        <canvas id="gauge" width="400" height="400"></canvas>
        <script src="http://ajax.googleapis.com/ajax/libs/
jquery/1.8.2/jquery.min.js"></script>
        <script type="text/javascript" src="example.js"></script>
    </body>
</html>
```

2. Then write our gauge plugin code in `example.js`:

    ```
    (function($) {
    ```

3. This is a support function that replaces `Array.forEach` and works on both single items and arrays. Our gauge will support multiple stripes, needles, and ticks, but it should also be able to work when a single one is provided:

    ```
    function eachOrOne(items, cb) {
        return (items instanceof Array ? items : [items]).map(cb);
    }
    ```

4. The following is a generic function that rotates the point `pt` around the center `c` (the angle amount is `a`). Direction is clockwise:

    ```
    function rotate(pt, a, c) {
        a = - a;
        return { x: c.x + (pt.x - c.x) * Math.cos(a) - (pt.y-c.y)
    * Math.sin(a),
                 y: c.y + (pt.x - c.x) * Math.sin(a) + (pt.y-c.y)
    * Math.cos(a) };
    }
    ```

5. The following is our gauge plugin

    ```
    $.gauge = function(target, options) {

        var defaults = {
            yoffset: 0.2,
            scale: {
                type: 'linear',
                values: [1, 200],
                angles: [0, Math.PI]
            },
            strip: {
                scale: 0, radius: 0.8, width: 0.05,
                color: "#aaa", from: 0, to: 200
            },
            ticks: {
                scale: 0, radius: 0.77, length: 0.1, width: 1,
    color: "#555",
                values: {from: 0, to:200, step: 10},
            },
            labels: {
                scale: 0, radius: 0.65,
                font: '12px Verdana', color: "#444",
                values: {from: 0, to:200, step: 20}
            },
            needle: {
    ```

```
                    scale: 0, length: 0.8, thickness: 0.1,
                    color: "#555", value: 67
              }
        };
```

By default, our gauge has the following:

- ❑ Is offset 20% from the top
- ❑ Has a linear scale with a value range 1 to 200, angle range 0 to 180 degrees,
- ❑ Has a single strip at 80% or total radius with a width of 5% of total radius colored with gray and going from 0 to 200.
- ❑ Has a single `ticks` array going from 0 to 200 with `step` 10
- ❑ Has labels from 0 to 200 with step 20
- ❑ Has a single needle set at value 67

6. We allow the user to override options and to specify more than one of any of the components mentioned previously:

```
var options = $.extend(true, {}, defaults, options);
for (var key in defaults) if (key != 'yoffset')
      options[key] = eachOrOne(options[key], function(item)
{
            return $.extend(true, {}, defaults[key], item);
      });
var $target = $(target);
var ctx = $target[0].getContext('2d');
```

7. We construct our `scale` function and replace our objects specifying ranges of values with actual arrays. Note that instead of a `range` object, you can also specify an actual array:

```
options.scale = eachOrOne(options.scale, function(s) {
      return $.gauge.scale(s);
});
eachOrOne(options.ticks, function(t) {
      return t.values = $.gauge.range(t.values);
});
eachOrOne(options.labels, function(l) {
      return l.values = $.gauge.range(l.values);
});
```

8. The following is the drawing code:

```
function draw(options) {
```

9. We will use the gauge center as a reference point and will clear the canvas:

```
var w = $target.width(), h = $target.height(),
    c = {x: w * 0.5, y: h * (0.5 + options.yoffset)},
    r = w * 0.5,
    pi = Math.PI;
ctx.clearRect(0, 0, w, h);
```

10. Then we'll draw all the strips (one or more) as arcs:

```
// strips
eachOrOne(options.strip, function(s) {
    var scale = options.scale[s.scale || 0];
    ctx.beginPath();
    ctx.strokeStyle = s.color;
    ctx.lineWidth = r * s.width;
    ctx.arc(c.x, c.y, s.radius * r, scale(s.to),
scale(s.from), true);
    ctx.stroke();
});
```

11. Then draw all the ticks (we use very short, very thick arcs as ticks). Our `scale` function turns the values in `range` to angles:

```
// ticks
eachOrOne(options.ticks, function(s) {
    var scale = options.scale[s.scale || 0];
    ctx.strokeStyle = s.color;
    ctx.lineWidth = r * s.length;
    var delta = scale(s.width) - scale(0);
    s.values.forEach(function(v) {
        ctx.beginPath();
        ctx.arc(c.x, c.y, s.radius * r,
            scale(v) + delta, scale(v) - delta, true);
        ctx.stroke();
    });
});
```

12. Then we draw the labels. We determine the position by placing it at the right-most vertically-centered position, then rotating it counter-clockwise by the amount scaled with the value:

```
// labels
ctx.textAlign    = 'center';
ctx.textBaseline = 'middle';
eachOrOne(options.labels, function(s) {
    var scale = options.scale[s.scale || 0];
    ctx.font = s.font;
```

```
            ctx.fillStyle = s.color;
            s.values.forEach(function(v) {
                var pos = rotate({x: c.x + r * s.radius,
y:c.y},

                     0 - scale(v), c);
                ctx.beginPath();
                ctx.fillText(v, pos.x, pos.y);
                ctx.fill();
            });
        });
```

13. Finally, we draw the needles. The needles are made of a circle centered at the central rotation point of the gauge and a triangle extending from there. We rotate all three triangle points the same way we rotate the label centers:

```
        // needle
        eachOrOne(options.needle, function(s) {
            var scale = options.scale[s.scale || 0];
            var rotrad = 0 - scale(s.value);
            var p1 = rotate({x: c.x + r * s.length, y: c.y},
rotrad, c),
                 p2 = rotate({x: c.x, y: c.y + r*s.
thickness/2}, rotrad, c),
                 p3 = rotate({x: c.x, y: c.y - r*s.
thickness/2}, rotrad, c);
            ctx.fillStyle = s.color;
            ctx.beginPath();
            ctx.arc(c.x, c.y, r * s.thickness / 2, 0, 2*Math.
PI);
            ctx.fill();
            ctx.beginPath();
            ctx.moveTo(p1.x, p1.y);
            ctx.lineTo(p2.x, p2.y);
            ctx.lineTo(p3.x, p3.y);
            ctx.fill();
        });
    }
    draw(options);
```

14. After drawing the whole gauge, the gauge function returns a function that can be used to change the gauge needle value(s) and redraw it:

```
        return function(val, i) {
            i = i || 0;
            options.needle[i].value = val;
            draw(options);
        }
    };
```

15. These are common helper functions. The `range` function creates an array of values, while `scale` creates a function that scales values from one range to another. Both support logarithmic scales:

```
$.gauge.range = function(opt) {
    if (opt instanceof Array) return opt;
    var arr = [], step = opt.step;
    var last = opt.from;
    for (var k = opt.from; k <= opt.to; k+= step)
        arr.push(opt.log ? Math.pow(opt.log, k) : k);
    return arr;
};
$.gauge.scale = function(opt, f) {
    if (opt.type == 'linear') opt.type = function(x) { return
x; };
    else if (opt.type == 'log') opt.type = Math.log;
    var f = opt.type,
        v0 = f(opt.values[0]),
        v1 = f(opt.values[1]);
    return function(v) {
        return (f(v) - v0) / (v1 - v0)
                * (opt.angles[1] - opt.angles[0]) + Math.PI +
opt.angles[0];
    };
}
}(jQuery));
```

The anonymous function is invoked with the jQuery object as a parameter that, in the scope of the function, becomes $. This is a typical way to construct jQuery plugins with their own private scope, and to make jQuery available as $ within that scope regardless of whether $ is the same as jQuery in the global namespace.

16. We will draw our gauge in `example.js`. The following is the content:

```
$(function() {
    var g = $.gauge("#gauge", {
        scale: {
            angles: [-0.3, Math.PI+0.3],
            values: [0, 220]
        },
        strip: [
            { from: 0,   to: 140, color:"#ada" },
            { from: 140, to: 180, color:"#dda" },
            { from: 180, to: 220, color:"#d88" }
        ],
        ticks: [{
```

```
                color: "rgba(0,0,0,0.33)",
                values: { from: 0, to: 220, step:10 },
                length:0.05, radius:0.8, width:0.3
            }, {
                color: "rgba(0,0,0,0.33)",
                values: { from: 0, to: 220, step:20 },
                length:0.11, radius: 0.77, width:0.3
            }],
            labels: {
                color: "#777",
                values: { from: 0, to: 220, step:20 },
                radius: 0.62
            },
            needle: { color:"#678" }
        });
        g(25);
    });
```

How it works...

We specified a linear scale for the gauge with angles going slightly below the middle, and speed values in the range 0 to 220. We created three strips, the green one in the range 0 to 140 km/h, a yellow one in the range 140 to 180 km/h, and a red one in the range 180 to 220 km/h. We're going to use two sets of strips: one larger every 20 km/h and one smaller on every 10 km/h, both semi-transparent. Finally, we add a needle with a bluish tint.

At the end, we can set our gauge value with the returned function, which we use to set it at 25 km/h.

Displaying a tree

In this recipe, we will take a look into how to display data in a tree-like layout. We are going to visualize a small family tree of Linux represented via JSON file. Additionally, will be using the D3.js file for manipulating the DOM to display the data.

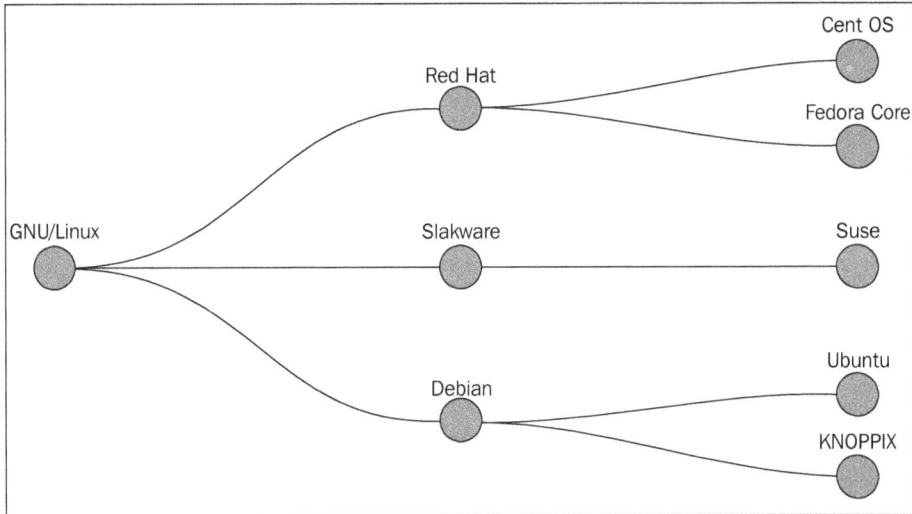

Getting ready

First, we need to have the data that is going to be used for the visualization. We need to get the `tree.json` file that is part of the examples for this recipe.

How to do it...

We will write the HTML and the backing JavaScript code that should generate data from a JSON file:

1. Let's first take a look a the structure of the JSON data:

```
{
  "name": "GNU/Linux",
  "url": "http://en.wikipedia.org/wiki/Linux",
  "children": [
    {
      "name": "Red Hat",
      "url": "http://www.redhat.com",
      "children": [ .. ]
    } ]
  ...
}
```

Each object has a name attribute representing the distribution name, a `url` attribute that has a link to the official web page, and the optional `children` attribute that can contain a list of other objects.

2. Next step would be to create the page using the HTML5 doctype, and adding the dependency to `D3.js` and a CSS file called `tree.css`:

```
<!DOCTYPE html>
<html>
  <head>
    <title>Linux Tree History</title>
    <script src="http://d3js.org/d3.v2.js"></script>
    <link type="text/css" rel="stylesheet" href="tree.css"/>
  </head>
```

3. In the body section, we are going to add a `<div>` tag having an `id` called `location` that we are going to use as placeholder, and additionally include a JavaScript file called `tree.js` that will be used to include the logic for mapping the data:

```
<body>
  <div id="location"></div>
  <script type="text/javascript" src="tree.js"></script>
</body>
</html>
```

4. Let's start with creating the display area in the `tree.js` file. First, we create the anonymous function that provides private state of the variables used inside:

```
(function() {
```

5. We then set up the size of the generated image with given `width` and `height`. For simplicity, we set them to fixed values:

```
var width = 1000,
        height = 600;
```

6. Afterwards, we set up a standard D3 layout tree:

```
var tree = d3.layout.tree()
        .size([height, width - 200]);
var diagonal = d3.svg.diagonal()
        .projection(function(d) {
          return [d.y, d.x];
        });
```

7. As we need to designate and create the actual SVG, we pick the location using the id previously chosen in the HTML called `location`, and append SVG element:

```
var vis = d3.select("#location").append("svg")
        .attr("width", width)
        .attr("height", height)
        .append("g")
        .attr("transform", "translate(60, 0)");
```

8. We also need to read out the data from `tree.json` and somehow create nodes and links with the given hierarchy:

```
d3.json("tree.json", function(json) {
    var nodes = tree.nodes(json);
    vis.selectAll("path.link")
            .data(tree.links(nodes))
            .enter().append("path")
            .attr("class", "link")
            .attr("d", diagonal);
    var node = vis.selectAll("g.node")
            .data(nodes)
            .enter().append("g")
            .append("a")
            .attr("xlink:href", function(d) {
                return d.url;
              })
            .attr("class", "node")
            .attr("transform", function(d) {
                return "translate(" + d.y + "," + d.x + ")";
              });

    node.append("circle")
            .attr("r", 20);

    node.append("text")
            .attr("dx", -19)
            .attr("fill", "white")
            .attr("dy", -19)
            .style("font-size", "20")
            .text(function(d) {
              return d.name;
            });
```

9. We can style the page using CSS, picking color for the link background of the page and the circle:

```
.node circle {
    fill: #fc0;
    stroke: steelblue;
    stroke-width: 1px;
}
.link {
  fill: none;
  stroke: #fff;
  stroke-width: 5.0px;
}
body{
    background-color: #000;
}
```

How it works...

The line `d3.layout.tree()` creates a new tree layout with default settings, where it is assumed that each input in the data element has a child array.

With `d3.svg.diagonal()`, we create a generator with default accessor functions. The returned function can generate the path data for a cubic Bézier connecting the nodes where we have tangents for smoothing the line.

> More information on Bézier curve can be found at `http://en.wikipedia.org/wiki/Bézier_curve`. There is some mathematics behind it, but the simplest explanation would be that it is a line affected by certain points making it a good pick to define curvy lines.

As we wanted to have the tree from left to right instead of the the default, which is from top to bottom, we need to change the default behavior by doing a projection:

```
var diagonal = d3.svg.diagonal()
        .projection(function(d) {
            return [d.y, d.x];
        });
```

The function will use `[d.y, d.x]` instead of the default `[d.x,d.y]`. One thing that you may have noticed is the `.append("g")` function that adds the SVG g element, which is a container element used for grouping together various related elements. We can have multiple nested elements inside, one within another, to an arbitrary depth, allowing us to create groups on various levels:

```
<g>
     <g>
     <g>
      </g>
     </g>
    </g>
```

To read the JSON data we've used the following:

```
d3.json("tree.json", function(json) { … }
```

That does an AJAX call to the `tree.json` resource.

> Note that, by default, your browser will not allow cross-domain requests. This includes requests to your local filesystem. To overcome this, please use a local web server explained in *Appendix A, Installing Node.js and Using npm*. Another option is to use JSONP as a great workaround, because with this security restriction there are some shortcomings. In *Chapter 8, Communicating with Servers*, we cover the issues and the reasoning behind these restrictions.
>
> For more information, take a look at the W3C page at `http://www.w3.org/TR/cors/`.

We then automatically map the data from the JSON file with `tree.nodes(json)`, where some assumptions are made on what we have inside the data; for example, we can have a parent node or children nodes.

After that, we selected all the `path.link` using W3C selectors that resemble a lot like the jQuery ones:

```
vis.selectAll("path.link")
```

Using `.data`, we bind them with link information that is returned by `tree.links`:

```
.data(tree.links(nodes))
```

What happens in the background is that D3's tree layout has a `links` function that accepts an array of nodes, and returns an array of objects representing the links from parent to child for each of these nodes. Links for the leafs will not be created. The information stored in the returned object has a `source` or the parent node and `target` or the child node. Now, in the following part, there is the .enter() function that's very much D3 magic. What happens is that, for every element in the array that is part of .data([theArray]) and has no corresponding DOM element found in the selection, it simply "enters inside the data" allowing us to use .append, .insert, .select, or .empty operators. In our case, we want to create SVG path elements having a CSS class of `link` and a d attribute calculated using the diagonal function we previously defined:

```
.enter()
.append("path")
.attr("class", "link")
.attr("d", diagonal)
```

So, for each data element, it will create `<path class='link'
d='dataCalucatedByDiagonal' />`.

The SVG path element is a concept used to represent a line drawing that we would do with a pen, for example, having various types of geometry and representation. The d attribute contains the path data designated with `moveto(M)`, `lineto(L)`, `curve(cubic and
quadratic besiers)`, `arc(A)`, `closepath(Z)`, `vertical lineto (V)`, and so on.

It's good to know what is generated by D3 for us in order to understand more completely how it works. Let's say we want to display a simple line:

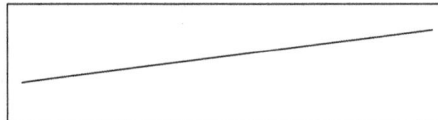

The SVG code would be as follows:

```
<svg xmlns="http://www.w3.org/2000/svg" version="1.1">
  <g style="stroke: red; fill: none;">
    <path d="M 10 30 L 200 10"/>
  </g>
</svg>
```

Examining the path data values, we can see that it means move `pen(M)` to `(10,30)` and draw `line(L)` to `(200,10)`.

In our example with the tree, we have the lines drawn using paths, so the next step would be to draw the nodes. We apply the same procedure where we select all the old `g.node` elements and enter the node data, but instead of creating the `<path/>` element, we just append `"g"` and additionally add an `<a>` element with the `<xlink:href>` attribute:

```
...
        .append("a")
        .attr("xlink:href", function(d) {
            return d.url;
        })
```

As we are already automatically iterating all the data nodes, we can access `d.url`, retrieving the URL for each node and setting it as a link to all the inner elements that we are going to add later.

Don't forget that we need to rotate the coordinates, because we want the tree to be displayed from left to right:

```
        .attr("transform", function(d) {
            return "translate(" + d.y + "," + d.x + ")";
        });
```

After this, we can append other elements to each of the elements, so in order to create the circle, we add the following:

```
    node.append("circle")
            .attr("r", 20);
```

That creates an SVG circle with radius of 20px, also, we append the `<text/>` element that will display the distribution name:

```
    node.append("text")
            .attr("dx", -19)
            .attr("dy", -19)
            . . .
```

Notice that we are moving the text element with `(-19,-19)` in order to avoid overlapping with the circle and the lines, and that is it.

There's more...

The first thing you must do is play around with the values that are constant, such as the image size or text offset. This will help you better understand how changes affect the layout. There are various different functions to generate the layout, you can create it in a radial fashion or make it dendrite-like.

There are various ways to add interaction where you can have updates on certain portion of the code, make some parts animated, or even include HTML inside the SVG.

LED scoreboard using web fonts

In this recipe, we are going create an LED scoreboard similar to the ones used in basketball games by making a clever use of HTML web fonts. The main goal of the recipe is to get introduced to web fonts and the features they offer.

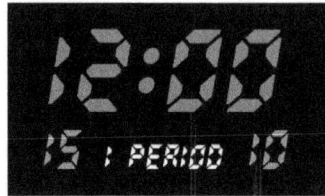

> [💡] The full specification on web fonts can be found on W3C at `http://www.w3.org/TR/css3-webfonts/`.

Getting ready

Before staring, you need to get the font we are going to use in this example. The files can be retrieved from the examples code, and they all have a RADIOLAND prefix.

How to do it...

To create the scoreboard, we will create an HTML page, a backing JavaScript code that will update the timers, and related data, as well as a CSS file that will use web fonts:

1. First, we will start with creation of the HTML page; in the `head` section, include `stylesheet.css` and a dependency to jQuery

    ```html
    <link rel="stylesheet" href="stylesheet.css" type="text/css" charset="utf-8">
    <script src="http://ajax.googleapis.com/ajax/libs/jquery/1.8.2/jquery.min.js"></script>
    ```

2. In the `body` part, add the `div` elements that we are going to use as placeholders for the scores and additionally include `scoreboard.js`:

    ```html
    <div class="counter"></div>
    <div class="score">
            <span class="home"></span>
             <span class="period"></span>
             <span class="guests"></span>
    </div>
    </div>
    <script type="text/javascript" src="scoreboard.js"></script>
    ```

3. We can now create the `stylesheet.css` file, defining first the web font that has the LED look:

```css
@font-face {
  font-family: 'RadiolandRegular';
  src: url('RADIOLAND-webfont.eot');
  src: url('RADIOLAND-webfont.eot?#iefix') format('embedded-
opentype'),
    url('RADIOLAND-webfont.woff') format('woff'),
    url('RADIOLAND-webfont.ttf') format('truetype'),
    url('RADIOLAND-webfont.svg#RadiolandRegular') format('svg');
  font-weight: normal;
  font-style: normal;
}
```

4. As the font is now defined as `RadiolandRegular`, we can refer to it directly:

```css
div.counter{
  font: 118px/127px 'RadiolandRegular', Arial, sans-serif;
  color: green;
}
    .score {
      font: 55px/60px 'RadiolandRegular', Arial, sans-serif;
      letter-spacing: 0;
      color: red;
      width: 450px;
    }

  .period {
      font: 35px/45px 'RadiolandRegular', Arial, sans-serif;
      color: white;
    }

  div.display {
      padding: 50px;
    }
```

5. We can proceed with the creation of the JavaScript that will be used and we'll use a mock object called `game` that has the game information. This object, in general, should be retrieved from a server using an AJAX call, but for simplicity, we are using some predefined values:

```javascript
var game = {
  periodStart: 1354650343000,
  currentPeriod: 1,
  score: {
    home: 15,
```

```
        guests: 10
    }
};
```

6. In order to have the logic for creation of our display object and for fetching the data separated, we can put it in a function:

```
function fetchNewData() {
    // server data
    var game = {
        periodStart: new Date().getTime(),
        //the server will return data like: periodStart:
1354838410000,
        currentPeriod: 1,
        score: {
          home: 15,
          guests: 10
        }
    };
    //return display data
    return {
        periodStart: game.periodStart,
        counter: '00:00',
        period: game.currentPeriod + ' Period',
        score: {
          home: game.score.home,
          guests: game.score.guests
        }
    };
}
```

7. We also create a `config` object where we can define game parameters, such as number of periods and minutes per period:

```
var config = {
    refreshSec: 1,
    periods: 4,
    minPerPeriod: 12
};
```

8. We then define the `updateCounter()` and `updateScore()` functions that will update the display and perform calculations for the timers. We are going to check if the current time is smaller that the start time of the game and set the timer to `00:00`. If current time is greater than the max possible, set the timer to max possible for a period:

```
function updateCounter() {
        var now = new Date(),
```

```
        millsPassed = now.getTime() - displayData.periodStart;

    if (millsPassed < 0) {
      displayData.counter = '00:00';
    } else if (millsPassed > config.minPerPeriod * 60 * 1000)
{
      displayData.counter = config.minPerPeriod + ':00';
    } else {
      //counting normal time
      var min = Math.floor(millsPassed/60000);
      if (min<10) {
        min = '0' + min;
      }
      var sec = Math.floor((millsPassed % 60000)/1000);
      if (sec<10) {
        sec = '0'+sec;
      }
      displayData.counter = min+':'+sec;
    }
    $('.counter').text(displayData.counter);
    $('.period').text(displayData.period);
```

9. Following that, we add a function that will update the score:

```
function updateScore(){
  $('.home').text(displayData.score.home);
  $('.guests').text(displayData.score.guests);
}
```

10. At the end, we can call the `setInterval` function that will call the updates every 500 milliseconds:

```
setInterval(updateCounter, 500);
setInterval(updateScore, 500);
```

How it works...

The HTML and JavaScript code are pretty straightforward in this recipe, but on the other hand, we are taking a deeper look at the CSS and the font files.

With the addition of the `@font-face` at-rule, we can specify online fonts to use in other other elements. By doing this, we allow the use of different fonts that are not available on the client machine.

In the definition of `@font-face`, we add `font-family`—a name definition that we can afterwards apply on any element. For example, consider the following example where we call our font `someName`:

```
@font-face {
  font-family: someName;
  src: url(awesome.woff) format("woff"),
       url(awesome.ttf) format("opentype");
}
```

You can notice the format definition named `format("woff")` next to `url` in this example as well as in our `stylesheet.css`. The following formats can be applied there:

- `.woff`: This stands for **Web Open Font Format** (**WOFF**), a format developed by Mozilla and is one of the newer standards around. The full specification is available on `http://www.w3.org/TR/WOFF/`. The format's goal is to provided alternative solutions to other formats that would be optimal for use in cases where we need a certain level of licensing. The format allows metadata to be attached to the file itself that can contain the license.

- `.ttf` and `.otf`: The **TrueType Font** (**TTF**) and the extended version **OpenType Font** (**OTF**) are some of the most widely used types. The standard for TrueType was developed by Apple Computers by the end of the 80s as a replacement of some of the PostScript standards. It provided the font developers with flexibility and control over how the fonts are shown to the user with many different sizes. Due to its popularity and features, it swiftly spreads over to other platforms such as Windows. OpenType is a successor to TrueType up on which it is based. The specification was developed by Microsoft with additions from Adobe Systems. The name OpenType is a registered trademark of Microsoft Corporation. Detailed specification can be found on `http://www.microsoft.com/typography/otspec/default.htm`.

- `.eot`: Embedded OpenType fonts are a form of OpenType fonts designed for use on web pages. The extensions done on the embedded versions are closely related to making copy protection. As the other fonts are easily copied, EOT gives only a subset of the available characters to the user, making it more difficult to copy the font fully. More information on EOT can be found on the W3C specification at `http://www.w3.org/Submission/EOT/`.

- `.svg` and `.svgz`: SVG and the gunziped version with extension `.svgz` can be used to represent fonts. The font definition is stored as SVG glyph allowing easy support. More on SVG fonts can be found on the specification at `http://www.w3.org/TR/SVG/fonts.html`. Unfortunately, this format is not supported in IE and Firefox at the time of writing.

There are few other attributes that can be used on `@font-face`, such as `font-style`, `font-weight`, and `font-stretch`. Also, we can specify a range of the characters used in Unicode by setting a value for `unicode-range`. Some examples for this taken from the specification are as follows:

- `unicode-range: U+0-7F;`: This is a code range for basic ASCII characters
- `unicode-range: U+590-5ff;`: This is a code range for Hebrew characters

One of the problems with web fonts is that no particular format is requested by the specification of CSS2. This often means that we need to offer several different formats to get identical experience across browsers.

> There a many `font-face` definition generators that simplify the creation of all of these possible options. One such is **FontSquirrel** (`http://www.fontsquirrel.com/tools/webfont-generator`).

Web fonts are becoming one of the most common building blocks of the Web, and as such, they should be always considered when we are in a need of a great looking typography. Images, SVG, Coufons, and similar types just don't play well with text. We might get great looking text using those, but the text will not be accessible by search engines, most of the accessibility software will ignore it, and it might even get the page size larger. On the other hand, using text allows us to do various CSS tweaks on the data where we can use selectors, such as `:first-letter`, `:first-line`, and `:lang`.

There's more...

Google has a good selection of fonts that we can use that are provided on `http://www.google.com/fonts/`. Besides the standard inclusion of fonts, they also have a JavaScript-based font loader. This loader solves the problem of seeing the fallback text rendering while the "real" font is loading, commonly known as **Flash of Unstyled Text** (**FOUT**). There, for example, we can do the following to include a font called `'Noto Sans'`:

```
<script type="text/javascript">
  WebFontConfig = {
    google: { families: [ 'Noto+Sans::latin' ] }
  };
  (function() {
    var wf = document.createElement('script');
    wf.src = ('https:' == document.location.protocol ? 'https' :
'http') +
        '://ajax.googleapis.com/ajax/libs/webfont/1/webfont.js';
    wf.type = 'text/javascript';
    wf.async = 'true';
    var s = document.getElementsByTagName('script')[0];
    s.parentNode.insertBefore(wf, s);
  })(); </script>
```

Afterwards, we can simply include it in CSS using `font-family: 'Noto Sans', sans-serif;`.

> More on the options for Google fonts can be found at `https://developers.google.com/fonts/`. As for the so-called FOUT and some of the ways to fight it there is more on an article by *Paul Irish* at `http://paulirish.com/2009/fighting-the-font-face-fout/`.

3
Animated Data Display

In this chapter we're going to cover the following recipes:

- ▸ Making a motion chart
- ▸ Displaying a force directed graph
- ▸ Making a live range chart filter
- ▸ Making an image carousel
- ▸ Zooming and panning a chart
- ▸ Using the web notifications API
- ▸ Creating interactive Geo charts from a dataset

Introduction

We are all living in an information age, where data is created in huge amounts every day. This excess amount of data is in dire need to be presented in a format that is accessible by the users.

This chapter will cover some common ways of doing animated data visualizations with minor interactions. Most of the examples will be data-driven documents, bounded to the page with D3 as well as with some other methods of animated data display.

> Throughout the book we use D3, so it is good to know some of the origins of it. Mike Bostock, the brilliant core author the library, has created it as an successor to a library that he created during his Ph.D. studies called Protovis, taking into account the web standards and making performance improvements. He also has an amazing visualizations list mostly done for the New York Times available at his site http://bost.ocks.org/mike/.

Making a motion chart

When working with a time-based data often you want to have a view, where the time changes will be visualized. One way of doing this is by using a motion chart that updates over time and that is what we will be creating with this recipe.

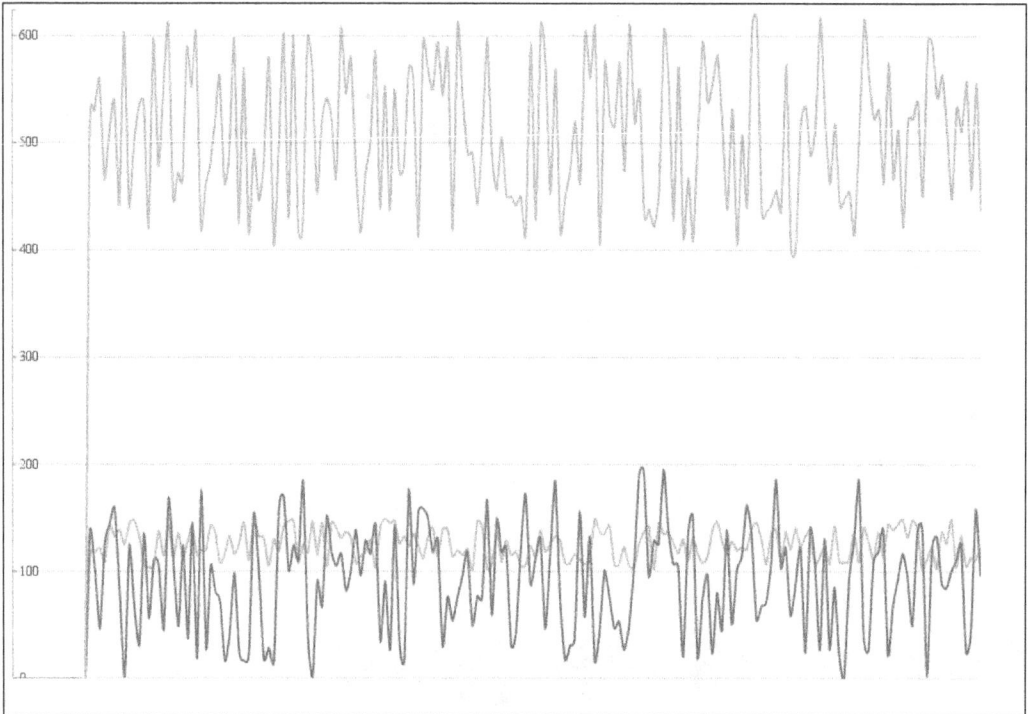

Getting ready

We will be using a toolkit for creating an interactive graph named **Rickshaw** that can be retrieved from `http://code.shutterstock.com/rickshaw/`, and is part of the example code as well. Besides that we also need `D3.js` to be included, because Rickshaw is built on top of it.

How to do it...

To create the recipe, we will add JavaScript code that will randomly generate data and create an interactive graph using Rickshaw.

1. First, we add the external JavaScript and CSS in the head section. By convention, we can put the vendor libraries in a separate folder `js/vendor/` and `css/vendor/`.

```
<!doctype html>
<head>
  <link type="text/css" rel="stylesheet"
    href="css/vendor/graph.css">
  <title>Motion chart</title>
  <script src="http://d3js.org/d3.v2.js"></script>
  <script src="js/vendor/rickshaw.js"></script>
</head>
```

2. We add the placeholders for the chart in the body section.

```
<div id="content">
  <div id="chart"></div>
</div>
```

3. We continue with the main part, the `js/example.js` file, where we first create a color palette, and then the refresh rate.

```
(function () {
  //create a color palette
    var palette = new Rickshaw.Color.Palette
      ({scheme: 'munin' });
  // we set the refresh rate in milliseconds
    var refreshRate = 500;
```

4. The next step is to create `Rickshaw.Graph` with SVG of size `900px` by `600px` and of the `line` type. We use the refresh rate we previously selected and the specified color palette.

```
// create graph
var graph = new Rickshaw.Graph({
  element: document.getElementById("chart"),
  width: 900,

height: 600,
  renderer: 'line',
  series: new Rickshaw.Series.FixedDuration(
    [
      { name : 'one' },
      { name : 'two' },
```

```
        { name : 'three' }
    ], palette, {
        timeInterval: refreshRate,
        maxDataPoints: 50
        }
    )
});
```

5. Following this we can add a Y axis to the created graph.

```
var yAxis = new Rickshaw.Graph.Axis.Y({
    graph: graph
});
```

Because we created the required objects, they can get rendered to the screen by calling .render on them.

```
graph.render();
yAxis.render();
```

6. We need data to display, so we will generate some random data, and add it to the graph. In order to add the data with a delay, use setInterval on a refreshRate period.

```
//random util
function getRandomInRange(n){
    return Math.floor(Math.random() * n);
}
// generate random data and add it to the graph
setInterval( function() {
    var data = {
        one: getRandomInRange(50) + 100,
        two: Math.abs(Math.sin(getRandomInRange(30)+1) ) *
            (getRandomInRange(100) + 100),
        three: 400 + getRandomInRange(110)*2
    };
    graph.series.addData(data);
    //update
    graph.render();   yAxis.render();
}, refreshRate );
```

At this point, we should be seeing something similar to the figure shown in the beginning of the recipe.

How it works...

The `Rickshaw.Color.Palette` we picked is with the scheme `munin`. There are also other palettes from which we can choose, such as `spectrum14` or `cool`. The palette is used in order to simplify and automate the picking of the colors for the graph. For example, if we manually call the `.color()` method multiple times.

```
palette.color()
```
```
"#00cc00"
```
```
palette.color()
```
```
"#0066b3"
```
```
palette.color()
```
```
"#ff8000"
```

It will always return the next color. Palette is a set of predefined colors that can be picked between given set of rules. For example, the original Nintendo Game Boy had four shades of green that could be used to display all the games. If we take a look at the implementation of the palettes in Rickshaw, we can notice that they are just a list of colors. The following is a snippet from Rickshaw source code definition of the palette `cool`:

```
this.schemes.cool = [
  '#5e9d2f',
  '#73c03a',
  '#4682b4',
  '#7bc3b8',
  '#a9884e',
  '#c1b266',
  '#a47493',
  '#c09fb5'
];
```

If we take a look at the `Rickshaw.Graph` creation, besides the SVG size, we picked the element with the ID `chart`, where the graph will get rendered.

```
element: document.getElementById("chart")
```

Additionally, we set the `renderer` type to `line`, but it can also be set to `area`, `stack`, `bar`, or `scatterplot`, depending on the result.

For the `series` property we use the following code snippet:

```
series: new Rickshaw.Series.FixedDuration([
  {name: 'one'},
  {name: 'two'},
  {name: 'three'}
  ], palette, {
```

```
    timeInterval: refreshRate,
    maxDataPoints: 50
    })
```

The first argument is the array with data names, after that comes the palette, and last is the options object where we set the update `timeInterval`. Additionally, `maxDataPoints` was set to `50`, and that one designates how many samples of data are currently displayed, meaning that we would display the last 50 objects.

Later on, we called the `.render()` method on the `graph` and `yAxis` objects for the first time, and afterwards, in the `setInterval()` method we called for re-rendering of them on every data change. The data for rendering we constructed had the following format:

```
var data = {
  one: someNumber,
  two: someNumber,
  three:  someNumber
  };
```

The preceding format represents a value for the three lines at the specific point of time.

This data object is passed into the series using the `addData()` method defined for `Rickshaw.Series.FixedDuration` that sets the latest update for the `series` property.

```
graph.series.addData(data);
```

If we need to get the current data for all the displayed frames, we could call the `graph.series.dump()` method.

That for example will return the following result:

```
Object:
  color: "#00cc00"
  data: Array[50]
  name: "one"
```

There's more...

There are various ways to customize the `chart` ID: filter information, add controls, or feed the data from a remote server. If we want to attach a legend, we can simply create such an object before the graph is rendered, and attach it to our graph object.

```
var legend = new Rickshaw.Graph.Legend({
  element: document.getElementById('legend'),
  graph: myGraph
  });
```

Displaying a force directed graph

In this recipe, we will create a graph with some of the characters of the play *Hamlet* by *William Shakespeare*. The idea is to visualize the connections between the characters in a fun and interactive way. The type of graph that will be visualized is known as **force directed** graph.

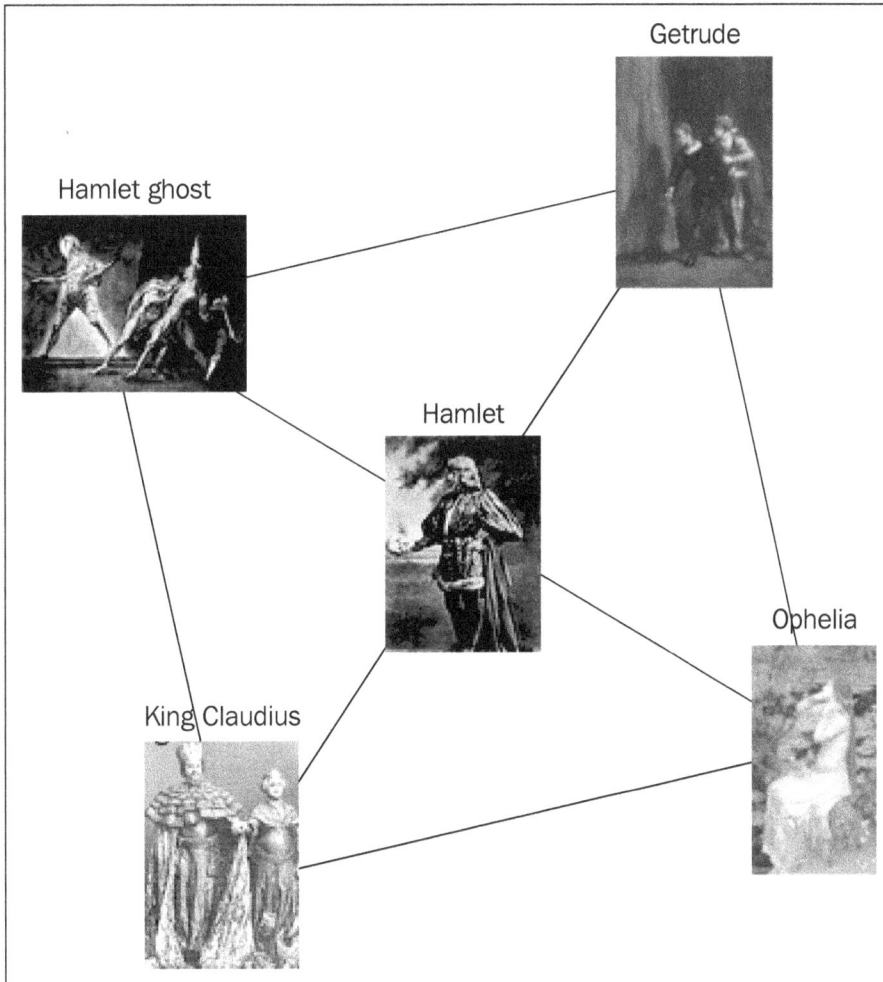

Getting ready

In order to visualize the connections between the characters, they need to be stored somehow. There is a sample `data.json` file that is a part of the code examples that you can use. Although we do encourage you to create your own sample data or at least play around with the existing one, but for the purpose of simplicity, we will be using the one provided in the code examples.

How to do it...

We will be creating a JSON file to contain the relation and image information, the HTML, and the accompanying JavaScript.

1. First, we can start with the creation of the data for the recipe. We can define the `nodes` list, where the object would be placed with the properties `name` that will designate the name of the node, **icon** will be the URL of the image, and group will be

```
{
  "nodes": [
    {
      "name": "Hamlet",
       icon":"http://upload.wikimedia.org/
          wikipedia/commons/thumb/4/4e/
             Bernhardt_Hamlet2.jpg/
                165px-Bernhardt_Hamlet2.jpg"
    },
    {
      "name": "King Claudius",
      "icon": "http://upload.wikimedia.org/
          wikipedia/commons/thumb/b/b4/
             Massalitinov_and_Knipper_in_Hamlet_1911.jpg/
                167px-Massalitinov_and_Knipper_in_Hamlet_1911
                   .jpg"
    },
```

2. After adding the nodes in the data, we also need information about how they are connected. To do that we will add a list of `links` to the model.

```
"links": [
  {
    "source": 1,
    "target": 0
  }
  {
    "source": 3,
    "target": 0
  }
]
```

3. Now we can proceed with the creation of the HTML file. For this implementation we will be using D3.js, so we need to include it and also setup two CSS classes, one for the link and the other for the node text.

```
<script src="http://d3js.org/d3.v2.min.js"></script>
<style>
.link {
  stroke: #aaa;
}
.node text {
  pointer-events: all;
  font: 14px sans-serif;
  cursor: pointer;
  user-select: none;
}
</style>
```

4. After this, we can start adding the parts in the main script. As in the previous examples, we will first add the SVG into the body element with some predefined size.

```
(function (){
  var width = 960,    height = 600;
  var svg = d3.select("body").append("svg")
  .attr("width", width)
  .attr("height", height);
}
```

5. Now we can create the layout for the graph.

```
var force = d3.layout.force()
.gravity(.04)
.distance(350)
.charge(-200)
.size([width, height]);
```

6. The next step is to map the data from the JSON document with the force layout and create all of the links and nodes.

```
d3.json("data.json", function(json) {
  force.nodes(json.nodes)
  .links(json.links)
  .start();
  var link = svg.selectAll(".link")
  .data(json.links)
  .enter().append("line")
  .attr("class", "link");
  var node = svg.selectAll(".node")
  .data(json.nodes)
```

```
        .enter().append("g")
        .attr("class", "node")
        .call(force.drag);
    }
```

7. We then append `image` from the model, defined as `icon` and `text` with the name of the node.

```
node.append("image")
.attr("xlink:href", function(d){return d.icon;})
.attr("x", -32)
.attr("y", -32)
.attr("width", 100)
.attr("height", 100);

node.append("text")
.attr("dx", -32)
.attr("dy", -32)
.text(function(d) { return d.name });
```

8. Also on force changes and updates, we will set up a listener that will update the links and nodes positions.

```
force.on("tick", function() {
    link.attr("x1", function(d) { return d.source.x; })
    .attr("y1", function(d) { return d.source.y; })
    .attr("x2", function(d) { return d.target.x; })
    .attr("y2", function(d) { return d.target.y; });

    node.attr("transform", function(d)
        { return "translate(" + d.x + "," + d.y + ")"; });
    });
}());
```

How it works...

First, we will take a look at the CSS, and more specifically at `pointer-events` that we have set to `all`. This setting makes the element to be the target of mouse-events, when the pointer is in the interior or over the perimeter, and can only be used on the SVG elements. In order to disable the selection of the text, we use the CSS property `user-select`, and set it to the value of `none`.

> user-select is not consistent across browsers, and in order to use it, we can add browser specific CSS hack, such as the following:
>
> ```
> -webkit-touch-callout: none;
> -webkit-user-select: none;
> -khtml-user-select: none;
> -moz-user-select: none;
> -ms-user-select: none;
> user-select: none;
> ```

The layout used for this recipe is d3.layout.force() that does not create a fixed visual representation, but instead we define the parameters, such as friction, distance, and gravity strength. Depending on the data and mouse interactions, we get different views.

```
var force = d3.layout.force()
.gravity(.04)
.distance(350)
.charge(-200)
.size([width, height]);
```

When constructing the layout after setting the parameters and the data information about the links and nodes, we need to call the start() method.

```
force.nodes(json.nodes)
.links(json.links)
.start();
```

We want to create the g element for all the nodes from our data, and set the appropriate CSS class node.

```
var node = svg.selectAll(".node")
.data(json.nodes)
.enter().append("g")
.attr("class", "node")
.call(force.drag);
```

Also, add a behavior to allow interactive dragging using .call(force.drag).

The g element represents a container that can be used to group other elements. Transformations that are applied to the g element are also performed on all of its child elements. This feature makes the element a good pick for organizing different section of view blocks.

> More on the g element can be found in the SVG specification from http://www.w3.org/TR/SVG/struct.html#Groups.

The `force.drag()` method is predefined in the `d3.layout.force()` method. Drag event is fixed to work on `mouseover` to allow catch of moving nodes. When the `mousedown` event is received, the nodes are dragged to the mouse position. Interesting is that this behavior supports the touch events from mobile devices, such as iOS or Android. In order to disable the click events for the nodes while dragging, `mouseup` is captured and stopped from propagating.

To create an image for the nodes, we add SVG `image` tag with `xlink:href` to the URL from the data stored in `d.icon`.

```
node.append("image")
.attr("xlink:href", function(d){return d.icon;})
```

In order to have the update from the layout, there are `tick` events that are dispatched on each tick of the visualization. In order to keep the elements updated, we added a listener for the event.

```
force.on("tick", function() {
  link.attr("x1", function(d) { return d.source.x; })
  .attr("y1", function(d) { return d.source.y; })
  .attr("x2", function(d) { return d.target.x; })
  .attr("y2", function(d) { return d.target.y; });
  node.attr("transform", function(d)
    { return "translate(" + d.x + "," + d.y + ")"; });
  });
```

The listener sets the correct positions for the movements to the `link` and `node`.

There's more...

One of the more obvious options here is to add more interactions to the visualization. Nodes can be made collapsible and links can be added to the nodes. Relationships between the nodes can be set to more fine-grained levels There are ways to make the data refresh over time and reload certain portions of the graph. If needed, there can be preset expected layout, so that the node will try to confirm a certain positioning.

> Learn more on D3 force layout and the related functionality from
> `https://github.com/mbostock/d3/wiki/Force-Layout`.

Making a live range chart filter

When working with large amounts of data, we usually want to add some way of filtering or picking up what data to show. This recipe will cover a simple range filter for the graph and a chart that displays time-varying series of data.

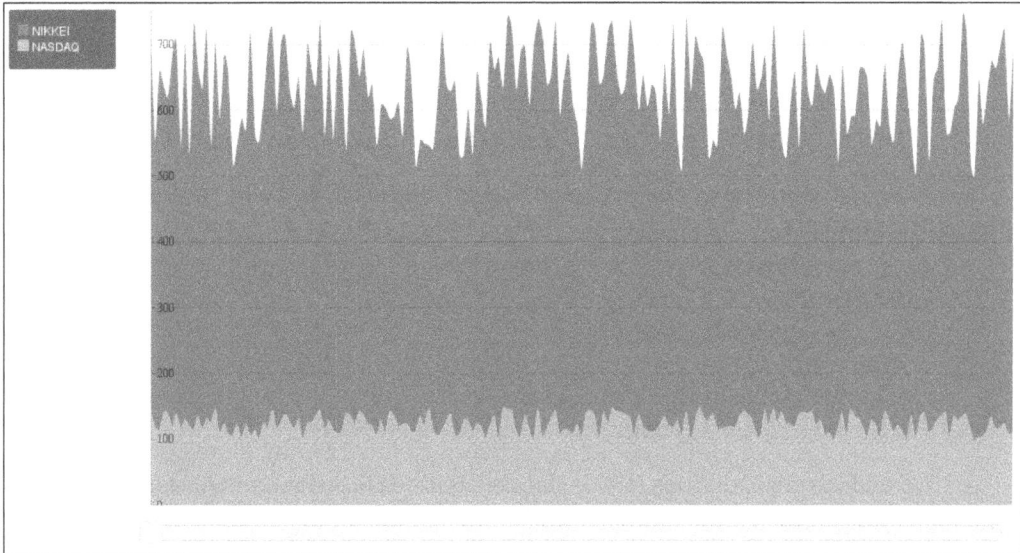

Getting ready

We will be using the same toolkit from the *Making a motion chart* recipe for creating interactive graphs. The necessary library Rickshaw can be retrieved from `http://code.shutterstock.com/rickshaw/`, and is part of the example code as well. Besides that we also need D3, because Rickshaw works on top of it.

How to do it...

We will create an HTML page containing a JavaScript file while generating a random data for the graph, and also add additional filtering elements.

1. First, we will make an HTML page and include the required CSS by the libraries.

    ```
    <!DOCTYPE html>
      <html>
        <head>
          <link type="text/css" rel="stylesheet"
            href="css/vendor/graph.css">
    ```

```
        <link type="text/css" rel="stylesheet"
          href="css/vendor/legend.css">
        <link rel="stylesheet" type="text/css"href="http:
          //code.jquery.com/ui/1.9.2/themes/base/
            jquery-ui.css">
        <link type="text/css" rel="stylesheet"
          href="css/main.css">
      </head>
```

2. Notice that we add an additional file `legend.css` that contains the layout information about the graph legend. We can then add our custom CSS file.

```
<link type="text/css" rel="stylesheet" href="css/main.css">
```

3. The HTML placeholders for the graph, legend, and slide will be the regular `div` elements.

```
<div id="content">
<div id="chart"></div>
<div id="legend"></div>
</div>
<div style="clear:both"></div>
<div id="slider"></div>
```

4. We add the dependencies for the libraries. Besides Rickshaw and its dependency D3, we are going to add jQuery and jQuery UI, because we will be using controls from there. And now, we can proceed to the main JavaScript, and start with defining the color palette and the refresh rate.

```
var refreshRate = 300;
var palette = new Rickshaw.Color.Palette
   ( { scheme: 'munin' } );
```

5. The next step is to create the graph in the chart element with `900px` by `500px` size.

```
var graph = new Rickshaw.Graph( {
   element: document.getElementById("chart"),
   width: 900,
   height: 500,
   renderer: 'area',
   series: new Rickshaw.Series.FixedDuration([{
     color: palette.color(),
     name: 'NASDAQ'
   },
   {
     color: palette.color(),
     name: 'NIKKEI'
   }], palette, {
     timeInterval: refreshRate,
```

```
    maxDataPoints: 200,
     timeBase: new Date().getTime() / 1000
   })
 });
```

6. As for the `slider` property, Rickshaw provides us with a ready control that we can connect to the graph we created.

```
var slider = new Rickshaw.Graph.RangeSlider({
   graph: graph,
   element: $('#slider')
});
```

7. To have a Y axis drawn, we can create it, and can connect it to our graph.

```
var yAxis = new Rickshaw.Graph.Axis.Y({
   graph: graph
});
```

8. For creation of a legend on the colors and names of the data samples displayed, there is a control that we can use and connect with our graph as well, while we also specify the element where it will get rendered.

```
var legend = new Rickshaw.Graph.Legend({
   graph: graph,
   element: $('#legend').get(0)
});
```

9. Because this example has a time-series component, we will generate random data. After the generation of the data, we call `graph.series.addData(data)` and re-render the `graph` and `yAxis` property. This generation, data update, and rendering happens on every `refreshRate` milliseconds.

```
function getRandomInRange(n) {
   return Math.floor(Math.random() * n);
}
setInterval( function() {
   var data = {
     one: getRandomInRange(50) + 100,
     two: 400 + getRandomInRange(110)*2
   };
   graph.series.addData(data);
   graph.render();
   yAxis.render();
}, refreshRate );
```

How it works...

Let's take a look at the graph's series input parameters.

```
series: new Rickshaw.Series.FixedDuration([{
  color: palette.color(),
  name: 'NASDAQ'
  }, {
  color: palette.color(),
  name: 'NIKKEI'
  }], palette,
```

Besides the graph data we also have a `name` and a `color` property. Now, the first thing you might ask yourself is, why have a `color` property and input a palette as well? Well, we do this in order to enable the other plugins to be able to read this information.

One of these plugins is `Rickshaw.Graph.Legend` that constructs a legend-box displaying info for each of the data streams.

We also add a range-filtering on the X axis with `Rickshaw.Graph.RangeSlider`.

```
var slider = new Rickshaw.Graph.RangeSlider({
  graph: graph,
  element: $('#slider')
});
```

In the background, the `slider` property uses jQuery UI control that is set to `range:true`. The minimum and maximum values are used from the current graph data. The `slider` property has a `slide` event that is used to limit the sample size displayed on the graph.

Because there is data being added constantly to the graph, the `slider` properties min and max values are set accordingly by an event from the graph. These are some of the considerations that you need to keep in mind while you are developing a custom control.

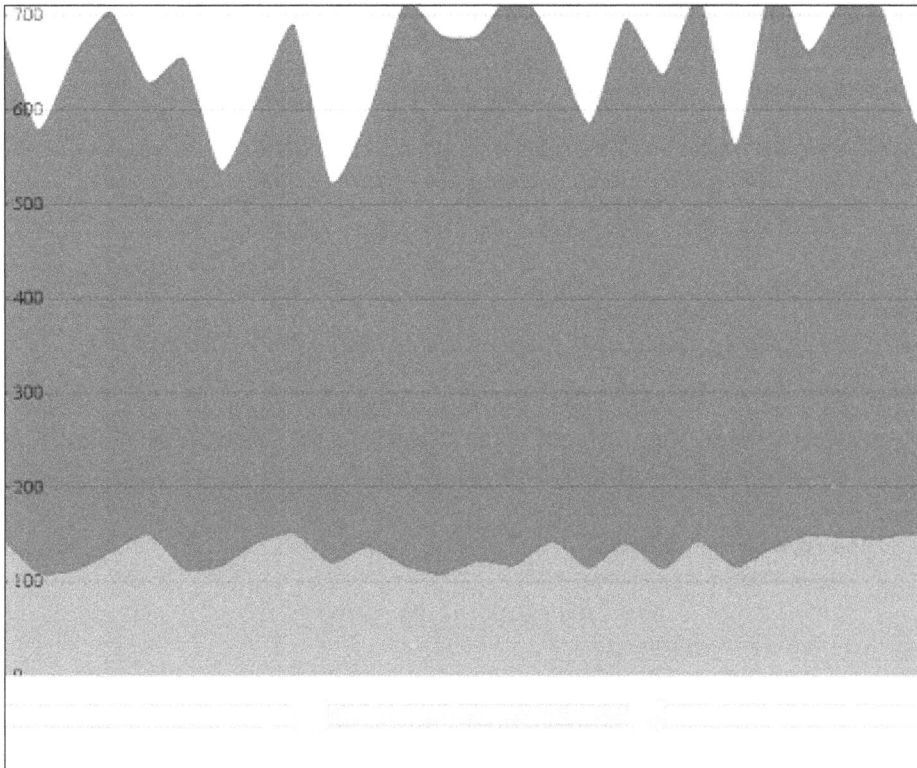

Slider set to only show a given portion of time. Because the time changes the slider is moved alongside with the data.

Making an image carousel

Image carousels are among the most popular marketing and showcase tools used on websites. They can also be used to show image galleries or presentations.

In this recipe we're going to build an image carousel. It will support automatic timed transitions that stop if the user moves over the carousel area. It will have a navigation area consisting of control rectangles denoting the currently active images and the number of remaining images.

This will be a 3D carousel utilizing HTLM5 features, such as CSS3 3D transforms.

Getting ready

We will need three images in the directory along with our code. They should be named `1.jpg`, `2.jpg`, and `3.jpg` respectively.

How to do it...

We will be creating the image carousel by using jQuery, HTML5, and CSS transformations.

1. First, we will create an HTML page with a carousel and the gray image controls. We're going to position the controls in the middle-bottom section of the carousel.

```
<!DOCTYPE html>
<html>
  <head>
    <title>Image carousel</title>
    <style type="text/css">
```

2. To get a 3D view that has depth, the main container must have a `perspective` property. It denotes the distance of the viewer from the screen. It will make nearby things look larger, and distant things look smaller.

```
#carousel {
  perspective: 500px;
  -webkit-perspective: 500px;
  position:relative; display:inline-block;
  overflow:hidden;
}
```

3. We're going to place all our images inside the rotator, then rotate the rotator itself. To do this, rotations on the rotator must preserve the 3D transforms of the child elements.

4. Additionally, both the rotator and the images will have a transition animation. We specify this by adding the `transition` property. In our example, transitions will work on transforms and will be one second long.

```
#rotator {
  transform-style: preserve-3d;
  -webkit-transform-style: preserve-3d;
  position:relative;
  margin:30px 100px;
  width:200px; height:200px;
  transition: transform 1s;
  -webkit-transition: -webkit-transform 1s;
}
#rotator img {
  position:absolute;
  width: 200px; height:200px;
  transition: transform 1s;
  -webkit-transition: -webkit-transform 1s;
}
#controls {
  text-align: center;
```

```
  position:absolute;
  left:0; bottom:0.5em;
  width:100%;
}
#controls span {
  height: 1em; width: 1em;
  background-color:#ccc;
  margin: 0 0.5em;
  display: inline-block;
}
  </style>
</head>
<body>
  <div id="carousel">
    <div id="rotator">
      <img class="image" src="1.jpg">
      <img class="image" src="2.jpg">
      <img class="image" src="3.jpg">
      </div>
    <div id="controls"></div>
  </div>
  <script src="http://ajax.googleapis.com/ajax/libs/jquery
    /1.8.2/jquery.min.js"></script>
  <script type="text/javascript" src="example.js">
</script>
</body>
</html>
```

5. The code that animates the carousel and makes the controls clickable will be in example.js.

```
(function() {
  $("#carousel").on('mouseover', pause);
  $("#carousel").on('mouseout', start);
  var position = 0;
  var all = $("#carousel").find('.image');
  var total = all.length;
```

6. We will place all the images in their appropriate position in the 3D space, each one rotated by a multiple of an angle and moved by a calculated amount. For more information see the *How it works...* section of this recipe.

```
var angle = (360 / total);
var deg2radfac = 2 * Math.PI / 360;
var zMovement = $("#rotator").width() / 2 *
  Math.tan(deg2radfac * angle / 2);
all.each(function(k) {
```

```
    var trans = 'rotateY(' + (angle * k).toFixed(0) + 'deg)
      '
    + 'translateZ('+ zMovement.toFixed(0) + 'px)';
    $(this).css('transform', trans);
    });
    $("#rotator").css('transform', 'translateZ
      ('+ (0 - zMovement).toFixed(0) + 'px)');
```

7. For each image we add a control marker, which can activate that image.

```
for (var k = 0; k < all.length; ++k) {
  $('<span />').attr('data-id', k).appendTo("#controls");
}
$("#controls").on('click', 'span', function() {
  changeTo(position = $(this).attr('data-id'));
});
ctrls = $("#controls span");
start();
```

8. Finally, let's write the functions that change the position of the carousel. The `change` function changes the position by `dir` elements, and `changeTo` changes the position directly to the specified element. Then we can start our carousel timer.

```
function change(dir) {
  dir = dir || 1;
  position += dir;
    if (position >= all.length) position = 0;
    else if (position < 0) position = 0;
    changeTo(position);
  }
function changeTo(position, cb) {
  ctrls.css({'opacity': 0.33});
  ctrls.eq(position).css({'opacity': 1});
  $("#rotator").css('transform',
  'translateZ('+ (0 - zMovement).toFixed(0) + 'px) ' +
  'rotateY(' + (angle * position).toFixed() + 'deg) ');
  }
function start() { timer = setInterval(change, 5000); }
function pause() {
  if (timer) { clearInterval(timer); timer = null; }
  }
}());
```

How it works...

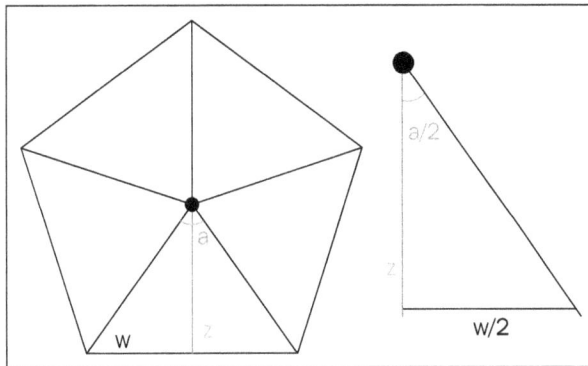

Building our carousel depends on the number of images we're going to use. To get a better sense of what exactly happens when we apply our transforms, lets look at the top view of a carousel. The preceding figure shows a carousel with five sides. Each side is translated away from the center point by a distance z, then rotated by an angle a multiple times. The angle can be calculated as follows: `a = 360 / number Of sides`.

The translation z however is slightly harder to calculate. To do that, we need to look at the triangle that consists of z and half of the sides width. By applying a trigonometric equation `tan(a/2) = (w/2) / z` we can calculate `z = w/2 / tan(a/2)`.

To rotate the carousel, we rotate the `rotator` parent by an angle a every 5 seconds. The user is allowed to click on the controls to change the rotation.

We also move `rotator` in the opposite direction by z to make the distance of the front element in the carousel the same, as if it hasn't been translated.

We hope that this recipe added some fun and freshness into the slightly dull topic of carousel making, by using some new HTML5 features, which will surely wow the users.

> Some of the CSS3 features are not widely available as of this writing. Internet Explorer 9, which otherwise does support a lot of HTML5 doesn't have them, though they're available in Internet Explorer 10. Before using these techniques, review the target browser requirements.

Zooming and panning a chart

The charts we discussed in the preceding chapter of this book were static. As such, they're great for visualizing limited quantities of data. However, when the dataset grows too large, users might be needed to interactively choose the range of data shown in the chart.

To enable this, we're going to make a chart that is capable of interactive controls, such as zooming and panning. The Flot chart library easily supports this with its navigation plugin.

In this recipe, we're going to show a one week temperature history at 30 minute increments. We're going to allow the user to zoom and pan the history.

Getting ready

We'll need to download Flot from the official website `http://www.flotcharts.org/` and extract the contents to a separate folder `flot`.

How to do it...

To create this recipe, we will add Flot, jQuery, and create an HTML file.

1. First, we create a basic HTML page with a placeholder for our chart. We're also going to include jQuery (needed by Flot), Flot itself, and the Flot navigate plugin. Flot needs to draw the chart canvas a placeholder `div`, so we're going to provide one. The placeholder needs to have `width` and `height` specified via CSS; otherwise Flot may fail to draw the chart correctly.

```
<!DOCTYPE HTML>
<html>
  <head>
    <title>Chart example</title>
  </head>
  <body>
    <div id="chart" style="height:200px;
      width:800px;"></div>
    <script src="http://ajax.googleapis.com/ajax/libs/
      jquery/1.8.2/jquery.min.js"></script>
    <script src="flot/jquery.flot.js"></script>
    <script src="flot/jquery.flot.navigate.js"></script>
    <script type="text/javascript" src=
      "example.js"></script>
  </body>
</html>
```

2. We're going to add our code in `example.js`.

```javascript
$(function() {
  var now   = Date.now();
  var hour = 60 * 60 * 1000, day = 24*hour;
  var weekAgo = now - 7*day;
  var zoomOut = null;

  function getData(cb) {
    var temperatures = [];
    // Generate random but convincing-looking data.
    for (var k = 24 * 7; k >= 0; --k)
    temperatures.push([now - k*hour,
      Math.random()*2 + 10*Math.sin(k/4 + 2)]);
    cb(temperatures);
  }

  getData(function(data) {
    var p = $.plot("#chart", [{data: data}], {
      xaxis: {
        mode: 'time',
        zoomRange: [day / 2, 7 * day],
        panRange: [weekAgo, now]
      },
    yaxis: { zoomRange: false,   panRange: false },
    zoom: { interactive: true },
      pan:  { interactive: true }
    });
  zoomOut = p.zoomOut.bind(p);
  });
  $('<input type="button" value="zoom out">')
  .appendTo("#chart")
  .click(function (e) {
    e.preventDefault();
    zoomOut && zoomOut();
  });
});
```

How it works...

To draw the chart, first we wrote the function `getData` to generate some convincing looking random data of temperature that rises during the day and falls during the night. Because it is callback based, we can replace this function with one that fetches the data from a server.

The plot drawing function `$.plot` takes three arguments. The first is the plot placeholder, the second is an array of series we need to draw, and the third are drawing options. We're going to pass only one series.

The new additions to our chart are to the plot options and the zoom-out button. We specify the zoom and pan range in the axes options. Our Y axis doesn't support zooming and panning, so it has been disabled.

The `zoomRange` option specifies the minimum and maximum range of the full plot when zooming. For example, our options specify that the plot will zoom to show at least half a day and at most a week in its full range.

The `panRange` option specifies the minimal minimum and maximal maximum on the X axis. In our example, we specify that the user cannot pan the chart to make its minimum value go below `weekAgo`, and cannot pan it to make its maximum value go above `now`.

Finally, we specify that zooming and panning will be interactive. This means that the user can zoom-in using double-click, and can pan it by dragging with the mouse.

To allow the user to reset the zoom, we add a `zoomOut` button, which calls the `zoomOut` function. We need to update this function whenever we redraw the plot, because the object returned from the `$.plot` call changes. This way multiple `getData` calls are allowed.

With this, we've added interactivity to our charts, allowing the user to customize the range of data they would like to view. Flot navigation works with all kinds of charts; be sure to check out the preceding chapter to see an overview of some of the chart types that are supported.

Using the web notifications API

Web notifications are one of the newer features added into modern browsers. They are intended as alerts for the user outside of the web page context. The idea is for them to be browsers intended, for example, when using a mobile browser notification could go into the home screen of the device. On the desktop usually they show up on the right-corner of the screen, at least on most desktop environments.

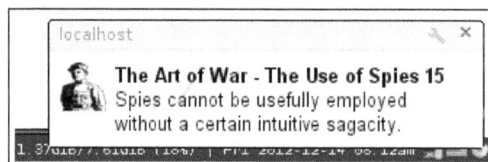

Getting ready

For the purpose of this example, we will be using data derived from Project Gutenberg `http://www.gutenberg.org/`. The data are the tips from the chapter *Use of spies* from *Sun Tzu's -Art of war* and can be found in this recipe code example under `data.json`.

How to do it...

To create this recipe we will create an HTML file, and use jQuery for simplicity.

1. First, we can start with the HTML part, where we just create a simple `button` and a `div` element with the ID `fallback` that we are going to use, if the browser does not support notifications.

```
<body>
  <button id="show">Show quote</button>
  <div id="fallback" ></div>
  <script src="http://ajax.googleapis.com/ajax/libs/
    jquery/1.8.2/jquery.min.js"></script>
  <script src="js/notification.js"></script>
  <script src="js/display.js"></script>
</body>
```

2. Let's first create the `notification.js` file that we will use as utility to create `simpleNotifations.show(data)`. The first check we have to do is verify support for `webkitNotifications`, the only full implementation at the time of writing.

```
var simpleNotification = (function () {
  var my = {};
  my.show = function (data) {
    if (window.webkitNotifications) {
      //check if there is a support for webkitNotifications
      if (window.webkitNotifications.checkPermission()
        == 0) {
        var notification = webkitNotifications
          .createNotification(data.icon, data.title,
            data.body);
        notification.show();
        //set timeout to hide it
        setTimeout(function(){
        notification.cancel();
      }, data.timeout);
    } else {
      webkitNotifications.requestPermission(function () {
        //call the same function again
        my.show(data);
```

```
            });
        }
    }
```

3. Next is the check for the real-standard-based web notification object, where in future, as browsers implement it more and more, it should be the first one.

```
else if (window.Notification) {
    if ("granted" === Notification.permissionLevel()) {
        var notification = new Notification(data.title, data);
        notification.show();
    } else if
    ("default" === Notification.permissionLevel() ) {
        Notification.requestPermission(function () {
            //call the same function again
            my.show(data);
        });
    }
}
```

4. Finally the case; if there is no support for any type of notification by the system we just use a callback to handle this case, where we also close the utility.

```
}else{
    //Notifications not supported, going with fallback
    data.errorCallback();
    }
};
return my;
}());
```

5. Next, we can continue with creating the `display.js` file that will get a random quote from the data, and call the previously defined `simpleNotification.show()` method. First we will do the fetching.

```
function fetchRandomQuote(location,data){
    $.ajax(
        {
            url:location,
            dataType:'json',
            success: function(result){
                var quoteNumber = Math.floor(Math.random()*26)+1;
                var obj = result.quotes[quoteNumber];
                for(var key in obj){
                    data.title += key;
                    data.body = obj[key];
                }
```

```
              simpleNotification.show(data);
          }}
        );
      };
```

6. Because we want some default behavior for all the notifications, such as icon, default
   message, or fallback function, we do the callout with a default `data` object.

```
$(document).ready(function() {
  $("#show").click(function (){
    var data = {
      icon: "images/war.png",
      title: "The Art of War - The Use of Spies ",
      body: "text",
      timeout : 7000,
      errorCallback: function(){
        $("#fallback").text(this.body);
        }
      };
    fetchRandomQuote('js/data.json',data);
  });});
```

How it works...

We will take a deeper look at the `notification.js` file, where most of the notification logic
is. The check tests we did on the notifications `if (window.webkitNotifications)` and
`if (window.Notification)` try to see if there is such object in the browser. If no such
object is there, this means there is no support for that type of notification. While on the other
hand, if the `if` condition was met, this means we have support, and can ask for permission.

```
if (window.webkitNotifications.checkPermission() == 0)
```

After that, we are free to create the notification and show it with the given parameters for
`icon`, `title`, and body.

```
var notification = webkitNotifications
  .createNotification(data.icon, data.title, data.body);
notification.show();
```

If we want the notification to hide after a given timeout, we add the following function:

```
setTimeout(function(){
  notification.cancel()
}, data.timeout);
```

On the other hand, if we do not have the permission to display a notification, we need to request it from the user, where we can do the call to our function once again.

```
webkitNotifications.requestPermission(function () {
  my.show(data);
}
```

> The request for the permission must come from a user-triggered event on some HTML element. In our case this is the `onClick` function on the button. More specifically the jQuery click `$("#show").click(function (){ ...}.`

We don't need to get into too much details for the fetching of the data, but in our default object we have the `icon` parameter with the value `images/war.png` that we will get used for the notification, as well as the `fallback` function and the `timeout` configuration.

```
var data = {
  icon: "images/war.png",
  title: "The Art of War - The Use of Spies ",
  body: "text",
  timeout : 7000,
  errorCallback: function(){
    $("#fallback").text(this.body);
  } };
```

> At the time of writing, Chrome is the only browser with full support for the notifications for quite some time, but Safari 6.0 and Firefox 22 Aurora also have initial implementations.
>
> The full specifications for web notifications can be found from `http://www.w3.org/TR/notifications/`.

Creating interactive Geo charts from a dataset

In this recipe, we will see how to create cool-looking interactive Geo charts, and how to use them for the display of data. These are becoming very common for the display of statistics on larger geographical area, usually from election results or global warming effects. In order to have a map covering multiple different countries, we will visualize the member and member applicant stats of the Commonwealth of Nations.

> The Commonwealth of Nations is a voluntary association of
> 54 independent sovereign states (one of whose membership
> is currently suspended). Most are former British colonies,
> or dependencies of these colonies. No one government in
> the Commonwealth exercises power over the others, as in a
> political union. Rather, the relationship is one of an international
> organization through which countries with diverse social, political,
> and economic backgrounds are regarded as equal in status, and
> cooperate within a framework of common values and goals, as
> outlined in the Singapore Declaration, which can be read from
>
> `http://en.wikipedia.org/wiki/Member_states_of_`
> `the_Commonwealth_of_Nations`.

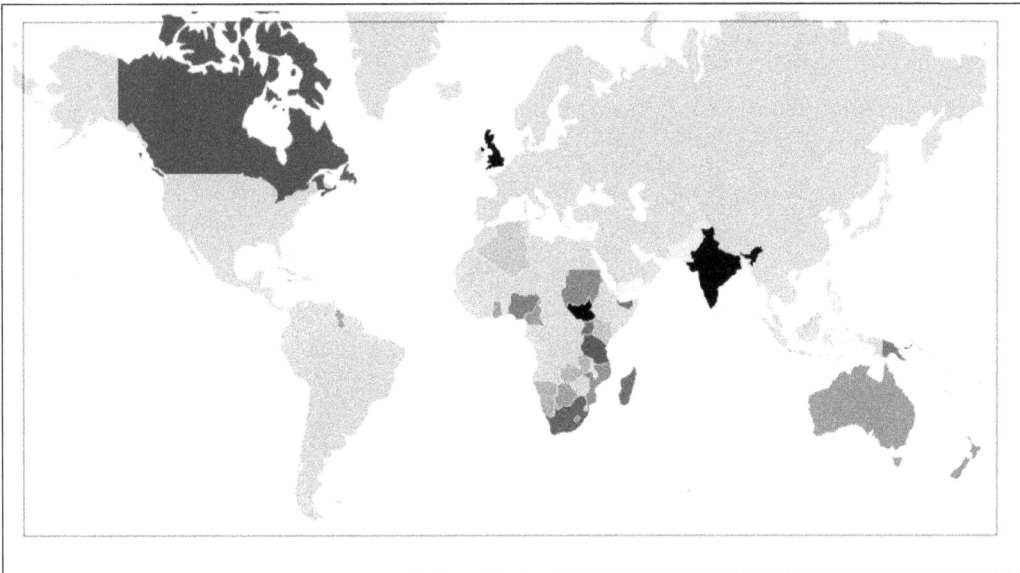

Getting ready

There are JSON object with definition of boundaries for valorous areas and scale levels mostly derived from the public domain dataset available at `http://www.naturalearthdata.com/downloads/`.

In our case, we use a `world-data.json` file that can be found as part of the code examples.

How to do it...

After getting the `world-data.json` file. we can start by creating the HTML and JavaScript files.

1. Let's first take a look at this country boundaries data in the `world-data.json` file for example, at the Bahamas.

```
{
    "type":"Feature",
    "properties":{
        "name":"The Bahamas"
    },
    "geometry":{
        "type":"MultiPolygon",
        "coordinates":[":[
            [
                [
                    [
                        -77.53466,
                        23.75975
                    ],
                    [
                        -77.78,
                        23.71
                    ], ...
            ]}}
```

In their properties we have the name of the country, and the geometry of the country represented as a polygon with multiple points.

> There are many different ways to create and represent the boundaries data. In order to create your own boundaries or get already available data, Open Street Map (`http://www.openstreetmap.org/`) is a great project that offers this options. For example, one of the tools called Osmosis can be used to get the vector data about certain objects at many different zoom levels from `http://wiki.openstreetmap.org/wiki/Osmosis`.

2. We can proceed with adding the CSS and dependencies to D3.js in the head.

```
<style>
  .frame {
    stroke: #333;
    fill: none;
    pointer-events: all;
  }
  .feature {
    stroke: #ccc;
  }
</style>
<script src="http://d3js.org/d3.v2.js"></script>
```

3. In the body part we directly start with the example.js file and define helpers with the data about the country names part of the euro-zone and utilities for generation of random numbers and colors.

```
<script>
var commonwealth = [
"Australia", "Algeria",
"The Bahamas", "Bangladesh",
"Belize", "Botswana",
"Brunei", "Cameroon",
"Canada", "Cyprus",
"Gambia", "Ghana",
"Guyana", "India",
"Jamaica", "Kenya",
"Lesotho", "Malawi",
"Malaysia", "Mozambique",
"Madagascar", "Namibia",
"New Zealand", "Nigeria",
"Pakistan", "Papua New Guinea",
"Rwanda", "Sierra Leone",
"Solomon Islands", "Somaliland",
"South Africa", "South Sudan",
"Sudan", "Sri Lanka",
"Swaziland", "United Republic of Tanzania",
"Trinidad and Tobago", "Yemen",
"Uganda", "United Kingdom",
"Vanuatu", "Zambia"
];

function random(number) {
  return Math.floor(Math.random()*number).toString(16)
```

```
        }
        function randomColor() {
            return "#"+random(255)+random(255)+random(255);
        }
```

4. There we add a utility function for getting a random color, if the country is part of the zone and #bbb, if not.

```
        function getColorForCountry(name){
            if(commonwealth.indexOf(name)<0){
                return "#bbb";
            }else {
                return randomColor();
            }
        }
```

5. Then to get the cool frame-like effect, we set the margins around it.

```
        var margin = {
            top: 10,    right: 10,
            bottom: 10,    left: 10
        },
            width = 960 - margin.left - margin.right,
            height = 500 - margin.top - margin.bottom;
```

6. Next we define the types of projection, zoom behavior, and path, where the zoom behavior add a callback on the `zoom` event to the `move()` method.

```
        var projection = d3.geo.mercator()
            .scale(width)
            .translate([width / 2, height / 2]);

        var path = d3.geo.path()
            .projection(projection);
        var zoom = d3.behavior.zoom()
            .translate(projection.translate())
            .scale(projection.scale())
            .scaleExtent([height, 10 * height])
            .on("zoom", move);
```

7. We create the SVG image with the previously set values for width and height, and call the zoom behaviors to get into the selected zoom level.

```
var svg = d3.select("body").append("svg")
  .attr("width", width + margin.left + margin.right)
  .attr("height", height + margin.top + margin.bottom)
.append("g")
  .attr("transform", "translate
    (" + margin.left + "," + margin.top + ")")
  .call(zoom);
```

8. First, we create the g element for the selected features of the map.

```
var feature = svg.append("g")
  .selectAll(".feature");
```

9. We then add the frame around the map by creating the SVG rectangle.

```
svg.append("rect")
  .attr("class", "frame")
  .attr("width", width)
  .attr("height", height);
```

10. Now we need to get the data from the world-data.json file, create the paths for the countries, and fill them with the appropriate color depending on whether d.properties.name is part of the needed group.

```
d3.json("js/world-data.json", function(data) {
  feature = feature
    .data(data.features)
    .enter().append("path")
    .attr("class", "feature")
    .attr("d", path)
    .style("fill", function(d)
      {return getColorForCountry(d.properties.name)});
  });
```

11. Finally, the move() function is called on zoom.

```
function move() {
  projection.translate(
    d3.event.translate).scale(d3.event.scale);
  feature.attr("d", path);
}
```

How it works...

First, `d3.geo.mercator()` constructs a **Mercator projection** from a spherical data representation.

> The Mercator projection is a cylindrical map projection created by Gerardus Mercator in 1569. It is very commonly used to represent maps, but it has the problem that the size and shape of the objects gets distorted as we move from the Equator towards the poles. More on Mercator projection can be found from `https://en.wikipedia.org/wiki/Mercator_projection` and `https://en.wikipedia.org/wiki/File:Cylindrical_Projection_basics2.svg`.

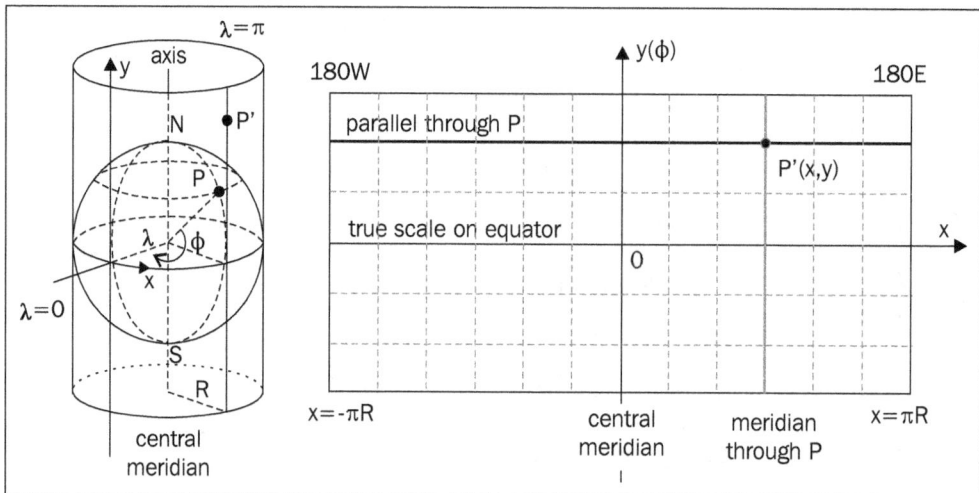

The `d3.geo.path()` method creates a new geographic generation with some predefined settings. We set this path generator to use our `projection` type.

```
var path = d3.geo.path()
    .projection(projection);
```

The `d3.behavior.zoom()` method enables us to add automatic zoom functionality to our `projection` type with the given scale and range of zoom in `scaleExtent`. Additionally, this creates a listener on the `zoom` event doing a call to the `move()` function.

```
d3.behavior.zoom()
    .scale(projection.scale())
    .scaleExtent([height, 10 * height])
    .on("zoom", move);
```

Main features that creates the counties is that we get the feature data from `world-data` and create the SVG path that actually represent individual countries, and we can then style and fill it with color.

```
d3.json("js/world-data.json", function(data) {
  feature = feature
    .data(data.features)
    .enter().append("path")
```

This type of map is also known as the choropleth map meaning a thematic map, where some statistical variable is displayed.

The file `js/world-data.json` contains the borders of each country with some metadata. The metadata is matched against our commonwealth list of countries. If they are a match, the country is colored. Note that there are few more countries that are not available in our map data.

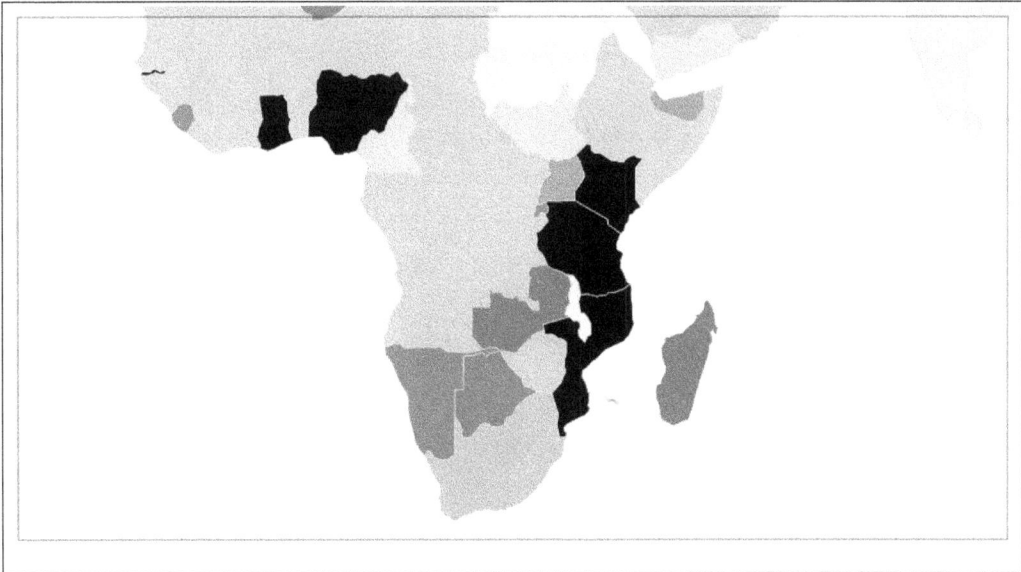

There's more...

When working with JavaScript and maps there are two formats that often pop up. One is GeoJSON (`http://www.geojson.org/`), a format for a variety of geographic data structures. The other is named TopoJSON (`https://github.com/mbostock/topojson`), and it is an extension of GeoJSON that encodes topology. TopoJSON uses line segments called arcs to get better characteristics than GeoJSON.

There is a company named CartoDB, `http://cartodb.com/` that specializes in the creation of maps, and while extensively using D3 in the background. They offer a free plan with a lot of options worth checking out, even though it is a commercial product.

4
Using HTML5 Input Components

In this chapter we will take a look at some of the great new element types added to HTML5. Topics covered are:

- ▸ Using the `text` input field
- ▸ Using `textarea`
- ▸ Inputting dates
- ▸ Inputting time
- ▸ Telephone input
- ▸ Range input filed
- ▸ Color picker input
- ▸ Using single-choice dropdowns
- ▸ Using multiple-choice select lists
- ▸ Getting geographical location input
- ▸ Using file inputs on client side
- ▸ Using drag-and-drop file area

Introduction

Forms are part of everyday web application development. We did lot of re-inventions to enable various input features. HTML5 adds few new input types and many different attributes and extensions to the existing structure. Most of these new stuff are already available in modern browsers and make life easier for all of us. For the things that are not there yet, we use a fallback that works on legacy systems. There is no good reason why you should not start using at least some of the features today.

> There are various ways to determine support for HTML5 features. Many sites provide a list of supported features but some of them worth mentioning are `http://caniuse.com/` and `http://html5please.com/`. You can often refer to them to get up to date information if you are not interested in adding fallback's.

Using the text input field

We will take a look at one of the basic examples of using input data with HTML `<input type="text">`. This input type automatically removes line breaks from the input values, so it's intended for single line text usage as shown in the following screenshot:

How to do it...

In the body section of the HTML document, we will create a form where the inputs with type `text` will be placed:

1. First we add the most basic input type `text`:

```
<form>
  <p>
    First name  <input name="firstname" type="text">
  </p>
```

2. Following that, we add one where audio input will be enabled:

```
  <p>
    Speak up <input name="quote" type="text" x-webkit-speech
speech>
  </p>
```

3. Also add one with the `placeholder` attribute and one with the `autofocus` attribute:

```
  <p>
    Last name: <input name="lastname" type="text"
placeholder="John Doe">
  </p>
  <label>
    Comment <input name="comment" type="text" title="This
      is area to insert your opinion" autofocus >  </label>
```

4. At the end, we add `submit` and close the form:

```
  <input type="submit" >
</form>
```

How it works...

The `<input name="firstname" type="text" >` element is the most basic HTML input element, where on submitting the form, the query parameter will be:

```
?firstname=someText&...
```

The next input element has an attribute `x-webkit-speech speech` that is, Chrome specific attribute allowing speech input, which means you can insert text using your microphone.

> Note that this will unlikely become standard since it relies on Google server-side processing for speech and as such is far from open web. In order to have widespread acceptance open speech providers should available.

For the third input element, we used the `placeholder` attribute that adds a beautiful hint inside the input field.

One new attribute added in HTML5 is `autofocus`. It is the Boolean valued attributes that allow us to specify what form control should have initial focus once the page gets loaded. We used the the single word syntax in our case but `autofocus="true"` will do the same trick. An additional thing to note here is that this can be appliqued on only one form element since that is the element that will get the initial focus and also it cannot be applied to `input type="hidden"`, since it does not make much sense to do so.

There's more...

If we are using our own fallback method for inserting voice data we can simply check if there is support for it in the current one in order to support other browsers:

```
var hasSupportForSpeach =
    document.createElement("input").webkitSpeech != undefined;
```

There is also an event being triggered that we can use for the voice input:

```
onwebkitspeechchange="myOnChangeFunction()"
```

> The open alternative for speech input that is developed is the **Web Speech API**. The main goal of it is to provide developers with a means to have speech input and output as text to speech. The API definition does not include implementation on where the recognition will be done, meaning server-side or client-side implementations are up to the vendor. More on the API on `https://dvcs.w3.org/hg/speech-api/raw-file/tip/speechapi.html`.
>
> The incubator working group that took care of the initial requirements and specification regarding speech integration in HTML5 can be found on: `http://www.w3.org/2005/Incubator/htmlspeech/`.

Using textarea

In this recipe we will take a look at the `textarea` element and create a simple form to show some of the attributes that can be used. `textarea` is intended for use as a multiple line plain-text editing control.

How to do it...

We will create an example `form` to demonstrate some of the uses of the `textarea` element:

1. First we add a `texarea` element with the `placeholder` attribute set:

```
<form>
  <label>Short info: <textarea placeholder="some default
    text"></textarea>
  </label>
```

2. Then we add a textarea with the `rows` and `cols` attributes set:

```
<label>
  Info with default size set: <textarea  rows="4" cols="15"
    placeholder="some default text"></textarea>
</label>
```

3. Then we add one with `maxlength` set:

```
  <label>
    Max area limited to 5 characters <textarea maxlength="5"
      placeholder="Inset text here limit 5 char"></textarea>
  </label>
```

4. Then we add one with the `title` attribute set:

```
  <label>
    Tip on hover <textarea maxlength="5" title="add an super
      awesome comment"></textarea>
  </label>
```

5. Finally we add `submit` and close the `form`:

```
  <input type="submit"/>
</form>
```

How it works...

The first example is a regular `<textarea />` element allowing text with multiple lines and line breaks. We can additionally use attributes, such as `rows` and `cols` to enable some initial size. This can also be achieved by setting initial size via CSS:

```
textarea{
    width:300px;
    height:100px;
}
```

Most of the new browsers now have a small dragable right corner for a text area, enabling the user to resize it. This resizability for the text area can be disabled by setting `max-width` and `max-height` in CSS.

We can also limit the number of characters that can be inserted using the `maxlength` attribute, like setting it to maximum of 5 characters in our example `maxlength="5"`.

There is also the attribute `title` that can be used to add hint to the user about the input filed.

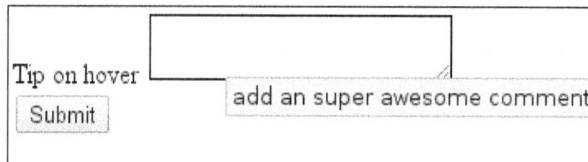

Tip on hover

add an super awesome comment

Submit

Attributes such as `title`, `maxlength`, and `placeholder` are not exclusive to `textarea`, but they can be used in other elements as well. For example, the `title` attribute is one of the global ones in HTML5 and can be added on any element. We could have the flowing snippet:

```
<input type="text" autofocus maxlength="10"
placeholder="Awesome">
```

More on the input attributes and the global element attributes can be found at the website `http://www.whatwg.org/specs/web-apps/current-work/multipage/elements.html#global-attributes`.

Inputting dates

Before HTML5 we were forced into creating custom controls that always had some missing features or were not compatible with some browsers. Now, there are separate input types for dates, and in this recipe we will see how to use them. They are unfortunately still not fully implemented across various user agents, but then everyone is slowly catching up.

How to do it...

We will simply create a basic HTML document and create a form in the body element:

1. First in the body section add `form` and inside it a `date input` element:

```
<form>
  <label>
    Select date  <input name="theDate" type="date">
  </label>
```

2. Similarly we add an input element for `month` and `week`:

```
<label>
  Select month <input name="theMonth" type="month">
</label>
<label>
  Select week <input name="theWeek" type="week">
</label>
```

3. At the end we add a simple `submit` and close the `form`:

```
  <input type="submit" />
</form>
```

How it works...

Depending on your browser's support you will either get an empty input field or a full-fledged date input control:

`<input type="week" />` rendered on Opera v12.11

On form submit, the parameters being sent by the form are valid strings:

```
?theDate=2012-12-21&theMonth=2012-12&theWeek=2012-W5
```

The creation and numbering on the dates, weeks, and months is in accordance to the ISO 8601 that is widely accepted in most programming languages, or at least there is a standardized way of representation and access to the data. There is also an option to specify the `min` and `max` attributes that should be valid date, month, and week strings accordingly, as well as `step` that will define the step of the selection control, and is defaulted to `1`.

Inputting time

In this recipe we will take a look at how to use time input controls and how they are combined with date selections. The general idea is to have the user agent render a clock that can be used as input. There are options to include the time zone and to have plain time representation and will try them out by creating a simple form as shown in the following screenshot:

How to do it...

Similar to the other examples, we create a form containing few input elements:

1. First we start the form and add the `time` input element:

```
<form>
  <label>
    Select time <input name="time" type="time" >
  </label>
```

2. We add a `datetime-local` input:

```
  <label>
    Date and time local <input name="datetime-local"
      type="datetime-local" >
  </label>
```

3. Also we add a `datetime` input:

```
  <label>
    Select date and time <input name="datetime"
      type="datetime" >
  </label>
```

4. Finally we add submit and close the form

```
    <input type="submit">
</form>
```

How it works...

On form submission, the values selected are added as query parameters in the URL, for example:

```
/?time=00%3A00%3A00.00&datetime-local=2012-11-
02T12%3A00&datetime=2012-12-21T12%3A00Z/
```

The `time` parameter here has a value of `00:00:00`, where the `%3A` is the `:` character URL encoded.

Similarly, the `2012-11-02T12%3A00` value for `datetime-local` is actually `2012-11-02T12:00` giving the date and time in the parameters following the `YYYY-MM-DDThh:mm:ss` pattern.

As for the `datetime` variable the format of the string is `YYYY-MM-DDThh:mm:ssTZD`, where we have the additional information about the time zone.

Since we have a correct context for our input elements, when opened on a browser that has good support the control will be optimized.

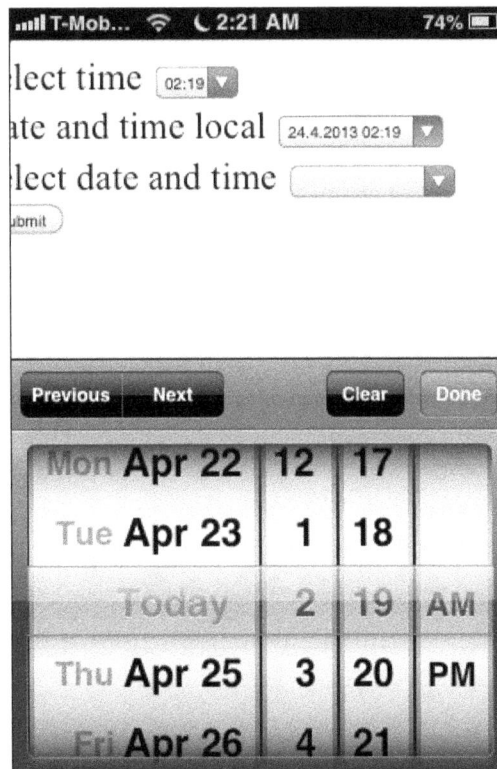

Telephone input

In this recipe, we will take a look at the input type for telephone numbers. Due to the very different telephone number formats between countries, the phone input does not require any specific pattern, if not explicitly specified. If we are required to have some specific pattern, we can do various types of validations as discussed in detail in *Chapter 6, Data Validation*.

The main advantage of using a text input type is to be more semantically correct, and as such to bring about more optimization on mobile devices.

How to do it...

As the preceding related recipes, we simply add the `input` element in the body of the HTML document:

```
<form>
   <label>
      Insert phone <input type="tel" >
   </label>
<input type="submit" >
</form>
```

How it works...

When you try it out on a first look, it seams like it is a regular `input type="text"` element. But this one now is more semantically correct. Now why is this important, or why should we care about it?

Mobile devices will pick this as a phone number and automatically open the numeric keyboard like the Android device displayed in the following screenshot:

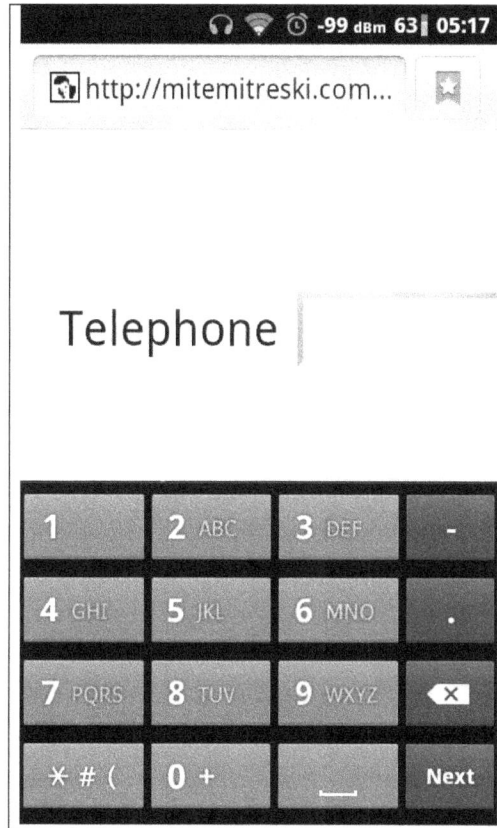

There's more...

There are also `input type="url"`, `input type="search"`, and `input type="email"` that give semantic to the elements, allowing mobile devices to pick up the correct keyboard. They also can have additional validations and logic about how the data can be inserted, allowing more type specific functions. Some of them will be covered in the validation-related recipes.

In HTML5 for all input types, it was added an attribute called `inputmode` that is derived from the term **Input modalities**. These attributes provides hints to the browser on what kind of keyboard should be used. The attributes can have the following values:

- **verbatim**: This value specifies alphanumeric characters that can commonly be used with the intention to be non-prose text such as usernames, keywords, or passwords.
- **latin**: This value specifies Latin input in the user's input in the user's preferred language with typing helpers like text prediction on mobile devices.
- **latin-name**: This value specifies same rules as `latin` but for names.

> ▸ **latin-prose**: This value specifies the same rules as `latin` but with complete typing helpers intended to be used in implementations like email, chat, or comments.

> ▸ **full-width-latin**: This value specifies same as `latin-prose`, but for the user's secondary language.

> ▸ **kana, katakana**: This value specifies **kana** or **romaji** input, typically **hiragana** input, using full-width characters, with support for converting to **kanji**. As for **katakana**, it is another form related to this. All of these are intended for Japanese input text. More about Japanese writing systems can be found on: `http://en.wikipedia.org/wiki/Japanese_writing_system`.

> ▸ **numeric**: This value specifies numeric characters input for digits 0-9 including the user-selected thousand separator and character for indicating negative numbers. The purpose for this is to input numeric codes, such as some street numbers or credit cards. If we are sure that we use numbers the input `type="number"` should be preferred, since it is more semantically correct.

> ▸ **tel, email, url**: This value can be used giving the same hints as we have used for the corresponding input types. We should prefer the input types in these values.

Browsers don't provide support for all of the states and have a fallback mechanism. Again here the states mostly makes sense for mobile or special purpose devices.

Range input field

We sometimes want to input a value that is something the user picks from a given range of values using a "slider". In order to enable this in HTML5 the `<input type="range" >` was added allowing imprecise control for setting the element's value.

How to do it...

With few simple steps, we will create few range controls that use different features of HTML5:

1. We start by adding an HTML page using the following part of the `body` text:

```
<form>
  <label>
    Select the range <input name="simpleRange" type="range" />
  </label>
  <br/>
  <label>
    Select within range <input id="vertical"
      name="simpleRangeLimited" min="20" max="100" type="range"
        />
  </label>
  <br/>
  <label>
```

```
      Custom step <input id="full" name="simpleRangeSteped"
        type="range" value="35" min="0" max="220" step="5" />
    </label>
    <span id="out"> </span>
    <br/>
    <label>
      Temperature scale
      <input min="0" max="70" type="range" name="themp"
        list="theList">
    </label>
      <datalist id="theList">
        <option value="-30" />
        <option value="10" label="Low" />
        <option value="20" label="Normal" />
        <option value="45" label="High" />
        <option value="some invalid Value" />
      </datalist>
    <br/>
    <input type="submit" />
  </form>
```

2. And in order to show one of the sliders vertically, we can add CSS in the `head` tag of HTML:

```
#vertical {
    height: 80px;
    width: 30px;
};
```

3. We can also display the value that is selected using JavaScript:

```
<script
  src="http://ajax.googleapis.com/ajax/libs/jquery/1.8.2/jquery.
min.js">
</script>
<script type="text/javascript">
  (function($){
    var val = $('#full').val();
    var out  = $('#out');
    out.html(val);
    $('#full').change(function(){
      out.html(this.value);
    });
  }($));
</script>
```

How it works...

The `type = "range"` is picked up by the browser and the a slider is created where the value for `min` is `0` and value for `max` is `100` having a `step` of 1.

In order to display it vertically, set width and height using CSS. To make it work on Chrome, since the change of rendering via size is not yet implemented, you can add the following code in CSS, forcing it to be displayed vertically:

```
-webkit-appearance: slider-vertical;
```

If we want to have a small display updated directly by changing the slider, we can achieve this with JavaScript, by adding an event listener to the input range element:

```
$('#full').change(function(){
   out.html(this.value);
});
```

There is also an option to connect the `input type="range"` element with a `datalist` that will create ticks with the predefined options:

```
<datalist id="theList">
<option value="-30" />
<option value="10" label="Low" />
<option value="20" label="Normal" />
<option value="45" label="High" />
<option value="some invalid Value" />
</datalist>
```

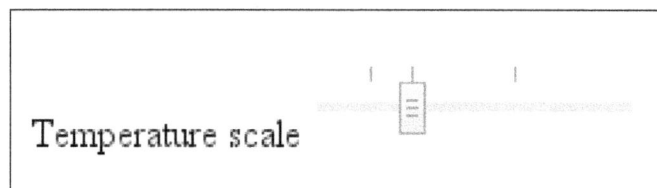

The options in the `datalist` element can have invalid values or values outside the range that is specified with the attributes min and max, and as such will be ignored. On the other hand, the values that are valid will add a marker on the slider where they are selectable.

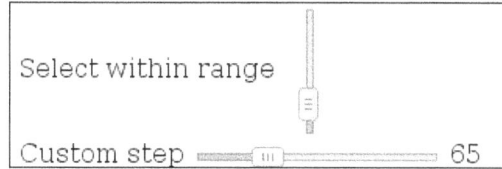

There is also an optional `label` attribute to the `datalist` that can be added, and should render the text next to the markers displayed. This feature with the display of labels is not supported by the browsers, but is part of the specification.

There 's more...

At the time of writing, neither Firefox nor IE had full support for the `type="range"` element, and as a workaround, we can use JavaScript to add basic support. There is already a utility script allowing a workaround available on `http://frankyan.com/labs/html5slider/` and source is also available on `https://github.com/html5-ds-book/html5slider` slider. In order to enable it, you just include the `html5slider.js`, and the magic happens.

Color picker input

As one of the new input types, we have the the the `input type="color"` element, which lets you pick a color and the chosen color will have its simple colors representation that we are used to. The color representation has a more popular name of hexadecimal color representation, and in this recipe, we will see a simple example on how to use it by creating a form with color picker:

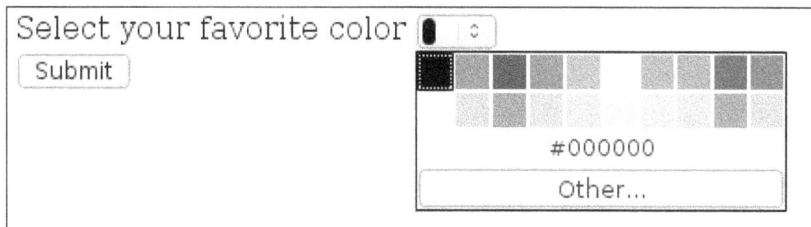

How to do it...

We will create a simple form where we will have a color picker added in a form that is part of the HTML body:

```
<form>
  <label>
    Select your favorite color <input type="color" value="#0000ff"
      >
  </label>
  <input type="submit" >
</form>
```

How it works...

The color input type gets picked up and the currently selected color is shown. On clicking the color, we can select a menu directly from the systems color picking control.

Value selected is represented as a simple color string having a # character and six character representation that is a case-insensitive hexadecimal string.

In case this is not supported in the browser, we can have a custom way of handling it. One of the ways to check for the support is to use the modenrizer.js method:

```
<script
  src="http://cdnjs.cloudflare.com/ajax/libs/modernizr/2.6.2/
modernizr.min.js"></script>
<script type="text/javascript">
  if(!Modernizr.inputtypes.color){
    //do a different method of color picking
    console.log("Browsers has no support for color going with
      fallback")
  }
</script>
```

It allows us to implement a fallback while the other browsers catch up with the implementation.

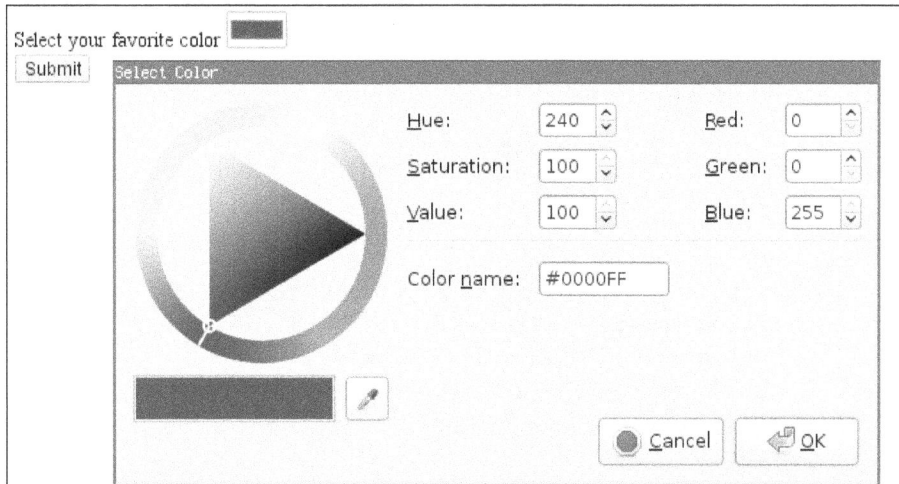

Using single-choice dropdowns

Single-choice dropdowns are a standard HTML component. Their usage, although straightforward, can sometimes be frustrating, both for the developer and the user. The browser requires that a "selected" attribute is added to the selected item. To set the value of the `select` element programmatically, the code must first find the item which is presently selected and remove its "selected" attribute, then find the item that has the specified value and add a "selected" attribute to it.

However, the developer might want an easier way to specify the value of the dropdown field. Simply adding an attribute containing the value should be enough. In this recipe, we're going to solve this problem by adding a new attribute to dropdowns.

How to do it...

Let's get started.

1. We will create an HTML page with a dropdown. In HTML, dropdowns are made with a `select` element. To add selection options, we add one or more option elements inside the `select` element. Normally, we would specify the pre-selected option by adding a selected attribute to it:

```
<select name="dropdown">
  <option value="1">First</option>
  <option value="2" selected="selected">Second</option>
  <option value="3">Third</option>
</select>
```

2. However, this can be inconvenient to generate on the server side or to generate with a template on the client side. More often than not, our list elements are static--its just the value that changes. To simplify templating, we can do it differently in our `index.html`:

```
<!DOCTYPE HTML>
<html>
  <head>
  <title>Dropdown</title>
  </head>
  <body>
    <select name="dropdown" data-value="2">
      <option value="1">First</option>
      <option value="2">Second</option>
      <option value="3">Third</option>
    </select>
    <script
      src="http://ajax.googleapis.com/ajax/libs/jquery/1.8.2/
jquery.min.js">
    </script>
    <script type="text/javascript" src="example.js">
    </script>
  </body>
</html>
```

3. Then we can set the value in `example.js`:

```
$(function() {
  $('body').on('change', 'select[data-value]', function() {
    $(this).attr('data-value', $(this).val()); });
  window.updateDropdowns = function() {
    $('select[data-value]').each(function() {
      $(this).val($(this).attr('data-value'));
    });
  }
  updateDropdowns();
});
```

How it works...

The code in `example.js` runs when the page is loaded. At that point, it finds all select elements that have a data-value attribute, and sets the selected option using jQuery's versatile function `$.fn.val`. Additionally, it binds a global event for all present and future select items that have a data-value attribute, which syncs that value to the actual value.

This is a more natural model for single-choice dropdowns.

There's more...

Its important to note that this code will not work properly with client-side generated HTML, which was generated after the page was loaded. To handle this case, the `updateDropdowns` method is to be called after new `select` elements are added to the page.

Using multiple-choice select lists

Select lists can be made to allow users to select multiple elements.

Multiple-choice select lists have a special serialization model. In this recipe we're going to look at how that model works and how to use it.

We're going to create a page with a form containing a multiple-choice select list. This form will send a `GET` request to another page where we're going to extract the selected items via JavaScript.

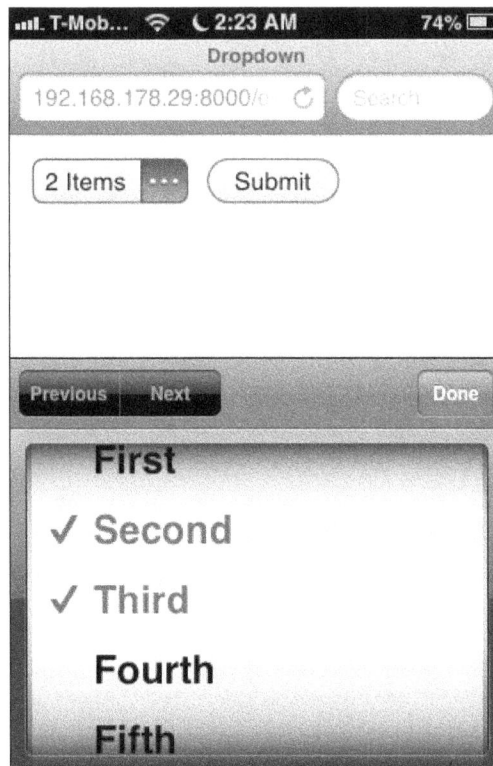

How to do it...

Follow these steps:

1. Create a basic page with a form that has a multiple select list as shown in the following code snippet:

```
<!DOCTYPE HTML>
<html>
  <head>
    <title>Dropdown</title>
  </head>
  <body>
    <form method="get" action="result.html">
      <select name="multi" multiple>
        <option value="1">First</option>
        <option value="2">Second</option>
        <option value="3">Third</option>
        <option value="4">Fourth</option>
        <option value="5">Fifth</option>
      </select>
      <input type="submit" value="Submit">
    </form>
  </body>
</html>
```

2. Then we will create the page that receives the list and displays the selected values as follows:

```
<!DOCTYPE HTML>
<html>
  <head>
    <title>Dropdown</title>
  </head>
  <body>
    <div id="result">
    </div>
    <script
      src="http://ajax.googleapis.com/ajax/libs/jquery/1.8.2/
jquery.min.js"></script>
    <script type="text/javascript" src="example.js">
    </script>
  </body>
</html>
```

3. Here is the `example.js` code snippet that displays the result:

```
$(function() {
  var params = window.location.search.substring(1).split('&').
    map(function(param) {
      var nameval = param.split('=');
      return { name: nameval[0], value: nameval[1] };
    });
    console.log(params);
    var selectValues = params.
    filter(function(p) { return p.name == 'multi'; }).
      map(function(p) { return p.value; })
    $("#result").text("Selected: " + selectValues.join(','));
});
```

How it works...

The address generated by the form submission looks as follows:

```
result.html?multi=2&multi=3
```

This format breaks many assumptions that popular frameworks make about the nature of form data. Often they treat form data as a dictionary, where a single name has a single value. In this case however, the data can't be put into such a dictionary because multi-select lists generate multiple parameters with the same name and different values.

Instead, we treat the parameters as a list, which enables us to extract and filter both values.

Getting geographical location input

One of the exciting new features in HTML5 is the geolocation API (`http://www.w3.org/TR/geolocation-API/`). It allows the developer to ask for the user's location. This API allows the developer to get geographic coordinates, such as latitude and longitude.

Before this API developers had to rely on more crude methods, such as GeoIP databases. These methods produced results that had poor accuracy. Depending on the user's browser, device, and the availability of GPS on it, the geolocation API could give results with a few meters accuracy.

In this recipe, we're going to display the user's location on a map. To do this, we're going to use the **Leaflet** library. The use of this library to show maps is covered in the *Displaying a map* recipe, *Chapter 2*, *Display of Graphical Data*.

How to do it...

Let's get started.

1. We're going to create a HTML page with a map placeholder, which will include the leaflet library (both CSS and JS files) and our code for getting and displaying the user's location, located in `example.js` as shown in the following code snippet:

```
<!DOCTYPE HTML>
<html>
  <head>
    <title>Geolocation example</title>
     <link rel="stylesheet"
       href="http://cdn.leafletjs.com/leaflet-0.4/leaflet.css"
         />
     <!--[if lte IE 8]>
       <link rel="stylesheet"
         href="http://cdn.leafletjs.com/leaflet-0.4/leaflet.
ie.css" />
       <![endif]-->
  </head>
  <body>
    <div id="map" style="height:480px; width:640px;"></div>
      <script
        src="http://ajax.googleapis.com/ajax/libs/jquery/1.8.2/
jquery.
          min.js"></script>
      <script src="http://cdn.leafletjs.com/leaflet-0.4/leaflet.
js"></script>
      <script type="text/javascript"
        src="example.js"></script>
  </body>
</html>
```

2. And we're going to add the following code in `example.js`:

```
$(function() {
  var map = L.map('map').setView([51.505, -0.09], 13)

  L.tileLayer('http://{s}.tile.openstreetmap.org/{z}/{x}/{y}.
    png',{
    attribution:'Copyright (C) OpenStreetMap.org',
    maxZoom:18
    }).addTo(map);

  if ("geolocation" in navigator) {
    var marker = L.marker([51.5, -0.09]).addTo(map);
```

```
      var watchId = navigator.geolocation.watchPosition(function(pos
ition) {
        var userLatLng = new L.LatLng(position.coords.latitude,
          position.coords.longitude);
        marker.setLatLng(userLatLng);
        map.panTo(userLatLng);
        });
      }
      else alert("Sorry, geolocation is not supported in your
        browser");
    });
```

How it works...

The geolocation API is available through the `geolocation` object that can be found in the navigator object. There are multiple methods available, as follows:

- `getCurrentPosition`: This method calls its callback function parameter one time after a location is obtained

- `watchCurrentPosition`: This method calls its first callback function parameter every time the location information is updated and returns a watcher ID

- `clearWatch`: This method removes the watch callback by clearing it using our returned watcher ID

In our example, we use `watchCurrentPosition`, and provide it with a callback, which sets the marker's position. The user will first be asked to give the website a permission to access his or her location. After the permission is given and a location is found, our callback will be called with a position object.

The position object contains the properties `timestamp` and `coords`. The `coords` property is an object containing `latitude` and `longitude` information. The `timestamp` property is a UNIX UTC timestamp denoting the time of the location information update.

There's more...

This example will not work when opened directly as a file. To view the example, a local server must be started in the same directory. For more information on how to start a local server, see *Appendix, Installing and using http-server*.

Using file inputs at the client side

HTML has always lacked a convenient method to read the user's files. Before HTML5, the only way to access user files on the client side was to use an input element of type file, upload that file to the server then send it back to the browser.

HTML5 brings the ability to read user files locally, inside the user's browser using JavaScript code. The implementation is an extension of the functionality of a file input element with additional API.

In this recipe, we're going to display a text file that is selected by the user by using the new HTML5 file API (`http://www.w3.org/TR/FileAPI/`).

How to do it...

Let's write the code.

1. Create an HTML page with a file `input` field and a content `div` to show the contents of the selected file:

    ```html
    <!DOCTYPE HTML>
    <html>
      <head>
        <title>File API example</title>
      </head>
      <body>
        <input type="file" id="file" value="Choose text file">
          <div id="content"></div>
            <script
              src="http://ajax.googleapis.com/ajax/libs/jquery/1.8.2/
    jquery.min.js"></script>
              <script type="text/javascript"
                src="example.js"></script>
      </body>
    </html>
    ```

2. Then we're going to add the code to read the selected file in `example.js`:

    ```javascript
    $(function() {
      $("#file").on('change', function(e) {
    ```

    We can read the selected file from the input element's files property.

    ```javascript
    for (var k = 0; k < this.files.length; ++k) {
      var f = this.files[k];
    ```

3. To read the contents, we use a `FileReader` object. We need to instantiate it, tell it what file to read (and in what way it should read it depending on its type), then attach an event listener when the reading completes that will access the file contents. This is done as follows:

```
var fr = new FileReader();
  if (f.type && f.type.match('image/.+'))
    fr.readAsDataURL(f);
  else
    fr.readAsText(f);
```

4. By the time the `onload` function is called, the variable `f` will change to be set to the value of the last file for each of the `onload` calls. To avoid this, we capture the variable using an anonymous function pattern.

```
(function(f) {
  fr.onload = function(e) {
```

5. The listener is called with an event, which in its target property contains our result or the text of the whole file.

```
if (f.type && f.type.match('image/.+'))
  $("<img />").attr('src', e.target.result)
  .appendTo("#content");
else
  $("<pre />").text(e.target.result)
  .appendTo("#content");
}
}(f));
}
});
});
```

How it works...

The HTML5 file API consists of two new additions:

▶ The file input element has a files property which contains a list of the selected files.

▶ A new type of object called `FileReader` exists that allows us to read the selected files in different ways by using its methods. Among others there are `readAsBinaryString`, `readAsText`, `readAsDataURL`, and `readAsArrayBuffer`. It also provides us with event listeners, which we can set to get the file contents when it is loaded or when an error occurs.

To display the text file, we use the reader's `readAsText` property. As a result, the file data is provided to the `onload` listener of the reader. The content of the file is a simple string that we append to the `div` content inside an element that displays preformatted text.

For retrieving images, we call `readAsDataURL`, and then easily create a new image element whose `src` attribute is set to that data URL. Then we add this element inside the content `div`.

If a folder is selected our recipe will display the entire contents of the folder, both text and images.

There's more...

Its possible to specify filters for the file selection dialog, which limits the category of the file. For example, adding `accept="image/*"` will tell the browser that the input expects images of any type, while adding `accept="image/jpeg"` will tell the browser that the input expects only JPEG images. This filter is based on media types. More information about available media types can be found at `http://www.iana.org/assignments/media-types`.

> Although IE9 supports a lot of HTLM5 features, the HTML5 file API is not supported. Support was added in IE version 10.

Using a drag-and-drop file area

With HTML5 we have another alternative for reading user files: we can use drag-and-drop areas. Often users find drag-and-drop intuitive and prefer it to other editing and manipulation methods.

Drag-and-drop also enable the user to drag elements from a different window or tab into ours, meaning they have more uses than regular file upload buttons.

In this recipe, we're going to make a drag-and-drop area for images. It will work both with dragged files and with images dragged from a different window or tab.

> More information about the HTML5 drag-and-drop specification can be found at `http://www.whatwg.org/specs/web-apps/current-work/multipage/dnd.html`.

How to do it...

Let's write the code.

1. We're going to create an HTML page with a drop area. To make the area easier to drop to, we're going to add some padding, margin, and border to it.

   ```
   <!DOCTYPE HTML>
   <html>
     <head>
       <title>File API example</title>
   ```

```html
    <style type="text/css">
      #content {
        padding:0.5em;
        margin:0.5em;
        border: solid 1px; #aaa;
      }
    </style>
  </head>
  <body>
    <div id="content"><p>Drop images here</p></div>
    <script
      src="http://ajax.googleapis.com/ajax/libs/jquery/1.8.2/
jquery.min.js"></script>
    <script type="text/javascript"
      src="example.js"></script>
  </body>
</html>
```

2. Then we're going to add the code to read the dropped files or images from another website in `example.js`.

```javascript
$(function() {
  $("#content").on('drop', function(e) {
```

The default browser action on drop is to navigate to the dropped item. We want to prevent this from happening.

```javascript
    e.preventDefault();
    e.stopPropagation();
    var files = e.originalEvent.dataTransfer.files;
```

3. We're going to read images as `DataURLs` and text files as text with our file reader.

```javascript
for (var k = 0; k < files.length; ++k) {
  var f = files[k];
  var fr = new FileReader();
    if (f.type && f.type.match('image/.+'))
      fr.readAsDataURL(f);
    else
      fr.readAsText(f);
```

4. Capturing each file inside a closure allows us to reference it from the a sync `onload` callback. There we append it to the content element as shown in the following code snippet:

```javascript
(function(f) {
  fr.onload = function(e) {
    if (f.type && f.type.match('image/.+'))
      $("<img />").attr('src', e.target.result)
```

```
      .appendTo("#content");
   else
      $("<pre />").text(e.target.result)
      .appendTo("#content");
   }
 }(f));
}
```

5. Alternatively, if the item was dragged from a different window or tab, we need to read it from the items property. We're looking for an item of type `text/html` as follows:

```
var items = e.originalEvent.dataTransfer.items;
for (var k = 0; k < items.length; ++k) {
  if (items[k].type == 'text/html') {
    items[k].getAsString(function (html) {
      $(html).appendTo("#content");
    });
  }
}
});
});
```

How it works...

In the first part of `example.js`, we used the standard HTML5 API. You can read more about it in the previous recipe *Using file inputs on the client-side--*in short, it allows us to read files as text or `DataURLs` and put them in the document.

This part of the code supports both image files and text files.

The second part is slightly different and is called only when dragging elements or images from a different website. It works on any `draggable` HTML element—this element will also be added to our content page as HTML. The image data will not be accessible.

In combination, the API described here is very powerful for use in online rich text, UI, or graphic editors. We can combine it with image uploading services or with our own panels containing various pre-made elements which we can drop inside the drop area.

There's more...

As can be seen in this recipe, the HTML5 drag-and-drop API is not limited to just files. By setting the `draggable="true"` attribute, any element on any page can be made dragable.

The `dragstart` event will be fired on the `draggable` element as soon as the dragging starts. As we move the element over potential drop targets, the `dragenter`, `dragover`, and `dragleave` events will be fired. Finally, the `drop` event that we used in this recipe is fired when the element is dropped, as well as `dragend`.

Finally, to get fine, programmatic control over the content of the dragged object, the `DataTransfer` object can be used. For example, the following `dragStart` handler placed on a `draggable` element:

```
function onDragStart(e) {
    e.dataTransfer.setData('text/html', '<p>Hello world</p>');
}
```

will cause the browser to place the specified HTML content inside the dragged object.

The best feature of custom HTML5 `draggable` elements is the compatibility with other applications in the system. Dragable objects can "travel" outside the browser into other applications, such as mail clients, image editors, and so on. As a result, HTML5 apps are one step closer to becoming first-class citizens inside the operating system.

5
Custom Input Components

In this chapter, we will cover the following:

- ▶ Using contentEditable for basic rich text input
- ▶ Advanced rich text input
- ▶ Creating a drop-down menu
- ▶ Creating custom dialogs
- ▶ Creating autocomplete for input
- ▶ Creating a custom single-selection list
- ▶ Creating a multiple-selection list
- ▶ Geographic location input using maps

Introduction

So far, we presented several different ways for getting input from the user. HTML5 offers many new features that enable the functionality of input components that was previously done with JavaScript.

Often, there comes the need to extend this standard functionality. In this chapter, we will see ways for creating some custom input components and using the already available ones, where we add additional functions to extend or simplify the end user experience.

Using contentEditable for basic rich text input

With the new `contentEditable` attribute in HTML5, we can turn every element into an editable rich text field. In theory, this could enable us to write complex rich text editors that would work right inside the browser.

Among other things, the new APIs can be used to send editing commands. This is done using the `document.execCommand` function, which takes a command string as the first argument, and options as the third.

In practice, every browser vendor implements the interface slightly differently. However, most modern browsers are fully compliant.

You can test your browser's compliance at `http://tifftiff.de/contenteditable/compliance_test.html`; however, the test doesn't take into account the possibility that some browsers might act differently on the same command.

In this recipe, we're going to make a very simple `contentEditable` field that supports few commands (paragraph style, undo/redo, bold/italic/underline, bullets, and numbered lists).

How to do it...

We will create an HTML page with a `contentEditable` div inside.

1. We're going to add some padding to the div to make it easier to click. Above the div, we're going to place our formatting buttons and a dropdown:

```
<!DOCTYPE HTML>
<html>
    <head>
        <title>Simple rich text editor</title>
        <style type="text/css">
            #edit { margin: 0.5em 0.1em; padding:0.5em;
            border: solid 1px #bbb; }
        </style>
    </head>
    <body>
    <div>
        <select class="btn style">
            <option value="P">Normal</option>
        </select>
        <button class="btn undo">Undo</button>
        <button class="btn redo">Redo</button>
        <button class="btn bold">B</button>
```

```html
        <button class="btn italic">I</button>
        <button class="btn under">U</button>
        <button class="btn bullet">Bullet</button>
        <button class="btn number">Number</button>
    </div>
    <div id="edit" contentEditable="true">
    </div>
    <script src="http://ajax.googleapis.com/ajax/libs/jquery/1.8.2/
jquery.min.js"></script>
    <script type="text/javascript" src="example.js"></script>
    </body>
</html>
```

2. Then we can make the editing controls work in our `example.js` file:

```javascript
$(function() {
    var editCommand = function(cmd, arg) { return document.
execCommand(cmd, true, arg); };
```

3. We're going to put all our `editCommand` bindings in an object:

```javascript
var bindings = {
    '.undo': editCommand.bind(this, 'undo'),
    '.redo': editCommand.bind(this, 'redo'),
    '.bold': editCommand.bind(this, 'bold'),
    '.italic': editCommand.bind(this, 'italic'),
    '.under': editCommand.bind(this, 'underline'),
    '.bullet': editCommand.bind(this, 'insertUnorderedList'),
    '.number': editCommand.bind(this, 'insertOrderedList')
};
```

4. Then we will apply them to the appropriate edit controls:

```javascript
for (var key in bindings) $(key).on('click', bindings[key]);
```

5. Finally, we will define and add additional paragraph styles:

```javascript
var styles = {
    'Heading 1': 'H1',
    'Heading 2': 'H2',
    'Heading 3': 'H3',
};
for (var key in styles)
    $('<option>').html(key).attr('value', styles[key]).
appendTo('.style');

$('.style').on('change', function() {
    editCommand('formatBlock', $(this).val());
});
});
```

How it works...

The `document.execCommand` function allows us to send commands to the currently active `contentEditable` field. These commands work just as toolbar buttons would in a regular rich text editor. For example, the command "bold" toggles the boldness of the text; applied the second time, it restores the text back to its original state. The function takes the following three arguments:

> ▸ `commandName`: This is the name of the command to execute.

> ▸ `showDefaultUI (boolean)`: This tells the browser if it should show a default user interface related to the command to the user, if such interface is needed.

> ▸ `Value`: This provides an argument for the command that depends on the type of the command. For example, bold, italic, and underline takes a `boolean` value.

In this recipe, we're not tracking the state at the current selection of cursor. We're going to leave that kind of tracking for a recipe where we will create a more advanced version of the editor. However, it's worth mentioning here that we can use the `document.queryCommandState` function to retrieve the state pertaining to the command at the current cursor position (or if there is an active selection of the current selection).

Advanced rich text input

While the basic `contentEditable`-based rich text input field is sufficient in most cases, sometimes it is not enough. We might want to allow the users to insert more complex objects such as images and tables.

In this recipe, we're going to make an advanced rich text editor that supports inserting images and basic tables.

We're going to build this editor based on the simple rich text editor demonstrated in the *Using contentEditable for basic rich text input* recipe.

Getting ready

We're going to start with the code from the *Using contentEditable for basic rich text input* recipe and improve upon it.

How to do it...

Let's write the code.

1. We're going to take the original `index.html` and `example.js` files but we will modify the HTML file. We're going to add two controls: a table button and a file picker to insert images:

```html
<!DOCTYPE HTML>
<html>
    <head>
        <title>Simple rich text editor</title>
        <style type="text/css">
            #edit {margin: 0.5em 0.1em;padding:0.5em;border:solid
1px #bbb;}
            #edit table td { border: solid 1px #ccc; }
        </style>
    </head>
    <body>
    <div>
        <select class="btn style">
            <option value="P">Normal</option>
        </select>
        <button class="btn undo">Undo</button>
        <button class="btn redo">Redo</button>
        <button class="btn bold">B</button>
        <button class="btn italic">I</button>
        <button class="btn under">U</button>
        <button class="btn bullet">Bullet</button>
        <button class="btn number">Number</button>
        <button class="btn table">Table</button>
        <input type="file" class="btn image">Image</input>
    </div>
    <div id="edit" contentEditable="true">
    </div>
    <script src="http://ajax.googleapis.com/ajax/libs/jquery/1.8.2/
jquery.min.js"></script>
    <script type="text/javascript" src="example.js"></script>
    <script type="text/javascript" src="example-table.js"></script>
    <script type="text/javascript" src="example-image.js"></script>
    </body>
</html>
```

2. To add tables to our rich text, we will create a new script called `example-table.js`. The table button will have dual functionality. One function will be changing the number of rows/columns in the currently active table. If there is no active table, it will insert a new one with the specified number of rows and columns. The following is the code in `example-table.js`:

```javascript
$(function() {
    var editCommand = function(cmd, arg) {
        return document.execCommand(cmd, true, arg);
    };
    $('.table').on('click', function() {
        var rows = prompt("How many rows?"),
            cols = prompt("How many columns?");
        var loc = document.getSelection().getRangeAt(0)
                .startContainer.parentElement;
        while (loc.id != 'edit'
            && loc.nodeName.toLowerCase() != 'table')
                loc = loc.parentElement;
        var isInTable = loc.nodeName.toLowerCase() == 'table';
        var contents;
        if (isInTable)
            contents = $(loc).find('tr').toArray().
map(function(tr) {
                return $(tr).find('td').toArray().map(function(td)
{
                    return td.innerHTML;
                });
            });
        var table = $('<table />');
        for (var k = 0; k < rows; ++k) {
            var row = $('<tr />').appendTo(table);
            for (var i = 0; i < cols; ++i) {
                var cell = $('<td />').appendTo(row);
                if (contents && contents[k] && contents[k][i])
                    cell.html(contents[k][i]);
                else cell.html(' ');
            }
        }
        if (isInTable) $(loc).remove();
        editCommand('insertHTML', table[0].outerHTML);
    });

});
```

3. To add images to our rich text, we will create a new script called `example-image.js`. The image picker will insert the user-selected image at the specified position. The following is the content of `example-image.js`:

```
$(function() {
    var editCommand = function(cmd, arg) {
        return document.execCommand(cmd, true, arg);
    };
    $(".image").on('change', function(e) {
        for (var k = 0; k < this.files.length; ++k) {
            var f = this.files[k];
            var fr = new FileReader();
            if (f.type && f.type.match('image/.+'))
                fr.readAsDataURL(f);
            else
                fr.readAsText(f);
            (function(f) {
                fr.onload = function(e) {
                    if (f.type && f.type.match('image/.+'))
                        editCommand('insertHTML',
                            $("<img />").attr('src',      e.target.
result)[0].outerHTML);
                }
            }(f));
        }
    });
});
```

How it works...

We added two new controls to the editor: the table control and the insert image control.

The table control asks the user to specify the number of rows and columns first. It figures out if the user is currently inside a table by inspecting the parent elements of the current cursor position. If a table is found, its content are remembered.

Afterward, a new table is constructed with the specified number of columns and rows. If the old table contained some content at that row/column position, that content is copied to the newly constructed cell. Finally, the old table is removed if present and the new table is added using the `insertHTML` command.

The image insertion control uses the HTML5 File API for file inputs to read image files selected by the user as data URLs. After reading them, it adds them to the content using the same `insertHTML` command.

There's more...

Using this method, it's easy to construct new controls that add any type of content to the `contentEditable` field. This enables us to create custom rich text or page editors with specialized functionality.

However, if the goal is to add a fully capable generic rich text editor to our page, we recommend using one of the many excellent editor components already available, such as TinyMCE (`http://www.tinymce.com/`).

Creating a drop-down menu

Drop-down menus are often used in web applications to show extended functionality. Actions that are used less often or useful to a small number of users can be added to the menu, resulting with a cleaner interface.

HTML5 and CSS3 allow us to build drop-down menus written entirely in CSS. We're going to create such a menu in this recipe.

Getting ready

Let's analyze the structure of a drop-down menu. A drop-down menu has an activation button that displays it and one or more items from the following:

- A regular (action) item
- A separator item
- A submenu item (that activates a sub-menu)

Our HTML element structure should reflect the drop-down menu structure. Our CSS code will control the positioning and display of the menu.

We're going to have three buttons showing slightly different, yet structurally same, menus.

The first will have the default behavior—drops down, is left-aligned with a submenu appearing on the right-hand side.

The second will have a modified behavior—right-aligned with a submenu appearing on the left-hand side.

Finally, the third will have a very different behavior; it will come above the button with submenus appearing to the right-hand side, but going up.

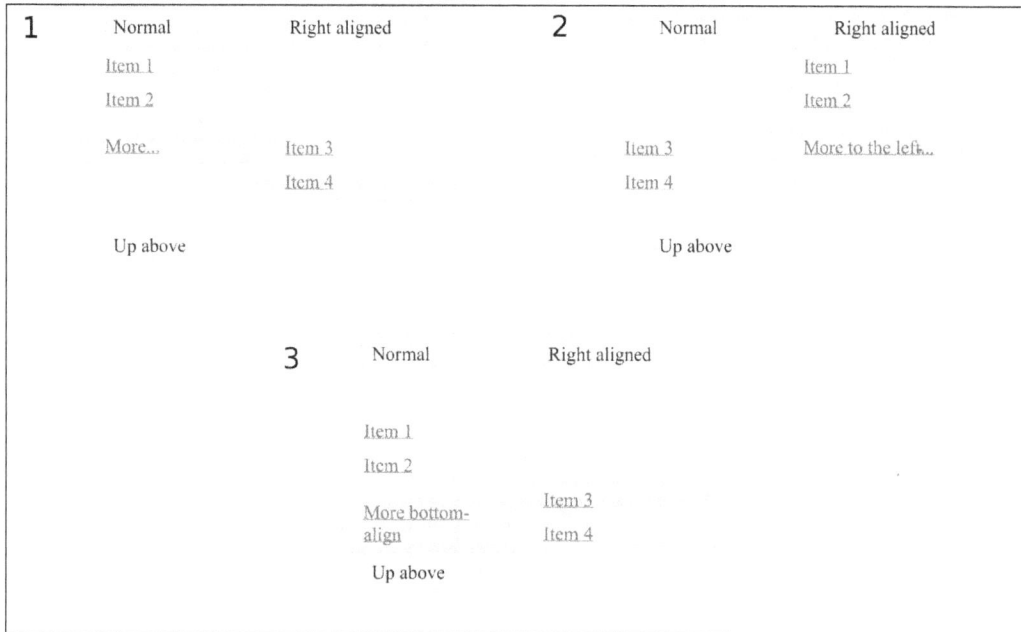

1	Normal	Right aligned	**2**	Normal	Right aligned
	Item 1				Item 1
	Item 2				Item 2
	More...	Item 3		Item 3	More to the left...
		Item 4		Item 4	
	Up above			Up above	

3	Normal	Right aligned
	Item 1	
	Item 2	
	More bottom-align	Item 3
		Item 4
	Up above	

How to do it...

To create the menu, we will use HTML and CSS.

1. Let's first create the menu structures in the HTML file. Essentially, it's the same structure discussed previously, copied three times with slight variations in styles, particularly on the unordered list elements that contain menus and submenus:

```
<!DOCTYPE HTML>
<html>
<head>
<title>Dropdown menu</title>
<link rel="stylesheet" type="text/css" href="example.css">
<style type="text/css">
.screen-bottom {
    position:fixed;
    bottom:3em;
}
</style>
</head>
```

```
<body>

<div class="dropdown-menu">
    <a class="btn">Normal</a>
    <ul class="menu">
        <li><a href="item1">Item 1</a>
        <li><a href="item2">Item 2</a>
        <li class="separator"></li>
        <li class="dropdown-menu">
        <a href="#" class="submenu">More...</a>
        <ul class="menu">
            <li><a href="item3">Item 3</a>
            <li><a href="item4">Item 4</a>
        </ul>
        </li>
    </ul>
</div>

<div class="dropdown-menu">
    <a class="btn">Right aligned</a>
    <ul class="menu right-align">
        <li><a href="item1">Item 1</a>
        <li><a href="item2">Item 2</a>
        <li class="separator"></li>
        <li class="dropdown-menu">
        <a href="#" class="submenu">More to the left...</a>
        <ul class="menu left-side">
            <li><a href="item3">Item 3</a>
            <li><a href="item4">Item 4</a>
        </ul>
        </li>
    </ul>
</div>


<div class="screen-bottom">
    <div class="dropdown-menu">
        <a class="btn">Up above</a>
        <ul class="menu up">
            <li><a href="item1">Item 1</a>
            <li><a href="item2">Item 2</a>
            <li class="separator"></li>
            <li class="dropdown-menu">
            <a href="#" class="submenu">More bottom-align</a>
```

```
            <ul class="menu bottom-align">
                <li><a href="item3">Item 3</a>
                <li><a href="item4">Item 4</a>
            </ul>
            </li>
        </ul>
    </div>
</div>
</body>
</html>
```

2. Then let's add the appropriate CSS for this menu in `example.css`. We're
   going to use a `border-box` sizing model. Unlike the regular model, where the
   borders and padding are outside the specified dimensions of the element (width
   or height), in the `border-box` model the padding and borders are included in
   the specified dimensions:

```css
.dropdown-menu * {
    -webkit-box-sizing: border-box; /* Safari/Chrome, WebKit */
       -moz-box-sizing: border-box; /* Firefox, other Gecko */
            box-sizing: border-box;
}
div.dropdown-menu {
    display:inline-block;
    position:relative;
    margin:0 1em;
}
```

3. We're going to add styling to the menu items that display the dropdowns as well as
   the menu itself. By default, the inner menu is absolutely positioned below the rest of
   the content:

```css
a.btn {
    padding: 0.5em 2em;
    background-color:#f1f1f1;
}
.dropdown-menu ul.menu {
    width:auto;
    background-color:#f9f9f9;
    border: solid 1px #ddd;
    display:none;
    position:absolute;
    top:50%;
    left:0;
    list-style:none;
```

```
        padding:0;
        min-width:170px;
    }
```

4. We need to make the menu show on hover when the button is active:

```
    .dropdown-menu:hover > ul.menu,
    .dropdown-menu:active > ul.menu {
        display:block;
    }
```

5. We need submenus to be positioned relative to their parent items:

```
    .dropdown-menu > ul.menu > li {
        position:relative;
    }
```

6. We'll set the style of a regular items and a separator item:

```
    .dropdown-menu > ul.menu > li:hover {
        background-color:#eee;
    }
    .dropdown-menu > ul.menu > li > a {
        padding:0.3em 1.5em;
        display:block;
    }
    .dropdown-menu > ul.menu > li.separator {
        height:0.01em;
        margin:0.3em 0;
        border-bottom: solid 1px #ddd;
    }
```

7. Regular submenus will be positioned slightly differently: in-line with their parent item but 90% from the left-hand side:

```
    li.dropdown-menu ul.menu {
        left:90%;
        right:auto;
        top:0em;
    }
```

8. Lastly, we apply the specialized styles for right-aligned and roll-up menus, as well as submenus that are bottom-aligned with their parent:

```
    .dropdown-menu ul.menu.right-align {
        left:auto;
        right:0;
    }
    .dropdown-menu ul.menu.up {
        top: auto;
```

```
        bottom:50%;
    }
    li.dropdown-menu ul.menu.left-side {
        right: 90%;
        left: auto;
    }
    li.dropdown-menu ul.menu.bottom-align {
        top:auto;
        bottom:0;
    }
```

How it works...

To display our menus dynamically, we use the `hover` and `active` CSS pseudo-selectors. They enable us to style elements differently when the cursor is hovering over them or when the elements are marked as `active`. Putting the entire menu inside the menu item allows us to display it by using these selectors on the menu item.

To position the menus and submenus, we use a combination of a `position:relative` parent menu item and `position:absolute` submenu child items. When we use this combination, our child positioning attributes are relative to the first relative parent, namely, the item.

This allows us to place the menu anywhere: below the parent by default or above as an option (for submenus, to the right by default, to the left as an option). It also allows us to align the submenu any way we like: left by default, right as an option (for submenus, top-aligned by default, bottom-aligned as an option).

These combinations should allow us to construct menus at arbitrary locations without worrying that the menu might go off-screen.

Creating custom dialogs

Custom dialogs can be used for all kinds of user input. We can ask the user to fill a form (for example, a login form can be displayed as a dialog). We can also use them to ask the user to accept or decline some action that requires immediate attention (for example, a dialog asking the user "Are you sure you want to delete the selected items?").

As we can theoretically display any other page segment in a dialog, it would be great if we had a single flexible method to do it. The easiest way to attain flexibility is to split the dialog into three parts: view, model, and controller.

In this recipe, we're going to create a general dialog. It will consist of a view (HTML that supports JavaScript templating), a model (available from the template), and a list of event bindings that make the controller.

This is an advanced recipe. If you're not familiar with **Embedded JavaScript Templates** (**EJS**), we recommend reading the EJS recipes in *Chapter 9, Client-side Templates*, before reading this recipe.

Login to continue	X

Invalid password

User: jack.r

Pass: •••••••

Login

Getting ready

We're going to use John Resig's simple implementation of EJS-like templates. It's a compiler that converts EJS templates to JavaScript functions. We're not going to explain the compiler—it's sufficient to know that it takes the ID of the element containing the template content and returns a template function. This function gives an HTML output when applied to an object.

The following is the template compiler function:

```
// Simple JavaScript Templating
// John Resig - http://ejohn.org/ - MIT Licensed
(function(){
  var cache = {};

  this.tmpl = function tmpl(str, data){
    // Figure out if we're getting a template, or if we need to
    // load the template - and be sure to cache the result.
    var fn = !/\W/.test(str) ?
      cache[str] = cache[str] ||
        tmpl(document.getElementById(str).innerHTML) :

      // Generate a reusable function that will serve as a template
      // generator (and which will be cached).
      new Function("obj",
        "var p=[],print=function(){p.push.apply(p,arguments);};" +

        // Introduce the data as local variables using with(){}
```

```
"with(obj){p.push('" +

    // Convert the template into pure JavaScript
    str
      .replace(/[\r\t\n]/g, " ")
      .split("<%").join("\t")
      .replace(/((^|%>)[^\t]*)'/g, "$1\r")
      .replace(/\t=(.*?)%>/g, "',$1,'")
      .split("\t").join("');")
      .split("%>").join("p.push('")
      .split("\r").join("\\'")
  + "');}return p.join('');");

  // Provide some basic currying to the user
  return data ? fn( data ) : fn;
};
})();
```

The original article explaining JavaScript Micro-Templating can be found at
http://ejohn.org/blog/javascript-micro-templating/.

How to do it...

We're going to write the page code and the dialog library.

1. Let's create a file named index.html. It will contain a secret div area and a template for a login dialog with the ability to pre-fill username and the ability to show an error message:

```
<!DOCTYPE HTML>
<html>
    <head>
        <title>Simple rich text editor</title>
        <link rel="stylesheet" type="text/css" href="dialog.css">
        <style type="text/css">
        .dialog.tmplExample .button-area { margin-top: 20px; text-
align:right; }
        .dialog.tmplExample p.error.hidden { display:none; }
        .dialog.tmplExample p.error { color:#c00; }
        div.secret { display:none; }
        </style>
    </head>
    <body>
    <div>
```

```
            <div class="secret">
                Welcome to the secret place, where only authenticated
users may roam.
            </div>
        </div>
        <script id="tmplExample" type="text/html">
            <p class="error hidden"></p>
            <p><label for="user">User:</label>
               <input name="user" type="text" value="<%= user %>" ></p>
            <p><label for="pass">Pass:</label>
               <input name="pass" type="password" value="<%= pass %>"
></p>
            <p class="button-area">
                <button class="login" type="button">Login</button>
            </p>
        </script>
        <script src="http://ajax.googleapis.com/ajax/libs/jquery/1.8.2/
jquery.min.js"></script>
        <script type="text/javascript" src="tmpl.js"></script>
        <!--<script type="text/javascript" src="dialog.js"></script>-->
        <script type="text/javascript" src="example.js"></script>
        </body>
</html>
```

2. To see how we would like the dialog API to work, we're going to create `example.js` next. It will immediately show a login dialog that will close once a correct password is input, then the secret content will be shown. Otherwise, an error message will be displayed inside the dialog:

```
$(function() {
    dialog("tmplExample", {title: 'Login to continue', user:
'jack.r', pass: ''}, {
        'button.login => click': function(dialog, ev) {
            var data = dialog.data();
            if (data.pass == 'secret') { dialog.close(); $('.
secret').show(); }
            else { dialog.find('p.error').text('Invalid
password').show(); }
        }
    });
});
```

3. Next let's create `dialog.js`. It should export a function called `dialog` that takes three arguments: the ID of the dialog template, the data to fill into the template, and an object containing event bindings:

```
(function () {
    window.dialog = function(template, data, bindings) {
```

1. First, build the `dialog` chrome:

```
var holder = $("<div />").addClass('dialog')
        .addClass(template);
var titlebar = $("<div />").addClass('title')
        .appendTo(holder);
var titletext = $("<span />").addClass('titletext')
        .appendTo(titlebar);
var close = $("<span />").addClass('close')
        .html('x').appendTo(titlebar);
var form = $("<form />").addClass('dialog')
        .appendTo(holder);
```

2. Fill it with the templated HTML, set the title, and display it:

```
form.html(tmpl(template, data));
$(titletext).text(data.title || "Dialog");
holder.appendTo('body');
```

3. Apply the bindings that are in the `selector => event` format:

```
for (var key in bindings) if (bindings.
hasOwnProperty(key))
        (function(key) {
            var selectorEvent = key.split(/\s+=>\s+/);
            form.find(selectorEvent[0]).on(selectorEvent[1],
                function() {
                    var args = [].slice.call(arguments);
                    args.unshift(self);
                    bindings[key].apply(this, args);
                });
        }(key));
```

4. Build the `dialog` object to return. Provide the `find()` function for fields, the `data()` function to extract all form data as a JSON object, as well as event binding and close functions:

```
var self = {};
self.find = form.find.bind(form);
self.data = function() {
    var obj = {};
    form.serializeArray().forEach(function(item) {
```

```
                              if (obj[item.name]) {
                                  if (!(obj[item.name] instanceof
    'array'))
                                      obj[item.name] = [ obj[item.name] ];
                                  obj[item.name].push(item.value);
                              }
                              else obj[item.name] = item.value;
                          });
                          return obj;
                      }
                      self.close = function() {
                          holder.trigger('dialog:close');
                          holder.remove();
                      };
                      self.on = holder.on.bind(holder);
                      close.on('click', self.close);
                      return self;
                  };
              }());
```

5. Finally, we will customize the positioning and style of the dialog in `dialog.css`:

```css
div.dialog {
    position:fixed;
    top:10%;
    left: 50%;
    margin-left: -320px;
    width:640px;
    height:auto;
    border: solid 1px #ccc;
    background-color:#fff;
    box-shadow: 2px 2px 5px #ccc;
}
div.dialog div.title { border-bottom: solid 1px #eee; }
div.dialog div.title span { padding: 0.5em 1em;
display:inline-block; }
div.dialog div.title span.close { float: right; cursor:
pointer; }
div.dialog form.dialog { padding: 1em; }
```

How it works...

To make a flexible dialog library, we split the data needed to show the dialog into view, model, and controller.

The `tmpl.js` library provides a function that processes an EJS template using the provided model object. The innards of this function are out of the scope of this recipe.

Our `dialog` function constructs a chrome containing a title bar, a Close button, and a form. Afterwards, it fills out the form with the template and data. Finally, it applies our bindings to the content of this form. The bindings are in the jQuery `selector => event` format and can be used to respond to any kind of user input.

This function returns a `dialog` object (constructed in the variable self). The object provides the following convenience functions:

- `find`: This allows the user to find elements within the form using selectors
- `data`: This extracts all data inputs into the form as an easy-to-use JSON object
- `close`: This closes the dialog
- `on`: This allows the user to add extra bindings (for example, the `dialog:close` event)

The object also provides a convenience event named `dialog:close` that gets triggered when the dialog is closed.

We style this dialog using `dialog.css`. The dialog is positioned with a pure CSS-based positioning method: using fixed-width and negative margins, we avoid the need to read the width of the window, and hence manage to fully avoid using JS.

The flexible templating language allows us to create dialog content of any complexity, while the `bindings` syntax allows full control over of all user input. We can simplify the creation of some common dialogs by providing the template and some, or all, of the bindings.

With this generic method, creating simple message boxes, generic text prompts, or complex dialog forms with a variable number of fields are all equally easy.

Creating autocomplete for input

One common functionality usually related to search fields or input is that we can guess the text after typing some of the data. This can be any field that we have in our database such as employee names. In this recipe, we will take a look at some of the possible ways to create autocomplete for input; it is up to you to decide what is best fit for your use case.

Getting ready

In this example we are going to use a sample JSON file that will simulate a result returned by a REST API. The file can be retrieved from the examples, and it's with the name `countries.json` where we have a list of objects—mapping of countries with their corresponding languages. In the example, we will use both **jQueryUI** (`http://jqueryui.com/`) and a library called **Chosen** (`https://github.com/harvesthq/chosen`). Why use both? Well, we can use either of them, or none, but the idea here is to show different ways of creating a good user experience with list selection. Additionally, as we will be simulating the REST service, we need a server running; more on this is available in *Appendix A, Installing Node.js and Using npm*.

How to do it...

For the example, we will use HTML and accompanying JavaScript and CSS:

1. We will first start with the `head` section and add the CSS dependencies for jQueryUI and Chosen. Also, we add a small CSS section in which we will define the size of the single selectors for Chosen:

   ```
   <head>
       <meta charset="utf-8">
       <title>Autocomplete</title>
   ```

```
    <link rel="stylesheet" href="//cdnjs.cloudflare.com/ajax/
libs/jqueryui/1.10.2/css/lightness/jquery-ui-1.10.2.custom.css"
type="text/css" media="all">
    <link rel="stylesheet" type="text/css" href="//cdnjs.
cloudflare.com/ajax/libs/chosen/0.9.11/chosen.css">
    <style type="text/css">
      .marker{
        width:350px;
      }
    </style>
  </head>
```

2. Next, we can add the body part of the HTML where we will create the form. First, we will create a block that will have an input text filed that shall be connected to a list of suggested fruits:

```
<div>
        <label>
          Pick your favorite fruit <input name="favFruit"
type="text" list="fruit" placeholder="Example:'Apple'">
        </label>
        <datalist id="fruit">
          <option value="apple" label="Apple"></option>
          <option value="apricot"></option>
          <option value="banana"></option>
          <option value="berries"></option>
        </datalist>
      </div>
```

3. The next input field is for the selection of country, where we will be using the Chosen type of selector that will have auto complete as part of the control:

```
    <div>
        <label for="country">Your country </label>
        <select id="country" name="country" data-
placeholder="Choose a Country..." class="marker">
            <option value=""></option>
            <option value="United States">United States</option>
            <option value="United Kingdom">United Kingdom</option>
            <option value="Afghanistan">Afghanistan</option>
            <option value="Aland Islands">Aland Islands</option>
            <option value="Andorra">Andorra</option>
            <option value="Angola">Angola</option>
            <option value="Anguilla">Anguilla</option>
            <option value="Antarctica">Antarctica</option>
            <option value="Antigua and Barbuda">Antigua and
Barbuda</option>
        </select>
    </div>
```

4. Another input element is for language selection. We are going to make it using the JSON data retrieved from the server, or a JSON file in our case. Also, we are going to add an input for occupation and a Submit button:

```
<div>
    <label for="language">Language</label>
    <input type="text" id="language" name="language"
placeholder="Example: English"/>
    </div>
    <div>
    <label for="occupation">Occupation</label>
    <input type="text" id="occupation" name="occupation"
placeholder="Example: prog">
    </div>
    <div>
     <input type="submit">
    </div>
```

5. Don't forget that this block needs to be part of a `form` in order to be submitted. One other option is to have the element specify a `form` attribute:

```
<input type="text" id="occupation" name="occupation"
placeholder="Example: prog" form ="someFormId" >
```

6. This sets who is the owner of the given element, allowing us to place the element anywhere in the document. The restriction here is that we can have only one form for a given element.

7. The next part is to include the external vendor JavaScripts for jQuery, jQueryUI and Chosen:

```
<script src="//cdnjs.cloudflare.com/ajax/libs/jquery/1.8.3/jquery.
min.js"></script>
 <script src="//cdnjs.cloudflare.com/ajax/libs/chosen/0.9.11/
chosen.jquery.min.js"></script>
 <script src="//cdnjs.cloudflare.com/ajax/libs/jqueryui/1.10.2/
jquery-ui.min.js" type="text/javascript"></script>
```

8. After that, we can start the jQuery selections and logic:

```
$(function() { ...}
```

9. To enable Chosen for elements, we select them and call the plugin directly on them; it's as simple as that:

```
$(".marker").chosen();
```

10. Another option is to use the jQueryUI `autocomplete` plugin. One way is to have the data locally, and then apply it on some selection:

```
var occupation = ["programmer","manager","doctor","designer"];
    $("#occupation").autocomplete({
        source:occupation,
        minLength:2,
        delay:200
    });
```

11. In the configuration of the component, the `source` attribute can accept a list of possible string options, and the `minLength` attribute designates the minimal number of characters that should be inserted before the autocomplete is triggered. The `delay` can be set in milliseconds between a keystroke and a search on the source data.

> Note that setting the delay to `low` can create a bad side-effect of making a lot requests to the data source.

12. The data can also be on a remote server and retrieved as source to the plugin where some additional filtering can be applied:

```
$("#language").autocomplete({
    source: function (request, response) {
    //matcher for terms filtering on client side
    var matcher = new RegExp( "^" + $.ui.autocomplete.
escapeRegex( request.term ), "i" );
            //simulate a server side JSON api
    $.getJSON("countries.json?term=" + request.term,
        function (data) {
    response($.map(data, function (value, key) {
      for(var name in value) {
        var result = {};
          if(matcher.test( value[name])){
            result.label=value[name]+" "+name;
            result.value=value[name];
            return result;
          }
        }
      })
     );
    });
    },
    minLength: 2,
    delay: 200
    });
```

How it works...

The simplest case is one where we use the standard HMTL5 tags in order to get autocomplete. There we have the following code:

```
<input name="favFruit" type="text" list="fruit"
placeholder="Example:'Apple'" />
```

This `list="fruit"` attribute connects the input filed to the `datalist`. This attribute is used to identify a list of predefined options that will be suggested to the user.

The other option was to use Chosen, a JavaScript plugin that enables user-friendly selections. This can be achieved by the following simple HTML:

```
<select id="country" name="country" data-placeholder="Choose a
Country..." class="marker">
    <option value=""></option>
    <option value="United States">United States</option>
    <!-- … Other options -->
</select>
```

This will be picked up by the plugin using jQuery Selector to activate the plugin element:

```
$(".marker").chosen();
```

Chosen will automatically style the selection and add autocomplete, and if we have the `data-placeholder` attribute set, it will mimic the standard behavior of the HTML5 `placeholder` attributes.

> Note that, for simplicity, other countries are removed, in practical use cases you can use a list of countries defined in ISO 3166-1 (http://www.iso.org/iso/country_codes.htm) and the corresponding Wikipedia article http://en.wikipedia.org/wiki/ISO_3166-1.

Another option is to use the jQueryUI autocomplete component. That is why we are going to analyze in more detail an example with a server-side data source. There are three options to go with:

- **Client-side filtering**: We get the entire JSON document, or any other document for that matter, and we filter the data on the client side. This is generally a great approach if possible. This might not be the case for every situation. The data containing the list could be huge. Consider the autocomplete feature on a search engine, the possible result list is huge there.

- ▶ **Server-side filtering**: We get only a portion of the data filtered by some query parameter. The filtering is done on the server, making it slower in most of the cases. Making additional request adds some additional lagging even if the data is returned instantly without doing to much processing, which may not be the case.

- ▶ **Server-side and client-side filtering**: When working with large datasets, a combination of the both methods may be our best way. We could only ask the server for more data only if a certain threshold is met.

> As as side note, it is worth mentioning that if we are creating a search input field, it is semantically correct to use the HTML5 `input type="search"`. This control enables a single-line input filed and can have the `autosave` attribute added to enable the out-of-the-box dropdown of previously searched terms. The code would be as follows:
>
> ```
> <input id="mySearchField" type="search" autosave>
> ```

In order to use the data that is retrieved from the server as the user types, we can use a function in the `source` attribute of the configuration:

```
source: function (request, response) {
```

In the `request` object, we can get the current data inserted in the `input` element via the `request.term` attribute. We can then create a regex matcher if we like to filter the data on the client side like in our case, as we always will access the same JSON file:

```
var matcher = new RegExp( "^" + $.ui.autocomplete.escapeRegex(
request.term ), "i" );
```

After that, we read the data using an Ajax call to the service:

```
$.getJSON("countries.json?term=" + request.term, function (data) {
```

Please note that most of the REST API's have their own functionality for filtering usually via `request` parameters, in our case we don't have that, but to illustrate we could easily do something like the following:

```
'countries.json?term=' + request.term
```

So the callback function receives the JSON data, but as we get all the data unfiltered, we do that using `jQuery.map( arrayOrObject, callback( value, indexOrKey ) )` that translates all the items in the new array from the original array of objects following the rules defined in the `callback` function.

In our case, the JSON has the following format:

```
[
  {
    "Afghanistan": "Pashto"
  },
  {
    "Albania": "Albanian"
  }
  ...
]
```

In order to filter the data using the `language` names, we should return a sublist of those objects that match our criteria defined in the `matcher`:

```
function (data) {
  response($.map(data, function (value, key) {
    for(var name in value) {
    var result = {};
    if(matcher.test( value[name])){
        result.label=value[name]+" "+name;
        result.value=value[name];
        return result;
      }
    }
  }));
  }
```

You may notice that the result returned has the `label` and `value` properties; this is because it is one of the possible formats for the `source` where we have an array of objects like these.

If we are to compare the jQueryUI method of handing data versus the Chosen library, we can conclude that jQueryUI is more flexible when working with different data sources. On the other hand, Chosen, in a way, just styles the standard HTML elements and is more compliant than doing clever hacks. Additionally, Chosen is very focused on doing few things very nicely, and makes a great user experience while not having the baggage that comes with a size-heavy library such as jQueryUI.

There's more...

The `list` attribute can be used on all input types except for `hidden`, `checkbox`, `radio`, `file`, or `button` types where it gets ignored. When you think about it, it makes a lot sense not to work those types because there is not much practical use in having autocomplete on them.

If we need to have the same behavior on older browsers, or to have a fallback mode, we can place that content in the `datalist` element:

```
<datalist id="fruits">
 <label>
  or select on from this list of element:
  <select name="Fallback">
   <option value="">
   <option>Apple</option>
   <option>Orange</option>
   <!-- ... -->
  </select>
 </label>
</datalist>
```

This data will not be displayed if the `datalist` element is supported, enabling us to add support for legacy browsers.

There are various other data sources that can be used with jQueryUI autocomplete, such as JSONP or XML, for example.

Creating a custom single-selection list

In the previous recipe, we used Chosen. In this recipe, we will take a deeper look into the creation of simple select boxes, making one the most user-friendly way pickers out there.

Getting ready

In this recipe, we will use Chosen (`https://github.com/harvesthq/chosen`) and its dependency jQuery by adding them from a CDN.

How to do it...

We create an HTML file and the accompanying JavaScript code:

1. First, we will start with the head section of the HTML, where we will include the Chosen CSS style:

```
<head>
    <meta charset="utf-8">
    <title>Single select list</title>
    <link rel="stylesheet" type="text/css" href="//cdnjs.
cloudflare.com/ajax/libs/chosen/0.9.11/chosen.css">
    <style type="text/css">
        .drop-down{
```

```
            width: 250px;
        }
    </style>
  </head>
```

2. We are going to create a simple form where the user can select their favorite programming language and job title. To do that, we add `select` elements with several available options:

```html
<form>
    <div>
      <label>
        Favorite programming language:
        <select id="programming" data-placeholder="Your favorite
programming language" class="drop-down">
            <option value=""></option>
            <option>Java</option>
            <option>Python</option>
            <option>Clojure</option>
            <option>C</option>
            <option selected>Java Script </option>
            <option>Lisp</option>
            <option>Pascal</option>
            <option>VB</option>
        </select>
      </label>
    </div>
```

3. The possible options can be grouped using the `optgroup` element:

```html
<div>
      <label>
        You consider your self to be a:
        <select id="occupation" data-placeholder="Occupation"
class="drop-down">
            <optgroup label="Software">
                <option>Java developer</option>
                <option>Node developer</option>
                <option>Software Achitect</option>
                <option selected>Engineer</option>
                <option>Manager</option>
            <optgroup>
            <optgroup label="Hardware">
              <option>Semiconductor</option>
              <option>Manager</option>
              <option>Computer Hardware Engineer</option>
            </optgroup>
```

```
        </select>
      </label>
    </div>
```

4. And at last, we just add a simple submit for the form:

```
<input type="submit" />
</form>
```

5. In order to include Chosen, we add their implementation from a CDN:

```
<script src="//cdnjs.cloudflare.com/ajax/libs/jquery/1.8.3/
jquery.min.js"></script>
    <script src="//cdnjs.cloudflare.com/ajax/libs/chosen/0.9.11/
chosen.jquery.min.js"></script>
```

6. To designate to what element should have Chosen applied, we use jQuery selection:

```
$(function() {
  $("#programming").chosen({
    allow_single_deselect:true
  });
  $("#occupation").chosen();
});
```

How it works...

The best thing about Chosen is its simplicity; we just select the elements with jQuery and apply the plugin. There is an option allowing deselect that we can enable during creation of these kind of elements:

```
$("#programming").chosen({allow_single_deselect:true});
```

> Note that Chosen can be used with **Prototype JS** instead of jQuery; there the selection of elements would be new Chosen(someElement);.

Also, we can add an attribute named data-placeholder that will contain default text, such as Occupation, as in our example. If this is not specified, it will default to Select Some Option for single select.

> On select elements, the browser assumes the first element to be selected if selectedIndex is not specified or if there is no option with the selected attribute. In order to allow none selected, we can set the first option blank, thus enabling the data-placeholder text support.

There's more...

If you need to use data for the options that will change after the initial creation of Chosen, you can update the component dynamically and then trigger the `liszt:updated` event on the selected field. The `liszt:updated` event is a Chosen-specific internal event. Chosen, after calling the event, will rebuild the list based on the updated content. For example, on an element with ID as `countries`, the triggering would be as follows:

```
$("#form_field").trigger("liszt:updated");
```

Creating a multiple-selection list

Chosen can be used to create beautiful-looking multiple selections. In this recipe, we will create a form for a menu ordering that uses this type of selections in a form.

Getting ready

This recipe will contain the same parts as *Creating a custom single-selection list*, and build upon them.

How to do it...

We start by having the same base as *Creating a custom single-selection list*, and add the following parts:

1. First, we add the selections that will have the `drop-down` CSS class we created in the head section:

```
            <div>
        <label for="cocktails">Place the order for cocktails</label>
        <select id="cocktails" data-placeholder="Add cocktails"
    multiple class="drop-down" name="cocktails">
            <option value=""></option>
            <option>Black Velvet</option>
            <option>Moonwalk</option>
            <option>Irish coffee</option>
            <option>Giant Panda</option>
            <option selected>Jungle Juice</option>
            <option selected>Mojito</option>
            <option selected disabled>Joker</option>
            <option disabled>Long Island Iced Tea</option>
            <option disabled>Kamikaze</option>
        </select>
    </div>
```

2. We can also use grouping of the options for the `select` element having sections, such as `Starters` and `Pizza`:

```
<div>
        <label for="food">Select the food order</label>
        <select id="food" data-placeholder="Select some off the menu
    element" multiple class="drop-down" name="food">
        <optgroup label="Starters">
                <option>White Pizza</option>
                <option>Calzone</option>
          <optgroup>
          <optgroup label="Pizza">
                <option>Chees and Tomato</option>
                <option>Garden Veggie</option>
                <option>Pepperoni</option>
          <optgroup>
          <optgroup label="Salads">
            <option>House Salad</option>
            <option>Cezar Salad</option>
            <option>Sopska</option>
          </optgroup>
        </select>
    </div>
```

3. Simply select all elements that have the `drop-down` CSS class and enable Chosen for them:

```
<script type="text/javascript">
$(function() {
 $('.drop-down').chosen();
 }
</script>
```

How it works...

Painless setup is one of the main features for Chosen so the JavaScript part is fairly simple because we only have a basic selection of elements. Options can be selected before the page is rendered to the user by having the `selected` attribute on options, such as `Mojito`. They can also be disabled from selection by using the `disabled` attribute, so in our case, the option `Long Island Iced Tea` will not appear in the selection.

Optgroups, selected states, multiple attributes, as well as other attributes are respected just like the standard HTML5 behavior. This means that we are not required to expect something special or do some customization on the server side handling for the forms.

Geographic location input using maps

Since the introduction of the HTML5 geolocation API, reading the user's location became much simpler. However, sometimes we might want to allow the user to correct or verify his location or to specify a location different than their own.

In this chapter, we're going to make a location input that allows the user to specify a location by marking it on a map.

Our location picker will be represented as a link. Upon clicking the link, the user will have the option to search for their location using an input field, and then select the location by clicking on the map.

As with all our map recipes, we're going to use the popular Leaflet (`http://leafletjs.com/`) map library.

Getting ready

We would like our map input to behave similar to most input fields. We're going to use a drop-down style mechanism, similar to most date picker components. The user will click on a link to modify the location, and a map dropdown will appear as a result. After the user makes their selection, the dropdown will disappear.

We're also going to add a search box to aid the user in finding the desired location on the map. To do this, we will use **Nominatim** (`http://nominatim.openstreetmap.org/`), a free geocoding service provided by OpenStreetMap. The following is an example of how a Nominatim JSON response looks like:

```
[{
    [snip]
    "lat": "52.5487969264788",
    "lon": "-1.81642935385411",
    "display_name": "135, Pilkington Avenue, Castle Vale, Birmingham,
West Midlands, England, B72 1LH, United Kingdom",
    [snip]
}]
```

It's an array of search results containing various data among which the data that we will need, such as latitude, longitude, and display name, are present.

How to do it...

Let's write the code.

1. As always, we start with our HTML page. Our input field consists of three components: the link to be clicked, a hidden input field containing latitude and longitude data, and a map-based location picker. The map and search box are not included in the HTML—they're created on demand.

   To make the map drop down below the link, it's positioned relatively to its container. To make autocomplete links appear on separate lines, their display style is set to `block`.

```
<!DOCTYPE HTML>
<html>
    <head>
        <title>Location input using a map</title>
        <style type="text/css">
            div[data-input-map] {
                position:relative;
            }
            div[data-map] {
                width: 480px;
                height: 320px;
                position:absolute;
                top:100%;
                left:0;
            }
            div[data-results] a {
                display:block;
```

```
            }
        </style>
        <link rel="stylesheet" href="http://cdn.leafletjs.com/
leaflet-0.4/leaflet.css" />
        <!--[if lte IE 8]>
        <link rel="stylesheet" href="http://cdn.leafletjs.com/
leaflet-0.4/leaflet.ie.css" />
        <![endif]-->
    </head>
    <body>
        <div data-input-map>
            <a href="#">Set location</a>
            <input data-location type="hidden" name="location"
value="51.5,-0.09" />
        </div>
        <script src="http://ajax.googleapis.com/ajax/libs/
jquery/1.8.2/jquery.min.js"></script>
        <script src="http://cdn.leafletjs.com/leaflet-0.4/leaflet.
js"></script>
        <script type="text/javascript" src="example.js"></script>
    </body>
</html>
```

2. In order to make this picker work, the following code is added in `example.js`:

```
$('body').on('click', '[data-input-map] > a', function(e) {
    e.preventDefault();
    var par = $(this).parent();

    // Read the current location of the input
    var location = par.find('[data-location]');
    var latlng = location.val().split(',').map(parseFloat);

    // Create the map element and center the map at the current
    // location. Add a marker to that location.
    var mape = $('<div data-map />')
        .appendTo(par)[0];
    var map = L.map(mape).setView(latlng, 13)
    L.tileLayer('http://{s}.tile.openstreetmap.org/{z}/{x}/{y}.
png',{
        attribution:'Copyright (C) OpenStreetMap.org',
        maxZoom:18
    }).addTo(map);
    var marker = L.marker(latlng).addTo(map);

    // Update the location when a new place is clicked.
```

```
map.on('click', function(e) {
    marker.setLatLng(e.latlng);
    location.val([e.latlng.lat, e.latlng.lng].join(','));
    setTimeout(function() {
        $(mape).remove();
        inpe.remove();
    }, 500);
});

// Given a street address return a list of locations with
// names and latlngs using the nominatim service.
function findLocation(query, callback) {
    $.ajax('http://nominatim.openstreetmap.org/search', {
        data: { format: 'json', q: query },
        dataType: 'json'
    }).success(function(data) {
        callback(data.map(function(item) {
            return {
                latlng: [item.lat, item.lon],
                name: item.display_name
            };
        }));
    });
}


// Add a search box
var inpe = $('<input type="text" data-search />')
    .appendTo(par);
delaySearch = null;

// Fire a search 1 second after the input stops changing,
// displaying the results in a list
inpe.on('keydown keyup keypress', function() {
    if (delaySearch) clearTimeout(delaySearch);
    delaySearch = setTimeout(function() {
        par.find('div[data-results]').remove();
        var autocomplete = $('<div data-results />')
            .appendTo(par);
        findLocation(inpe.val(), function(results) {
            results.forEach(function(r) {
                $('<a href="#" />')
                    .attr('data-latlng', r.latlng.join(','))
                    .text(r.name).appendTo(autocomplete);
            });
```

```
                        // When a result is picked, center the map there
and
                        // allow the user to pick the exact spot.
                        autocomplete.on('click', 'a', function(e) {
                            e.preventDefault();
                            var latlng = $(this).attr('data-latlng')
                                .split(',');
                            map.setView(latlng, 13);
                            autocomplete.remove()
                        });
                    });
            }, 1000);
        });


});
```

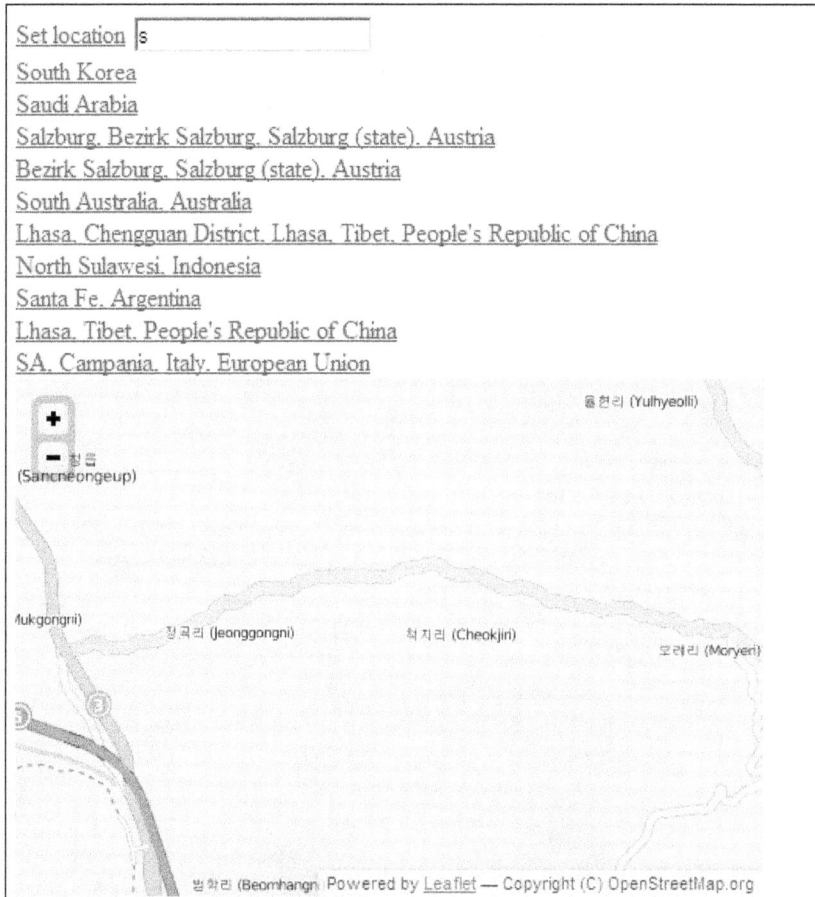

How it works...

The code found in `example.js` enables the user to click on the **Set location** link and choose a location using the map. The `click` event binding is added to the document body to make it easier to add a new location input to the page.

We parse the latitude and longitude from the hidden input field and then create a map centered at those coordinates with a marker placed at the same place.

When the user clicks on the map, the location is updated and the map is removed after 500 milliseconds. This should be long enough for the user to notice that his change was successfully applied.

Additionally, we added a search box next to the clicked link. When the user types in a search query inside, a search is performed by making an Ajax request to Nominatim. To avoid overloading the service, the search is delayed by 1 second; if the user types something before that second passes, the query is canceled and a new one is scheduled for sending 1 second later.

Upon fetching the results, the code displays them as a list of links. When clicked, they will reposition the map to be centered at the exact location of the clicked search result. The list of search results will be removed and the user will be allowed to select the exact location.

6
Data Validation

In this chapter, we will cover the following recipes:

- ▸ Validating text by length
- ▸ Validating numbers by range
- ▸ Using the built-in pattern validation
- ▸ Advanced use of built-in constraints and custom validations
- ▸ Calculating password strength
- ▸ Validating US zip codes
- ▸ Using asynchronous server-side validation
- ▸ Combining client-side and server-side validation

Introduction

Forms usually expect the user to behave in a certain way and to insert data as requested. This is where data validations come in. Server-side validation is always a must to do and form validation at the client side should be considered.

Validation makes the application user-friendly, saves time and bandwidth. Client-side and server-side validation complement each other and they should be used always. In this chapter, we are going to look at some new mechanisms provided mostly for client-side checks by HTML5 as well as how to tackle some common problems.

Validating text by length

One of the most basic checks at the client side is the length of the text being inserted or submitted with the form. This is often left out, but it is one of the checks that must be done and not just at the client side. Imagine if we had no restriction on any of our inputs, a few large texts could overload the server without making much effort.

How to do it...

Let's create a simple HTML form that will contain a few different inputs on which we will apply some constrains:

1. Head of the page is a standard one, so we will directly go into creating the form, first adding the `name` input limited to `20` characters as follows:

    ```
    <form>
        <div>
            <label>
                Name <input id="name" type="text" name="name"
    maxlength="20" title="Text is limited to 20
    chars"placeholder="Firstname Lastname" >
            </label>
        </div>
    ```

2. After that we will add another `input` field that initially has an invalid value, longer than the one specified for testing purpose, as follows:

    ```
        <div>
            <label>
                Initially invalid <input value="Some way to long value"
    maxlength="4" name="testValue" title="You should not have more
    than 4 characters">
            </label>
        </div>
    ```

3. Additionally, we will add the `textarea` tag that will have the `spellcheck` attribute added as follows:

    ```
        <div>
            <label>
                Comment <textarea spellcheck="true" name="comment"
    placeholder="Your comment here"> </textarea>
            </label>
        </div>
    ```

4. After that we will add two buttons, one for submitting the form and another for enabling the JavaScript fallback validation as follows:

```
<button type="submit">Save</button>
<button id="enable" type="button">Enable JS validation</button>
```

5. Since we are going to test out a fallback version using the jQuery Validate plugin, we will add the dependency for those two libraries and include our own `formValidate.js` file that will be defined later:

```
<script src="//cdnjs.cloudflare.com/ajax/libs/jquery/1.8.3/jquery.min.js"></script>
<script src="//cdnjs.cloudflare.com/ajax/libs/jquery-validate/1.10.0/jquery.validate.min.js"></script>
<script src="formValidate.js" ></script>
```

6. We also need to select the form that is to be submitted and add the JavaScript-based validations using the plugin, when the button for enabling the fallback is clicked:

```
$("#enable").click(function(){
  $("#userForm").validate({
    rules: {
      name : "required",
      comment: {
        required: true,
        minlength: 50
      }
    },
    messages: {
      name: "Please enter your name",
      comment: {
        required: "Please enter a comment",
        minlength: "Your comment must be at least 50
          chars long"
      }
    }
  });
});
```

Note that we also add the messages that will be shown on validation errors.

The button for enabling JavaScript is used only for demonstrative purpose, in a real application you are probably going to have it as a fallback or as the only approach. Since we are only checking for maximum length, validation should not be a problem unless we previously have rendered the HTML with incorrect values. As for the message for validation, at the time of writing it is supported in all of the modern browsers and IE 10, but none of the mobile browsers have added support for it yet. We can first check that if the browsers support the spellcheck attribute, and then act accordingly:

```
if ('spellcheck' in document.createElement('textarea'))
{
    // spellcheck is supported
} else {
    //spellchek is not supported
}
```

How it works...

Initially, we will take a look at the `maxlength` attribute. As you would expect the browsers do not allow this type of constraint to be broken by user input, they generally stop the input after the maximum has been inserted.

So the question is how can this constraint be violated?

Well, if the rendered HTML is invalid to start with or if the data was changed programmatically, then the form will be submitted without validation. This is actually the specified behavior; there is a dirty flag that designates if the input was from the user or not. In our case, as long as we don't change anything in the input labeled **Initially invalid**, the form will get submitted successfully. On the other hand, when the user changes some of the data in that element the form fails with a validation error, as shown in the following screenshot:

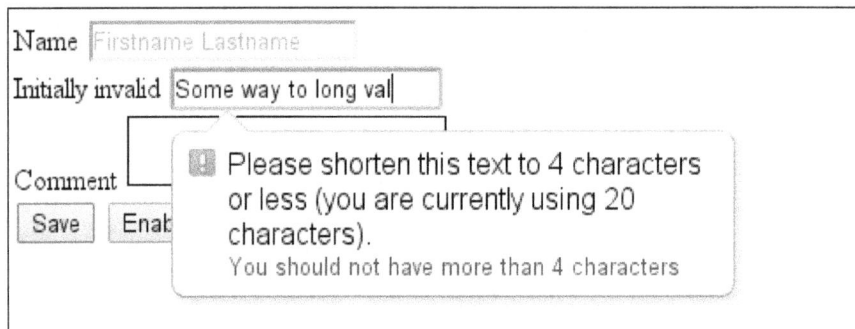

validation pop up as shown on Chrome Version 28 development release

In the validation error pop up displayed beside the error message will have the contents of the `title` attribute, meaning that this attribute has another usage besides the standard hint. This message box looks differently on various browsers.

Even though the major control when enabling grammar and spellchecker on the browsers is up to the user, there is an attribute called `spellcheck`, that can be added to hint the browser to do spelling checks. In our example, the comment would look like the following screenshot:

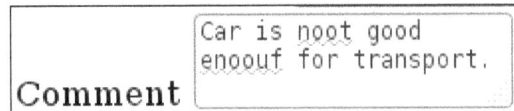

Comment | Car is noot good enoouf for transport.

This attribute is inheritable and can be combined with the `lang` attribute. For example, if we have the following snippet:

```
<html lang="en">
<body spellcheck="true">
  <textarea></textarea>
  <div lang="fr">
    <textarea></textarea>
      <input type="text">
  </div>
</body>
</html>
```

In the example we have multiple different languages used. Since the page has the `lang="en"` attribute set, the English dictionary will be used for all elements that are nested inside. And because the `div` element has the `lang="fr"` attribute, all the nested elements (`textarea` and `input type = text`) will be checked against the French dictionary.

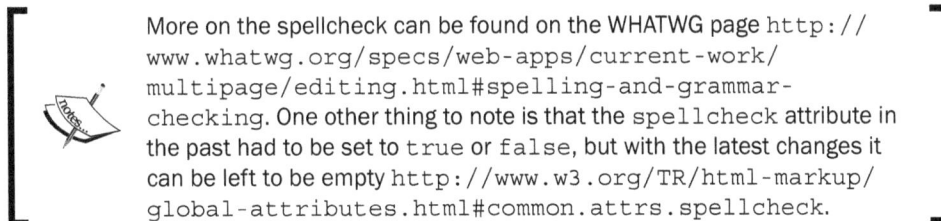

> More on the spellcheck can be found on the WHATWG page `http://www.whatwg.org/specs/web-apps/current-work/multipage/editing.html#spelling-and-grammar-checking`. One other thing to note is that the `spellcheck` attribute in the past had to be set to `true` or `false`, but with the latest changes it can be left to be empty `http://www.w3.org/TR/html-markup/global-attributes.html#common.attrs.spellcheck`.

Why do we say that the user has the full control? Well, if the user had always picked spellcheck in the browser or never checked, that option overrides the behavior that comes with this tag. This attribute can be applied to text input related elements, as well as the elements whose content has been made editable.

Fallback or in a way different approach is to use JavaScript to validate for the text length. Because there is no `minlength` attribute in HTML5, there is no standard way of validation for minimal length. Therefore, we are going to use jQuery Validation plugin. There is a way to do this also by using the `pattern` attribute and regex, but that we are going to discuss in detail later in the *Using built-in pattern validation* recipe in this chapter.

To enable the validation, we select the form and set the rules by specifying the validation rule, where the keys are the form parameter names, and values are the applied validation checks:

```
$("#userForm").validate({
    rules: {
        name : "required",
        comment: {
            required: true,
            minlength: 50
        }
    },
```

After that, we add the message for each individual check, where again the keys are the form parameter names as follows:

```
messages: {
    name: "Please enter your name",
    comment: {
        required: "Please enter a comment",
        minlength: "Your comment must be at least 50 chars long"
    }
```

The validation rules will also include the original attributes added to the form elements. In our case, the input labeled **Initially invalid** has the `maxlength` attribute, and this will be added as part of other rules that are part of the JavaScript configuration. Also, the rules that are defined in JavaScript can be moved to be a part of appropriate form elements. Finally, the result of the JavaScript version should look something like the following screenshot:

There's more...

The style of the side text displayed by the jQuery Validation plugin in our example is the same as labels. There is a simple CSS class named `.error` added when there are validation errors, also there is an option to execute function when validation problem happens or is removed. This can be done while configuring the validate element as follows:

```
highlight: function(currentElement) {
    console.log("error on " +currentElement );
}, unhighlight: function(currentElement) {
    console.log("no more error on " +currentElement );
}
```

As far the topic of styling validation messages and elements is concerned, they will be discussed later in this chapter.

Validating numbers by range

When it comes down to numbers in forms, the basic validation is to check if the number is in a given range. For achieving this, there are the `min` and `max` attributes that should be applied to input types number, range, and date/time related inputs.

How to do it...

We will create a form containing a few input elements that need to have a range restriction, as follows:

1. First of all, we will start by creating the form with a number `input` field for age, limiting it to minimum of `18`, as given in the following code snippet:

```
<form>
  <div>
    <label>
      Age <input id="age" type="number" name="name" min="18" max="140" />
    </label>
  </div>
```

2. We will add the `range` input for the `Bet` value the user would place as follows:

```
  <div>
    <label>
      Bet <input id="deposit" value="1000" type="range" name="deposit" min="0" max="2000" />
      <output id="depositDisplay">1000</output>
    </label>
  </div>
```

3. Also, we include inputs limited with `min`, `max`, and `step` as follows:

```
<div>
  <label>
    Doubles <input value="4" type="number" name="doubles"
min="0" step="5" max="10" title="The value should be multiple of
5"/>
  </label>
</div>
<div>
  <label>
    Awesomeness <input id="awesomeness" value="11" type="range"
name="awesomeness" min="0" step="3" max="50" />
    <output id="awesomenessDisplay">10</output>
  </label>
</div>
```

4. After that, we will add the dependency for jQuery, our `example.js`, and an input `submit` as follows:

```
<input type="submit" />
</form>
  <script src="//cdnjs.cloudflare.com/ajax/libs/jquery/1.8.3/
jquery.min.js"></script>
  <script src="example.js"> </script>
```

5. We will also just link the range input with the output field in order to have a simple display in the `example.js` script, as follows:

```
$(function() {
  $('#deposit').change(function() {
    $('#depositDisplay').html(this.value);
  });

  $('#awesomeness').change(function() {
    $('#awesomenessDisplay').html(this.value);
  });
});
```

How it works...

As you might expect, the range for the age 18 to 140 is expected by the user, and if that input is not in that range we get an underflow constraint violation that will display the appropriate (**The value must be greater than or equal to {min}**) message. Similarly, we get an overflow constraint violation with the message, **Value must be less than or equal to {max}**.

For the input type `range`, there is no way for the user to get outside the range or even to trigger the step mismatch validation error. The step mismatch error should only be triggered if the initial value was not within the `min` value and some multiples of the `step` attribute:

```
<input value="11" type="range" name="awesomeness" min="0" step="3"
max="50" />
```

Here `11` should not be valid, because the value of the `step` attribute is `3`, and there is no way of getting to `11` using a slider, but the value is initially as such, so we should get an validation error, but this is browser specific. Most of the current versions of the browsers just correct the initially selected value while rendering.

If we try to submit the form for the **Doubles** input we should get a validation message, as shown in the following screenshot:

Here we receive the message because the value is `4`, but the constrains are `min="0"` `step="5"` `max="10"`, meaning that the value entered must be a multiple of `5`.

The user cannot get a validation message using the input type `range`, but this can happen using an input type `number`, since the user can manually Insert data here.

Using the built-in pattern validation

In order to create more complex validation, we need to use JavaScript. To ease the development, the `pattern` attribute was introduced for the `input` fields. This enables us to use regex for making validation checks, and in this recipe we will take a look at some of the elements that can be used in it.

How to do it...

In this example, we will create a form using simple HTML as follows:

1. First, we will add the form directly in the `body` section, starting with the **Username** field:

   ```
   <div>
     <label>
       Username: <input type="text" title="only letters allowed"
   name="username" pattern="^[a-zA-Z]+$" />
     </label>
   </div>
   ```

2. Then, we will add **Phone** as follows:

   ```
   <div>
     <label>
       Phone <input type="tel" name="phone" pattern="[\+]?[1-9]+"
   />
     </label>
   </div>
   ```

3. We will include `url` for **Webpage** as follows:

   ```
   <div>
     <label>
       Webpage <input type="url" name="webpage" />
     </label>
   </div>
   ```

4. We will add the **Emails** and **Gmail** input as follows:

   ```
   <div>
     <label>
       Emails <input type="email" name="emails" multiple required
   />
     </label>
   </div>
   <div>
     <label>
     Gmail <input type="email" name="emails" pattern="[a-z]+@gmail.
   com" maxlength="14"/>
     </label>
   </div>
   ```

How it works...

The `pattern` attribute, if specified, uses an earlier version of the JavaScript regex. Whole text must be matched against the given expression. For our example, we used loose validation, where, for example, for input type `tel`, we allow numbers and optional leading + specified by the pattern `[\+]?[1-9]+`.

Some of the other input types, such as `URL` and `email` use their built-in validation. All mails must match the following regex:

```
/^[a-zA-Z0-9.!#$%&'*+/=?^_`{|}~-]+@[a-zA-Z0-9-]+(?:\.[a-zA-Z0-9-]+)*$/
```

Now this is very permissive so we can add additional validations as we added in the input labeled **Gmail**. Constrains can be combined, or if some attribute accepts multiple entries all of these will get validated according the constrains, as we did in the following e-mails example:

Emails ex@examples.com,a

Gmail

Subm ⬚ Please enter a comma separated list of email addresses.

Also remember that we need to add a hint using title or placeholder or any other way, because the user will get the **Please match the requested format** message by default, and will not know what is he or she doing wrong.

There's more...

There is a site named `http://html5pattern.com/` that is intended as the source of regularly used input patterns. It's definitely a good resource, and we encourage you to visit it.

Advanced use of built-in constraints and custom validations

So far, we have already used some of the built-in validation mechanisms. Now we are going to take a deeper look at some of them, and how we can add our own customization. We will change the style and apply some more advanced checks as well, when we will see how we can disable validation on certain elements by creating a form that has most of these features.

> The current working draft version for the form validation can be found at `http://www.whatwg.org/specs/web-apps/current-work/multipage/forms.html#client-side-form-validation`.

How to do it...

We will create a form that will have error messages styled using CSS, and custom validation using HTML and JavaScript as follows:

1. We will start off by creating the head section, where we will include `example.css`, where the CSS file will contain selectors for the `input` elements with valid, invalid, optional, and required state:

```
<head>
  <title>Built In Validation</title>
  <link rel="stylesheet" href="example.css">
</head>
```

2. The next step is to create the `example.css` file. The `valid.png` image can be found in the source examples. In real life, you would probably not use all of these states to style the look of the forms, but we added it here in order to show what can be done:

```
input:invalid {
    background-color: red;
    outline: 0;
}
input:valid {
    background-color: green;
    background: url(valid.png) no-repeat right;
    background-size: 20px 15px;
    outline: 0;
}
input:required{
  box-shadow: inset 0 0 0.6em black;
}
input:optional{
  box-shadow: inset 0 0 0.6em green;
}
```

> CSS `box-shadow` is not fully supported in legacy browsers, for example IE 8. The specification for `box-shadow` can be found at `http://www.w3.org/TR/css3-background/#box-shadow`.

3. Following the `head` section, we will start with adding the form elements in the `body` section. First, we will add the `name` and `nickname` fields, making them `required`, and for which later we will ensure not to have the same value:

```
<div>
  <label>
    Name <input required name="name" x-moz-errormessage="We need
this."/>
```

```
    </label>
  </div>
  <div>
    <label>
    Nickname <input required name="nickname"/>
    </label>
  </div>
```

4. We can also include two date/time related inputs, one for `week` and other for `month`, where we will limit the weeks from second week of 2013 to second week of 2014 and allow every other month to be selected:

```
    <div>
    <label>
      Start week <input type="week" name="week" min="2013-W02"
max="2014-W02" required />
    </label>
  </div>
  <div>
    <label>
      Best months <input value="2013-01" type="month" step="2"
name="month" />
    </label>
  </div>
```

5. Also, we will add three buttons: one for submitting the form, another for checking the validity using JavaScript, and one more for submitting without validation and constraint checks:

```
    <button type="submit">Save</button>
    <button type="submit" formnovalidate>Save but don't validate</
button>
    <button type="button">Check Validity</button>
```

6. Outside the form, we will add one `div` element for displaying some log information:

```
    <div id="validLog"></div>
```

7. As for the JavaScript, we add the dependency for jQuery and include `example.js`:

```
    <script src="//cdnjs.cloudflare.com/ajax/libs/jquery/1.8.3/
jquery.min.js"></script>
    <script src="example.js"></script>
```

8. In the `example.js` file, we will add an event for the check validity button, where we will print the `ValidityState` value to `validLog`, on the validation errors of each of the form elements:

```
    $(function() {
      var attemptNumber = 1;
```

```
$("button[type=button]").click(function(){
  var message = (attemptNumber++)+"#<br/>";
  var isValid = $('form')[0].checkValidity();
  if(isValid){
    message += "Form is valid";
  }else{
    $("input").each(function( index ) {
      var validityState = $(this)[0].validity;
      var errors = "";
      If(!validityState.valid){
        message += "Invalid field <b> " + $(this).
attr("name")+"</b>: ";
        for(key in validityState){
          if(validityState[key]){
            errors += key+" ";
          }
        }
        message += "  " + errors + " <br />";
      }
    });
  }
  message += "<hr />";
  $("#validLog").prepend(message);
});
```

9. To add custom validation, we will use the `.setCustomValidity()` method, so it will check if the `name` and `nickname` values are the same, and if so, we will add validation error, and if they are not, we will remove the custom check:

```
$("input[name='nickname']").change(function(){
  if($(this).val() === $("input[name='name']").val()){
    $(this)[0].setCustomValidity("You must have an awesome
nickname so nickname and name should not match");
  }else{
  $(this)[0].setCustomValidity("");

});
$("input[name='name']").change(function(){
  if($(this).val() === $("input[name='nickname']").val()){
  $(this)[0].setCustomValidity("Nickname and name should not
match");
  }else{
  $(this)[0].setCustomValidity("");
  }
});
```

How it works...

The `required` attribute marks the HTML element inside the form, required to have a value before the form can be submitted. The first field that will not have a value would get focused upon submission and a hint with a message would be shown to the user:

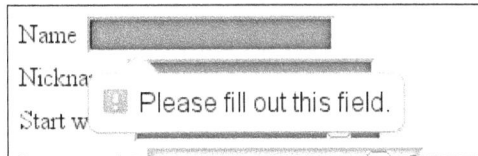

There are several ways to customize the message displayed to the user on Firefox; we can use the `x-moz-errormessage` attribute. In our case, this is `x-moz-errormessage="We need this."`, but this will only work there. On Chrome, the `title` attribute gets additionally displayed beside the standard message, but the original message stays. Another way for changing the message would be to set the value using JavaScript:

```
<input type="text" required="required" oninvalid="this.
setCustomValidity('Please put some data here')">
```

As for styling the form elements, there are the CSS pseudo class selectors `:required` and `:optional`.

> In WebKit, there are browser-specific CSS selectors that can be used to style the hint box, which are as follows:
>
> `::-webkit-validation-bubble {...}`
> `::-webkit-validation-bubble-message {...}`
>
> But because they are browser-specific, they are not very helpful in a practical use case.

The `min`, `max`, and `step` attributes can be used on date-related input types and not just on numbers. The default step is one day for date type, one week for week types, and so on. If we set a different step than the default one, for example on the month input if we have the step with value two, the user will not be able to select every other month from the DatePicker control, but he or she can still enter the wrong date in text, triggering `stepMismatch`.

Because validation is triggered before the form is submitted, and if the input is invalid, the `submit` event is never called. If we need to have a way of submitting data without validation, we can do that by using the `formnovalidate` attribute as follows:

```
<button type="submit" formnovalidate>Save but don't validate</button>
```

We may sometimes need to access the `validityState` value of an element from JavaScript; for that purpose there is a `checkValidity()` method executed on the form and the input elements in the form. As the name suggests, it checks the state of elements, and when it is called on the form, all the child elements are checked for validation and additionally, we can call the method on each individual element, for example `input`, `select`, or `textarea`. In our case for the form, it was as follows:

```
$('form')[0].checkValidity();
```

The `$('form')[0]` element gives us the wrapped DOM element of the selected jQuery's object, this can also be done by calling `.get()` on the selected element. Each element has a `validitystate` value that we can read as follows:

```
$("input").each(function(index) {
    var validityState = $(this)[0].validity;
...
```

There are several built-in checks we can access at this point that are properties of the `validityState` object: `valueMissing`, `typeMismatch`, `patternMismatch`, `tooLong`, `rangeUnderflow`, `rangeOverflow`, `stepMismatch`, `badInput`, and `customError`. Each of these will return `true` if there is such constraint violation. In the example code for this recipe, we just print out the name of the constraint violation to the log.

What happens if we have fields that depend on each other or when we need to implement some custom validation logic? No problem there we are covered, we can use the `setCustomValidity()` method on each of the fields that depend. In our case, we wanted the input for the `name` and `nickname` variables to be different. So we added change listener and if they are the same we just set the message with `customValidity("your message here")` and when we need to remove the violation, we set the message to be an empty string:

```
$("input[name='nickname']").change(function(){
    if($(this).val() === $("input[name='name']").val()){
        $(this)[0].setCustomValidity("You must have an awesome nickname
so nickname and name should not be the same");
    }else{
        $(this)[0].setCustomValidity("");
    }
});
```

Additionally, there are two more CSS pseudo selectors for `:valid` and `:invalid` that we will be used to style elements, depending on their `validityState` value.

The specification for client-side form validation can be found at: `http://www.whatwg.org/specs/web-apps/current-work/multipage/forms.html#client-side-form-validation`. As for the constraints API, more info is found at `http://www.whatwg.org/specs/web-apps/current-work/#the-constraint-validation-api`.

One important thing to note is that all the browsers do not have full support for all the features. IE 9, for example, has no support for any of the constrains as well as none of the new input types. More on current browsers support can be found at `http://caniuse.com/#search=form%20vali` and `http://www.quirksmode.org/compatibility.html`.

There's more...

If we want to use some of the attributes to disable the entire form from validating, we can set the form attribute called `novalidate`. For example, this will disable the checks, but allow use of `min` and `max` for input type range.

There is an another way to disable the standard browser hint box and create a custom one:

```
$('form').each(function(){
  $(this)[0].addEventListener('invalid', function(e) {
    e.preventDefault();
    console.log("custom popup");
  },true);
});
```

Several questions should be thought through before using built-in constraints:

▶ Do we need to know when the user has clicked on the **Submit** button?

▶ Do we need client-side validation for browsers that don't support the Form Validation API yet?

If we need to know when the user has tried to submit the form, we can attach event listener for click rather than submit. As for legacy browsers, we may choose to rely on server-side validation that must be present, but if we don't want to lose functionality at the client side, there are some ways of doing this by adding webshim, `http://afarkas.github.com/webshim/demos/index.html`.

Calculating password strength

A lot of websites display the strength of the password chosen by the user on their registration forms. The goal of this practice is to help the user choose a better, stronger password which cannot be guessed or brute-forced easily.

In this recipe, we're going to make a password strength calculator. It will determine the password strength by calculating the number of brute-force attempts that a potential attacker must make before guessing the password. It will also warn the user if his password is in a list of 500 commonly used passwords.

Getting ready

Before we begin, its important to look at how we're going to calculate the number of brute-force attempts that an attacker must make. We're going to take a look at two factors: the length of the password and the size of the character set used by the user.

The size of the character set can be determined as follows:

* ▶ If the user adds a lowercase alphabet letter in his password, the size of the character set grows by 26 (the number of letters in the alphabet)
* ▶ Additional 26 are added if the user uses an uppercase letter anywhere except at the beginning of the password
* ▶ 10 characters are added if the user adds a number
* ▶ 24 characters are added if the user adds a special character such as dot, comma, braces, ampersand, and so on
* ▶ 20 characters are added if the user uses a unicode character not found in other tables

How to do it...

Let's write the HTML and JavaScript code:

1. Create a simple HTML page with a `password` input, then add a `div` element, which we will update with the password strength result. Common passwords will be included via a script named `common-passwords.js`:

```
<!DOCTYPE HTML>
<html>
    <head>
        <title>Password strength calculator</title>
    </head>
    <body>
    <input type="password" id="pass" value="" />
    <div id="strength">0 (very poor)</div>
```

```
    <script src="//cdnjs.cloudflare.com/ajax/libs/jquery/1.8.2/
jquery.min.js"></script>
    <script type="text/javascript" src="common-passwords.js"></
script>
    <script type="text/javascript" src="example.js"></script>
    </body>
</html>
```

The `common-passwords.js` script is not included here, but can be found in the supplementary code.

2. The code checking the logic is in `example.js`:

```
$(function() {
    function isCommon(pass) {
      return ~window.commonPasswords.indexOf(pass);
    }

    function bruteMagnitude(pass) {
      var sets = [
      { regex: /\d/g, size: 10 },
      { regex: /[a-z]/g, size: 26 },
      { regex: /[A-Z]/g, size: 26 },
      { regex: /[!-/:-?\[-`{-}]/g, size: 24 },
      ];
      var passlen = pass.length,
      szSet = 0;

      sets.forEach(function(set) {
        if (set.regex.test(pass)) {
          szSet += set.size;
          pass = pass.replace(set.regex, '');
        }
      });
      // other (unicode) characters
      if (pass.length) szSet += 20;
      return passlen * Math.log(szSet) / Math.LN10;
    }

    var strengths = ['very poor', 'poor', 'passing', 'fair',
        'good', 'very good', 'excellent'];

    function strength(pass) {
        if (isCommon(pass) || !pass.length) return 0;
        var str = bruteMagnitude(pass);
        return str < 7  ? 0 // very poor
```

```
                    : str < 9   ? 1 // poor       - 10 million - 1 billion
                    : str < 11 ? 2 // passing      - 1 billion - 100 billion
                    : str < 13 ? 3 // fair         - 100 billion - 10
          trillion
                    : str < 15 ? 4 // good         - 10 trillion - 1
          quadrillion
                    : str < 17 ? 5 // very good - 1-100 quadrillion
                    : 6;           // excellent - over 100 quadrillion
          }
```

3. Update the `div` element indicating password strength when a key is pressed in the `password` field:

    ```
        $('#pass').on('keyup keypress', function() {
          var pstrength = strength($(this).val());
          $("#strength").text(pstrength + ' (' + strengths[pstrength]
    + ')');
          });
    });
    ```

How it works...

The calculation is split into two parts: checking for password commonality and password complexity.

We check if the password is common simply by checking if it can be found in the `commonPasswords` array provided by `common-password.js`. `Array#indexOf` returns 1 if the entry was not found. The bitwise not operator ~ turns that value into zero, which evaluates to false. All the other numbers greater than or equal to 0 will have negative values, which are true values. Thus, the entire expression returns true if the password is found in the array.

In the `bruteMagnitude` function we calculate the password's brute-force order of magnitude using the `passwordLength` and character `setsize` methods:

```
magnitude = log10(setSize passwordLength) = passwordLength *
log10(setSize)
```

This is an approximate order of magnitude of the number of passwords that a brute-force password attacker must try to guess the password.

Based on this information, we can now give an actual password strength. If the password is among the top 500 common passwords, it will be classified as poor. Otherwise it will be classified according to its brute force magnitude using the following table:

Magnitude	Number of passwords	Rating
Less than 7	Less than 10 million	Very poor
7 to 8	10 million to 1 billion	Poor
9 to 10	1 billion to 100 billion	Passing
11 to 12	100 billion to 10 trillion	Fair
13 to 14	10 trillion to 1 quadrillion	Good
15 to 17	1 to 100 quadrillion	Very good
Greater than 17	Greater 100 quadrillion	Excellent

The classification, along with the descriptive text will be updated on every key press and displayed to the user below the password field.

Validating US zip codes

Validating zip codes at the client side can be useful on web pages with address forms.

Entering numbers is an error-prone process. It would be great for the user if we could provide some kind of basic immediate validation to inform them of a possible error in their data entry.

On the other hand, a satisfyingly complete zip code database has a non-trivial size. Loading the complete database at the client side might be difficult and non-optimal.

In this recipe, we're going to write a client-side zip code validation function. In the process, we're going to learn what it takes to convert a non-trivial zip code database to a smaller representation which can be loaded at the client side.

Getting ready

Let's download the zip code database file first. The `unitedstateszipcode. org` website provides a free zip code database in a CSV format (`http://www. unitedstateszipcodes.org/zip-code-database/`).

We're going to extract a smaller database from this file which can be loaded at the client side. To do this, we're going to write a Node.js script, so make sure you have Node.js installed. Download Node.js from `http://nodejs.org/`, explained in *Appendix A, Installing Node.js and Using npm*.

> Node.js is a platform built on top of Chrome's V8 JavaScript engine, meant for writing fast asynchronous network applications. It comes with a great module manager called npm and a registry containing tens and thousands of module libraries.

How to do it...

In the same directory with `zip_code_database.csv`, we're going to create a new Node.js script. To process a CSV file, we're going to use a CSV parsing library.

1. From a command prompt in the same directory, let's install the node module CSV by running the following command:

   ```
   npm install csv
   ```

2. Then we're going to make `createdb.js`, which will parse the CSV file and extract the minimum amount of data from it, US state, and zip code:

   ```javascript
   var csv = require('csv');
   var zips = {};
   csv().from.path('zip_code_database.csv').on('record', function(zc)
   {
       // column 0 is zipcode; column 5 is state
       // column 12 is country, 13 is decomissioned (0/1)
       // filter non-decmissioned US zipcodes
       if (zc[12] == 'US' && !parseInt(zc[13])) {
         zips[zc[5]] = zips[zc[5]] || [];
         zips[zc[5]].push(parseInt(zc[0].trim(), 10));
       }
   }).on('end', function() {
   ```

3. At this point, we have a usable array of zip codes. However, if we were to write them all directly, it would result in a fairly large 400 KB JSON array, 150 KB when compressed with GZIP. Many of the valid zip code numbers are sequential. We can take advantage of this and represent them as ranges instead. By applying this technique we get a 115 KB file, 45 KB when compressed. This size seems a lot more acceptable:

   ```javascript
   var zipCodeDB = [];
   function rangify(arr) {
     var ranges = [], first = 0, last = 0;
     for (var k = 0; k < arr.length; ++k) {
       var first = arr[k];
       while (arr[k] + 1 >= arr[k + 1] && k < arr.length - 1)
   ++k;
       var last = arr[k];
       ranges.push(first != last? [first, last]:[first]);
   ```

```
        first = last = 0;
    }
    return ranges;
}
```

4. The final representation will be a JSON array sorted by the `state` name. Every element in this array represents a state and contains two attributes: state name and a list of valid zip codes represented as numbers, or zip code ranges represented as two-dimensional arrays:

```
var list = [];
for (var state in zips) if (state != 'undefined') {
    list.push({state: state, codes: rangify(zips[state])});
}
list = list.sort(function(s1, s2) {
    return s1.state < s2.state ? -1
        : s1.state > s2.state ?  1
        :0;
});
console.log('window.zipCodeDB =', JSON.stringify(list));
}
```

5. Running this script in the command line from the same directory `node createdb.js > zipcodedb.js` will result with the `zipcodedb.js` file, which contains the database. Here is a sample of the database JSON:

```
window.zipCodeDB = [{
    "state": "AA",
    "codes": [34004, 34006, 34008, 34011, [34020, 34025],
        [34030, 34039], 3404, ...]
},
...
]
```

6. We can now use this database to create the basic validator by including it in our `index.html` page. The page will contain a simple state selection dropdown and a zip code field. Below the zip code field will be the validation message:

```
<!DOCTYPE HTML>
<html>
    <head>
        <title>Zip code validation</title>
    </head>
    <body>
    <p>State: <select id="state"></select></p>
    <p>Zipcode: <input type="text" id="zipcode" value="" /></p>
    <div id="validate">Invalid zipcode</div>
```

```
    <script src="//cdnjs.cloudflare.com/ajax/libs/jquery/1.8.2/
jquery.min.js"></script>
    <script type="text/javascript" src="zipcodedb.js"></script>
    <script type="text/javascript" src="example.js"></script>
    </body>
</html>
```

7. Finally, we're going to write a `lookup` function to check if a given zip code is in our database, which we're going to use to validate the user input as they type. We will populate the states dropdown using the same database:

```
$(function() {

    function lookup(zipcode) {
      function within(zipcode, ranges) {
        for (var k = 0; k < ranges.length; ++k)
        if (zipcode == ranges[k]
        || (ranges[k].length > 1
        && ranges[k][0] <= zipcode
        && zipcode <= ranges[k][1])) return k;
        return -1;
        }
        for (var k = 0; k < window.zipCodeDB.length; ++k) {
          var state = window.zipCodeDB[k],
          check = within(zipcode, state.codes);
          if (~check) return state.state;
        }
        return null;
    }

    window.zipCodeDB.forEach(function(state) {
      $('<option />').attr('value', state.state)
      .text(state.state).appendTo('#state');
    });

    $("#zipcode").on('keypress keyup change', function() {
      var state = lookup($(this).val());
      if (state == $("#state").val())
      $('#validate').text('Valid zipcode for ' + state);
      else $('#validate').text('Invalid zipcode');
    });
});
```

How it works...

To validate zip codes at the client side, we first had to convert our database to a smaller size.

The downloaded database contained a lot of extra data such as city to zip code mappings, zip code types, time zone and geographic coordinates, as well as decommissioned zip codes. We removed the extra data, leaving only the US zip codes that are still in use along with their state.

To reduce the database even further, we represented longer valid zip code ranges as arrays containing the first and the last number in the range. This helped to reduce the database size further to a reasonable size as compared to the size of a medium website image.

To use the database, we wrote a simple `lookup` function that checks if the zip code is inside the list of values of `zipcode` and `ranges` in any of the states and returns the state if found.

The validation information updates automatically while the user is entering the zip code.

Using asynchronous server-side validation

Many validation checks can only be performed at the server side. The following are the examples:

▶ When validating a user registration form, we need to check if the entered username is available

▶ When the user enters a postal address, we might need to ask an external service to verify if the address is correct

The problem with server-side validation checks is that they need to be asynchronous. As a result, they cannot be written in JavaScript as functions that return validation results.

To solve this problem, in this recipe we're going to make a validator that uses the continuation-passing style. The example has a username input field that is validated against the server. The server checks if the username is available for registration or already occupied by another user.

Getting ready

We're going to briefly look at the continuation-passing style. It's a style used by most of the JavaScript libraries for asynchronous operations, for example, server communication. For example in jQuery, instead of writing the following code:

```
data = $.getJSON('/api/call');
doThingsWith(data);
```

We write as follows:

```
$.getJSON('/api/call', function(data) {
    doThingsWith(data);
});
```

We can apply the same transformation to a validation function as follows:

```
var errors = validate(input)
if (errors.length) display(errors);
```

This will become:

```
validate(input, function(errors) {
    if (errors.length) display(errors);
});
```

This means we also need to change the `validate` function. For example, if we had as follows:

```
function validate(input) {
    if (condition(input))
        return [{message: "Input does not satisfy condition"}];
    else return [];
}
```

After transforming it to the continuation-passing style we will have:

```
function validate(input, callback) {
    condition(input, function(result) {
        if (result) callback([{message: "Input does not satisfy
condition"}]);
        else callback([]);
    });
}
```

This enables us to use the server-side calls, for example, $.getJSON in our validation function as follows:

```
function validate(input, callback) {
    $.getJSON('/api/validate/condition', function(result)
        if (result) callback([{message: "Input does not satisfy
condition"}]);
        else callback([]);
    });
}
```

Now we can use our server-side validator from the browser.

How to do it...

We're going to write the HTML page containing the form to be validated and the JavaScript code that implements the validation.

1. Let's start with the HTML page. It must contain a form with a username input and a validation result with red text hidden by default:

```
<!DOCTYPE HTML>
<html>
<head>
<title>Async validation</title>
<style type="text/css">
p[data-validation-error] {
    display:none;
    color:red;
}
</style>
</head>
<body>
<form>
    <p>Username:</p>
    <p><input name="user" id="user" value="" /></p>
    <p data-validation-error="user"></p>
</form>
<script src="//cdnjs.cloudflare.com/ajax/libs/jquery/1.8.2/jquery.
min.js"></script>
<script type="text/javascript" src="example.js"></script>
</body>
</html>
```

2. The validation code will be in `example.js` – it contains a function that simulates an `async` server call, a function that used to delay the execution of the `async` server call to prevent multiple calls, and a function that displays the validation result:

```
$(function() {
    function validate(name, callback) {
      // Simulate an async server call
      setTimeout(function() {
        callback(~['user', 'example'].indexOf(name) ?
        'Username is already in use' : null);
        },500);
    }
    function createDelayed(ms) {
      var t = null;
      return function(fn) {
```

```
            if (t) clearTimeout(t);
            t = setTimeout(fn, ms);
            };
        };
        var delayed = createDelayed(1500);

        var user = $('input[name="user"]'),
        form = user.parents('form');
        user.on('keyup keypress', function() {
            delayed(validate.bind(null, $(this).val(), function
    callback(err) {
            var validationError = form.find('p[data-validation-
    error="user"]');
            console.log(validationError);
            if (err) validationError.text(err).show();
            else validationError.hide();
        }));
        });
    });
```

How it works...

The code in the `validate` function from `example.js` simulates a server call by using the `setTimeout` function. It would be easy to replace this code with a real call to the server validation API using something similar to `jQuery.getJSON` to get the validation results.

The `createDelayed` function creates a `delayer` object. The `delayer` object wraps the function to be delayed. It is different from `setInterval`, because if the `delayer` object is called again before the delay expires, the previous timeout will be canceled and restarted. This helps us to avoid overloading the server with requests on every single keystroke, instead the request is sent `1500ms` after the user stops typing.

We call the `delayer` object on every user keypress, binding "`this`" to `null`, the first argument to the current value of the input field, and the `callback` function to a function that shows the returned validation error if it exists.

Combining client-side and server-side validation

When dealing with real web forms we usually need to do various kinds of validation on multiple fields. Some fields may only need checks that can be performed at the client side, while some might also require server-side validation.

In this recipe, we're going to design and implement our own validation plugin that supports asynchronous validation. It will work similarly to jQuery Validate. We're also going to implement some basic validation methods such as `required`, `minLength`, and `remote`.

We're going to use these methods on a simple user registration form, which will be blocked from submission until the user enters valid data in all fields.

Getting ready

The first step in our design process is to design the data structures that will be used in our validator. We're going to make an API similar to jQuery Validate, which takes a configuration object as its parameter. However, we're going to opt into a more modern, HTML5 approach where the validation rules are embedded into the HTML as follows:

```
<form data-avalidate>
  <input name="field"
      data-v-ruleName="ruleParam" name="user" value="" />
  <span data-v-error="ruleName">{parameterized} rule error</span>
</form>
```

In order to support this rule and message structure, Validate will utilize validation plugins.

Each plugin will have a unique name.

The plugin will be a function that takes three parameters: the element being, the rule parameters object, and a `callback` function to call when the validation is complete. The `callback` function will take two arguments: the first will indicate if the field is valid and the second will contain the message parameters.

The plugin will prevent the submission of the form unless it verifies the validity of all the fields.

How to do it...

Let's write the HTML and JavaScript code.

1. The `index.html` page will contain the form with its validation rules embedded. Note that we can also mix in standard HTML form validation, for example via the `required` attribute as follows:

```
<!DOCTYPE HTML>
<html>
<head>
<title>Async validation</title>
<style type="text/css">
[data-v-error] { display:none; color:red; }
label { width: 10em; display:inline-block; text-align: right; }
</style>
</head>
<body>
  <form data-avalidate>
    <p>
    <label for="user">Username:</label>
    <input name="user"
      required
      data-v-minlen="6"
      data-v-server="/api/validate/unique"
      value="" />
    <span data-v-error="minlen">Must be at least {minlen}
characters long</span>
    <span data-v-error="server">{username} is already in use</
span>
    </p>

    <p>
    <label for="email">Email:</label>
    <input name="email" type="email"
      required
      data-v-minlen="6"
      data-v-server="/api/validate/email"
      value="" />
    <span data-v-error="server">{email} is already in use</span>
    </p>

    <p><label for="pass">Password:</label>
    <input name="pass" type="password"
      required
```

```
      data-v-minlen="8"
      data-v-strength="3"
      value="" />
    <span data-v-error="minlen">Must be at least {minlen}
characters long</span>
    <span data-v-error="strength">Strength is {strength}</span>
    </p>

    <p><label for="pass2">Password (again):</label>
    <input name="pass2" type="password"
      required
      data-v-equals="pass"
      value="" />
    <span data-v-error="equals">Must be equal to the other
password</span>
    </p>

    <input type="submit">

</form>
<script src="//cdnjs.cloudflare.com/ajax/libs/jquery/1.8.2/jquery.
min.js"></script>
<script type="text/javascript" src="avalidate.js"></script>
<script type="text/javascript" src="avalidate-plugins.js"></
script>
</body>
</html>
```

> The interesting part about this HTML file is that there are no other scripts included besides `avalidate.js` and `avalidate-plugins.js`, yet they provide full validation to this form.

2. Let's see the code that we need to add to `avalidate.js`:

```
;(function($) {
```

To properly execute asynchronous validation we need to be able to the delay the request until the user stops typing. To do this we use `createDelayed` – it creates timeouts which reset themselves on each call:

```
function createDelayed(ms) {
  var t = null;
  return function(fn) {
    if (t) clearTimeout(t);
    t = setTimeout(fn, ms);
  };
}
```

`showError` displays the appropriate error besides the form, filling it with templated text. The first time it runs, it moves the template out of the `error` element inner text and adds into a new attribute:

```
function showError(error, strings) {
  var tmpl;
  if (!error.attr('data-v-template')) {
    tmpl = error.text().toString();
    error.attr('data-v-template', tmpl);
  } else tmpl = error.attr('data-v-template');
  for (var key in strings)
    tmpl = tmpl.replace('{'+key+'}', strings[key]);
  error.text(tmpl).show();
}
```

`elementVerifier` executes on an element. It looks up all verifier plugins specified by the `data-v-pluginName` attributes, reads the plugin options from the attribute, and then runs the async plugin.

3. When all the plugins finish verifying, it marks the element as valid if no errors were found. Otherwise it displays the errors as they appear:

```
function elementVerifier() {
  var isValid = true, waiting = 0, field = this;
  $.each(this.attributes, function(i, attr) {
    if (!attr.name.match(/data-v-/)) return;
    var plugin = attr.name.toString().replace('data-v-',''),
    options = attr.value;

    ++waiting;
    $.avalidate[plugin].call(field, options, function (valid,
strings) {
      var error = $(field).parent().find('[data-v-
error="'+plugin+'"]');
      if (!valid) {
        showError(error, strings);
        isValid = false;
      }
      else error.hide();
      if (!--waiting && isValid)
      $(field).attr('data-valid', 1);
    });
  });
}
```

4. `setupFormVerifier` enables the validation process on a certain form by binding to all changes, keyboard and mouse events that happen in its fields. It creates a separate `delayer` variable for every element and runs the `elementVerifier` object with that `delayer`. Finally, it forbids the form submission unless all the fields are marked as valid by the `elementVerifier` object:

```
function setupFormVerifier(form) {
    form.on('change keyup mouseup', 'input,textarea,select',
function() {
        var $this = $(this)
        var delayer = $this.data('avalidate');
        if (!delayer) {
          delayer = createDelayed(800);
          $this.data('avalidate', delayer);
        }
        $this.attr('data-valid', 0);
        delayer(elementVerifier.bind(this));
        }).on('submit', function(e) {
            var all = $(this).find('input,textarea,select').
filter('[type!="submit"]'),
            valid = all.filter('[data-valid="1"]');
            if (all.length != valid.length)
            e.preventDefault();
        });
    }
```

5. The following is the part that makes everything work without manual intervention. We listen to all the events arriving on the document `body` object, and if an event arrives at a form that is supposed to have validation enabled but doesn't, we run `setupFormVerifier` on it (once):

```
$(function() {
    $('body').on('submit change keyup mouseup', 'form[data-
avalidate]', function() {
        if (!$(this).attr('data-avalidate-enabled')) {
          setupFormVerifier($(this));
          $(this).attr('data-avalidate-enabled', 1)
        }
    });
    });
}(jQuery));
```

6. The plugins are much easier to write. Here is `avalidate-plugins.js`. Note that the server plugin is simulated with `setTimeout`. The same principles apply when making an AJAX call:

```
;(function($) {

    $.avalidate = {};
    $.avalidate.equals = function(name, callback) {
        var other = $(this).parents('form').
find('[name="'+name+'"]').val();
        callback($(this).val() === other, {});
    };
    $.avalidate.minlen = function(len, callback) {
        callback($(this).val().length >= len || $(this).text().
length >= len, {minlen: len});
    };
    $.avalidate.server = function(param, cb) {
        setTimeout(function() {
            var val = $(this).val();
            if (~param.indexOf('mail'))
            cb('test@test.com' != val, {email: val });
            else
            cb('username' != val, { username: val });
        }.bind(this), 500);
    };
    $.avalidate.strength = function(minimum, cb) {
        cb($(this).val().length > minimum, {strength: 'Low'});
    };

}(jQuery));
```

How it works...

This validator takes advantage of the new HTML5 data attribute features. HTML5 does include some great new validation options by adding input element attributes and types, but they're not enough. To solve this, we follow the HTML5 model and add our own data attributes for validation methods and validation error messages.

To make these new data attributes work we need to load JavaScript code. One of the pitfalls of JavaScript-initialized elements is the need to call the initialization functions whenever we add a new element on the page. This plugin successfully avoids the pitfall by using the new jQuery binding APIs. Instead of binding to the forms directly, the listener is attached to the document body object. As such, it works with all the form elements including the newly added ones.

The flexible plugins enable easy extension of the validator without modifications to the core. Adding a new validation rule is as simple as adding a new function.

Finally, our error messages can have user-friendly templates filled with optional message strings provided by the validators.

> You may have noticed that the JavaScript files start with a semicolon character (;). This makes them safer for concatenation and minification. If we prepend a script that ends with a value (treated as a function call while the entire contents of the script without a semicolon) to another that is wrapped within parenthesis, the value will be will be treated as an argument to that function call. To avoid this, we prepend a semicolon before the parenthesis, terminating any previous statements that may be missing a semicolon.

7
Data Serialization

In this chapter, we will cover the following recipes:

- Deserializing JSON to JavaScript objects
- Serializing objects to JSON strings
- Decoding base64 encoded binary data
- Encoding binary data or text to base64
- Serialization of binary data into JSON
- Serializing and deserializing cookies
- Serializing form into request strings
- Reading XML documents with DOMParser
- Serializing of XML document at the client side

Introduction

One of the basic concepts of data storage and transmission is serialization. We are going to go through some of the ways to prepare the data for either sending to another environment or saving it permanently. Besides that we will see the ways for reading some of the data serialized by another computer environment.

Deserializing JSON to JavaScript objects

The simplest of all cases is reading JSON data into JavaScript objects. Data formatted in this way is of lightweight and additionally it is a subset of JavaScript. There are several ways to read this data and we will take a look at how this can be done by creating a simple JSON snippet and then converting it to JavaScript objects.

How to do it...

This example will be simple enough to be a script in an HTML file or even executed on a firebug or developer tools console:

1. We first need the following serialized JSON string:

```
var someJSONString = '{"comment":"JSON data usually is retrieved
from server","who":"you"}';
```

2. There are few different ways to do this without adding external JavaScript dependency, one is through the use of `eval`, the other is through the use of `json`:

```
var evalData =   eval('(' + someJSONString + ')');
var jsonData =   JSON.parse(someJSONString);
```

3. After this we will try to access some of the attributes form the deserialized object:

```
document.writeln(someJSONString.who + " access without
conversion <br/>" );
document.writeln(jsonData.who + " with parse <br/>" );
document.writeln(evalData.who + " with eval <br/>");
```

Upon execution, the first `document.writeln` method should return `undefined`, because we are trying to access property on a JSON string that is not yet deserialized, while on the other two we should get the value you.

How it works...

JSON is language independent format but at the same time JSON is JavaScript, meaning that we can use the `eval` function. Now that it is very simple since this is a top level function, and it accepts string as input that will get evaluated. If the string passed as an argument has JavaScript statements `eval` will perform those. This can be a dangerous thing just because it executes the code passed to it. If it is used on a code you don't trust, then you might get exploits from potentially malicious third party. For most use cases of `eval`, there are good alternatives already there. Debugging also can be very hard when we use `eval`, so it's something we should avoid in most cases.

When it comes to JSON parsing, on most of the modern browsers we can use the `JSON.parse(text [, reviver])` statement that has been added to JavaScript 1.7. This function parses a string as JSON and has the optional argument for having a `reviver`, a function that can transform the value being produced by parsing. For example, if we wanted to append `"a?"` to each on the values, we can define something as follows:

```
var transformed = JSON.parse(someJSONString, function(key, val) {
  if (key === "") return val;
  return val +' a?';
});
```

Now, if we try to access `transformed.who` we will get `"you a?"`. The final object will contain the following information:

```
{comment: "JSON data usually is retrieved from server a?", who: "you
a?"}
```

Meaning that each of the values of the original string that was parsed had the value `'a?'` appended to it and the key at given iteration took the values `comment` and `who`.

If the `reviver` function returns `undefined` or `null` for a given value, that property will get deleted, so it can be used as a filtering mechanism.

There's more...

What will happen in case of older browsers that don't support JSON natively. There are two simple options, we can just include JSON 2 or JSON 3:

```
<script src="//cdnjs.cloudflare.com/ajax/libs/json3/3.2.4/json3.
min.js"></script>
```

```
<script src="//cdnjs.cloudflare.com/ajax/libs/json2/20121008/json2.
js"></script>
```

JSON 3 is a polyfill that is compatible with almost all of the JavaScript platforms and in a way, it's the newer implementation of JSON 2 and this is what we should use. There are several inconsistencies and special cases that were not handled correctly by JSON 2, although at the time of writing the older version was more widespread. Additionally, JSON 3 parser does not use `eval` or `regex`, making it more secure and giving it performance benefits in mobile were this can be significant.

If you already have jQuery in your project that you can use `jQuery.parseJSON( json )` similarity Prototype JS has it's own implementation, `String#evalJSON()`.

One common error is the use of single quotes instead of double quotes. Most implementation of JSON do not allow the use of single quote, this was probably done for simplicity. To quote Douglas Crockford: JSON's design goals were to be minimal, portable, textual, and a subset of JavaScript. The less we need to agree on in order to interoperate, the more easily we can interoperate.

Serializing objects to a JSON string

The reverse of the previous recipe is to serialize JavaScript objects into JSON string. Similarly the same rules about having browser support for JSON applies but again this is not a problem in most of the browsers. One way would be to manually create the string, but that is just a way to error-prone and messy browsers, so we will try out some of the methods available out there.

How to do it...

In the following example we use only JavaScript, so we can place it inside a simple script tag in an HTML file:

1. First need data in order to serialize it to string, so we will create a simple JavaScript object:

```
var someJSON = {
  "firstname":"John",
  "lastname":"Doe",
  "email":"john.doe@example.com"
};
```

2. We create another object where we are going to have the `toJSON()` function:

```
var customToJSON = {
  "firstname":"John",
  "lastname":"Doe",
  "email":"john.doe@example.com",
  toJSON: function () {
  return {"custom":"rendering"};
  }
};
```

3. In order to convert the JavaScript object to a string we will use the `JSON.stringify(value [, replacer [, space]])` function:

```
var jsonString = JSON.stringify(someJSON);
var jsonStringCustomToJSON = JSON.stringify(customToJSON);
```

4. After that we will try out the other arguments for that same function where, for the `replacer`, we will create a list of allowed properties and for the third argument, we will try two different options:

```
var allowedProperties=["firstname","lastname"];
var jsonCensured = JSON.stringify(someJSON ,
allowedProperties);
var jsonCensured3Spaces = JSON.stringify(someJSON,allowedProp
erties,30);
var jsonCensuredTab = JSON.stringify(someJSON,allowedProperti
es,"\t");
```

5.   We can than simply write the output to the document object:

```
document.writeln(jsonString + "  <br/>" );
document.writeln(jsonStringCustomToJSON + "  <br/>" );
document.writeln(jsonCensured + "  <br/>" );
document.writeln(jsonCensured3Spaces + "  <br/>" );
document.writeln(jsonCensuredTab + "  <br/>" );
```

How it works...

The JSON `stringify` method accepts three arguments, where the last two are optional. When used with only one argument it will return a JSON string form the JavaScript object, where if some of the properties are undefined inside an object, then it is omitted or censored to null when found in array. If there is a `toJSON()` function defined inside the object than that function is used to select the object that will get converted. This allows the objects to define their own JSON representation. In our case, the evaluated version of `JSON.stringify(customToJSON)` will be as follows:

```
{"custom":"rendering"}
```

The full function definition of `stringify` is as follows:

```
JSON.stringify(value[, replacer ] [, space])
```

We can use `replacer` to filter attributes that will get white listed. The `replacer` can be an array of `String` and `Number` objects that will serve as an allowed list of parameters.

The `space` argument can be added and have a value of type `String` or a `Number`. If it is a `Number`, it indicates the number of space characters to use as white spaces. In our examples this can be seen if you open the generated HTML in the browser. If the `space` argument is a `String`, then the first 10 characters of the value passed are used as white spaces for creation of the JSON.

One thing to note is that the order of the serialized attributes is not guaranteed for non-array objects. You must not rely on ordering of properties within the object after the object is serialized. Now serialization might not be the most accurate definition of the process because of this, so that is why this is called as stringification commonly.

There's more...

Again we have the similar problems for older user agents that don't support JSON. For that use we would recommend JSON 3:

```
<script src="//cdnjs.cloudflare.com/ajax/libs/json3/3.2.4/json3.
min.js"></script>
```

Also you should not use the `stringify` function for debugging purposes since as we previously mentioned it converts undefined objects in a specific way, so you might get a wrong conclusion by doing so. This wrong conclusion is only related to the order and JSON compatibly, but it is fully valid to use it for general debugging of objects.

Decoding base64 encoded binary data

Until very recently, JavaScript didn't have any native support for storing binary data types. Most binary data was handled as strings. Binary data that could not be handled using strings (for example, images) was handled as base64 encoded strings.

> Base64 is a method to encode binary data by converting groups of bytes into groups of base64 numbers. The goal is to avoid data loss by safely representing binary data using only printable characters which will not be interpreted in a special way.

HTML5 has much better support for binary data, it can be stored and manipulated using the `ArrayBuffer` class and the typed array classes. However, legacy libraries and API may still use base64 data. In order to do more efficient binary processing in modern browsers, we might want to convert this data into array buffers.

In this recipe, we're going to write a conversion function that converts base64 encoded strings to array buffers.

Getting ready

To write this function, first we need to understand how base64 encoding works.

The usual way to access binary data is one byte at a time. A byte has 8 bits. If we try to assign a digit interpretation to a byte, it would be capable of representing 2 ^ 8 = 256 different digits. In other words, a byte could represent a single base 256 digit.

We need to represent binary data as base64 digits. They are represented by the letters A-Z, a-z, 0-9, +, and / – a total of 64 characters, enough to store 6 bits of data per character. To do this, we will have to take groups of 6 bits from the binary data. The lowest common denominator of 6 bits and 8 bits are 24 bits, which means that every group of 3 bytes are represented by a group of 4 base64 digits.

We can conclude that the decoding process will take all four groups of base64 encoded digits and produce 3 bytes from each group.

But what happens if the total number of bytes isn't divisible by 3? Base64 uses an additional character "=" (the equal sign) to denote the number of bytes missing from the last group. A single character is added at the end of the string to indicate that the last group has 1 byte less (only two in the last group). Two of them are added when there are 2 bytes less (only one byte in the last group).

Now that we have understood how base64 works, we're ready to write a base64 decoder.

How to do it...

Let's get started.

1. Create an `index.html` page containing a text field to input `text` and two `div` elements. One of the elements will be used to display the base64 string , while the other will be used to display the decimal values of the converted bytes:

```html
<!DOCTYPE HTML>
<html>
    <head>
      <title>Text to base64 and binary</title>
    </head>
    <body>
    <input type="text" id="text" value="Enter text here">
    <div id="base64"></div>
    <div id="bytes"></div>
    <script src="http://ajax.googleapis.com/ajax/libs/jquery/1.8.2/
jquery.min.js"></script>
    <script type="text/javascript" src="atobuf.js"></script>
    <script type="text/javascript" src="example.js"></script>
    </body>
</html>
```

2. Create `example.js` and put the code that will apply the changes on the page as the user types the text:

```javascript
$(function() {
    $("#text").on('keyup keypress', function() {
      var base64 = btoa($(this).val()),
      buf = atobuf(base64),
      bytes = new Uint8Array(buf),
      byteString = [].join.call(bytes, ' ');
      $("#base64").text(base64);
      $("#bytes").text(byteString);
    });
}
```

3. Create `atobuf.js`, which exports a function taking a base64 string and returns an ArrayBuffer object with the decoded bytes:

```
(function(exports) {
    var key = {};
    'ABCDEFGHIJKLMNOPQRSTUVWXYZabcdefghijklmnopqrstuvwxyz
0123456789+/='
        .split('').forEach(function(c, i) {
            key[c] = i;
        });

    exports.atobuf = function atobuf(b64str) {
        var b64l = b64str.length,
            bytes = b64l / 4 * 3;
        if (b64str[b64str.length - 1] == '=') bytes -= 1;
        if (b64str[b64str.length - 2] == '=') bytes -= 1;

        var buf = new ArrayBuffer(bytes),
            arr = new Uint8Array(buf),
            at = 0;

        for (var k = 0; k < bytes; k+=3) {
            var e1 = key[b64str[at++]],
                e2 = key[b64str[at++]],
                e3 = key[b64str[at++]],
                e4 = key[b64str[at++]];

            var b1 = (e1 << 2) | (e2 >> 4),
                b2 = ((e2 & 0xF) << 4) | (e3 >> 2),
                b3 = ((e3 & 0x3) << 6) | e4;

            arr[k]   = b1;
            if (k+1<bytes) arr[k+1] = b2;
            if (k+2<bytes) arr[k+2] = b3;
        }

        return buf;
    };

}(typeof(exports) !== 'undefined' ? exports : this));
```

How it works...

The code in `index.html` and `example.js` is fairly straightforward we set up a page to easily preview and test the results of our conversion function. To store the bytes, we create a `Uint8Array` object over the passed buffer. This is a new kind of array type introduced in HTML5, which enables us to read the individual bytes in the `ArrayBuffer` object as unsigned 8 bit integers.

A point worth noting is that a `Uint8Array` object doesn't have the `join` method. This is why we "borrow" the method from an empty array by writing `[].join.call(bytes, ' ')`, which calls the `join` method (ordinarily belonging to the empty array) as if it were a method of the object bytes.

Inside `atobuf.js` we export the `atobuf` function either as a CommonJS module (done by attaching to the `exports` object) or as a function attached to the global object.

To make the conversion faster, we predefine a conversion dictionary that maps the characters to their appropriate numeric values.

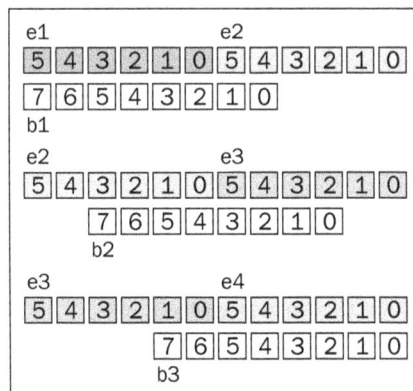

Let's see how the bit manipulation code works. The encoded values have 6 bits, while the decoded values have 8 bits. While reading the explanation, note that the bits are enumerated from right to left, with bit 0 being the right-most bit, bit 1 the second-right-most bit, and so on.

For the first decoded byte, we need the 6 bits stored in the first encoded value positioned as bits 2 to 7 in the decoded value. That's why we shift them two places to the left. We also need bits 4 and 5 from the second encoded value for the first decoded value, positioned as bits 0 and 1. This means we need to shift them to the right by four places.

For the second byte, we need bits 0 to 3 from the second encoded value positioned as bits 4 to7 in the decoded value. To do this, we zero out bits 4 and 5 using a binary AND operation and shift the rest four places to the left. We also need bits 2 to 5 from the third encoded value as bits 0 to 3, so we need to shift them two places to the right.

For the third byte, we need bits 0 to1 from the third encoded value at places 6 to7, which means using AND to zero out the rest and shifting six places to the left. The bits on the last encoded value are all in the right place at the third byte, so we take them as they are.

Encoding binary data or text into base64

HTML5 support for binary data is through an `ArrayBuffer` object, the related type arrays. When it comes to transmitting that data, usually the way to do this is via base64. This is used mostly for dealing with textual data but with the rise of the usage of Data URI, base64 becomes more and more relevant. In this recipe, will see how to encode data using this scheme.

How to do it...

We will create an HTML file where we will use a `canvas` element, which will generate some data that will get encoded into base64:

1. In order to have binary data, we will create an image using canvas, so we add a `canvas` element:

```html
<!doctype html>
<html>
  <head>
    <meta charset="utf-8">
    <title>Binary data to Base64</title>
  </head>
  <body>
    <canvas id="myCanvas" width="100" height="100"></canvas>
```

2. We can have some input field that could be used to show the text encoding:

```html
<input type="text" id="text" placeholder="Insert some text">
```

3. Following that element we can place two output elements, one for the encoded binary data from the image and one for the encoded text:

```html
<div>
  <b> Text Base64:</b>
  <output id="content"></output>
</div>
<hr />
<div>
  <b> Image Base64:</b>
  <output id="imgBase"></output>
</div>
```

4. We then include the dependency to jQuery and `example.js`:

```
    <script src="http://ajax.googleapis.com/ajax/libs/
jquery/1.8.2/jquery.min.js"></script>
    <script type="text/javascript" src="example.js"></script>
```

5. Since we have included the `example.js` file, we can then proceed to creating logic for encoding the data. In order to have some binary data, we will create an image of a square with canvas:

```
var canvas = $('#myCanvas')[0],
context = canvas.getContext('2d');
context.beginPath();
context.rect(0, 0, 100, 100);
context.fillStyle = 'green';
context.fill();
var imgdata = context.getImageData(0,0, 200, 200);
```

> The current method definitions for `CanvasRenderingContext2D` can be found at WHATWG: `http://www.whatwg.org/specs/web-apps/current-work/multipage/the-canvas-element.html#canvasrenderingcontext2d`.

6. In order to create base64 encoded data, we are going to convert the array to string, so that we can define a function as follows:

```
function arrayToString(inputArray){
    var stringData = '';
    var bytes = new Uint8ClampedArray(inputArray);
    var length = bytes.byteLength;
    for (var i = 0; i < length; i++) {
      stringData += String.fromCharCode(bytes[i]);
    }
    return stringData;
}
```

7. Now we can call that function and use the internal `btoa()` method that accepts string that will get encoded:

```
var stringData = arrayToString(imgdata.data);
var b64encoded = btoa(stringData);
```

8. To demonstrate that we can go back now, we will use `atob` to decode the base64 encoded string data:

```
var originalStringData = atob(b64encoded);
```

9. Now in order to get back from the decoded string data to the original binary array we need to define a function as follows:

```
function stringToArray(raw){
  var rawLength = raw.length;
  var array = new Uint8ClampedArray(new ArrayBuffer(rawLength));
   for(i = 0; i < rawLength; i++) {
     array[i] = raw.charCodeAt(i);
   }
  return array;
}
```

10. After that we can call that function on our decoded data:

```
var originalArray = stringToArray(originalStringData);
```

11. We will just print the base64 encoded string on to the page:

```
$("#imgBase").text(b64encoded);
```

12. Due to certain assumptions made by the base64 algorithm, UTF is not initially supported. There is a workaround for this, created by Johan Sundström that takes advantage of standard functions and makes UTF possible:

```
function utf8ToB64(str) {
    return window.btoa(unescape(encodeURIComponent(str)));
}

function b64ToUtf8(str) {
    return decodeURIComponent(escape(window.atob(str)));
}
```

13. This is only of interest to us for textual data, so we can try it out by connecting the input field with the output tag where we will have a base64 encoded text:

```
$("#text").keyup(function(e) {
    var currentValue = $(this).val();
    $("#content").val(utf8ToB64(currentValue));
});
```

How it works...

The modern browsers have support for `atob("base64encoded")` and `btoa("stringToBeEncoded")`. These methods allow encoding and decoding of base64 strings. We use `btoa()` to encode string data and we get result that has ASCII character A-Z, a-z, 0-9, and the symbols (/, +, =) making the data convenient for transport. The data range restriction comes at a price, the encoded data is now larger than the original binary stream with about 33 percent of overhead. On the other hand, the encoded data is usually more compressible, so the gzip will more or less even up the size.

> JavaScript typed arrays provide a way for accessing raw binary data much more efficiently than using the standard types. They are supported in all of the modern browsers and IE 10. More on typed arrays can be found on MDN: `https://developer.mozilla.org/en-US/docs/JavaScript/Typed_arrays`.

To the test binary data encoding, we took array generated from HTML canvas. To retrieve the binary array representation there, we used the following statement:

```
context.getImageData(0,0, 200, 200);
```

This returns `ImageData` object that contains properties width, height, and data. The data attributes is represented as an `Uint8ClampedArray` object. These type of arrays are similar to the standard `Array` object, where each of the items is an 8 bit (1 byte) unsigned integer. All the values stored in this array are in the range 0 to 255, which is perfect for colors. In our case, we can see the values stored in the array by logging with `console.log()`, and we get values as follows:

```
[0,128,0,255,0,128,0,255 …]
```

The 0 is for red, 128 is for green, and the third 0 is for blue, the 255 value on the other hand is for the opacity level. Since we want to encode the data of the array to base64 we cannot simply call `btoa(theArray)`, since we only store the `toString` value and not the whole array:

[Object Uint8ClampedArray]

> If we are to compare `Uint8array` with `Uint8ClampedArray` the main difference is the first uses modulo shortening when inserted value that is out of range and the clamped one well clamps the values. For example, if we were to to set the value 300 to a 255 limited it will become 255 for `Uint8ClampedArray` but 45 for the other. Similarly the value -1 will be clamped to 0. More info about `Uint8ClampedArray` can be found at:
>
> `http://www.khronos.org/registry/typedarray/specs/latest/#7.1`

The main reason why we added `arrayToString` is to create a string for us that we can latter use in `btoa`. Similarly we would need `stringToArray` that will revert the transformation.

When it comes to text the core functions `btoa()`/`atob()` don't have support for Unicode. If we try to convert characters with a value larger than `"\u0100"` we will get:

Error: InvalidCharacterError: DOM Exception 5

As a fix for this we added methods `utf8ToB64()` and `b64ToUtf8()`.

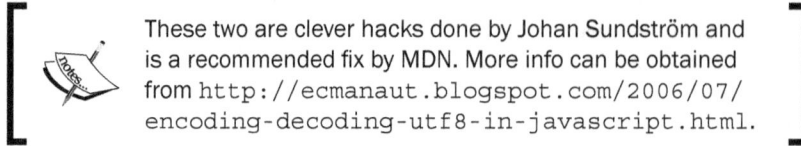

> These two are clever hacks done by Johan Sundström and is a recommended fix by MDN. More info can be obtained from `http://ecmanaut.blogspot.com/2006/07/encoding-decoding-utf8-in-javascript.html`.

The hack takes advantage of standard function pairs `encodeURIComponent()`/`decodeURIComponent()` and `escape()`/`unescape()`.

How does this combination of `encodeURICompoenent` and `unescape` work?

Here is an example of how this method works:

```
> encodeURICompoenent(" ");
"%20"
```

The result we are getting is a percent-encoded string, where the UTF-8 characters are replaced with the appropriate percent representation. Now we could use just `encodeURIComponent`, since percent encoding uses only ASCII characters:

```
> "\u2197"
"⬀"
> encodeURIComponent("\u2197")
"%E2%86%97"
> btoa(encodeURIComponent('\u2197'));
"JUUyJTg2JTk3"
```

But there is a drawback with this approach and that is the resulting percent-encoded string is lot bigger the initial one, and since base64 adds additional overhead it can easily become huge.

The `escape` and `unescape` functions are deprecated, since they don't work for non ASCII characters but in our case the input is valid, and as such, they can be used. As for future versions they are not a part of the standards but they will probably stay. The `unescape` function returns the ASCII string for the specified hexadecimal encoded value. The benefit of using this is now we have representation that is a smaller string. Another great thing about this hack is it uses multiple encoding functions available by the browser to extend standard functionality.

There's more...

When it comes to user agent support, IE is the only current browser that has not yet included `btoa()` and `atob()`, but this was only valid for versions older than IE 10. In order to enable it on unsupported user agents we can use a polyfill. There are several different polyfills for this, but we can use the one called `base64.js`, (`https://bitbucket.org/davidchambers/base64.js`).

There is an interesting async resource loader called `yenope.js`, that is very fast and allows custom checks. If we want to include `base64.js` we can test for the existence of the needed functions and if it's not then it will automatically include it.

```
yepnope({
    test: window.btoa && window.atob,
    nope: 'base64.js',
    callback: function () {
        //safe to use window.btoa and window.atob
    }
});
```

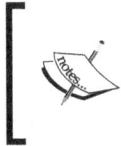

> Yepnope is one of the many conditional resource loaders, but it is one of the simple ones. The `yepnope` function is the core of the entire loader. As such it is very small and integrated in Modernizer; more info can be found at `http://yepnopejs.com/`.

Serializing binary data into JSON

When working with REST API's if you need to include binary data as part of the JSON, then one of the simplest ways is to use base64. Images and similar resources should most likely exist as separate resources but they can also be part of the JSON document as well. In this recipe, we are going to cover a simple example of including image in JSON document.

How to do it...

We will generate some binary data from a `canvas` element and serialize it to JSON:

1. We start by creating an HTML file, where we can place a simple `canvas`, a `div` element for output, and includes jQuery together with the script will be created afterwards:

```html
<!doctype html>
<html>
  <head>
    <meta charset="utf-8">
    <title>Binary data to json</title>
    <style type="text/css">
      div {
        word-wrap: break-word;
      }
    </style>
  </head>
  <body>
    <canvas id="myCanvas" width="75" height="75"></canvas>
```

```
      <hr />
      <div>
        <output id="generatedJson"> </output>
      </div>
      <script src="http://ajax.googleapis.com/ajax/libs/
jquery/1.8.2/jquery.min.js"></script>
        <script type="text/javascript" src="example.js"></script>
      </body>
    </html>
```

2. In the `example.js` script we can create a simple circle on the `canvas` element:

```
var canvas = $('#myCanvas')[0],
    context = canvas.getContext('2d');
context.beginPath();
context.arc(50, 50, 20, 0, Math.PI*2, true);
context.closePath();
context.fillStyle = 'green';
context.fill();
var imgdata = context.getImageData(0,0, 50, 50);
```

3. Then we define the same `arrayToString` function we used in the *Serializing binary data or text in base64* section:

```
function arrayToString(inputArray){
  var stringData = '',
  len = inputArray.byteLength;
  for (var i = 0; i < len; i++) {
    stringData += String.fromCharCode(inputArray[i]);
  }
  return stringData;
}
```

4. We then encode the data and create a JavaScript object while also creating two data URI form the `canvas` element, one `jpeg`, and the other `png`:

```
var imageEncoded = btoa(arrayToString(imgdata.data));
var jsObject = {
  "name":"pie chart or not a pie...chart",
  "dataURL" : {
    "jpeg": canvas.toDataURL('image/jpeg'),
    "png": canvas.toDataURL('image/png')
  },
  "image" : imageEncoded
};
```

5. In order to create the JSON object we can use `JSON.stringify` and then print the result to the `generatedJson` div:

```
var jsonString = JSON.stringify(jsObject, null , 2);
  $("#generatedJson").text(jsonString);
```

How it works...

The code is very similar to the previous recipe, we created a simple circle using 2D context for canvas:

```
context.beginPath();
context.arc(50, 50, 20, 0, Math.PI*2, true);
context.closePath();
```

Then we got the binary data from the image and applied the same logic like in the *Encoding binary data or text into base64* recipe. One specific feature is the use of Data URI that simply create a base64 encoded rendering of the image in the specified format. In our case we created a rending in `jpeg` and `png`. If you copy out the data contained in

```
"dataURL" : {
    "jpeg": "copy data rendered here",
    "png":"or copy data from here"
  }
```

and paste it into the browsers URL selection, it will render the image. Data URI will be looked into in great details in chapter titled *Data storage*.

There's more...

The base 64 encoding can be used with XML to store more complex or binary data. Because the character base of the encoding does not interfere with the parsing, no CDATA sections are needed.

There are plenty of other format for exchange of binary data with the server such as BSON, Base32 or Hessian. Base64 is most commonly used since it's very simple and it easy to integrate.

One great usage of base64 is to store the text into a URL parameter making the text easy to get represented and reconstructed, you can see that on `http://hashify.me`.

Serializing and deserializing cookies

Despite all the advances made in HTML5, browsers still have a very strange cookie API. The way it works is error-prone and inconsistent with the normal semantics of JavaScript.

The global `document` object has a `cookie` property, if a string is assigned to it, it magically adds the specified cookie to the list of cookies. When an attempt to read the cookie is made, a different value containing all the cookies is returned.

This API is not very useful without a wrapper. In this recipe, we're going to wrap this API in a wrapper that actually makes sense. We're going to test this wrapper by making a form page that saves itself on every modification (preserving the data after a page reload) for two minutes.

Getting ready

Let's find out how `document.cookie` works. We can set a cookie as follows:

```
document.cookie = "name=test; expires=Fri, 18 Jan 2023 00:00:00 GMT;
path=/";
```

This sets a cookie for the whole domain of the current website called test, expiring on January 18 2023. Now if we try to read from `document.cookie` we will get `"name=test"`, which means that all the extra data has been stripped out. If we continue by adding another cookie:

```
document.cookie = "otherName=test; expires=Fri, 18 Jan 2023 00:00:00
GMT; path=/"
```

And then try to access `document.cookie`, we get both cookies:

```
"name=test; otherName=test"
```

To actually clear the cookie we will need to set the `expires` date in the path as follows:

```
document.cookie = "otherName=test; expires=Fri, 18 Jan 2000 00:00:00
GMT; path=/"
```

And then we're back to `document.cookie` containing `"name=test"`.

Finally, if we omit the `expires` date, we're going to get a cookie that lasts until the user closes the browser or until we clear it by setting its expire date in the past:

```
document.cookie = "otherName=test; path=/"
```

But what happens if the value contains the character `;`? The cookie value will be cut off at this character and the next parameter (expire date or path) will be ignored. Fortunately, we can work around this by using `encodeURIComponent` to encode the value.

Now we have enough information to write our cookie handling library.

How to do it...

Let's write the code:

1. Create the form page in `index.html`, it will contain three text fields and include our cookie wrapper script and formsaving script:

```
<!DOCTYPE HTML>
<html>
<head>
<title>Cookie serialization</title>
</head>
<body>
<form method="post">
    <input type="text" name="text1" value="Form data will be
saved"><br>
    <input type="text" name="text2" value="in the cookie
formdata"><br>
    <input type="text" name="text3" value="and restored after
reload">
</form>
<script src="http://ajax.googleapis.com/ajax/libs/jquery/1.8.2/
jquery.min.js"></script>
<script type="text/javascript" src="cookie.js"></script>
<script type="text/javascript" src="example.js"></script>
</body>
</html>
```

2. Create `cookie.js`, which implements and exports the cookie API. It will have the following function:

   ❑ `cookie.set(name, value, options)`: This function sets the value of a cookie. The value can be an arbitrary object as long as it can be serialized by `JSON.stringify`. Available options are `expires`, `duration`, and `path`.

```
(function(exports) {

    var cookie = {};

    cookie.set = function set(name, val, opt) {
      opt = opt || {};
      var encodedVal = encodeURIComponent(JSON.
stringify(val)),
        expires = opt.expires  ? opt.expires.toUTCString()
        : opt.duration ? new Date(Date.now()
                                    + opt.duration * 1000).
toUTCString()
```

```
                        : null;

           var cook = name +'=' + encodedVal + ';';
           if (expires) cook += 'expires=' + expires;
           if (opt.path) cook += 'path=' + opt.path;
           document.cookie = cook;
        };

     cookie.del = function(name) {
        document.cookie = name + '=deleted; expires='
        + new Date(Date.now() - 1).toUTCString();
     }
     cookie.get = function get(name) {
        var cookies = {};
        var all = document.cookie.split(';').
   forEach(function(cs) {
        var c = cs.split('=');
        if (c[1])
        cookies[c[0]] =
        JSON.parse(decodeURIComponent(c[1]));
        });
     if (name)
        return cookies[name]
        else
        return cookies
     };

     exports.cookie = cookie;
  }(typeof(exports) !== 'undefined' ? exports : this));
```

3. Create `example.js` to test the new cookie API. It loads the form data when the document loads and saves it when it's changed:

```
$(function() {
    var savedform = cookie.get('formdata');
    savedform && savedform.forEach(function(nv) {
      $('form')
      .find('[name="'+nv.name+'"]')
      .val(nv.value);
    });
    $('form input').on('change keyup', function() {
      cookie.set('formdata', $('form').serializeArray(),
      {duration: 120});
    });
});
```

How it works...

Our API implements several convenient functions to deal with cookies.

The `cookie.set` function allows us to set a cookie. It takes three parameters: name, value, and options.

The value is serialized with `JSON.stringify`, and then encoded using `encodeURIComponent`. As a result we can store any object that can be serialized with `JSON.stringify` (there are however size limits which vary between browsers).

The options parameter is an object which can contain three properties: expires, duration, and path. The `expires` property is the date when the cookie should expire. Alternatively, `duration` can be provided – it is the duration that the cookie should last in seconds. If both of these are omitted, the cookie will last until the end of the current browser session. Finally, the `path` property is a string specifying the path where the cookie is available. The default is the current path.

There's more...

Cookies should not be used to store large amount of data. Most browsers limit the cookie size at 4 KB per cookie. Some browsers limit the total size of all cookies to 4 KB. Data stored inside cookies is transferred with every request made to the server, increasing the total use of bandwidth.

For larger data we can use local storage instead. More information can be found in *Chapter 10, Data Binding Frameworks*.

Note that this example doesn't work when opened on a local filesystem. To make it work, a local HTTP server must be run. See appendix for more information on how to run a simple HTTP server.

Serializing a form into request strings

A common task when working with forms is the need to create the actual request string. There are several different ways to do this, the first thing that comes to mind is just to select each individual form element and get it's value, and then create the string by appending the name attributes with the values. This is very error prone, so we are going to take a look at a better solution using `jQuery.serialize()`.

How to do it...

As usual we can start with the HTML:

1. First we add basic the `head` section and an output element where the generated request string will be shown:

```html
<!doctype html>
<html>
  <head>
    <meta charset="utf-8">
    <title>JavaScript objects to form data</title>
  </head>
  <body>
    <label><b>Generated string:</b></label>
    <output id="generated">none</output>
    <hr/>
    <output id="generatedJson">none</output>
    <hr/>
```

2. Then we can proceed with creating a simple form, where we add input for full name, e-mail, and percentage of awesomeness:

```html
    <form id="theForm">
      <label>Full name</label>
      <input type="text" id="fullName" name="fullName"
placeholder="Some Name">
      <label>Email address </label>
      <input type="email" id="email" name="email"
placeholder="example@example.com">
      <label>Percent of awesomeness </label>
      <input type="number" id="awesomeness" name="awesomeness"
value="50" min="1" max="100">
      <br/>
      <input type="submit">
    </form>
```

3. Following that we can include the needed JavaScript dependencies to jQuery and our `example.js` script:

```html
  <script src="http://ajax.googleapis.com/ajax/libs/jquery/1.8.2/
jquery.min.js"></script>

    <script src="example.js"></script>
```

4. We can then proceed to creating the `example.js` file, where on every update of the form elements the form is serialized:

```
$(function() {
$("#theForm").keyup(function(){
    var theForm = $("#theForm"),
    parameterArray = theForm.serializeArray();
    $("#generated").text(theForm.serialize());
    $("#generatedJson").text(JSON.stringify(parameterArray));
    });
});
```

How it works...

The `.serialize()` function converts form elements and their values into a percent-encoded string. Percent-encoding is often called URL encoding and is a way to represent information in a URI-friendly way. As such, it is a core part in most of the forms that are used and it has an MIME type of `application/x-www-form-urlencoded`.

If we have a button in the form it will not be considered as part of the generated string, because that button was not clicked in order to submit the form. Additionally, values from the checkboxes and radio buttons are only part of the generated string if they are checked.

On the other hand if we need some JSON representation then we can use `.serializeArray()`, a function that will create a JavaScript array. After having this array of elements we can create a JSON using `JSON.stringify()`. The default JSON representation may not be very useful in most cases but we can easily restructure and filter the elements.

The `.serializeArray()` and `.serialize()` functions save only "successful controls" as defined by the W3C (`http://www.w3.org/TR/html401/interact/forms.html#h-17.13.2`), where you will get same behavior as if the form was submitted regularly with a button click.

There's more...

The first thing to note is that data from file select elements is not serialized using these two methods. For this purpose and other similar use cases, the `FormData` object was introduced in `XMLHttpRequest Level 2`. This object allows the creation of a set of key/value pairs in order to be sent using `XMLHttpRequest`. The data that will be created using this method gets sent in the same way as standard submit, where the encoding was set to `"multipart/form-data"`.

We saw in our example the creation of JSON objects from the form elements can get messy even with using `.serializeArray()`. In order to simplify things and enable easy creation of more complex JSON directly from the elements `form2js`, `https://github.com/maxatwork/form2js` was created. A small example on how this works would be to create a simple person object:

```
{
    "person" :
    {
        "contact" :
        {
            "email" : "test@example.com",
            "phone" : "0123456789"
        }
    }
}
```

To achieve this we only create the definition in the `name` attribute and the script handles everything else:

```
<input type="email" name="person.contact.email" value="test@example.
com" />
<input type="text" name="person.contact.phone" value="0123456789" />
```

There is a standard JavaScript version and a jQuery plugin for this library. It also has other features such as having array of objects or custom field handlers.

Reading XML documents with DOMParser

While `XMLHttpRequest` allows us to both download and parse XML documents, sometimes we might want to parse XML data documents manually. For example, manual parsing would enable us to include arbitrary XML data (for example, XML-based templates) inside the page in a `script` tag. This can help to reduce the number of requests sent to the browser.

In this recipe, we are going to read a simple XML document from a `textarea` input and parse it using `DOMParser`, and then display the result as a tree.

How to do it...

Let's write the test HTML page and the parser:

1. Create `index.html`, it should contain a `textarea` element to input XML (a sample XML document is included), a placeholder for the document `body` object, and some CSS styles for the document tree:

```
<!DOCTYPE HTML>
<html>
<head>
<title>Deserializing XML with DOMParser</title>
<style type="text/css">
div.children { padding-left: 3em; }
h3 { padding:0; margin:0; }
.children .text { padding-top: 0.5em; }
.attribute .name { padding-left: 1.5em; width:5em;
    display:inline-block; font-weight:bold; }
.attribute .value { padding-left: 1em; font-style:oblique; }
</style>
</head>
<body>
<textarea rows="11" cols="60">
&lt;?xml version=&quot;1.0&quot; encoding=&quot;UTF-8&quot; ?&gt;
&lt;root&gt;
    Text in document
    &lt;element attribute=&quot;value&quot; foo=&quot;bar&quot;
/&gt;
    &lt;bold weight=&quot;strong&quot;&gt;Text in element&lt;/
bold&gt;
    &lt;list&gt;
        &lt;item&gt;item text 1&lt;/item&gt;
        &lt;item&gt;item text 2&lt;/item&gt;
    &lt;/list&gt;
&lt;/root&gt;
</textarea>
<div id="tree">
</div>
<script src="http://ajax.googleapis.com/ajax/libs/jquery/1.8.2/
jquery.min.js"></script>
<script type="text/javascript" src="example.js"></script>
</body>
</html>
```

2. Create `example.js`, and add the code that parses the document and converts it into an HTML tree:

```
$(function() {
  function parseDocument(text) {
    function displayElement(e) {
      var holder = $("&div />").addClass('element');
      $("<h3 />").text(e.nodeName).appendTo(holder);
      if (e.attributes && e.attributes.length) {
        var attrs = $("<div />").addClass('attributes')
        .appendTo(holder);
        for (var a = 0; a < e.attributes.length; ++a) {
          var nameval = e.attributes[a];
          var attr = $("<div />").addClass('attribute')
          .appendTo(attrs);
          $('<span />').addClass('name')
          .text(nameval.name).appendTo(attr);
          $('<span />').addClass('value')
                     .text(nameval.value).appendTo(attr);
        }
      }
      if (e.childNodes.length) {
        var children = $("<div />").appendTo(holder)
        .addClass('children');
        for (var c = 0; c < e.childNodes.length; ++c) {
          var child = e.childNodes[c];
          if (child.nodeType == Node.ELEMENT_NODE)
                     displayElement(child).appendTo(children);
               else if (child.nodeType == Node.TEXT_NODE
                      || chilc.nodeType ==
                                    Node.CDATA_SECTION_NODE)
                     $("<div />").addClass('text')
                          .text(child.textContent)
                          .appendTo(children);
          }
        }
        return holder;
    }
    var parser = new DOMParser();
    var doc = parser.parseFromString(text, 'application/xml');
    window.doc = doc;
    return displayElement(doc.childNodes[0]);
  }
  function update() {
    $('#tree').html('')
```

```
        parseDocument($('textarea').val()).appendTo('#tree');
    }
    update();
    $('textarea').on('keyup change', update);
});
```

How it works...

To parse an XML document, we create a new `DOMParser` object and call the `parseFromString` method. We specify the document type as application/xml – the parser can also parse `text/html` and return an `HTMLDocument` element, or `image/svg+xml` returning an `SVGDocument` element.

The resulting document has a very similar API to the one found in `window.document` (the same DOM API is available). We create a recursive function that iterates all the children of the root element and generates HTML. It constructs headers for the element names, span elements for the attribute names and values, div elements for the text nodes, and calls itself to generate HTML to display element nodes. The result is a DOM tree:

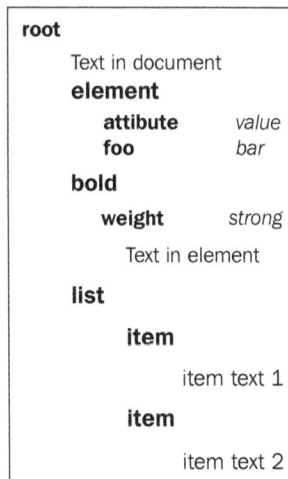

```
root
    Text in document
    element
        attribute      value
        foo            bar
    bold
        weight         strong
            Text in element
    list
        item
            item text 1
        item
            item text 2
```

Serialization of XML document at the client side

JSON is extremely simple to use than JavaScript; there are lot of REST services already out there that use XML. In this recipe we are going to create a simple form that will construct an XML document using the DOM API for XML.

How to do it...

Let's start:

1. First we create a simple HTML document:

```
<!doctype html>
<html>
  <head>
    <meta charset="utf-8">
    <title>Create XML from JavaScript objects</title>
  </head>
  <body>
    <output id="log"> </output>
```

2. After this we are going to include a KML document inside the text, in a real life application this will probably get loaded by AJAX, but for simplicity we will add the data directly:

```
<kml id="test" xmlns="http://www.opengis.net/kml/2.2">
  <Document>
    <name>Red Pyramid</name>
    <description><![CDATA[]]></description>
    <Style id="style1">
      <IconStyle>
        <Icon>
          <href></href>
        </Icon>
      </IconStyle>
    </Style>
    <Placemark>
      <name>Red Pyramid</name>
      <styleUrl>#style1</styleUrl>
      <Point>
        <coordinates>31.206320,29.808853,0.000000</coordinates>
      </Point>
    </Placemark>
  </Document>
</kml>
```

> You may have noticed the use of **KML (Keyhole Markup Language)** in this recipe. Originally this was a format developed by a company acquired by Google, but now its is an international open standard. This format is widely used for describing placemarks and locations. More info can be found at:
>
> `https://developers.google.com/kml/documentation/`

3. Following this block we can just include the JavaScript `example.js`:

```
    <script src="example.js"></script>
  </body>
</html>
```

4. We will create a simple XML document form scratch and serialize it to a string. The code will simply retrieve a section of the HTML document where we have the KML data serializing it to a string, and then displaying the data in the text area:

```
;(function() {
 var doc = document.implementation.createDocument("","root",
null),
        node = doc.createElement("someNode");
   doc.documentElement.appendChild(node);

   document.getElementById('first')
   .appendChild(
     document.createTextNode(
       new XMLSerializer()
     .serializeToString(doc))
   );

   var kml = document.getElementById('test');
   document.getElementById('second')
   .appendChild(
     document.createTextNode(
       new XMLSerializer()
       .serializeToString(kml))
   );
}());
```

How it works...

The core of this example is the `XMLSerializer()` method, that can be used to convert DOM subtree or the entire document into text. The object is supported by most of the modern browsers and IE 9+, but for older versions, you need to use some fallback similar to the following one:

```
function xmlStringify(someXML) {
    if (typeof XMLSerializer !== 'undefined') {
      return (new XMLSerializer()).serializeToString(someXML);
    }
    // fallback for IE
    if (someXML.xml) {
      return someXML.xml;
    }
    //Not supported
}
```

Standard DOM manipulation can be used to create an XML document. The same thing applies for jQuery where we have out-of-the-box functionality for the creation of documents. Things only get more complicated if we need to work with larger documents or do extensive work with XML. Most of the REST services these days have some sort of content negotiation, so usual JSON is an available and a better option.

There's more...

There is also a functionality called JXON(`https://developer.mozilla.org/en-US/docs/JXON`), which stands for JavaScript XML Object Notation is a generic name for the API related to creation and use of XML documents in JavaScript. This basically defines a convention for a two-way conversion between JSON and XML.

While working extensively with XML, XPath can be your best friend. It enables a very flexible way of accessing specific parts of the documents that match certain pattern.

> **XPath (XML Path Language)** is a query language for selecting nodes in an XML document. Much like SQL, it provides certain calculation functions. There is an extensive documentation on MDN at `https://developer.mozilla.org/en-US/docs/XPath` as well as the specification documents at `http://www.w3.org/TR/xpath20/`.

8
Communicating with Servers

In this chapter, we're going to cover the following topics:

- ▶ Creating an HTTP GET request to fetch JSON
- ▶ Creating a request with custom headers
- ▶ Versioning your API
- ▶ Fetching JSON data with JSONP
- ▶ Reading XML data from the server
- ▶ Using the FormData interface
- ▶ Posting a binary file to the server
- ▶ Creating an SSL connection with Node.js
- ▶ Making real-time updates with Ajax Push
- ▶ Exchanging real-time messages using WebSockets

Creating an HTTP GET request to fetch JSON

One of the basic means of retrieving information from the server is using HTTP GET. This type of method in a RESTful manner should be only used for reading data. So, GET calls should never change server state. Now, this may not be true for every possible case, for example, if we have a view counter on a certain resource, is that a real change? Well, if we follow the definition literally then yes, this is a change, but it's far from significant to be taken into account.

Opening a web page in a browser does a GET request, but often we want to have a scripted way of retrieving data. This is usually to achieve **Asynchronous JavaScript and XML** (**AJAX**), allowing reloading of data without doing a complete page reload. Despite the name, the use of XML is not required, and these days, JSON is the format of choice.

A combination of JavaScript and the `XMLHttpRequest` object provides a method for exchanging data asynchronously, and in this recipe, we are going to see how to read JSON for the server using plain JavaScript and jQuery. Why use plain JavaScript rather than using jQuery directly? We strongly believe that jQuery simplifies the DOM API, but it is not always available to us, and additionally, we need have to know the underlying code behind asynchronous data transfer in order to fully grasp how applications work.

Getting ready

The server will be implemented using Node.js. Please refer to *Appendix A, Installing Node.js and Using npm*, on how to install Node.js on your machine, and how to use npm. In this example, for simplicity, we will use **restify** (`http://mcavage.github.io/node-restify/`), a Node.js module for creation of correct REST web services.

How to do it...

Let's perform the following steps.

1. In order to include `restify` to our project in the root directory of our server side scripts, use the following command:

   ```
   npm install restify
   ```

2. After adding the dependency, we can proceed to creating the server code. We create a `server.js` file that will be run by Node.js, and at the beginning of it we add `restify`:

   ```
   var restify = require('restify');
   ```

3. With this `restify` object, we can now create a server object and add handlers for `get` methods:

   ```
   var server = restify.createServer();
   server.get('hi', respond);
   server.get('hi/:index', respond);
   ```

4. The `get` handlers do a callback to a function called `respond`, so we can now define this function that will return the JSON data. We will create a sample JavaScript object called `hello`, and in case the function was called having a parameter index part of the request it was called from the `"hi/:index"` handler:

```
function respond(req, res, next) {
  console.log("Got HTTP " + req.method + " on " + req.url + "
responding");
  var hello = [{
    'id':'0',
    'hello': 'world'
  },{
    'id':'1',
    'say':'what'
  }];
  if(req.params.index){
    var found = hello[req.params.index];
    if(found){
      res.send(found);
    } else {
      res.status(404);
      res.send();
    }
  };
  res.send(hello);
  addHeaders(req,res);
  return next();
}
```

5. The following `addHeaders` function that we call at the beginning is adding headers to enable access to the resources served from a different domain or a different server port:

```
function addHeaders(req, res) {
  res.header("Access-Control-Allow-Origin", "*");
  res.header("Access-Control-Allow-Headers", "X-Requested-With");
};
```

6. The definition of headers and what they mean will be discussed later on in the chapter. For now, let's just say they enable accesses to the resources from a browser using AJAX. At the end, we add a block of code that will set the server to listen on port 8080:

```
server.listen(8080, function() {
  console.log('%s listening at %s', server.name, server.url);
});
```

7. To start the sever using command line, we type the following command:

   node server.js

8. If everything went as it should, we will get a message in the log:

   ```
   restify listening at http://0.0.0.0:8080
   ```

9. We can then test it by accessing directly from the browser on the URL we defined `http://localhost:8080/hi` or see the communication using some of the tools discussed in *Appendix A, Installing Node.js and Using npm*.

Now we can proceed with the client-side HTML and JavaScript. We will implement two ways for reading data from the server, one using standard XMLHttpRequest and the other using jQuery.get(). Note that not all features are fully compatible with all browsers.

1. We create a simple page where we have two div elements, one with the ID data and another with the ID say. These elements will be used as placeholders to load data form the server into them:

   ```
   Hello <div id="data">loading</div>
   <hr/>
   Say <div id="say">No</div>s
   <script src="http://ajax.googleapis.com/ajax/libs/
   jquery/1.8.2/jquery.min.js"></script>
   <script src="example.js"></script>
   <script src="exampleJQuery.js"></script>
   ```

2. In the example.js file, we define a function called getData that will create a AJAX call to a given url and do a callback if the request went successfully:

   ```
   function getData(url, onSuccess) {
     var request = new XMLHttpRequest();
     request.open("GET", url);
     request.onload = function() {
       if (request.status === 200) {
         console.log(request);
         onSuccess(request.response);
       }
     };
     request.send(null);
   }
   ```

3. After that, we can call the function directly, but in order to demonstrate that the call happens after the page is loaded, we will call it after a timeout of three seconds:

   ```
   setTimeout(
       function() {
         getData(
           'http://localhost:8080/hi',
   ```

```
            function(response){
                console.log('finished getting data');
                var div = document.getElementById('data');
                var data = JSON.parse(response);
                div.innerHTML = data[0].hello;
            })
        },
        3000);
```

4. The jQuery version is a lot cleaner, as the complexity that comes with the standard DOM API and the event handling is reduced substantially:

```
    (function(){
    $.getJSON('http://localhost:8080/hi/1', function(data) {
        $('#say').text(data.say);
    });
    }())
```

How it works...

At the beginning, we installed the dependency using `npm install restify`; this is sufficient to have it working, but in order to define dependencies in a more expressive way, npm has a way of specifying it. We can add a file called `package.json`, a packaging format that is mainly used for for publishing details for Node.js applications. In our case, we can define `package.json` with the flowing code:

```
{
    "name" : "ch8-tip1-http-get-example",
    "description" : "example on http get",
    "dependencies" : ["restify"],
    "author" : "Mite Mitreski",
    "main" : "html5dasc",
    "version" : "0.0.1"
}
```

If we have a file like this, npm will automatically handle the installation of dependencies after calling `npm install` from the command line in the directory where the `package.json` file is placed.

`Restify` has a simple routing where functions are mapped to appropriate methods for a given URL. The HTTP GET request for '/hi' is mapped with `server.get('hi', theCallback)`, where `theCallback` is executed, and a response should be returned.

When we have a parameterized resource, for example in `'hi/:index'`, the value associated with `:index` will be available under `req.params`. For example, in a request to `'/hi/john'` to access the `john` value, we simple have `req.params.index`. Additionally, the value for index will automatically get URL-decoded before it is passed to our handler. One other notable part of the request handlers in `restify` is the `next()` function that we called at the end. In our case, it mostly does not makes much sense, but in general, we are responsible for calling it if we want the next handler function in the chain to be called. For exceptional circumstances, there is also an option to call `next()` with an `error` object triggering custom responses.

When it comes to the client-side code, `XMLHttpRequest` is the mechanism behind the async calls, and on calling `request.open("GET", url, true)` with the last parameter value as `true`, we get a truly asynchronous execution. Now you might be wondering why is this parameter here, isn't the call already done after loading the page? That is true, the call is done after loading the page, but if, for example, the parameter was set to `false`, the execution of the request will be a blocking method, or to put it in layman's terms, the script will pause until we get a response. This might look like a small detail, but it can have a huge impact on performance.

The jQuery part is pretty straightforward; there is function that accepts a URL value of the resource, the data handler function, and a `success` function that gets called after successfully getting a response:

```
jQuery.getJSON( url [, data ] [, success(data, textStatus, jqXHR) ] )
```

When we open `index.htm`, the server should log something like the following:

Got HTTP GET on /hi/1 responding

Got HTTP GET on /hi responding

Here one is from the jQuery request and the other from the plain JavaScript.

There's more...

XMLHttpRequest Level 2 is one of the new improvements being added to the browsers, although not part of HTML5 it is still a significant change. There are several features with the Level 2 changes, mostly to enable working with files and data streams, but there is one simplification we already used. Earlier we would have to use `onreadystatechange` and go through all of the states, and if the `readyState` was 4, which is equal to `DONE`, we could read the data:

```
var xhr = new XMLHttpRequest();
xhr.open('GET', 'someurl', true);
xhr.onreadystatechange = function(e) {
  if (this.readyState == 4 && this.status == 200) {
    // response is loaded
  }
}
```

In a Level 2 request however, we can use `request.onload = function() {}` directly without checking states. Possible states can be seen in the table:

State name	Numeric value	Description
UNSENT	0	Object created
OPENED	1	The `open` method was called
HEADERS_RECEIVED	2	All redirects have been followed and all headers of the final object are now available
LOADING	3	The response is being revived
DONE	4	Data has been received or something went wrong during transfer, for example infinite redirects

One other thing to note is that `XMLHttpRequest` Level 2 is supported in all major browsers and IE 10; the older `XMLHttpRequest` has a different way of instantiation on older versions of IE (older than IE 7), where we can access it through an ActiveX object via new `ActiveXObject("Msxml2.XMLHTTP.6.0");`.

Creating a request with custom headers

The HTTP headers are a part of the `request` object being sent to the server. Many of them give information about the client's user agent setup and configuration, as that is sometimes the basis of making description for the resources being fetched from the server. Several of them such as `Etag`, `Expires`, and `If-Modified-Since` are closely related to caching, while others such as `DNT` that stands for "Do Not Track" (`http://www.w3.org/2011/tracking-protection/drafts/tracking-dnt.html`) can be quite controversial. In this recipe, we will take a look at a way for using the custom `X-Myapp` header in our server and client-side code.

Getting ready

The server will be implemented using Node.js, so you can refer to *Appendix A, Installing Node.js and Using npm* on how to install Node.js on your machine, and how to use npm. In this example, again for simplicity, we will use restify (`http://mcavage.github.io/node-restify/`). Also, monitoring the console in your browser and server is crucial in order to understand what happens in the background.

How to do it...

1. We can start by defining the dependencies for the server side in `package.json` file:

```
{
  "name" : "ch8-tip2-custom-headers",
  "dependencies" : ["restify"],
  "main" : "html5dasc",
  "version" : "0.0.1"
}
```

2. After that, we can call `npm install` from the command line that will automatically retrieve `restify` and place it in a `node_modules` folder created in the root directory of the project. After this part, we can proceed to creating the server-side code in a `server.js` file where we set the server to listen on port 8080 and add a route handler for `'hi'` and for every other path when the request method is HTTP OPTIONS:

```
var restify = require('restify');
var server = restify.createServer();
server.get('hi', addHeaders, respond);
server.opts(/\.*/, addHeaders, function (req, res, next) {
  console.log("Got HTTP " + req.method + " on " + req.url + " with
headers\n");
  res.send(200);
  return next();
});
server.listen(8080, function() {
  console.log('%s listening at %s', server.name, server.url);
});
```

> In most cases, the documentation should be enough when we write the application's build onto Restify, but sometimes, it is a good idea to take a look a the source code as well. It can be found on `https://github.com/mcavage/node-restify/`.

3. One thing to notice is that we can have multiple chained handlers; in this case, we have `addHeaders` before the others. In order for every handler to be propagated, `next()` should be called:

```
function addHeaders(req, res, next) {
  res.setHeader("Access-Control-Allow-Origin", "*");
  res.setHeader('Access-Control-Allow-Headers', 'X-Requested-With,
X-Myapp');
  res.setHeader('Access-Control-Allow-Methods', 'GET, OPTIONS');
  res.setHeader('Access-Control-Expose-Headers', 'X-Myapp,
X-Requested-With');
  return next();
};
```

The `addHeaders` adds access control options in order to enable cross-origin resource sharing. **Cross-origin resource sharing** (**CORS**) defines a way in which the browser and server can interact to determine if the request should be allowed. It is more secure than allowing all cross-origin requests, but is more powerful than simply allowing all of them.

4. After this, we can create the handler function that will return a JSON response with the headers the server received and a hello world kind of object:

```
 function respond(req, res, next) {
   console.log("Got HTTP " + req.method + " on " + req.url + " with
 headers\n");
   console.log("Request: ", req.headers);
   var hello = [{
     'id':'0',
     'hello': 'world',
     'headers': req.headers
   }];
   res.send(hello);
   console.log('Response:\n ', res.headers());
   return next();
 }
```

We additionally log the request and response headers to the sever console log in order to see what happens in the background.

5. For the client-side code, we need a plain "vanilla" JavaScript approach and jQuery method, so in order to do that, include `example.js` and `exampleJquery.js` as well as a few `div` elements that we will use for displaying data retrieved from the server:

```
 Hi <div id="data">loading</div>
 <hr/>
 Headers list from the request: <div id="headers"></div>
 <hr/>
 Data from jQuery: <div id="dataRecieved">loading</div>
 <script src="http://ajax.googleapis.com/ajax/libs/
 jquery/1.8.2/jquery.min.js"></script>
 <script src="example.js"></script>
 <script src="exampleJQuery.js"></script>
```

6. A simple way to add the headers is to call `setRequestHeader` on a `XMLHttpRequest` object after the call of `open()`:

```
 function getData(url, onSucess) {
   var request = new XMLHttpRequest();
   request.open("GET", url, true);
   request.setRequestHeader("X-Myapp","super");
   request.setRequestHeader("X-Myapp","awesome");
```

```
    request.onload = function() {
      if (request.status === 200) {
        onSuccess(request.response);
      }
    };
    request.send(null);
  }
```

7. The `XMLHttpRequest` automatically sets headers, such as `"Content-Length"`,`"Referer"`, and `"User-Agent"`, and does not allow you to change them using JavaScript.

> A more complete list of headers and the reasoning behind this can be found in the W3C documentation at `http://www.w3.org/TR/XMLHttpRequest/#the-setrequestheader%28%29-method`.

8. To print out the results, we add a function that will add each of the header keys and values to an unordered list:

```
getData(
  'http://localhost:8080/hi',
  function(response){
    console.log('finished getting data');
    var data = JSON.parse(response);
    document.getElementById('data').innerHTML = data[0].hello;
    var headers = data[0].headers,
        headersList = "<ul>";
    for(var key in headers){
      headersList += '<li><b>' + key + '</b>: ' + headers[key]
+'</li>';
    };
    headersList += "</ul>";
    document.getElementById('headers').innerHTML = headersList;
  });
```

9. When this gets executed. a list of all the request headers should be displayed on a page, and our custom `x-myapp` should be shown:

host: localhost:8080
connection: keep-alive
origin: http://localhost:8000
x-myapp: super, awesome
user-agent: Mozilla/5.0 (X11; Linux x86_64) AppleWebKit/537.27
(KHTML, like Gecko) Chrome/26.0.1386.0 Safari/537.27

10. The jQuery approach is far simpler, we can use the `beforeSend` hook to call a function that will set the `'x-myapp'` header. When we receive the response, write it down to the element with the ID `dataRecived`:

```
$.ajax({
    beforeSend: function (xhr) {
      xhr.setRequestHeader('x-myapp', 'this was easy');
    },
    success: function (data) {
      $('#dataRecieved').text(data[0].headers['x-myapp']);
    }
```

11. Output from the jQuery example will be the data contained in `x-myapp` header:

    Data from jQuery: this was easy

How it works...

You may have noticed that on the server side, we added a route that has a handler for `HTTP OPTIONS` method, but we never explicitly did a call there. If we take a look at the server log, there should be something like the following output:

```
        Got HTTP OPTIONS on /hi with headers
        Got HTTP GET on /hi with headers
```

This happens because the browser first issues a **preflight request**, which in a way is the browser's question whether or not there is a permission to make the "real" request. Once the permission has been received, the original GET request happens. If the `OPTIONS` response is cached, the browser will not issue any extra preflight calls for subsequent requests.

The `setRequestHeader` function of `XMLHttpRequest` actually appends each value as a comma-separated list of values. As we called the function two times, the value for the header is as follows:

```
    'x-myapp': 'super, awesome'
```

There's more...

For most use cases, we do not need custom headers to be part of our logic, but there are plenty of API's that make good use of them. For example, many server-side technologies add the `X-Powered-By` header that contains some meta information, such as `JBoss 6` or `PHP/5.3.0`. Another example is Google Cloud Storage, where among other headers there are `x-goog-meta`-prefixed headers such as `x-goog-meta-project-name` and `x-goog-meta-project-manager`.

Versioning your API

We do not always have the best solution while doing the first implementation. The API can be extended up to a certain point, but afterwards needs to undergo some structural changes. But we might already have users that depend on the current version, so we need a way to have different representation versions of the same resource. Once a module has users, the API cannot be changed at our own will.

One way to resolve this issue is to use a so-called URL versioning, where we simply add a prefix. For example, if the old URL was `http://example.com/rest/employees`, the new one could be `http://example.com/rest/v1/employees`, or under a subdomain it could be `http://v1.example.com/rest/employee`. This approach only works if you have direct control over all the servers and clients. Otherwise, you need to have a way of handling fallback to older versions.

In this recipe, we are going implement a so-called "Semantic versioning", `http://semver.org/`, using HTTP headers to specify accepted versions.

Getting ready

The server will be implemented using Node.js, so you can refer to *Appendix A, Installing Node.js and Using npm* on how to install Node.js on your machine and how to use npm. In this example, we will use restify (`http://mcavage.github.io/node-restify/`) for the server-side logic to monitor the requests to understand what is sent.

How to do it...

Let's perform the following steps.

1. We need to define the dependencies first, and after installing `restify`, we can proceed to the creation of the server code. The main difference with the previous examples is the definition of the `"Accept-version"` header. restify has built-in handling for this header using **versioned routes**. After creating the server object, we can set which methods will get called for what version:

   ```
   server.get({ path: "hi", version: '2.1.1'}, addHeaders, helloV2,
   logReqRes);
   server.get({ path: "hi", version: '1.1.1'}, addHeaders, helloV1,
   logReqRes);
   ```

2. We also need the handler for the HTTP OPTIONS, as we are using cross-origin resource sharing and the browser needs to do the additional request in order to get permissions:

   ```
   server.opts(/\.*/, addHeaders, logReqRes, function (req, res,
   next) {
   ```

```
    res.send(200);
    return next();
});
```

3. The handlers for Version 1 and Version 2 will return different objects in order for us to easily notice the difference between the API calls. In the general case, the resource should be the same, but can have different structural changes. For Version 1, we can have the following:

```
function helloV1(req, res, next) {
  var hello = [{
    'id':'0',
    'hello': 'grumpy old data',
    'headers': req.headers
  }];
  res.send(hello);
  return next()
}
```

4. As for Version 2, we have the following:

```
function helloV2(req, res, next) {
  var hello = [{
    'id':'0',
    'awesome-new-feature':{
      'hello': 'awesomeness'
    },
    'headers': req.headers
  }];
  res.send(hello);
  return next();
}
```

5. One other thing we must do is add the CORS headers in order to enable the `accept-version` header, so in the route we included the `addHeaders` that should be something like the following:

```
function addHeaders(req, res, next) {
  res.setHeader("Access-Control-Allow-Origin", "*");
  res.setHeader('Access-Control-Allow-Headers', 'X-Requested-With, accept-version');
  res.setHeader('Access-Control-Allow-Methods', 'GET, OPTIONS');
  res.setHeader('Access-Control-Expose-Headers', 'X-Requested-With, accept-version');
  return next();
};
```

> Note that you should not forget to the call to `next()` in order to call the next function in the route chain.

6. For simplicity, we will only implement the client side in jQuery, so we create a simple HTML document, where we include the necessary JavaScript dependencies:

```
Old api: <div id="data">loading</div>
<hr/>
New one: <div id="dataNew"> </div>
<hr/>
<script src="http://ajax.googleapis.com/ajax/libs/
jquery/1.8.2/jquery.min.js"></script>
<script src="exampleJQuery.js"></script>
```

7. In the `example.js` file, we do two AJAX calls to our REST API, one is set to use the Version 1 and other to use Version 2:

```
$.ajax({
    url: 'http://localhost:8080/hi',
    type: 'GET',
    dataType: 'json',
    success: function (data) {
    $('#data').text(data[0].hello);
    },
    beforeSend: function (xhr) {
    xhr.setRequestHeader('accept-version', '~1');
    }
});
$.ajax({
    url: 'http://localhost:8080/hi',
    type: 'GET',
    dataType: 'json',
    success: function (data) {
    $('#dataNew').text(data[0]['awesome-new-feature'].hello);
    },
    beforeSend: function (xhr) {
    xhr.setRequestHeader('accept-version', '~2');
    }
});
```

Notice that the `accept-version` header contains values ~1 and ~2. These designate that all the semantic versions such as 1.1.0 and 1.1.1 1.2.1 will get matched by ~1 and similarly for ~2. At the end, we should get an output like the following text:

Old api:grumpy old data
New one:awesomeness

How it works...

Versioned routes are a built-in feature of restify that work through the use of `accept-version`. In our example, we used Versions `~1` and `~2`, but what happens if we don't specify a version? restify will do the choice for us, as the the the request will be treated in the same manner as if the client has sent a `*` version. The first defined matching route in our code will be used. There is also an option to set up the routes to match multiple versions by adding a list of versions for a certain handler:

```
server.get({path: 'hi', version: ['1.1.0', '1.1.1', '1.2.1']},
  sendOld);
```

The reason why this type of versioning is very suitable for use in constantly growing applications is because as the API changes, the client can stick with their version of the API without any additional effort or changes needed in the client-side development. Meaning that we don't have to do updates on the application. On the other hand, if the client is sure that their application will work on newer API versions, they can simply change the request headers.

There's more...

Versioning can be implemented by using custom content types prefixed with `vnd` for example, `application/vnd.mycompany.user-v1`. An example of this is Google Earth's content type KML where it is defined as `application/vnd.google-earth.kml+xml`. Notice that the content type can be in two parts; we could have `application/vnd.mycompany-v1+json` where the second part will be the format of the response.

Fetching JSON data with JSONP

JSONP or JSON with padding is a mechanism of making cross-domain requests by taking advantage of the `<script>` tag. AJAX transport is done by simply setting the `src` attribute on a `script` element or adding the element itself if not present. The browser will do an HTTP request to download the URL specified, and that is not subject to the same origin policy, meaning that we can use it to get data from servers that are not under our control. In this recipe, we will create a simple JSONP request, and a simple server to back that up.

Getting ready

We will make a simplified implementation of the server we used in previous examples, so we need Node.js and restify (`http://mcavage.github.io/node-restify/`) installed either via definition of `package.json` or a simple install. For working with Node.js, please refer to *Appendix A, Installing Node.js and Using npm*.

How to do it...

1. First, we will create a simple route handler that will return a JSON object:

```
function respond(req, res, next) {
  console.log("Got HTTP " + req.method + " on " + req.url + "
responding");
  var hello = [{
    'id':'0',
    'what': 'hi there stranger'
  }];
  res.send(hello);
  return next();
}
```

2. We could roll our own version that will wrap the response into a JavaScript function with the given name, but in order to enable JSONP when using restify, we can simply enable the bundled plugin. This is done by specifying what plugin to be used:

```
var server = restify.createServer();
server.use(restify.jsonp());
server.get('hi', respond);
```

3. After this, we just set the server to listen on port 8080:

```
server.listen(8080, function() {
  console.log('%s listening at %s', server.name, server.url);
});
```

4. The built-in plugin checks the request string for parameters called `callback` or `jsonp`, and if those are found, the result will be JSONP with the function name of the one passed as value to one of these parameters. For example, in our case, if we open the browser on `http://localhost:8080/hi`, we get the following:

```
[{"id":"0","what":"hi there stranger"}]
```

5. If we access the same URL with the `callback` parameter or a JSONP set, such as `http://localhost:8080/hi?callback=great`, we should receive the same data wrapped with that function name:

```
great([{"id":"0","what":"hi there stranger"}]);
```

This is where the P in JSONP, which stands for padded, comes into the picture.

6. So, what we need to do next is create an HTML file where we would show the data from the server and include two scripts, one for the pure JavaScript approach and another for the jQuery way:

```
<b>Hello far away server: </b>
<div id="data">loading</div>
<hr/>
```

```
<div id="oneMoreTime">...</div>
<script src="http://ajax.googleapis.com/ajax/libs/
jquery/1.8.2/jquery.min.js"></script>
<script src="example.js"></script>
<script src="exampleJQuery.js"></script>
```

7. We can proceed with the creation of `example.js`, where we create two functions; one will create a `script` element and set the value of `src` to `http://localhost:8080/?callback=cool.run`, and the other will serve as a callback upon receiving the data:

```
var cool = (function(){
  var module = {};

  module.run = function(data){
    document.getElementById('data').innerHTML = data[0].what;
  }

  module.addElement = function (){
    var script = document.createElement('script');
    script.src = 'http://localhost:8080/hi?callback=cool.run'
    document.getElementById('data').appendChild(script);
    return true;
  }
  return module;
}());
```

8. Afterwards we only need the function that adds the element:

```
cool.addElement();
```

This should read the data from the server and show a result similar to the following:

Hello far away server:
hi there stranger

From the `cool` object, we can run the `addElement` function directly as we defined it as self-executable.

9. The jQuery example is a lot simpler; We can set the datatype to JSONP and everything else is the same as any other AJAX call, at least from the API point of view:

```
$.ajax({
    type : "GET",
    dataType : "jsonp",
    url : 'http://localhost:8080/hi',
    success: function(obj){
      $('#oneMoreTime').text(obj[0].what);
    }
});
```

We can now use the standard `success` callback to handle the data received from the server, and we don't have to specify the parameter in the request. jQuery will automatically append a `callback` parameter to the URL and delegate the call to the `success` callback.

How it works...

The first large leap we are doing here is trusting the source of the data. Results from the server is evaluated after the data is downloaded from the server. There has been some efforts to define a safer JSONP on `http://json-p.org/`, but it is far from being widespread.

The download itself is a `HTTP GET` method adding another major limitation to usability. **Hypermedia as the Engine of Application State** (**HATEOAS**), among other things, defines the use of HTTP methods for the create, update, and delete operations, making JSONP very unstable for those use cases.

Another interesting point is how jQuery delegates the call to the `success` callback. In order to achieve this, a unique function name is created and is sent to the `callback` parameter, for example:

```
/hi?callback=jQuery182031846177391707897_1359599143721&_=1359599143727
```

This function later does a callback to the appropriate handler of `jQuey.ajax`.

There's more...

With jQuery, we can also use a custom function if the server parameter that should handle `jsonp` is not called `callback`. This is done using the flowing config:

```
jsonp: false, jsonpCallback: "my callback"
```

As with JSONP, we don't do `XMLHttpRequest` and expect any of the functions that are used with AJAX call to be executed or have their parameters filled as such call. It is a very common mistake to expect just that. More on this can be found in the jQuery documentation at `http://api.jquery.com/category/ajax/`.

Reading XML data from server

Another common data format for REST services is XML. If we have the option to choose a format, there are very small number of cases where JSON is not a better choice. XML is a better option if we need strict message validation using multiple namespaces and schemas, or for some reason, we use **Extensible Stylesheet Language Transformations** (**XSTL**). The biggest reason of all is the need to work with and support legacy environments that don't use JSON. Most of the modern server-side frameworks have a built-in support for content negotiation, meaning that depending on the client's request, they can serve up the same resource in different formats. In this recipe, we are going to create a simple XML server and use it from the client side.

Getting ready

For the server side, we will use Node.js with restify (`http://mcavage.github.io/node-restify/`) for the REST services, and xmlbuilder (`https://github.com/oozcitak/xmlbuilder-js`) for creating simple XML documents. To do this, we can use npm to install the dependencies or define a simple `package.json` file, such as the one available in the example files.

How to do it...

Let's follow these steps to demonstrate the use of XML.

1. The server code is similar to other restify-based examples that we created previously. As we just want to demonstrate the use of XML, we can create a simple structure with xmlbuilder:

```
var restify = require('restify');
var builder = require('xmlbuilder');
var doc = builder.create();
doc.begin('root')
  .ele('human')
    .att('type', 'female')
      .txt('some gal')
      .up()
  .ele('human')
    .att('type', 'male')
      .txt('some guy')
  .up()
  .ele('alien')
    .txt('complete');
```

2. The use of it is very straightforward; the `doc.begin('root')` statement creates the root of the document and the `ele()` and `att()` statements create an element and attribute accordingly. As we are always adding new parts on the level of nesting where we added the last one, in order to move the cursor on level up, we just call the `up()` function.

    In our case, the document that will be generated is as follows:

    ```
    <root>
      <human type="female">some gal</human>
      <human type="male">some guy</human>
      <alien>complete</alien>
    </root>
    ```

3. To create the route for the resource, we can create `server.get('hi', addHeaders, respond)`, where the `add` headers are the ones for CORS and the response will return the XML document we created as a string:

    ```
    function respond(req, res, next) {
      res.setHeader('content-type', 'application/xml');
      res.send(doc.toString({ pretty: true }));
      return next();
    }
    ```

4. restify does not have a direct support for `application/xml`; if we leave it like this, the server's response will be of type `application/octet-stream`. In order to add support, we will create the `restify` object and add a formatter that will accept XML:

    ```
    var server = restify.createServer({
      formatters: {
        'application/xml': function formatXML(req, res, body) {
          if (body instanceof Error)
            return body.stack;

          if (Buffer.isBuffer(body))
            return body.toString('base64');

          return body;
        }
      }
    });
    ```

    The server should be returning correct `content-type` and CORS headers together with the response data:

    ```
    < HTTP/1.1 200 OK
    < Access-Control-Allow-Origin: *
    < Access-Control-Allow-Headers: X-Requested-With
    ```

```
< content-type: application/xml

< Date: Sat, 02 Feb 2013 13:08:20 GMT

< Connection: keep-alive

< Transfer-Encoding: chunked
```

5. As we have the server ready, we can proceed with the client side by creating a basic HTML file in which we will include jQuery and a simple script:

```
Hello <div id="humans"></div>
<hr/>
<script src="http://ajax.googleapis.com/ajax/libs/jquery/1.8.2/
jquery.min.js">
</script>
<script src="exampleJQuery.js"></script>
```

6. For simplicity, we use `jQuery.ajax()`, where the value of `dataType` will be `xml`:

```
     (function(){
  $.ajax({
    type: "GET",
    url: "http://localhost:8080/hi",
    dataType: "xml",
    success: function(xml) {
      $("root > human", xml).each(function(){
        var p = $("<p></p>");
        $(p).text($(this).text()).appendTo("#humans");
      });
    }
  });
}())
```

How it works...

While most of the example code should be straightforward, the first thing you might be wondering is what is `application/octet-stream`? Well, it is an internet media type of a generic binary data stream. If we were to open the resource with a browser, it will ask us where to save it or with what application it should be opened.

The `formatter` we added in the `restify` implementation accepts a function with the request, response, and the body. It is the `body` object that is of most interest to us; we check if it is an instance of `Error` in order to somehow handle it. The other check that needs to be done is if the `body` is an instance of `Buffer`. JavaScript does not play very well with binary data, so a `Buffer` object was created to store raw data. In our case, we just return the body, as we already have constructed the XML. If we do a lot of processing like this, it might make sense to add formatting for JavaScript objects directly rather manually creating a string with XML data.

On the client side, we used `jQuery.ajax()` to get the XML, and when that happens, the `success` callback does not just receive text, but also accepts a DOM element that we can traverse using standard jQuery selectors. In our case, with `"root> human"`, we select all the `human` elements, and for the text inside, each of them appends a paragraph to `"#humans"`, just like working with HTML:

```
$("root > human", xml).each(function(){
    var p = $("<p></p>");
    $(p).text($(this).text()).appendTo("#humans");
});
```

There's more...

JXON (`https://developer.mozilla.org/en-US/docs/JXON`) is one good alternative when we have to support XML. Without standardization, it follows a simple convention to transform XML to JSON. Another good option for working with XML is to use XPath—the XML Path Language (`http://www.w3.org/TR/xpath/`), a query language that can be used to retrieve values from certain nodes or to select them for other manipulation. XPath is the simplest option in most of the use cases and as such, it should often be our first option.

Older versions of jQuery (before Version 1.1.2) had support of XPath out of the box but was later removed as the standard selectors are lot more powerful when doing HTML transformations.

ECMAScript for XML or commonly known as E4X is a programming language extension to enable native support for XML. Although it has several implementations available in the newest version of Firefox, it's getting removed.

Using the FormData interface

One of the new features added to `XMLHttpRequest` Level 2 (`http://www.w3.org/TR/XMLHttpRequest2/`) is the `FormData` object. This enables us to use a set of key-value pairs that can be sent using AJAX. The most common use is in sending binary files or any other large amount of data. In this recipe, we will create two scripts that will send `FormData`, one with a plain JavaScript and the other with jQuery, as well as the server-side code to support it.

Getting ready

The server will be done in Nodejs using restify (`http://mcavage.github.io/node-restify/`). In order to install the dependencies, a `package.json` file can be created where restify will be added.

How to do it...

1. The server should be able to accept `HTTP POST` with type `multipart/form-data;` that is why there is a built-in plugin for `restify` called `BodyParser`. This will block the parsing of the HTTP request body:

```
var server = restify.createServer();
server.use(restify.bodyParser({ mapParams: false }));
server.post('hi', addHeaders, doPost);
```

2. This switches the content type, and depending on it, does the appropriate logic for `application/json`, `application/x-ww-form-urlencoded`, and `mutipart/form-data`. The `addHeaders` parameter will be the same as we added in the other examples that enables CORS. For simplicity in our `doPost` handler, we just log the request body and return HTTP 200:

```
function doPost(req, res, next) {
  console.log("Got HTTP " + req.method + " on " + req.url + "
responding");
  console.log(req.body);
  res.send(200);
  return next();
}
```

3. For the client side, we create an HTML file that will have a simple script:

```
(function () {
var myForm = new FormData();
myForm.append("username", "johndoe");
myForm.append("books", 7);
var xhr = new XMLHttpRequest();
xhr.open("POST", "http://localhost:8080/hi");
xhr.send(myForm);
  }());
```

4. The jQuery way is a lot simpler; we can set `FormData` as part of the `data` attribute in `jQuery.ajax()` where additionally we need to disable data processing before we send and leave the original content type:

```
(function() {
  var formData = new FormData();
  formData.append("text", "some strange data");
  $.ajax({
    url: "http://localhost:8080/hi",
    type: "POST",
    data: formData,
    processData: false,  // don't process data
    contentType: false   // don't set contentType
  });
}());
```

How it works...

The transmitted data will have the same format as it would if we submitted a form that has the `multipart/form-data` encoding type. The need for this type of encoding comes from sending mixed data together with files. This encoding is supported by most of the web browsers and web servers. The encoding can be used for forms that are not HTML or even part of the browser.

If we take a look at request being sent, we can see that it has the following data:

```
Content-Length:239
Content-Type:multipart/form-data; boundary=----WebKitFormBoundaryQXGz
NXa82frwui6S
```

The payload will be as follows:

```
------WebKitFormBoundaryQXGzNXa82frwui6S
Content-Disposition: form-data; name="username"
johndoe
------WebKitFormBoundaryQXGzNXa82frwui6S
Content-Disposition: form-data; name="books"
7
------WebKitFormBoundaryQXGzNXa82frwui6S--
```

You may notice that each of these parts contain a `Content-Disposition` section with the name of the control that is an origin of the data or, in our case, the key we set in every append to the `FormData` object. There is also an option to set the content type on each individual part, for example, if we had an image from some control named `profileImage` then that part can be as follows:

```
Content-Disposition: form-data; name="profileImage"; filename="me.png"
Content-Type: image/png
```

The last call to `xhr.sent()` in `example.js` sets the content type automatically when we are sending an object of type `FormData`.

And if we need to support older legacy browsers that don't have `XMLHttpRequest` level 2, we can check if `FormData` is there and handle that case accordingly:

```
if (typeof FormData === "undefined")
```

The method we use as a fallback cannot be an AJAX call, but this should not be a problem as all the modern browsers IE<10 version don't have support for it.

Posting a binary file to the server

Posting text, XML, or JSON to the server is relatively easy, and most JavaScript libraries are optimized for that scenario.

Posting binary data is slightly trickier. Modern applications may need to be able to upload the generated binary files; examples include images drawn on an HTML5 canvas, ZIP files created with JSZip, and so on.

Additionally, it's convenient to be able to upload files selected using the HTML5 file API. We can do some interesting things with it, such as resumable file uploads by splitting the file into smaller parts and uploading every part separately to the server.

In this recipe, we're going to upload files selected by the user using a file input.

Getting ready

The server will be implemented using Node.js—you can download and install Node.js from `http://nodejs.org/`. The server will be implemented with the Node.js framework **Connect** (`http://www.senchalabs.org/connect/`).

How to do it...

Let's write the client and server code.

1. Create a file named `index.html`—the file upload page that includes a file input, upload button, a progress bar, and a message container:

```
<!DOCTYPE HTML>
<html>
<head>
<title>Upload binary file</title>
<style type="text/css">
.progress {
    position:relative;
    height:1em; width: 12em;
    border: solid 1px #aaa;
}
.progress div {
    position: absolute;
    top:0; bottom:0; left:0;
    background-color:#336699;
}
</style>
</head>
```

```
<body>
<input type="file"   id="file" value="Choose file">
<input type="button" id="upload" value="Upload"><br>
<p id="info"></p>
<div class="progress"><div id="progress"></div></div>
<script src="http://ajax.googleapis.com/ajax/libs/jquery/1.8.2/
jquery.min.js"></script>
<script type="text/javascript" src="uploader.js"></script>
<script type="text/javascript" src="example.js"></script>
</body>
</html>
```

2. Create a file named `uploader.js` that implements a binary file uploader. It posts the file to a specified URL and returns an object that enables the binding of progress events:

```
window.postBinary = function(url, data) {
    var self = {},
        xhr = new XMLHttpRequest();
    xhr.open('POST', url, true);
    xhr.responseType = 'text';
    self.done = function(cb) {
        xhr.addEventListener('load', function() {
            if (this.status == 200)
                cb(null, this.response)
            else
                cb(this.status, this.response)
        });
        return self;
    }
    self.progress = function(cb) {
        xhr.upload.addEventListener('progress', function(e) {
            if (e.lengthComputable)
                cb(null, e.loaded / e.total);
            else
                cb('Progress not available');
        });
        return progress;
    };
    xhr.send(data);
    return self;
};
```

3. Create a file named `example.js` that uses the API provided by `uploader.js` to add the upload functionality to the upload form:

```
$(function() {
    var file;
    $("#file").on('change', function(e) {
        file = this.files[0]
    });
    $("#upload").on('click', function() {
        $("#info").text("Uploading...");
        $("#progress").css({width:0});
        if (!file) {
            $("#info").text('No file selected')
            return;
        }
        var upload =  postBinary('/upload/' + file.name, file);
        upload.progress(function(err, percent) {
            if (err) {
                $("#info").text(err);
                return;
            }
            $("#progress").css({width: percent + '%'});
        });
        upload.done(function(err, res) {
            if (err) {
                $("#info").text(err + ' ' + res);
                return;
            }
            $("#progress").css({width: '100%'});
            $("#info").text("Upload complete");
        });

    });
});
```

4. Create a file named `server.js`—a Node.js server based on the Node.js Connect framework that handles the file uploads and serves the static files:

```
var path = require('path'),
    connect = require('connect'),
    fs = require('fs');

connect()
    .use('/upload', function(req, res) {
        var file = fs.createWriteStream(
            path.join(__dirname, 'uploads', req.url))
```

```
            req.pipe(file);
            req.on('end', function() {
                res.end("ok");
            });
        })
        .use(connect.static(__dirname))
        .listen(8080);
```

5. Open a command prompt from the directory where `server.js` is located and type the following commands to create a directory for the uploads, install the connect library, and start the server:

    mkdir uploads

    npm install connect

    node server.js

6. Navigate your browser to `http://localhost:8080` to test the example. All the created files (including `server.js`) should be in the same directory.

How it works...

The new `XMLHttpRequest` object in HTML5 has a `send` method that supports more types of data. It can accept `File`, `Blob`, and `ArrayBuffer` objects. We use this new functionality together with the HTML5 File API to upload the file selected by the user. You can find out more about this API in the *Using file inputs on the client side* recipe of *Chapter 4, Using HTML5 Input Components*.

The new API also provides an `upload` object, which is of type `XMLHttpRequestUpload`. It allows us to attach event listeners to monitor the upload progress. We use this functionality to show a progress bar for the upload.

The server accepts the uploads at `'/upload'` and saves the files to the `uploads` directory. Additionally, it serves the static files in the example directory.

There's more...

The new XHR API is only available in Internet Explorer 10 and up.

Some browsers may fail to fire upload progress events.

Creating an SSL connection with Node.js

Common security problems are so-called man-in-the-middle attacks, a form of eavesdropping in which the attacker makes independent connections to the victim and forwards the messages to the desired locations. The attacker must be able to intercept messages and change them on his own. This is only possible if the attacker can successfully impersonate the two involved parties. **Secure Socket Layer** (**SSL**) and it's successor **Transport Layer Security** (**TSL**) prevent these type of attacks by encrypting the data. In this recipe, we create a Node.js server using restify that has support for HTTPS.

Getting ready

We will use a certificate and a server private key in order to enable HTTPS. To generate this, we need OpenSSL (http://www.openssl.org/), a fully featured open source toolkit implementing SSL and TLS, as well as a general purpose cryptography library.

First, on the command line, generate an RSA (http://en.wikipedia.org/wiki/RSA_(algorithm)) private key:

```
openssl genrsa -out privatekey.pem 1024
```

```
[mmitresk@fs1 tmp]$ openssl genrsa -out privatekey.pem 1024
Generating RSA private key, 1024 bit long modulus
.........................................++++++
.....................++++++
e is 65537 (0x10001)
```

The actual key that will get generated should be something like the following:

```
[mmitresk@fs1 tmp]$ cat privatekey.pem
-----BEGIN RSA PRIVATE KEY-----
MIICXQIBAAKBgQDi2blbrjZO5G824CCA+LBx4Lto5KxOBdDsQa1FtBBvulx7c8iQ
qwu4t8VRrW5ZjFQlNDZCn8Gfi/A1jdMAmkp+7p78Dz/RhiqokmtvcUoSELbJGmWa
Ay+GydXwDEQlNv3Cr/3O8fR+BdKm+68oPFgRqqFFLk/OUMjmOB6tmQVTtwIDAQAB
AoGAUeoOzbVFtQO1v5oFAq1KgYSGB+Vy9qWRAI7is6XGvaGM3aM8jEjHbccmQEOg
6MMMa3bEFSC8+RC+B4iT5cbRGQCgYzRQWpAszO+ZBEXruzLga8j9NZwLl2G7Ijgc
8XLy4ujFg3vozUDXCIrgldVaMaTDxsVljR/DbL9vEsBSsvECQQD0qVKWjUyDBhVu
g9buDRhq57H/CL68VfxdhuVSZ56PEiHHHwn/4IR3bcn2PUHUmIz3TbuwC0c79GVf
IzZiAOe/AkEA7VOXbOkuvFZUrLZNEik+EtroJJnfXPK1c8c3QnnXWJdDXLku1/CA
f+fymn1C/ovJOKM8XOsRFDJdbkOrY75SCQJASQ36NCwy6Xi6k4pYdjKA1QMkGiQR
WAlQ1th9xzJbnRrr7RoukTIIO+UThixaaNG4XevfHDzx40whrNvF1FOy3wJBAMJ7
MNNip5FW5t/wKmvD8QE/7U736GRe1L99LdDAxennXiEd9bymaJLkOAnOslKftIbH
CJNHjUHQFm9muTNrYAkCQQCyQeSS34PcfS8znDtfX3gdqRxceOBawE36Cv/Q49nR
I2KGMT710eNx3RdbKlN2etH7SpQQlMtb3lWNvmWETHvX
-----END RSA PRIVATE KEY-----
```

The one you generated should be substantially longer.

> Note that the private key is called *private* for a reason, you should not have it in any version control system or have it accessible for everyone. This should be kept safe, as it is your real identification.

Next we will create a **Certificate Signing Request** (**CSR**) file using the private key that we just created with some additional information that will be prompted to enter:

```
openssl req -new -key privatekey.pem -out csr.pem
```

After filling out the form, we get a CSR file generated, which is intended for asking a Certificate Authority to sign your certificate. This file could be sent to them for processing and they would give us a certificate. As we are only creating a simple example, we will self-sign the file using our private key:

```
openssl x509 -req -in csr.pem -signkey privatekey.pem -out publiccert.pem
```

The `publiccert.pem` file is the one that we will use as a certificate in our server.

How to do it...

1. First we add the dependencies, and then we create an `options` object where we read out the key and the certificate that we generated:

```
var restify = require('restify');
var fs = require('fs');
// create option for the https server instance
var httpsOptions = {
  key: fs.readFileSync('privatekey.pem'),//private key
  certificate: fs.readFileSync('publiccert.pem')//certificate
};
```

> File IO in Node.js is provided using the `fs` module. This is a wrapper to the standard POSIX functionality. The documentation on it can be found at `http://nodejs.org/api/fs.html`.

2. We continue with the creation of the routes and handlers, and in order not to duplicate the logic for the two server instances, we create a common `serverCreate` function:

```
var serverCreate = function(app) {
  function doHi(req, res, next) {
    var name = 'nobody';
    if(req.params.name) {
      name = req.params.name;
    }
```

```
      res.send('Hi ' + name);
      return next();
    }
    app.get('/hi/', doHi);
    app.get('/hi/:name', doHi);
  }
```

3. Then we can use this function to create instances of the two servers:

```
serverCreate(server);
serverCreate(httpsServer);
```

4. We can set the standard server to listen to port `80` and the HTTPS version to port `443`:

```
server.listen(80, function() {
  console.log('started at %s', server.url);
});

httpsServer.listen(443, function() {
  console.log('started at %s', httpsServer.url);
});
```

5. Now we can call `node server.js` to start the servers and try to access the following pages from the browser:

    ❑ `http://localhost:80/hi/John`

    ❑ `http://localhost:443/hi/UncleSam`

How it works...

The first thing you might encounter when running the server is an error similar to the following:

```
Error: listen EACCES
    at errnoException (net.js:770:11)
    at Server._listen2 (net.js:893:19)
```

The problem here is that the server itself cannot bind to a port smaller than 1024 unless it has root or administrative privileges(as commonly known).

The HTTPS server we just created uses public key cryptography. Each peer has two keys: one public and one private.

> In cryptography, commonly the involved parties are called Alice and Bob, so we will use the same names. More on the topic can be found on Wikipedia at `http://en.wikipedia.org/wiki/Alice_and_Bob`.

Alice and Bob's public keys are shared with everyone, and their private keys are kept secret. In order for Alice to encrypt a message that she needs to sent to Bob, she needs Bob's public key and her private key. On the other hand, if Bob needs to decrypt the same message that he received from Alice, he needs her public key and his private key.

In TLS connections, the public key is the certificate. This is because it is signed to prove that the real owner is the person they are claiming to be; for example Bob. TSL certificates can be signed by a Certificate Authority that actuality confirms that Bob is who it claims to be. Firefox, Chrome, and other browsers have a list of root CA's that are trusted for issuing a certificate. This root CA may issue certificates to other signing authorities that sell them to the general public; very interesting business don't you think?

In our case, we self-signed our certificate so it is not trusted by the browsers, when we open it, we get the following lovely little page:

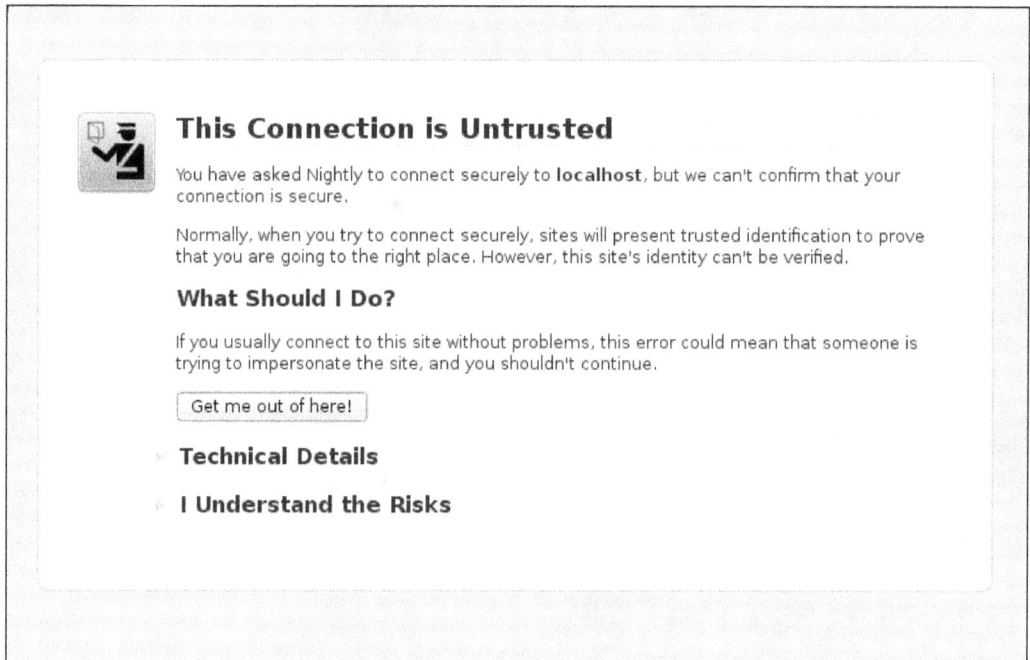

This Connection is Untrusted

You have asked Nightly to connect securely to **localhost**, but we can't confirm that your connection is secure.

Normally, when you try to connect securely, sites will present trusted identification to prove that you are going to the right place. However, this site's identity can't be verified.

What Should I Do?

If you usually connect to this site without problems, this error could mean that someone is trying to impersonate the site, and you shouldn't continue.

[Get me out of here!]

› **Technical Details**

› **I Understand the Risks**

This message will not appear when we use a CA-signed certificate, as we would have an authority recognized by our browser as a trusted one.

There's more...

Open Web Application Security Project, or OWASP (`https://www.owasp.org/`), has a comprehensive database of procedures of common security problems and pitfalls when creating web application. There you can find a great cheat sheet for security about HTML5 applications (`https://www.owasp.org/index.php/HTML5_Security_Cheat_Sheet`). When it comes to HTTPS, one common problem is having mixed content that does not always come from same protocol. One simple way to increase security is to have every request sent over TLS/SSL.

Making real-time updates with Ajax Push

Comet is a web model in which a long-held HTTP request allows the server to "push" data from the server to the browser without the need for the browser to make a request explicitly. Comet is known in many different names, Ajax Push, Server Push, Reverse Ajax two-way-web, and so on. In this recipe, we are going to create a simple server that sends or "pushes" its current time to client.

Getting ready

For this example, we will use Node.js and a library called **Socket.IO** (`http://socket.io/`). The dependency can be included in the `package.json` file or directly installed from npm.

How to do it...

Let's get started.

1. First, we will start with the server side, where we will add the needed `require` statements for Socket.IO, HTTP, and filesystem:

```
var app = require('http').createServer(requestHandler),
    io = require('socket.io').listen(app),
    fs = require('fs')
```

2. The server is initialized with `requestHandler`, where we will just serve an `index.html` file placed in the same directory that we will create a bit later:

```
function requestHandler (req, res) {
  fs.readFile('index.html',
    function (err, data) {
      if (err) {
        res.writeHead(500);
        return res.end('Error loading index.html');
      }
    res.writeHead(200);
```

```
    res.end(data);
    });
}
```

3. If the file cannot be read, it returns HTTP 500, and if everything is fine, it just returns the data, a very simplified handler. We set the server to listen on port 80 with `app.listen(80)` and afterwards we can continue with the Socket.IO-related configuration:

```
io.configure(function () {
  io.set("transports", ["xhr-polling"]);
  io.set("polling duration", 10);
});
```

Here we set the only allowed transport to be `xhr-polling` for the purpose of the example. Socket.IO has support for multiple different ways of sending server-side events to the client, so we disabled everything else.

> Note that in a real-life application, you probably will want to leave the other transport methods as they might be a better option for the given client or act as a fallback mechanism.

4. Afterwards, we can continue with the events. On every connection we get, we emit a `ping` event with some JSON data towards the client the first time, and on every received `pong` event, we wait for 15 seconds and then again send some JSON data with the current server time:

```
io.sockets.on('connection', function (socket) {
  socket.emit('ping', {
    timeIs: new Date()
  });
  socket.on('pong', function (data) {
    setTimeout(function(){
    socket.emit('ping', {
      timeIs: new Date()
    });
    console.log(data);
    }, 15000);
  });
});
```

5. Now on the client side, we will include the `socket.io.js` file, and as we are serving our `index.html` file from node, it will be added with the following default path:

```
<script src="/socket.io/socket.io.js"></script>
```

6. After that, we connect to `localhost` and wait for a `ping` event, and on every such event, we append a `p` element with the server time. We then emit a `pong` event to the server:

```
<script>
  var socket = io.connect('http://localhost');
  socket.on('ping', function (data) {
    var p = document.createElement("p");
    p.textContent = 'Server time is ' + data.timeIs;
    document.body.appendChild(p);
    socket.emit('pong', {
      my: 'clientData'
    });
  });
</script>
```

Now when we start the server and access `index.html` by opening `http://localhost`, we should be getting server updates without explicitly asking for them:

```
Server time is 2013-02-05T06:14:33.052Z
```

How it works...

If we don't set the only transport method to be Ajax pooling or xhr-polling, Socket.IO will attempt to use the best method available. Currently, there are several transports supported: WebSocket, Adobe Flash Socket, AJAX long polling, AJAX multipart streaming, Forever IFrame, and JSONP Polling.

Depending on the browser used, different methods might be better, worse, or not available, but it's safe to say that WebSockets are the future. Long polling is easier to implement on the browser side and works with every browser that supports `XMLHttpRequest`.

As the name suggests, long polling works with the client requesting the server for an event. This request is left open until the server has sent some new data to the browser or has closed the connection.

If we open up a console in our example, we can see that a request is done towards the server, but it is not closed as the response is not finished:

hOC6eXNTrdlhwO9aHcqX?t=1360049439710	GET	(pending)
/socket.io/1/xhr-polling		

As we configured the server-pulling duration to 10 seconds with `io.set("polling duration", 10)`, this connection will be closed and another is reopened. The first thing you might be wondering is why do we ever need to close the connections? Well, if we don't, the resources on the server will easy get depleted.

You may notice the closing and sending of the data in the server console:

```
    debug - xhr-polling received data packet 5:::{"name":"pong","args":
[{"my":"clientData"}]}
    debug - setting request GET /socket.io/1/xhr-polling/5jBJdDQ6Uc2ZYX
zZHcqd?t=1360050667340
    debug - setting poll timeout
    debug - discarding transport
```

One additional thing to note is that as soon as the connection is closed, either due to a response received or due to a timeout on the server side, a new one is created. The newly created request usually has a connection for the server waiting for it, resulting in a significant reduction of latency.

There's more...

Socket.IO has plenty of other features that we did not cover. One of them is the broadcasting of messages to all the connected clients. For example, to let everyone know that a new user connected, we can do the following:

```
    io.sockets.on('connection', function (soc) {
    soc.broadcast.emit('user connected');
    });
```

Even if we don't use Node.js, the comet technologies or "hacks" are available in most of the programming languages, and are a great way to improve the user experience.

Exchanging real-time messages using WebSockets

Before HTML5 Web Sockets, web applications that needed to implement real-time updates, such as chat messages and game moves, had to resort to inefficient methods.

The most popular method was to use long polling, where a connection to the server is kept open until an event arrives. Another popular method was streaming chunked blocks of JavaScript to an `iframe` element, also known as **comet streaming**.

HTML5 WebSockets enable the exchange of real-time messages with the web server. The API is much cleaner and easier to use, less error-prone, and provides lower message latency.

In this recipe, we're going to implement a simple chat system based on WebSockets. To make the system easier to extend, we're going to use dnode on top of the underlying WebSockets. The dnode library provides full callback-based RPC for multiple languages and platforms: Node.js, Ruby, Java, and Perl. Essentially, it enables us to call server-side code as if it were executing on the client side.

Getting ready

The server will be implemented using Node.js—you can download and install Node.js from `http://nodejs.org/`.

To prepare yourself, you will also need to install some node modules. Create a new directory for the recipe and type in the following commands to install node modules:

```
npm install -g browserify
npm install express shoe dnode
```

How to do it...

Let's write the client and the server.

1. Create the main chat page containing a list of messages, a list of users, and a text input box in `index.html`. The chat page is styled to fill the whole browser viewport.

```html
<!DOCTYPE HTML>
<html>
<head>
<title>Using websockets</title>
<style type="text/css">
#chat { position: absolute; overflow: auto;
    top:0; left:0; bottom:2em; right:12em; }
#users { position: absolute; overflow: auto;
    top:0; right: 0; width:12em; bottom: 0; }
#input { position: absolute; overflow: auto;
    bottom:0; height:2em; left: 0; right: 12em; }

#chat .name { padding-right:1em; font-weight:bold; }
#chat .msg { padding: 0.33em; }
</style>
</head>
<body>
<div id="chat">
</div>
<div id="users">
</div>
<input type="text" id="input">
<script src="http://ajax.googleapis.com/ajax/libs/jquery/1.8.2/
jquery.min.js"></script>
<script type="text/javascript" src="example.min.js"></script>
</body>
</html>
```

2. Create a file named chat.js—a chat room implementation in JavaScript. The chat() function creates a chat room and returns the public API of the chatroom, consisting of the join, leave, msg, ping, and listen functions.

```
function keysOf(obj) {
    var k = [];
    for (var key in obj)
        if (obj.hasOwnProperty(key))
            k.push(key);
    return k;
}
function chat() {
    var self = {},
        users = {},
        messages = [];


    // Identify the user by comparing the data provided
    // for identification with the data stored server-side
    function identify(user) {
        return users[user.name] && user.token
            == users[user.name].token;
    }
    // Send an event to all connected chat users that
    // are listening for events
    function emit(event) {
        console.log(event);
        for (var key in users) if (users.hasOwnProperty(key))
            if (users[key].send) users[key].send(event);
    }
    // This function resets the timeout countdown for a
    // specified user. The countdown is reset on every user
    // action and every time the browser sends a ping
    // If the countdown expires, the user is considered
    // to have closed the browser window and no longer present
    function resetTimeout(user) {
        if (user.timeout) {
            clearTimeout(user.timeout);
            user.timeout = null;
        }
        user.timeout = setTimeout(function() {
            self.leave(user, function() {});
        }, 60000);
    }

    // When a user attempts to join, he must reserve a
```

```
// unique name. If this succeeds, he is given an auth
// token along with the name. Only actions performed
// using this token will be accepted as coming from
// the user. After the user joins a list of users and
// past messages are sent to him along with the
// authentication information.
self.join = function(name, cb) {
    if (users[name]) return cb(name + " is in use");
    users[name] = {
        name: name,
        token: Math.round(Math.random() * Math.pow(2, 30))
    }
    resetTimeout(users[name]);
    emit({type: 'join', name: name});
    cb(null, { you: users[name], messages: messages,
        users: keysOf(users) });
}
// The leave function is called when the user leaves
// after closing the browser window.
self.leave = function(user, cb) {
    if (!identify(user)) return
    clearTimeout(users[user.name].timeout);
    delete users[user.name];
    emit({type: 'leave', name: user.name});
    cb(null);
}
// The message function allows the user to send a
// message. The message is saved with a timestamp
// then sent to all users as an event.
self.msg = function(user, text) {
    if (!identify(user)) return;
    resetTimeout(users[user.name]);
    var msg = {
        type: 'msg',
        name: user.name,
        text: text,
        time: Date.now()
    }
    messages.push(msg);
    emit(msg);
}
// The ping function allows the browser to reset
// the timeout. It lets the server know that the
// user hasn't closed the chat yet.
```

```
        self.ping = function(user) {
            if (identify(user))
                resetTimeout(users[user.name]);
        }
        // The listen function allows the user to provide
        // a callback function to be called for every event.
        // This way the server can call client-side code.
        self.listen = function(user, send, cb) {
            if (!identify(user)) return
            users[user.name].send = send;
        }
        return self;
    };
    module.exports = chat;
```

3. Let's create the Node.js script named `server.js`, implementing the web server:

```
var express = require('express'),
    http    = require('http'),
    chat    = require('./chat.js'),
    shoe    = require('shoe'),
    dnode   = require('dnode')
// Create an express app
var app = express();
// that serves the static files in this directory
app.use('/', express.static(__dirname));
// then create a web server with this app
var server = http.createServer(app);
// Create a chat room instance,
var room = chat();
// then create a websocket stream that
// provides the chat room API via dnode
// and install that stream on the http server
// at the address /chat
shoe(function (stream) {
    var d = dnode(room);
    d.pipe(stream).pipe(d);
}).install(server, '/chat');
// start the server
server.listen(8080);
```

4. Create a file named `example.js` to implement the chat client:

```
var shoe = require('shoe'),
    dnode = require('dnode');

$(function() {

    // Add a message to the message div
    function addMsg(msg) {
        var dMsg = $("<div />").addClass('msg'),
            dName = $("<span />").addClass('name')
                .text(msg.name).appendTo(dMsg),
            dText = $("<span />").addClass('text')
                .text(msg.text).appendTo(dMsg);
        dMsg.appendTo("#chat");
        $("#chat").scrollTop($("#chat")[0].scrollHeight);
    }

    // Re-display a list of the present users.
    function showUsers(users) {
        $("#users").html('');
        users.forEach(function(name) {
            $("<div />").addClass('user')
                .text(name).appendTo('#users');
        });
    }

    // Create a client-side web sockets stream
    // piped to a dnode instance
    var stream = shoe('/chat');
    var d = dnode();
    // When the remote chat API becomes available
    d.on('remote', function (chat) {
        // Attempt to join the room until a suitable
        // nickname that is not already in use is found
        function join(cb, msg) {
            var name = prompt(msg || "Enter a name");
            chat.join(name, function(err, data) {
                if (err) join(cb, err);
                else cb(data);
            });
        }
        join(function(data) {
            var me = data.you,
                users = data.users;
```

```
        // Show the users and messages after joining
        showUsers(users);
        data.messages.forEach(addMsg);
        // Allow the user to send messages
        $("#input").on('keydown', function(e) {
            if (e.keyCode == 13) {
                // sending works by calling the
                // remote's msg function.
                chat.msg(me, $(this).val());
                $(this).val('');
            }

        });
        // Tell the remote we're listening for
        // events
        chat.listen(me, function(e) {
            if (e.type == 'msg')
                return addMsg(e);
            if (e.type == 'leave')
                delete users[users.indexOf(e.name)];
            else if (e.type == 'join')
                users.push(e.name);
            showUsers(users);
        });
        // Tell the remote every 30 seconds that
        // we're still active
        setInterval(function() {
            chat.ping(me);
        }, 30000);

    });
  });
  // pipe dnode messages to the websocket stream
  // and messages from the stream to dnode
  d.pipe(stream).pipe(d);
});
```

5. Use `browserify` to create `example.min.js`:

    browserify example.js --debug -o example.min.js

6. Start the node server:

    node server.js

7. Navigate your browser to `http://localhost:8080` to test the example.

How it works...

We're not using the WebSockets API directly here. The reason for that is, it's not very easy to send responses to messages using the raw WebSockets—they don't support a request-response cycle. Because of that, it would be much harder to implement some of the RPC calls, such as asking the server if the name is available.

On the other hand, the dnode protocol supports passing local callbacks to remote functions, which in turn can pass callbacks of their own to the callbacks received and so on—resulting in a very powerful, full RPC implementation. This allows us to extend our application to meet new demands as they arise. As a bonus, the resulting API is much clearer and more expressive.

Here is what we did to implement a chatroom with dnode:

1. We created a simple object that uses continuation-passing style to return errors and values for all functions. This is our chatroom object and defines the RPC API for our application.

2. We defined a WebSockets server based on the `shoe` library that creates a new Node. js stream for every connected client. Then we installed it to the regular HTTP server at the `/chat` route.

3. We connected the two by piping every connected client stream to a newly created dnode stream based on the chatroom object.

That's all! Then, to use the API on the client, do the following:

1. We defined a WebSockets client based on the `shoe` library that connects to the HTTP server at the `/chat` route and creates a new Node.js stream when the connection is established.

2. We piped that stream to a newly created dnode client.

3. After establishing a connection, the dnode client received an object containing the API defined in step 1—all the functions are available.

> Find out more about dnode at `https://github.com/substack/dnode`.
>
> IE versions up to IE 9 don't support the WebSockets API. As of February 2013, the built-in browser in the latest version of Android (v 4.2) doesn't support the WebSockets API either.

9
Client-side Templates

In this chapter, we will cover the following recipes:

- Rendering objects using Handlebars
- Rendering objects using EJS
- Rendering objects using Jade
- Rendering arrays using Handlebars
- Rendering arrays using EJS
- Rendering arrays using Jade
- Simplifying templates with helpers in Handlebars
- Reusing templates with partials in Handlebars
- Reusing templates with partials in EJS
- Using filters in Jade
- Using mixins in Jade
- Using layouts and blocks in Jade

Introduction

Modern service apps are often built for multiple platforms, where only one of those platforms is the Web. Other platforms may include iOS, Android, and other websites that need to use the service through an API. Some of those platforms might not support HTML. They might also need to show different HTML for the same data or do preprocessing before displaying the data.

As a result, there has been a shift in web apps from using server-side HTML rendering to client-side HTML rendering. The service serves the serialized raw data (most often as JSON, sometimes XML) and the client decides how to display the data.

In this chapter we're going to take a look at several popular client-side template languages, each with a different approach to templating:

- ▶ EJS, which combines HTML with the full power of JavaScript
- ▶ Handlebars, which combines HTML with a succinct but more restricted block structures
- ▶ Jade, which replaces HTML syntax with a cleaner-looking version that has support for dynamic facilities

We're going to learn how to do some common tasks in each, such as displaying basic objects, displaying lists (or looping), and using partial templates.

Rendering objects using Handlebars

Handlebars is a template language that adds minimal syntax to HTML. Its goal is to minimize the amount of logic present in the template and force the passed model object to correspond to what should be rendered in the view.

In this recipe, we will demonstrate some of the advantages and shortcomings of Handlebars using a simple example. We're going to render a user greeting based on the time of the day.

Getting ready

We need to download Handlebars from `https://github.com/wycats/handlebars.js`. The browser version is in the `dist` directory. Create a directory for the example and copy `handlebars.js` to this directory, or download directly (on Linux):

```
wget https://raw.github.com/wycats/handlebars.js/master/dist/
handlebars.js
```

How to do it...

Let's write the code:

1. Create `index.html` containing a `name` input, a `greeting` placeholder, and the Handlebars template:

```
<!DOCTYPE HTML>
<html>
<head>
<title>Displaying objects with Handlebars</title>
</head>
<body>
<form method="post">
    <p>Name: <input id="name" type="text" name="name"
value="John"></p>
```

```
</form>
<div id="greeting">
</div>
<script id="template" type="text/x-handlebars-template">

{{#if evening}}
    Good evening,
{{/if}}
{{#if morning}}
    Good morning,
{{/if}}
{{#if day}}
    Hello,
{{/if}}
<b>{{name}}</b>

</script>
<script src="http://ajax.googleapis.com/ajax/libs/jquery/1.8.2/
jquery.min.js"></script>
<script type="text/javascript" src="handlebars.js"></script>
<script type="text/javascript" src="example.js"></script>
</body>
</html>
```

2. Create `example.js` to bind the template to the data and the view:

```
$(function() {
    var template = Handlebars.compile($('#template').html());
    function changeName() {
        var hour = new Date().getHours();
        $('#greeting').html(template({
            name: $("#name").val(),
            evening: hour > 18,
            morning: hour < 10,
            day: hour >= 10 && hour <= 18
        }));
    }
    $('#name').on('keypress keyup', changeName);
    changeName();
});
```

How it works...

We usually embed Handlebars templates inside an HTML page by adding them to a `script` element with a `type` attribute set to `text/x-handlebars-template`. The browser ignores scripts with unknown types, so we can be sure that the content is left intact.

Using the template is done in two phases. In the first phase, we need to compile the template text. This process results with a compiled template in the form of a JavaScript function being returned. In the second phase, we pass a model object as a parameter to that function (the compiled template) and get the HTML output.

Handlebars is a very opinionated and minimal templating language. The use of program logic, such as comparison operators inside the template is strictly forbidden. This is by design, and it is a good idea, if the business logic changes we don't need to update the template. For example, if we start considering the period from midnight to 2 a.m. as evening, we don't need to change the template – we only need to add the condition when creating the model, which we pass to Handlebars.

On the other hand, we can see that Handlebars sometimes goes a bit too far with its restrictions. For example, it doesn't support a case structure, enumerations or constructs such as `'else if'`. As a result, we must either resort to Boolean expressions for every possible state or keep the actual text or value inside the model. In some of those cases the model may interfere with information that belongs to the view.

Rendering objects using EJS

EJS is a template language that allows users to mix HTML and JavaScript inside the template. Similar to PHP and ERB, it works by adding extra tags to HTML which allow the user to "escape" from HTML to the programming language and use the full facilities of that language.

In this recipe, we're going to demonstrate EJS using a simple example. We're going to render a user greeting based on the time of the day.

Getting ready

We need to download EJS from `http://embeddedjs.com/` and extract `ejs_production.js` in our `recipe` folder.

How to do it...

Let's get started.

1. Create `index.html` containing a `name` input, a `greeting` placeholder, and an EJS `template`:

```html
<!DOCTYPE HTML>
<html>
<head>
<title>Displaying an EJS object</title>
</head>
<body>
<form method="post">
    <p>Name: <input id="name" type="text" name="name"
value="John"></p>
</form>
<div id="greeting">
</div>
<script id="template" type="text/ejs">
    <% if (hour > 18) { %>
        Good evening,
    <% } else if (hour < 10) { %>
        Good morning,
    <% } else { %>
        Hello,
    <% } %>
    <b><%= name %></b>
</script>
<script src="http://ajax.googleapis.com/ajax/libs/jquery/1.8.2/
jquery.min.js"></script>
<script type="text/javascript" src="ejs_production.js"></script>
<script type="text/javascript" src="example.js"></script>
</body>
</html>
```

2. Create `example.js` to bind the template to the data and the view:

```javascript
$(function() {
    var template = new EJS({
        text: $('#template').html()
    });
    function changeName() {
        $('#greeting').html(template.render({
            name: $("#name").val(),
            hour: new Date().getHours()
```

```
        }));
    }
    $('#name').on('keypress keyup', changeName);
    changeName();
});
```

How it works...

The common way to embed EJS templates inside the page is to add them inside a `script` element with a `type` attribute set to `text/ejs`. The browser ignores scripts with unknown types, so we can be sure that the content is left intact.

In-between the EJS opening and closing tags, `<% %>`, we can write any arbitrary JavaScript, which will be executed when rendering the template. The rest of the template is plain HTML. This makes EJS very easy to use.

When we want to print the value of a JavaScript expression, we use a different opening tag, `<%=`, which prints the expression value as plain text, escaping any HTML contained.

To use the template, we create a new EJS object. This calls the EJS compiler, which compiles the template into a more efficient form. Then we can call the `render` method of this object, passing it the variables (data model) to use when rendering the template.

There's more...

To print the value of an HTML expression without escaping we can use the `<%-` tag instead of the `<%=` tag. This enables us to insert the HTML code as DOM nodes (as against treating them as plain text).

Rendering objects using Jade

Jade is a clean, terse template language. It uses significant whitespace to denote block and element hierarchy. It supports many advanced features, for example, mixins, which are subtemplates and blocks, which are template sections replaceable by inheritance.

In this recipe, we're going to render a simple greeting using Jade. Later on in this chapter, we're going to look at some of the more advanced features.

Getting ready

We need to download `jade.min.js` in our `recipe` folder, available at `https://github.com/visionmedia/jade`.

How to do it...

Let's get started.

1. Create `index.html`, it will contain a small form asking the user for his or her name, a placeholder to render the greeting, and the greeting template:

```
<!DOCTYPE HTML>
<html>
<head>
<title>Displaying an object with Jade </title>
</head>
<body>
<form method="post">
    <p>Name: <input id="name" type="text" name="name"
value="John"></p>
</form>
<div id="greeting">
</div>
<script id="template" type="text/jade">

if hour > 18
    span Good evening,
else if hour < 10
    span
        | Good
        | morning,
else
    span Hello,
b= name

</script>
<script src="http://ajax.googleapis.com/ajax/libs/jquery/1.8.2/
jquery.min.js"></script>
<script type="text/javascript" src="jade.min.js"></script>
<script type="text/javascript" src="example.js"></script>
</body>
</html>
```

2. Create `example.js` to compile the template and bind it to the data and the view:

```
$(function() {
    var template = jade.compile(
        $('#template').html()
    );
    function changeName() {
```

```
            $('#greeting').html(template({
                name: $("#name").val(),
                hour: new Date().getHours()
            }));
        }
        $('#name').on('keypress keyup', changeName);
        changeName();
    });
```

How it works...

Jade templates are very similar to the resulting HTML structure. Our template produces a single span element containing the greeting text, and another b (bold) element containing the name of the user.

Jade supports conditionals. Their syntax looks exactly similar to the element syntax, except that they're not rendered. The condition doesn't need to be wrapped in parenthesis, but otherwise the Boolean expression is evaluated as the JavaScript code.

As shown in the "Good Morning" greeting, we can use the vertical pipe character to split the text into multiple lines

To display the contents of a variable (escaping HTML markup), we use the "=" (equals) character. If we don't want the content to be filtered we can use the character "-" (minus).

To use a Jade template, we compile it using jade.compile. This results with a template function. If we pass an object to this function, we're going to get a rendered HTML as the result. We display the HTML inside the #greeting element.

Rendering arrays using Handlebars

Displaying a list of objects is the most common reason we need a separate template language, otherwise we could easily get by with direct DOM manipulation. Handlebars has an easy, clean, and straightforward syntax for array iteration—the each construct, which works very similarly to the for each loops in other languages.

In this recipe, we're going to render a list of message objects. Each message object will have an author, arrival time, body, and read status. We're going to use a different style to distinguish between read and unread messages.

As usual in this chapter, the template will be included in the HTML file inside a script tag. However, the compilation can be called on any string that we choose; it is therefore possible to download the template data by sending a request to the server.

Getting ready

We need to download Handlebars from `https://github.com/wycats/handlebars.js`. The browser version is in the `dist` directory. Create a directory for the example and copy `handlebars.js` to this directory, or download directly (on Linux):

```
wget https://raw.github.com/wycats/handlebars.js/master/dist/
handlebars.js
```

How to do it...

Follow these steps:

1. Create `index.html`, it will contain a header, the Handlebars template, the placeholder to render the message list, and some styles for the list:

```html
<!DOCTYPE HTML>
<html>
<head>
<title>Rendering an array with EJS</title>
<style type="text/css">
.message {
    border-bottom:solid 1px #ccc;
    width: 250px;
    padding: 5px; }
.message p { margin: 0.5em 0; }
.message.unread { font-weight:bold; }
.message .date {
    float: right;
    font-style: italic;
    color: #999; }
</style>
</head>
<body>
<h2>Messages</h2>
<div id="list">
</div>
<script id="template" type="text/x-handlebars-template">

{{#each list}}
    <div class="message {{status}}">
        <p><span class="name">{{name}}</span>
        <span class="date">{{date}}</span></p>
        <p class="text">{{text}}</p>
    </div>
```

```
    {{/each}}

    </script>
    <script src="http://ajax.googleapis.com/ajax/libs/jquery/1.8.2/
    jquery.min.js"></script>
    <script type="text/javascript" src="handlebars.js"></script>
    <script type="text/javascript" src="example.js"></script>
    </body>
    </html>
```

2. Create `example.js` to display an example array in the placeholder element using the `template` variable:

```
$(function() {
    var template = Handlebars.compile($('#template').html());
    $('#list').html(template({list:[
        { status: 'read',   name: 'John', date: 'Today',
            text: 'just got back, how are you doing?' },
        { status: 'unread', name: 'Jenny', date: 'Today',
            text: 'please call me asap' },
        { status: 'read',   name: 'Jack', date: 'Yesterday',
            text: 'where do you want to go today?' },
    ]}));
});
```

How it works...

Handlebars have the `{{#each}}` helper, which iterates through the array passed as its first argument.

Inside the block, every member variable of the array element comes into the current scope and is directly accessible by name. This feature greatly simplifies this template because it avoids the repetition of the variable name inside the loop.

From this example we can see that we're not limited to using the variables inside the elements, we can also use them in the middle of attributes or anywhere else in the HTML.

Rendering arrays using EJS

One of the most common tasks when using a template language is to render a list of items. Since EJS is based on escaping to JavaScript, rendering lists can be done using the loop constructs in the language.

In this recipe, we're going to render a list of message objects. Each message object will have an author, arrival time, body, and read status. We're going to use a different style to distinguish between read and unread messages.

Getting ready

We need to download EJS from `http://embeddedjs.com/` and extract `ejs_production.js` in our `recipe` folder.

How to do it...

Let's get started.

1. Create `index.html`, it will contain a header, the EJS template, the placeholder to render the message list, and some styles for the list:

```html
<!DOCTYPE HTML>
<html>
<head>
<title>Rendering an array with EJS</title>
<style type="text/css">
.message {
    border-bottom:solid 1px #ccc;
    width: 250px;
    padding: 5px; }
.message p { margin: 0.5em 0; }
.message.unread { font-weight:bold; }
.message .date {
    float: right;
    font-style: italic;
    color: #999; }
</style>
</head>
<body>
<h2>Messages</h2>
<div id="list">
</div>
<script id="template" type="text/ejs">
<% for (var k = 0; k < list.length; ++k) {
    var message = list[k];  %>
    <div class="message <%= message.status %>">
        <p><span class="name"><%= message.name %></span>
        <span class="date"><%= message.date %></span></p>
        <p class="text"><%= message.text %></p>
    </div>
<% } %>
</script>
<script src="http://ajax.googleapis.com/ajax/libs/jquery/1.8.2/
jquery.min.js"></script>
```

```
<script type="text/javascript" src="ejs_production.js"></script>
<script type="text/javascript" src="example.js"></script>
</body>
</html>
```

2. Call the `render` function from `example.js` with some text data:

```
$(function() {
    var template = new EJS({
        text: $('#template').html()
    });
    $('#list').html(template.render({list:[
        { status: 'read',   name: 'John', date: 'Today',
            text: 'just got back, how are you doing?' },
        { status: 'unread', name: 'Jenny', date: 'Today',
            text: 'please call me asap' },
        { status: 'read',   name: 'Jack', date: 'Yesterday',
            text: 'where do you want to go today?' },
    ]})));
});
```

How it works...

In the `render` function we pass a model object containing an array of messages to the renderer.

To render the array we use a standard JavaScript `for` loop. We can add any valid JavaScript code between the opening and closing tags. In our example we assign a variable inside the body of the loop, and then use it throughout the template.

From the example it's clear that EJS allows you to escape to JavaScript at any point in the template text. Even escaping in HTML attributes is allowed (we are adding a class to our message that corresponds to the message status, read or unread) by escaping inside the `class` attribute.

There's more...

This example shows that EJS is almost as powerful as JavaScript itself. However, it's not recommended to write any business logic code inside the template. Instead, prepare your model object in a way that makes the template code straightforward to write.

Rendering arrays using Jade

Jade also supports rendering lists of items as other template languages. We can use the `each` construct to iterate through the elements in the array and output some HTML elements for each.

In this recipe, we're going to render a list of message objects. Each message object will have an author, arrival time, body, and read status. We're going to use a different style to distinguish between read and unread messages.

We're also going to use different backgrounds for odd and even rows.

Getting ready

We need to download `jade.min.js` in to our `recipe` folder available at `https://github.com/visionmedia/jade`.

How to do it...

Follow these steps:

1. Create `index.html` containing the CSS style, placeholder, and the template `script` element:

```
<!DOCTYPE HTML>
<html>
<head>
<title>Rendering an array with EJS</title>
<style type="text/css">
.message {
    border-bottom:solid 1px #ccc;
    width: 250px;
    padding: 5px; }
.message p { margin: 0.5em 0; }
.message.unread { font-weight:bold; }
.message.odd { background-color:#f5f5f5; }
.message .date {
    float: right;
    font-style: italic;
    color: #999; }
</style>
</head>
<body>
<h2>Messages</h2>
<div id="list">
```

```
</div>
<script id="template" type="text/jade">

each msg,i in list
  .message(class=msg.status + (i % 2?' odd':' even'))
    p
      span.name=msg.name
      span.date=msg.date
    p.text=msg.text

</script>
<script src="http://ajax.googleapis.com/ajax/libs/jquery/1.8.2/
jquery.min.js"></script>
<script type="text/javascript" src="jade.min.js"></script>
<script type="text/javascript" src="example.js"></script>
</body>
</html>
```

2. Create `example.js` to wrap the element and the template with some model data:

```
$(function() {
    var template = jade.compile($('#template').html());
    $('#list').html(template({list:[
        { status: 'read',   name: 'John', date: 'Today',
            text: 'just got back, how are you doing?' },
        { status: 'unread', name: 'Jenny', date: 'Today',
            text: 'please call me asap' },
        { status: 'read',   name: 'Jack', date: 'Yesterday',
            text: 'where do you want to go today?' },
    ]}));
});
```

How it works...

Besides allowing us to access the array element, the `each` construct in Jade can also provide the index of the element.

Using this index we demonstrate that Jade can support arbitrary expressions. We add an odd class to oddly-numbered messages, and an even class to evenly-numbered ones. Of course, it's better to use CSS pseudo-selectors to do this, for example:

```
.message:nth-child(odd) { ... }
.message:nth-child(even) { ... }
```

Jade allows us to omit the name of the element and only use a class and/or an ID attribute. In these cases the element is assumed to be a `div`.

We can append CSS style classes and an ID after the element tag. Jade will add the corresponding attributes to the element.

There's more...

Instead of concatenating the style classes, we can also pass a variable which contains an array of classes to add to the element.

Simplifying templates with helpers in Handlebars

While writing templates we often have the task of displaying common visual elements, such as alerts, dialogs, and lists. These elements may have a complex internal structure, and writing a template every time to map the model to this structure can be an error-prone and repetitive process.

Handlebars allows us to simplify the writing of templates containing common elements by replacing the template for the common element with a call to helpers.

In this recipe, we're going to write Handlebars helpers to render links, images, and unordered lists. We're going to display a list of people with their name, photo, and link to their profile.

Getting ready

We need to download Handlebars from `https://github.com/wycats/handlebars.js`. The browser version is in the `dist` directory. Create a directory for the example and copy `handlebars.js` to this directory, or download directly (on Linux):

```
wget https://raw.github.com/wycats/handlebars.js/master/dist/
handlebars.js
```

How to do it...

Follow these steps:

1. Create `index.html`, which will contain the list style, list placeholder, and list template. The template will utilize our new helpers:

```
<!DOCTYPE HTML>
<html>
<head>
<title>Helpers in Handlebars</title>
<style type="text/css">
li { padding:1em; }
```

```
li img { vertical-align:middle; }
</style>
</head>
<body>
<div id="list">
</div>
<script id="template" type="text/x-handlebars-template">

{{#ul list}}
    {{img image alt=name}} {{name}}
{{else}}
    No items found
{{/ul}}

</script>
<script src="http://ajax.googleapis.com/ajax/libs/jquery/1.8.2/
jquery.min.js"></script>
<script type="text/javascript" src="handlebars.js"></script>
<script type="text/javascript" src="example.js"></script>
</body>
</html>
```

2. Implement the helpers, and render the template in `example.js`:

```
$(function() {
    Handlebars.registerHelper('ul', function(items, options) {
        if (items .length) return '<ul>' + items.
map(function(item) {
            return '<li>' + options.fn(item) + '</li>';
        }).join('') + '</ul>'
        else
            return options.inverse(this);
    });

    Handlebars.registerHelper('img', function(src, options) {
        return new Handlebars.SafeString('<img src="' + src
            + '" alt="'+ (options.hash['alt'] || '')
            + '" title="'+ (options.hash['title'] || '')
            + '">');
    });

    var template = Handlebars.compile($('#template').html());

    $('#list').html(template({list:[
        { name: 'John',  image: '1.png'},
```

```
            { name: 'Jack',   image: '2.jpg'},
            { name: 'Jenny',  image: '3.jpg'},
        ]}));
    });
```

How it works...

Inside our template, we're using two new helpers, `ul` to display lists and the `img` tag to display images.

Handlebars has two different types of helpers: regular and block. Block helpers are invoked in the following format:

```
{{#helperName argument param=value otherparam=value}}
    body
{{else}}
    alternative
{{/name}}
```

When Handlebars encounters a block, it invokes its block function, which takes one or two arguments:

```
function helper(argument, options) {
    ...
}
```

If specified, the first argument is passed to the `helper` function. If the first argument is not available, the `options` argument becomes first.

The named parameters are also optional, and are available inside the `options` argument in the `hash` property that is, `options.hash`.

Next comes the mandatory block argument, available inside the `helper` function as `options.fn`. The block argument is a function that takes a context and returns the result of rendering the block with that context

The `else` block is also a block function (`options.inverse`). It is optional and can be omitted. If omitted, a default empty block function is passed as `options.inverse` instead.

In our example we pass the list contents to our `ul` helper. This helper uses the regular block on each item if there are items in the list; otherwise it uses the alternative block to display the empty list message.

The other type of helper is a regular helper and can be invoked as follows:

```
{{helperName argument param=value otherparam=value}}
```

Client-side Templates

Normal helpers work similarly, to the block helpers, except that they don't receive the block parameters. In our example, we pass the `alt` text to the rendered image as a named parameter.

Both types of helpers should return the rendered HTML.

In our `example.js` file, we register our two new helpers by calling `Handlebars.registerHelper`. This makes them available to all subsequent templates that we need to render. Afterwards, we can call `render` on the template with our data, which in turn invokes the helpers to generate the resulting HTML:

```
<ul>
    <li> <img src="1.png" alt="John" title=""> John </li>
    <li> <img src="2.jpg" alt="Jack" title=""> Jack </li>
    <li> <img src="3.jpg" alt="Jenny" title=""> Jenny </li>
</ul>
```

Reusing templates with partials in Handlebars

Handlebars partials are templates which can be invoked from other templates with a certain context.

One example use of a partial template is a user login box. Such a box would display the username, the number of unread notifications, and a logout link if the user is logged in; otherwise it would display regular login options which are available while using Facebook and Twitter.

Partial templates can be used instead of helpers when there are no parameters to be passed to the helper or when no complex logic is necessary. They're particularly useful when the amount of dynamically generated content is small and the amount of HTML is large. This is because inside partial templates, HTML can be written directly without the need to convert it to strings.

In this recipe, we're going to use partial templates to render a threaded conversation model. This example also demonstrates that partial templates can be re-used recursively from within themselves.

Getting ready

We need to download Handlebars from `https://github.com/wycats/handlebars.js`. The browser version is in the `dist` directory. Create a directory for the example and copy `handlebars.js` to this directory, or download directly (on Linux):

```
wget https://raw.github.com/wycats/handlebars.js/master/dist/
handlebars.js
```

326

How to do it...

Let's get started.

1. Create `index.html` which will contain the conversation placeholder, the main conversation template, and the recursive partial thread template:

```
<!DOCTYPE HTML>
<html>
<head>
<title>Partials in Handlebars</title>
<link rel="stylesheet" type="text/css" href="style.css">
</head>
<body>
<div id="list" class="conversation">
</div>

<script id="thread-template" type="text/x-handlebars-template">
    <div class="message">
        <img src="{{image}}">
        <span class="name">{{from}}</span>
        <span class="date">{{date}}</span>
        <p class="text">{{text}}</p>
    </div>
    <div class="replies">
        {{#each replies}}
            {{> thread}}
        {{/each}}
    </div>
</script>

<script id="template" type="text/x-handlebars-template">
<h2>{{topic}}</h2>
{{> thread}}
<p><input type="button" value="Reply"></p>
</script>

<script src="http://ajax.googleapis.com/ajax/libs/jquery/1.8.2/
jquery.min.js"></script>
<script type="text/javascript" src="handlebars.js"></script>
<script type="text/javascript" src="example.js"></script>
</body>
</html>
```

2. To style the displayed messages, create `style.css` and add the following CSS code:

```css
* { box-sizing: border-box; }
.conversation { width: 70ex; }
.message {
    background-color:#f5f5f5;
    padding: 5px;
    margin:5px 0;
    float:left;
    clear: both;
    width:100%; }
.message p {
    margin: 0 0 0.5em 0; }
.message .name {
    font-weight: bold; }
.message img {
    float: left;
    margin-right: 1em}
.message.unread {
    font-weight:bold; }
.message .date {
    margin-left:1em;
    float: right;
    font-style: italic;
    color: #999; }
.replies {
    margin-left:3em;
    clear:both; }
```

3. The rendering will be done from `example.js`:

```javascript
$(function() {

    Handlebars.registerPartial('thread', $("#thread-template").
html());

    var template = Handlebars.compile($('#template').html());

    $('#list').html(template({
        topic: "The topic of this conversation",
        from: 'John',
        image: '1.png',
        text: "I wrote some text",
        date: 'Yesterday',
        replies:[
            {from: 'Jack',
```

```
            image: '2.jpg',
            text: "My response to your text is favorable",
            date: 'Today' ,
            replies: [
                {from: 'John',
                    image: '1.png',
                    text: "Thank you kindly",
                    date: 'Today'}
            ]},
        {from: 'Jenny',
            image: '3.jpg',
            text: "I'm also going to chime in",
            date: 'Today' }
    ]})));
});
```

How it works...

The data structure of the message in this recipe is recursive. It contains the message details: the username and user photo, message text, and message date. But it also contains the replies to that message, which are messages themselves.

To render this structure we write a partial template for a single thread of conversation, specifying how to display the message details but also iterating through all the replies and invoking itself for every reply.

This partial template is then called once from the main template, resulting with a full conversation tree.

Handlebars partial templates are called with the variables from the current context. Partials work just the same as we do directly to replace the call to the partial with the contents of the partial template:

```
{{> partial}}
```

There's more...

Partial templates can be used for headers, footers, menus, or even recursively. It's a recommended practice to split large reusable sections of a website into partial templates to avoid copying and to making these sections easier to change and reusable.

Reusing templates with partials in EJS

Partial templates are larger sections of HTML which need to be included multiple times from multiple pages. Common uses for partial templates include headers, footers, site menus, login boxes, alerts, and so on.

The latest version of EJS doesn't natively support partial templates; they have been removed. However, there is another way to use other templates from within a template, by including the compiled template itself in the data model.

In this recipe, we're going to render a conversation thread using a recursive partial template written in EJS.

Getting ready

We need to download EJS from `http://embeddedjs.com/` and extract `ejs_production.js` in our `recipe` folder.

How to do it...

Let's get started.

1. Create `index.html`, which will contain the conversation placeholder, the main conversation template, and the recursive partial thread template:

```
<!DOCTYPE HTML>
<html>
<head>
<title>Partials in EJS</title>
<link rel="stylesheet" type="text/css" href="style.css">
</head>
<body>
<div id="list" class="conversation">
</div>

<script id="thread-template" type="text/ejs">
    <div class="message">
        <img src="<%= thread.image %>">
        <span class="name"><%= thread.from %></span>
        <span class="date"><%= thread.date %></span>
        <p class="text"><%= thread.text %></p>
    </div>
    <div class="replies">
        <% thread.replies && thread.replies.
forEach(function(reply) { %>
```

```
            <%= partial.render({thread:reply, partial:partial}) %>
        <% }); %>
    </div>
</script>

<script id="template" type="text/ejs">
<h2><%= thread.topic %></h2>
<%= partial.render({thread: thread, partial: partial}) %>
<p><input type="button" value="Reply"></p>
</script>

<script src="http://ajax.googleapis.com/ajax/libs/jquery/1.8.2/
jquery.min.js"></script>
<script type="text/javascript" src="ejs_production.js"></script>
<script type="text/javascript" src="example.js"></script>
</body>
</html>
```

2. Add the styles necessary to render the template in `style.css`:

```
* { box-sizing: border-box; }
.conversation { width: 70ex; }
.message {
    background-color:#f5f5f5;
    padding: 5px;
    margin:5px 0;
    float:left;
    clear: both;
    width:100%; }
.message p {
    margin: 0 0 0.5em 0; }
.message .name {
    font-weight: bold; }
.message img {
    float: left;
    margin-right: 1em}
.message.unread { font-weight:bold; }
.message .date {
    margin-left:1em;
    float: right;
    font-style: italic;
    color: #999; }
.replies {
    margin-left:3em;
    clear:both; }
```

3. Add the rendering code in `example.js`:

```
$(function() {
    var template = new EJS({
        text: $('#template').html()
    });

    var threadTemplate = new EJS({
        text:$("#thread-template").html()
    });
    $('#list').html(template.render({
        partial: threadTemplate,
        thread:{
            topic: "The topic of this conversation",
            from: 'John',
            image: '1.png', text: "I wrote some text",
            date: 'Yesterday',
            replies:[
                {from: 'Jack',
                    image: '2.jpg',
                    text: "My response to your text is favorable",
                    date: 'Today' ,
                    replies: [
                        {from: 'John',
                            image: '1.png',
                            text: "Thank you kindly",
                            date: 'Today'}
                ]},
                {from: 'Jenny',
                    image: '3.jpg',
                    text: "I'm also going to chime in",
                    date: 'Today' }
        ]}}));
});
```

How it works...

The message thread is a recursive data structure. It contains the message details (such as date, user, and text) and also the replies which are themselves message threads.

To make the partial template object available inside the template, we include it in the passed model. Then we can call it from the template, passing it further inside the model of the recursive partial thread template.

This partial template displays the message details, and then proceeds to call itself to render every reply if such replies are available. In each call we pass the partial template object to make it available within the next call.

The process ends when there are no more threads to be rendered, resulting with a complete message tree:

There is more...

Even though EJS doesn't natively support partials anymore, this recipe shows how we can still reuse EJS templates inside each other. We can easily extend this to full partial support by passing a table of all registered partials along with every model.

Using filters in Jade

Jade filters are powerful features which enable the users to use different markups inside Jade templates. Their primary use is to make templates even more succinct by enabling the user to use the appropriate tool for a particular section of the template.

In this recipe, we're going to use Jade filters to embed markdown inside our template and explain how filters work.

Getting ready

The client-side version of Jade `https://github.com/visionmedia/jade` is found in the `jade.js` file and does not support markdown filters out of the box. To add support for markdown we need edit this file and find the line that starts defining the `markdown` filter:

```
markdown: function(str){
  var md;

  // support markdown / discount
  try {
    ….
  }
  str = str.replace(/\\n/g, '\n');
  return md.parse(str).replace(/\n/g, '\\n').replace(/'/g,'&#39;');
},
```

And then replace it with the following function:

```
markdown: function(str){
  str = str.replace(/\\n/g, '\n');
  return markdown.toHTML(str).replace(/\n/g, '\\n').
replace(/'/g,'&#39;');
  },
```

This will inform Jade to use the globally defined markdown object, which we're going to provide by including an external markdown script.

How to do it...

Let's get started.

1. Create `index.html` which will contain the placeholder for our template and the template itself:

    ```
    <!DOCTYPE HTML>
    <html>
    ```

```html
<head>
<title>Using the markdown filter in Jade</title>
</head>
<body>
<h2>Rendered markdown</h2>
<div id="list">
</div>
<script id="template" type="text/jade">

#header
  | Hello
#content
  :markdown
    # Jade-markdown hybrid
    **Jade** simplifies the writing of HTML markup and dynamic
    templates. However, its not very good at simplifying the
    writing textual content that combines headings, paragraphs
    and images.

    This is where the **markdown** filter steps in. The filter
    allows you  to write text documents and easily embed
    [links](http://google.com) or images such as:

    ![Google](https://www.google.com/images/srpr/logo3w.png)

    Because filters are post-processed by Jade, we can easily
    add dynamic content such as the current date:
    #{new Date().toString()} or model #{prop} passed to the
    template function and have it processed by Jade.

</script>
<script src="http://ajax.googleapis.com/ajax/libs/jquery/1.8.2/
jquery.min.js"></script>
<script src="https://raw.github.com/spion/markdown-js/master/lib/
markdown.js"></script>
<script type="text/javascript" src="jade.js"></script>
<script type="text/javascript" src="example.js"></script>
</body>
</html>
```

2. Create the simple `example.js` file to bind the template to the element:

```javascript
$(function() {
    var template = jade.compile($('#template').html());
    $('#list').html(template({prop: 'properties' }));
});
```

How it works...

When Jade encounters the `:markdown` block, it passes the text found inside it to the markdown `filter` function which we previously created. This `filter` function calls the markdown-js to the HTML method that processes the markdown and generates HTML.

> **Rendered markdown**
>
> Hello
>
> ## Jade-markdown hybrid
>
> **Jade** simplifies the writing of HTML markup and dynamic templates. However, its not very good at simplifying the writing textual content that combines headings, paragraphs and images.
>
> This is where the **markdown** filter steps in. The filter allows you to write text documents and easily embed links or images such as:
>
> # Google
>
> Because filters are post-processed by Jade, we can easily add dynamic content such as the current date: Tue Apr 23 2013 12:56:56 GMT+0200 (CEST) or model properties passed to the template function and have it processed by Jade.

Using mixins in Jade

Similar to partial templates in other template languages, Jade mixins are smaller template pieces that can accept parameters. Mixins are useful when generating common HTML chunks such as alert boxes, dialogs, and menus.

In this recipe we're going to compare Jade's mixins with the partial templates found in the other template languages by reimplementing the threaded conversation template. This is a recursive template that renders a threaded conversation tree.

Getting ready

We need to download `jade.min.js` in our `recipe` folder, available at `https://github.com/visionmedia/jade`.

Let's get started.

1. Create `index.html` which will contain the conversation placeholder, the main conversation template, and the recursive partial thread template:

```
<!DOCTYPE HTML>
<html>
<head>
<title>Mixins in Jade</title>
<link rel="stylesheet" type="text/css" href="style.css">
</head>
<body>
<div id="list" class="conversation">
</div>

<script id="thread-template" type="text/jade">
</script>

<script id="template" type="text/jade">

mixin thread(thread)
  .message
    img(src=thread.image)
    span.name=thread.from
    span.date=thread.date
    p.text=thread.text
  .replies
    if thread.replies
      each reply in thread.replies
        +thread(reply)

h2=thread.topic
+thread(thread)
p
  input(type="button",value="Reply")

</script>

<script src="http://ajax.googleapis.com/ajax/libs/jquery/1.8.2/
jquery.min.js"></script>
<script type="text/javascript" src="jade.min.js"></script>
<script type="text/javascript" src="example.js"></script>
</body>
</html>
```

2. Create `example.js` to pass the data to the template:

```
$(function() {
    var template = jade.compile($('#template').html());
    $('#list').html(template({
        thread:{
            topic: "The topic of this conversation",
            from: 'John',
            image: '1.png',
            text: "I wrote some text",
            date: 'Yesterday',
            replies:[
                {from: 'Jack',
                    image: '2.jpg',
                    text: "My response to your text is favorable",
                    date: 'Today' ,
                    replies: [
                        {from: 'John',
                            image: '1.png',
                            text: "Thank you kindly",
                            date: 'Today'}
                ]},
                {from: 'Jenny',
                    image: '3.jpg',
                    text: "I'm also going to chime in",
                    date: 'Today' }
        ]}})));
});
```

3. Create `style.css` to style the conversation thread:

```
* { box-sizing: border-box; }
.conversation { width: 70ex; }
.message {
    background-color:#f5f5f5;
    padding: 5px;
    margin:5px 0;
    float:left;
    clear: both;
    width:100%;
}
.message p {
    margin: 0 0 0.5em 0; }
.message .name {
    font-weight: bold; }
.message img {
```

```
    float: left;
    margin-right: 1em}
.message.unread { font-weight:bold; }
.message .date {
    margin-left:1em;
    float: right;
    font-style: italic;
    color: #999; }
.replies {
    margin-left:3em;
    clear:both; }
```

How it works...

The message thread is a recursive data structure. It contains the message details (such as date, user, and text) and also the replies which are themselves message threads.

To render this structure we wrote a Jade mixin. The mixin takes the thread as an argument and displays its attributes as well as the text in the top node of the thread.

Finally, if there are replies inside the thread object, it iterates through all of those replies and recursively calls itself with each reply as an argument. Calling a mixin is done by prefixing the mixin name with the character "+".

The main template displays the topic of the top level message in a heading. Afterwards it invokes the mixin with the top level thread which results in the rendering of the complete thread tree.

Using layouts and blocks in Jade

To allow us to easily create different templates, Jade supports template inheritance. Jade's template inheritance allows us to define a master layout template, and then replace parts of this template by extending the master layout.

In this recipe we're going to use template inheritance to simulate a complete website, containing a header, a menu, some content, and a footer. The content will be split into two pages.

Getting ready

The client-side version of Jade does not support layouts and blocks. Specifying the template to extend requires access to the filesystem which is not available inside the browser. However, we can precompile the templates using browserify. To do this we're going to write a browserify plugin that registers a handler for the Jade files.

Let's install the prerequisites first. We're going to need `nodejs`, which can be downloaded from `http://nodejs.org/`. After installing node from a command prompt, we're going to install browserify Version 1 (Version 2 has no support for plugins as of now):

```
npm install -g browserify@1
```

Next, we shall create a new directory for our example:

```
mkdir example && cd example
```

In that directory we will install Jade (and markdown to add markdown support to Jade):

```
npm install jade markdown
```

How to do it...

Follow these steps:

1. Let's write the browserify plugin, `browserify.jade.js`:

```
var jade = require('jade');
module.exports = function(browserify) {
    browserify.register('jade', function(tmpl, file) {
        var fn =  jade.compile(tmpl, {
            client: true,
            filename:true,
            path: __dirname
        });
        return ["var jade = require('jade/lib/runtime.js');",
                'module.exports=',fn.toString()].join('');
    });
};
```

2. Then create `index.html`, which in this case is a simple placeholder for the content which will be filled by the templates:

```
<!DOCTYPE HTML>
<html>
<head>
<title>Blocks and layouts in Jade</title>
<link rel="stylesheet" type="text/css" href="style.css">
</head>
<body>
<div id="content">
</div>
<script src="http://ajax.googleapis.com/ajax/libs/jquery/1.8.2/
jquery.min.js"></script>
<script type="text/javascript" src="example.min.js"></script>
</body>
</html>
```

3. Then we can create `example.js`, which will load the two templates and make the menu clicks render a different template:

```
$(function() {
    var templates = {
        'layout':require('./layout.jade'),
        'example':require('./example.jade')
    };
    console.log(templates.layout.toString())
    $('body').on('click', 'a', function() {
        var template = templates[$(this).text().trim()];
        $("#content").html(template({}));
    });
    $("#content").html(templates.layout({}));
});
```

4. Here is the content of `layout.jade` (which also renders the menu):

```
#header
  | Welcome to example.jade
ul.menu
  block menu
    li
      a layout
    li
      a example
.content
  block content
    div
      p This is the default page
#footer
  | Copyright notice and extra links here
```

5. Add this to `example.jade`, which extends `layout.jade` by appending an item to the `menu` block and replacing the `content` block:

```
extends layout
block append menu
  li
    a new item
block content
  :markdown
    Different content with *markdown* support.
    This means [linking](http://google.com) is easy.
```

6. Let's add `style.css` to give it a nice look:

```
* { box-sizing: border-box; }
#content {
    max-width: 800px;
    margin: 0 auto; }
ul.menu {
    background-color: #ccc;
    margin: 0; padding:0; }
ul.menu li {
    display:inline-block;
    border-top: solid 1px #ddd;
    border-left: solid 1px #ddd;
    border-right: solid 1px #bbb; }
ul.menu li a {
    display: inline-block;
    cursor:pointer;
    padding: 0.5em 1em; }
.content {
    padding: 1em;
    background-color:#f5f5f5; }
#header {
    background-color:#333;
    color: #ccc;
    padding:0.5em;
    font-size: 1.5em; }
#footer {
    margin-top: 0.5em;}
```

7. Finally let's wrap it all into `example.min.js` by typing the following command in the command prompt:

```
browserify -p ./browserify-jade.js example.js -o example.min.js
```

How it works...

Let's start with `browserify-jade.js`.

This plugin works by registering the new file extension `'jade'` with browserify and telling it to invoke our transformation function with the contents of every jade file it encounters being required in our code. This means it will intercept both `require('layout.jade')` and `require('example.jade')`.

Our plugin function compiles the received template content using Jade, and then writes the code of the resulting JavaScript function. However to make sure that Jade helper functions are available for the generated template, it also includes `runtime.js` via require. This file contains the basic Jade library that all compiled templates need to work (adding it this way will cause browserify to include it in the final bundle).

How blocks and inheritance work:

To make a template an inheritable layout, all we need to do is place named blocks inside it. In our example we have two named blocks in `layout.jade` – one for the menu and one for the content.

Named blocks allow us extend the template and then replace parts of the content with our own. We do this in the `example.jade` file. This file inherits from layout, appends a new menu item to the menu block using "`block append`", and completely replaces the content block with its own written in markdown.

> It's also possible to prepend content to a block by simply using "`block prepend`".

When we run the `browserify` command, it combines the templates and `example.js` into a single file called `example.min.js`, which we include in our page:

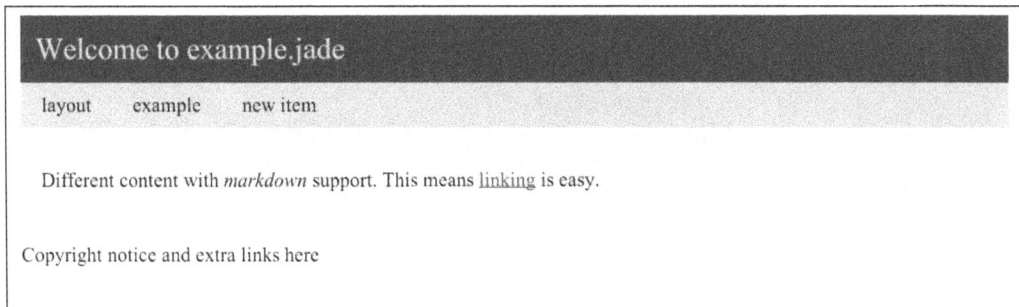

The result is a simple page with a heading, menu, content, and a footer block. When a link from the menu is clicked, the appropriate template is loaded and rendered on this page.

10
Data Binding Frameworks

In this chapter, we're going to cover the following topics:

- ▸ Creating a basic Angular view with data binding
- ▸ Rendering lists and using Angular controllers
- ▸ Routing, filters, and backend services in Angular
- ▸ Using Angular's client-side validation
- ▸ Making a chart component with Angular directives
- ▸ Structuring applications for Meteor.js
- ▸ Reactive programming and data in Meteor.js
- ▸ Live HTML and user-specific data in Meteor.js
- ▸ Security mechanisms in Meteor.js

Introduction

Within modern web applications, a lot of code is gradually moving from the server to the browser. As a result, new possibilities and challenges are emerging.

One such possibility is instant automated data binding. Client-side code enables us to bind model objects to parts of the web page. This means that changes in the model are automatically and instantly reflected in the view element displaying that model.

Additionally, a challenge in code organization also emerges. JavaScript does not provide adequate module facilities or code organization models that are needed in larger browser applications.

In this chapter, we're going to cover two complete frameworks that attempt to provide solutions to both challenges. These frameworks support a declarative, data-binding approach to writing web applications. At the same time, they provide modularization and organization facilities, allowing us to give a clear structure to our code—to separate it into models, views, controllers, or view-models and components.

The first half of the chapter will cover Angular—a framework coming from Google that provides client-side bindings, and can work with any server-side stack (Rails, Node.js, Django, and so on). It provides data binding+ and organizational facilities. We'll do the following in this chapter:

▶ Create basic Angular views with data binding

▶ Use Angular controllers to write a small list editing application

▶ Add validation to our application

▶ Create a simple markdown wiki using the Angular router and filters and define a local storage service

▶ Use directives to create a component that displays a chart

The second half will cover Meteor—a complete framework and platform that covers both the client and the server side, and also provides data binding and organizational facilities. Meteor is more of a truly different way of building web applications, and we will cover some of the following basics for it:

▶ Structuring your application Meteor style

▶ Basics of reactive programming, and how to work with data in Meteor

▶ Live HTML and user data

▶ Security and authentication

Creating a basic Angular view with data binding

Angular.js allows us to create views with automated data binding. This means that we can specify model objects whose properties will bind to element properties or content.

Automated data binding simplifies programming. Instead of adding event listeners to watch for changes inside our elements and then manually updating elements by adding classes, changing attributes, or modifying their content, we can simply change the model objects, and the elements will get updated automatically.

In this recipe, we're going to create a simple currency converter that converts USD to GBP using a fixed conversion rate.

Getting ready

Angular is available via CDN, so no downloading is necessary. We can simply include it to our page.

How to do it...

Let's write the Angular template.

Create a file named `index.html` that contains the following code:

```
<!doctype html>
<html>
  <head>
    <script src="https://ajax.googleapis.com/ajax/libs/
angularjs/1.0.5/angular.min.js"></script>
  </head>
  <body>
    <div ng-app>
      <label>Amount in USD:</label>
      $<input type="text" ng-model="usdValue" placeholder="Enter USD
amount">
      <hr>
      <label>Amount in GBP:</label><span ng-show="usdValue"> £
{{usdValue * 0.65}}</span>
    </div>
  </body>
</html>
```

How it works...

Our HTML page is not written in pure, standard HTML. There are a lot of new attributes added, and we're going to explain them in the following paragraphs.

The `ng-app` attribute tells Angular which part of our page should be managed by it. In our case, it's the only `div` element on the page. We could also put this tag on the HTML element, in which case the entire page will be controlled by Angular.

Inside the `div`, we have an input element with an `ng-model` attribute with the value `usdValue`. This attribute causes Angular to add a new property into the view's model called `usdValue`. The value of this property will automatically update to the value of the input field when the content changes. This property now becomes globally available inside the view.

Our span element contains an ng-show attribute with the value usdValue. This attribute will cause the span element to be shown only if usdValue has a non-falsy value. Examples of "falsy" values are null, empty string, undefined, and zero—for those values, the span element will be hidden.

Finally, inside the span we have both the currency and an expression placed within double curly braces. As this expression depends on the value of the usdValue variable, the contents of the span element will be automatically updated whenever that value changes.

The resulting binding connects the span element with the input field. Whenever the input field is changed, the model usdValue variable is automatically updated. This in turn causes both the visibility and the content of the span element to update automatically.

There's more...

The ng attributes are called **attribute directives** in Angular. Angular also allows you to write your own attribute directives.

> The ng attributes are non-standard, and HTML validators will complain when encountering them. To work around this, you can prefix them with the data prefix. For example, data-ng-model will validate fine, as custom attributes with the data prefix are standards-compliant.

Rendering lists and using Angular controllers

Angular allows us to interact with our view through code by letting us set a controller for the view. The controller can modify the view scope (the model) and call other operations, such as background services.

In this recipe, we're going to use a controller to write a simple to-do list.

How to do it...

Let's get started.

1. Create a file named index.html that will display a list of tasks, the form to add a new task, and the button to hide all the tasks:

```
<!doctype html>
<html ng-app>
<head>
<script src="https://ajax.googleapis.com/ajax/libs/
angularjs/1.0.5/angular.min.js"></script>
```

```
<script src="example.js"></script>
</head>
<body>
<div ng-controller="TodoListController">
    <ul>
        <li ng-repeat="task in tasks" ng-show="task.shown">
        <input type="checkbox" ng-model="task.complete">
        {{task.text}}
        </li>
    </ul>
    <form ng-submit="addTask()">
        <input type="text" placeholder="Write a task here..." ng-
model="taskToAdd">
        <input type="submit" value="Add">
    </form>
    <button ng-click="hideComplete()">Hide complete</button>
</div>
</body>
</html>
```

2. Create a file named `example.js` to define the controller for our to-do list:

```
function TodoListController($scope) {
    $scope.tasks = [
        {text: "Write a todo list",
            complete: false, shown: true },
        {text: "Save it to the backend",
            complete: false, shown: true },
    ];
    $scope.addTask = function() {
        $scope.tasks.push({
            text: $scope.taskToAdd,
            complete: false,
            shown:true
        });
        $scope.taskToAdd = "";
    };
    $scope.hideComplete = function() {
        $scope.tasks.forEach(function(t) {
            if (t.complete)
                t.shown = false;
        });
    };
}
```

How it works...

In this example, we declare that the Angular app is going to be our entire page by setting the `ng-app` attribute to the root element of the page.

The `div` element represents our view. This element has an `ng-controller` attribute that specifies the controller for the view. The controller is a function defined in the global scope of the window.

Inside this view, we use the `ng-repeat` directive to display our list of tasks inside list elements. Inside this list, there is a checkbox denoting the task completion state and the text of the task.

The `tasks` variable belongs to the view's scope. We expect the variable to contain an array of tasks, each having a `text` description, completion status in the `complete` field (bound to the checkbox of the task), and a `hidden` flag.

At the bottom of the page is the form used to add tasks to the list. Using the `ng-submit` attribute, we declare that this form should execute the `addTask()` function when submitted. In order to do this, we expect the scope to contain the `addTask()` function. The `text` field in this form is bound to the `taskToAdd` variable.

Finally, to hide the completed tasks, we have added a button to the page. By setting the value of its `ng-click` attribute to `hideCompleted()`, we tell the button to execute the `hideCompleted()` function when the button is clicked. For this, we expect that the scope of the view contains a `hideCompleted()` function.

How can we attach the necessary function and some data to the view?

To do this, we can use our controller function defined in `example.js`. The controller function is invoked when the view is loaded.

Inside this controller, there is no DOM manipulation code or DOM event bindings. Instead, what we have is a `$scope` parameter passed to the controller by Angular. This parameter represents the variable scope of the view. The controller simply attaches variables such as the `tasks` array to that scope, and the variable immediately becomes available to the view.

We also attach the `addTask()` and `hideCompleted()` functions to the scope. The code inside is fairly straightforward:

- addTask pushes a new task from the list with the content of the `taskToAdd` scope variable and then resets its value to an empty string. This will cause Angular to update the list of tasks and to reset the content of the `input` field bound to `taskToAdd`.

- hideCompleted goes through the list of tasks and sets the `hidden` flag to every completed task. As a result, the `ng-show` directive automatically causes the tasks marked as `hidden` to be hidden from the view.

There's more...

This example highlights the main differences when working with an automatic data binding framework.

Without automated data binding, we would need to manually pass data to the template render function, then set up event bindings for actions. The actions would manually pull data from the view, do the actual model manipulation, then call the render function again. This is an imperative approach to templating.

With automated data binding frameworks, inside the template we specify how its parts are connected with the model object. Then, to update the view, we simply manipulate or change the model and the view updates automatically to reflect those changes. This is a declarative approach to templating.

The only downside in this recipe is that our controller must be declared in the global variable scope. We're going to show how to avoid this in the next recipe.

Routing, filters, and backend services in Angular

To better utilize the browser's Back button functionality, as well as allow users to copy and paste links, Angular provides a router module. The router functions similarly to a server-side router, with the path appended in the URL after the hash along with query string parameters. It will redirect the user to the appropriate pair of controller and view.

Additionally, to share data between views and the server, we need to define a module for the backend storage. We're going to use HTML5 `localStorage` instead—the resulting code will be very similar.

In this recipe, we're going to build a simple markdown-based wiki that stores pages in local storage. Angular also supports filters, so we're going to write a markdown filter module.

How to do it...

Let's write our Angular app:

1. Create a file named `index.html` that will host the Angular application. It includes all the necessary scripts and sets up the `div` element that will host the views:

    ```
    <!doctype html>
    <html ng-app="wiki">
    <head>
    <link rel="stylesheet" type="text/css" href="style.css">
    ```

```
<script src="https://raw.github.com/spion/markdown-js/master/lib/
markdown.js"></script>
<script src="https://ajax.googleapis.com/ajax/libs/
angularjs/1.0.5/angular.min.js"></script>
<script src="https://ajax.googleapis.com/ajax/libs/
angularjs/1.0.5/angular-sanitize.min.js"></script>
<script src="edit-controller.js"></script>
<script src="view-controller.js"></script>
<script src="storage.js"></script>
<script src="markdown-filter.js"></script>
<script src="app.js"></script>
</head>
<body>
<div id="main" ng-view>
</div>
</body>
</html>
```

2. To display markdown, we're going to need a `markdown` filter. Define the Angular filter inside an Angular module called `markdown`, within `markdown-filter.js`:

```
angular.module('markdown', []).filter('markdown', function() {
    return function(input) {
        return input ? markdown.toHTML(input) : ''
    };
});
```

3. To store the wiki pages, we're going to need a storage module. Define a factory that creates `Storage` objects inside the module called `storage` in `storage.js`:

```
angular.module('storage', []).factory('Storage', function() {
    var self = {};
    self.get = function get(id) {
        var page = localStorage["page-"+id];
        if (page) return JSON.parse(page);
        else return {id: id, text: null};
    };
    self.save = function save(page) {
        var stringified = JSON.stringify(page);
        localStorage["page-"+page.id] = stringified;
    };
    return self;
});
```

4. Now let's define our wiki application inside `app.js`. Besides the `storage` and `markdown` modules, we're also going to use `ngSanitize` to display unsafe HTML. We're going to define two routes, one for editing and another for viewing pages:

```
var wwwApp = angular.module('wiki',
    ['storage', 'markdown', 'ngSanitize'])
    .config(['$routeProvider', '$locationProvider',
        function($routeProvider, $locationProvider) {
            $locationProvider
                .html5Mode(true).hashPrefix('!');
            $routeProvider.when('/edit/:page', {
                templateUrl: '../edit.html',
                controller: EditController
            })
            .when('/:page', {
                templateUrl: 'view.html',
                controller: ViewController
            })
        }]);
```

5. Let's define our viewing template in `view.html`. Besides displaying the article, it should also provide an edit link as well as a link to return to the main page:

```
<div ng-show="page.text"
    ng-bind-html-unsafe="page.text | markdown">
</div>
<br>
<a href="edit/{{page.id}}">Edit this page</a> -
<a href="./">Go to the start page</a>
```

6. Now let's define the viewing controller inside `view-controller.js`. It should load the displayed article from storage.

```
function ViewController($scope, $routeParams, Storage) {
    $scope.page = Storage.get($routeParams.page || 'index');
}
```

7. Add the editing template inside `edit.html`:

```
<div class="edit">
    <div class="left">
        <textarea ng-model="page.text"></textarea>
    </div>
    <div class="right"
        ng-bind-html-unsafe="page.text | markdown">
    </div>
</div>
<a ng-click="savePage()"
    href="../{{page.id}}">Save</a>
```

8. Then define the editing controller inside `edit-controller.js`; it should load the page from `storage` and define the `savePage()` method to save a page:

```
function EditController($scope, Storage, $routeParams) {
    $scope.page = Storage.get($routeParams.page);
    $scope.savePage = function() {
        Storage.save({id: $scope.page.id, text: $scope.page.
text});
    };
}
```

9. Finally, let's style things up by adding some CSS in `style.css`:

```
* { box-sizing: border-box; }
#main { padding: 0em 1em; }
.edit .left {
    float:left;
    width: 50%;
    padding-right: 1em; }
.edit .right {
    float: right;
    width: 50%;
    padding-left: 1em; }
.edit textarea {
    width: 100%;
    min-height: 24em;}
.edit input {
    width: 70%; }
.edit {
    float:left;
    width: 100%;
    clear:both; }
```

10. To run the application, run an HTTP server for the directory. Assuming you have Node.js installed (see *Appendix A, Installing Node.js and Using npm*), install `http-server`, and then run it in the `app` directory:

    npm install -g http-server

    http-server

11. Point your browser to `http://localhost:8080/` to see the result.

How it works...

The previous recipe defined a simple, single-controller application and as such, it had no real need for routing and modularization. This recipe, on the other hand, implements a more complex application with multiple views and controllers, as well as storage and filter modules.

Our Angular app begins in `app.js`—defined as a module called `wiki`, the same as the `ng-app` attribute of the `html` tag inside our `index.html` file. It contains the main glue code that loads our custom `markdown` and `storage` modules and sets up the controllers and views.

To configure our app, we load two objects: `$locationProvider` and `$routeProvider`:

```
['$routeProvider', '$locationProvider',  function($routeProvider,
$locationProvider) { … }]
```

The preceding loading syntax is the array syntax, where we define the module names to load as elements of the array; then we define the function taking these modules as arguments at the end of the array and the executing the code that uses them.

We use the `locationProvider` module to enable `html5mode`, where every URL looks as if it has been loaded as a separate page, containing no hashes. This mode requires the HTML5 browser history API. As a fallback, we define a prefix `!` to use after the hash and before the URL.

To define our routes, we use `routeProvider`. We declare that any `/edit/:page` URL will be handled by `EditController` and displayed with the `edit.html` template. The `:page` part of the URL is a URL parameter and matches any text—it will be accessible in the controller. We also define a `/:page` route used to view pages, which is handled by `ViewController` and is using the `view.html` template.

The `view` template contains a `div` element that is shown only if the page text is defined. The way we do this is using the `ng-bind-html-unsafe` directive. This directive allows us to bind an expression, which is evaluating to arbitrary HTML, to the element, which is exactly what we need for the `markdown` filter.

To use the filter we use the pipe character:

```
ng-bind-html-unsafe="page.text | markdown"
```

The editing link for the page is located at the bottom of the link, taking us to the editing view for this page. Similarly, on the edit page, we bind both the markdown text and the generated HTML to different elements. As a result, changing the textarea results with instant updates to the displayed HTML, giving us a live preview of the generated page.

Both the view and the edit controllers are fairly simple: the first controller loads the article from storage, while the second controller defines a `save()` function that saves the article back to the storage.

What is new in our controllers are the extra parameters they receive:

```
function EditController($scope, Storage, $routeParams) ...
function ViewController($scope, $routeParams, Storage) ...
```

These parameters cause Angular to inject the requested objects by passing them as parameters to the controllers. In this case, the `Storage` object is requested (defined in the `storage` module) and the `$routeParams` built-in object is requested. The order of the parameters doesn't matter, what matters is their names. We can avoid this behavior by using the array syntax:

```
var EditController = ['$scope', 'Storage', '$routeParams',
function($scope, Storage, $routeParams) { … }]
```

With the preceding syntax, Angular will inject the objects in the order specified by the array.

Defining a filter is simple. Inside `markdown-filter.js`, we define a new module called `markdown`. Then we declare that the module will provide a filter called `markdown`. To define a filter, we define a function that constructs and returns the filter. The returned filter should be a function taking a single input argument and returning the filtered output. Our `markdown` filter simply calls `markdown.toHTML` on the input argument.

The `storage` object is defined in a similar way in `storage.js`. Here we define a new module called `storage`. In this module, we define a constructor for a `Storage` object, which provides the `get()` and `save()` functions. Then we can inject our storage in any controller by adding an argument called `Storage`. In Angular, these injectable objects created by factories are usually called **services**.

There's more...

Using `ng-bind-html-unsafe` is not secure and may allow an attacker to write a page that injects arbitrary scripts that steal personal information or perform other actions on behalf of the user. To avoid this, the `$sanitize` service from the `ngSanitize` module should be used to process HTML whenever possible.

Using Angular's client-side validation

Angular extends the new HTML5 validation attributes on its own, and allows the users to add error conditions to the template. With these capabilities of Angular, we can add custom error messages and styles to our forms.

In this recipe, we're going to create a simple user registration form in Angular and then we'll add some validation rules to the form.

How to do it...

Let's perform the following steps:

Create a file named `index.html` that contains the registration form and the validation rules:

```
<!doctype html>
<html ng-app>
<head>
<script src="https://ajax.googleapis.com/ajax/libs/angularjs/1.0.5/
angular.min.js"></script>
<style type="text/css">
    form { display: block; width: 550px; margin: auto; }
    input[type="submit"] { margin-left: 215px; }
    span.err { color: #f00; }
    label { width: 120px; display:inline-block; text-align: right; }
</style>
</head>
<body>
<div>
    <form name="register">
        <p>
        <label for="user">User:</label>
        <input type="text" name="name" ng-model="user.name"
            required  ng-minlength="5" ng-maxlength="32">
        <span ng-show="register.name.$error.required" class="err">
            Required</span>
        <span ng-show="register.name.$error.minlength" class="err">
            Minimum 5 characters</span>
        <span ng-show="register.name.$error.maxlength" class="err">
            Maximum 32 characters</span>
        </p>

        <p>
        <label for="pass">Pass:</label>
        <input type="password" name="pass" ng-model="user.pass"
            required  ng-minlength="6" ng-maxlength="32"
            ng-pattern="/^(?=.*[a-zA-Z])(?=.*[0-9])/">
        <span ng-show="register.pass.$error.required" class="err">
            Required</span>
        <span ng-show="register.pass.$error.minlength" class="err">
            Minimum 6 characters</span>
        <span ng-show="register.pass.$error.maxlength" class="err">
            Maximum 32 characters</span>
```

```
        <span ng-show="register.pass.$error.pattern" class="err">
            Must have both letters and numbers</span>
        </p>

        <p>
        <label for="age">Age:</label>
        <input type="number" name="age" ng-model="user.age"
            required min="13">
        <span ng-show="register.age.$error.required" class="err">
            Required</span>
        <span ng-show="register.age.$error.min" class="err">
            Must be 13 or older</span>
        </p>

        <p>
        <label for="email">Email:</label>
        <input type="email" name="email" ng-model="user.email"
            required>
        <span ng-show="register.email.$error.required" class="err">
            Required</span>
        <span ng-show="register.email.$error.email" class="err">
            Not a valid email address</span>
        </p>

        <p>
        <label for="url">Website:</label>
        <input type="url" name="website" ng-model="user.website"
            required>
        <span ng-show="register.website.$error.required" class="err">
            Required</span>
        <span ng-show="register.website.$error.url" class="err">
            Not a valid website URL</span>
        </p>

        <input type="submit" value="Register" ng-
disabled="register.$invalid">
    </form>
</div>
</body>
</html>
```

How it works...

Angular adds validation support by extending the built-in HTML5 validation rules with newly added rules and properties. Let's look at the ones we're using inside our form:

Our first field is the user's username. Besides the HTML5 `required` attribute, we're also using two validation directives: `ng-minlength` and `ng-maxlength` to specify minimum and maximum username length.

Another addition by Angular is the ability to access the current validation state in the template from other separate elements. The error spans display the validation errors. However, they're only shown if the respective validation error has occurred.

To access the validation state, we can use the following format:

```
<formName>.<fieldName>.$error.<checkName>
```

For example, to check if the `user` field in the `register` form has a `minlength` error, we can use the following attribute:

```
register.user.$error.minlength
```

Similarly, we can use a `number` input field and check if the number is within the specified range with the `min` and `max` attributes. The appropriate `$error` fields have the names `$error.min` and `$error.max` respectively.

For the e-mail and the URL inputs, we can use the `$error.email` and `$error.url` fields respectively.

Finally, at the end of the form, in our Submit button, we use `ng-disable` to disable the submission of the form if there is an error in one of the fields. To check for errors, we can simply use the following syntax:

```
<formName>.$invalid
```

In our case is, it is as follows:

```
register.$invalid
```

The preceding code will return `true` if any of the validation rules in any field generates an error.

Making a chart component with Angular directives

Angular directives allow us to extend the HTML syntax in a very powerful way—by adding new attributes and elements. This allows us to create components that feel native: from date and time pickers to data grids, charts, and visualizations.

Such components can then be reused without adding initialization code to our controllers. We simply tell the component what model it should bind to and it will automatically update its appearance to reflect any changes in the model.

In this recipe, we're going to make a chart directive using Flot to draw our chart. In the process, we will learn about some of the many powerful features of Angular directives.

Getting ready

We need to download Flot from `http://www.flotcharts.org/` and extract the ZIP archive into our recipe directory, creating a sub-directory called `flot`.

How to do it...

Let's write the code.

1. Create a file named `index.html`. It will include all the necessary scripts and a view that displays a chart using our `chart` directive.

```
<!doctype html>
<html ng-app="chart">
<head>
<script src="https://ajax.googleapis.com/ajax/libs/
angularjs/1.0.5/angular.min.js"></script>
<script src="http://ajax.googleapis.com/ajax/libs/jquery/1.8.2/
jquery.min.js"> </script>
<script src="flot/jquery.flot.js"></script>
<script src="random.js"></script>
<script src="chart.js"></script>
<script src="controller.js"></script>
<script src="app.js"></script>
</head>
<body>
<div id="main" ng-controller="Controller">
    <chart style="display:block; width:800px; height:200px;"
        data="chart.data" options="chart.options">
</div>
</body>
</html>
```

2. To implement the controller, create a file named `controller.js`—it will set up the chart data and options. Additionally, it will update the chart data with randomly generated points every 50 milliseconds:

```
function Controller($scope, $timeout) {
    $scope.chart = {
        data: [getRandomData()],
        options: {lines: {fill:true}}
    };
    setInterval(function updateData(delay) {
        $scope.$apply(function() {
            $scope.chart.data[0] = getRandomData();
        });
    }, 50);
}
```

3. To create a random data generation function, create a file named `random.js` and add the following code:

```
(function() {
    var data = [], maximum = 200;
    window.getRandomData = function getRandomData() {
        if (data.length)
            data = data.slice(1);
        while (data.length < maximum) {
            var previous = data.length ? data[data.length - 1] :
50;
            var y = previous + Math.random() * 10 - 5;
            data.push(y < 0 ? 0 : y > 100 ? 100 : y);
        }
        var res = [];
        for (var i = 0; i < data.length; ++i)
            res.push([i, data[i]])
        return res;
    }
}());
```

4. Finally, write the `chart` directive in a file named `chart.js`:

```
angular.module('chart', []).directive('chart', function() {
    var dir = {};
    dir.restrict = 'E';
    dir.scope = {
        data: '&',
        options: '&'
    }
    dir.link = function(scope, el, attrs) {
```

```
            console.log(scope)
            var data = scope.data(),
                opts = scope.options(),
                flot = $.plot(el, data, opts);
            function updateOnData(newdata) {
                data = newdata;
                flot.setData(data);
                flot.setupGrid();
                flot.draw();
            };
            function updateOnOptions(options) {
                opts = options;
                flot = $.plot(el, data, opts);
            }

            scope.$watch('data()', updateOnData, {objectEquality:
    true});
            scope.$watch('options()', updateOnOptions,
    {objectEquality: true});
        }
        return dir;
    });
```

How it works...

This is a fairly regular Angular app with a `div` element that has a controller. The controller sets up a new object in the scope.

The `setInterval` call in the controller deserves a special mention. We're trying to modify a scope object outside of the usual functions called from the browser event loop by Angular.

> The browser event loop is a programming construct that waits for and dispatches events. Such events include mouse and keyboard events, timeouts and intervals set up by `setTimeout` and `setInterval`, script loading, image loading or `xmlhttprequest` completion, and so on.

All functions registered on the event loop by Angular are wrapped inside a scope application wrapper that notifies the scope that it should check itself for updates after execution. However, functions outside Angular, such as `setTimeout` and `setInterval`, don't do this wrapping, and we have to do it manually using the `$apply` function on the angular `$scope` object (`$scope.$apply`).

The `chart` directive factory is defined inside the `chart` module. The factory creates the directive, which is an object. Let's explain the properties of this object:

- ▸ `directive.restrict`: This restricts the directive to certain types. `E` means that the directive is restricted to elements. Additionally, three more possibilities are available: `A` for attributes, `C` for CSS classes, and `M` for a special comment form.
- ▸ `directive.scope`: This allows us to configure the attributes that define the local (isolate) scope of our directive. We can use the following different special characters for different kind of imports:
  - ❑ The `&` character means to interpret the attribute as an expression. It allows us to set up arbitrary one-way bindings and watch the expression for updates. To get the expression value, we need to call the imported scope variable as a function.
  - ❑ The `=` character means to interpret the attribute as a variable of another scope. This allows us to set up two-way data bindings.
  - ❑ The `@` character means to interpret the attribute as a string value. The string value of the attribute is returned.
- ▸ `directive.link`: This is called to link the directive with a new element. This is done once for every instance of the directive (in our case, every element). It allows us to define the code executed to render the new chart, as well as to set up scope watches to update the chart. It's called with the `scope`, `element`, and `attribute` parameters.

In our example, the `chart` directive is restricted to elements. Because we don't need two-way data bindings, using `&`, we interpret both the `data` and the `options` attributes as expressions. This allows the use of filters and other operations, which is very useful and not provided by the `=` interpretation.

Inside the `link` function, we render the initial chart. Because we interpreted both attributes as expressions, we need to invoke them as functions to get the values.

> Unlike in Angular controllers, the order of the parameters of our `link` function does matter and is always: `scope`, `element`, and `attributes`. This is because they are not processed by the Angular dependency injection system.

Setting up watches for expressions is also done slightly differently—the watch string is a function call.

Both `data` and `options` are complex objects whose content can be modified without changing the object itself. Because of this, we need to pass a third parameter to the `watch` function that specifies that object equality should be used when comparing the values of the watched expression. The default is to check the object reference, and it will not work for our chart.

When `data` or `options` are modified, we re-render our chart. Our `chart` element is now fully dynamic, as can be seen from the example that updates the data points every 50 milliseconds. Those updates immediately reflect on the chart.

There's more...

Besides the `directive.link` property, there is also `directive.compile`. It's only invoked once per directive, even if there are multiple instances. It allows us to transform a template inside our element and to include the content inside the directive. More properties are also available—detailed documentation can be found in the Angular guide on the official website at `http://angularjs.org/`.

Structuring applications for Meteor.js

The first promise made by Meteor.js is that it's a faster way of building web applications. Most of the web frameworks that are used today have a web server and a database on the same rack and send rendered HTML to the browsers. They all use standard request and response based development.

Nowadays, we also have a lot of smart clients: JavaScript-powered applications that run in the browser or native clients in Android or iOS. All of these are connected with the cloud; they all are aligned with either Google, Facebook, Twitter, or Amazon in one way or another.

Meteor provides a new way to have a code built around **Smart Packages**, code modules that can be executed on the client or server side or even both. Developers can pick the Smart Packages that they will use in their app. Meteor will create a bundle that is ready to be part of the cloud. In this recipe, we will construct a very basic Meteor application in order to see what is the Meteor's way of doing pretty much everything. One important thing to note about Meteor is that it is still work in progress, and should be treated as such.

Getting ready

At the time of writing, the officially-supported platforms are Mac OS and GNU/Linux. There is a preview installation for Windows available as an MSI installer package at `http://win.meteor.com/` where it should have the same functionality, but with a few more bugs and an uncomfortable shell. Official support for Windows is planned in the future, so that should not be a big problem.

For Linux and Mac, installation is done using command line:

```
curl https://install.meteor.com | /bin/sh
```

This command will run and install Meteor to your machine, but it only works for Debian-and RedHat-based distribution. If your OS is not in one of these categories, there is no need for worries, there is probably a package for Meteor that would be already part of your distribution repository, but it might be a few versions behind.

Meteor is built on top of Node.js and uses it's own system for managing packages. By default, it also uses MongoDB as a database.

How to do it...

1. After having Meteor installed, we can start by creating an application titled `simple`:

   `meteor create simple`

   This will create a folder called `simple`, and in it we should have files called `simple.html`, `simple.js`, `simple.css`, and a sub folder called `.meteor`.

2. To start the application, just type `meteor` in the folder:

   `meteor`

   `[[[[[ /the-example-location/simple ]]]]]`

   `Running on: http://localhost:3000/`

How it works...

Before digging into the code, we will take a look at some of the ideas behind Meteor. The creators promote the framework with their seven principles that mostly live up to your expectations:

Seven Principles of Meteor

Data on the Wire. Don't send HTML over the network. Send data and let the client decide how to render it.

One Language. Write both the client and the server parts of your interface in JavaScript.

Database Everywhere. Use the same transparent API to access your database from the client or the server.

Latency Compensation. On the client, use prefetching and model simulation to make it look like you have a zero-latency connection to the database.

Full Stack Reactivity. Make realtime the default. All layers, from database to template, should make an event-driven interface available.

> *Embrace the Ecosystem. Meteor is open source and integrates, rather than replaces, existing open source tools and frameworks.*

> *Simplicity Equals Productivity. The best way to make something seem simple is to have it actually be simple. Accomplish this through clean, classically beautiful APIs.*

Some of these principles are overblown but nonetheless, Meteor is certainly a new way of building web applications.

Let's get back to the generated code and start with `simple.js`:

```js
if (Meteor.isClient) {
  Template.hello.greeting = function () {
    return "Welcome to simple.";
  };

  Template.hello.events({
    'click input' : function () {
      // template data, if any, is available in 'this'
      if (typeof console !== 'undefined'){
        console.log("You pressed the button");
      }
    }
  });
}
if (Meteor.isServer) {
  Meteor.startup(function () {
    // code to run on server at startup
    });
}
```

The variables `Meteor.isServer` and `Meteor.isClient` are provided so that we can change the behavior depending on whether the code is running on the client or the server.

If we add `console.log("I'm running")` in the `server` section of `simple.js`, we can notice the server console reloading the server:

```
I'm running
```

This is basically how we create server code in Meteor, where we can choose if we would like to have a singe file or a whole bunch of other files. Meteor collects all the files we have in our project tree, with the exception for the `server` and `public` subdirectories. It minifies them, and they get served to each client.

Unlike Node.js' way of creating an asynchronous callback, Meteor uses a single thread per request, meaning that it should lead to somewhat more maintainable code.

If we take a look at `simple.html`, we have a simple template that uses the client code that is part of `simple.js`, where the appropriate `Template.hello.events` event and the data in `Template.hello.greeting` are used:

```
<head>
  <title>simple</title>
</head>
<body>
  {{> hello}}
</body>
<template name="hello">
  <h1>Hello World!</h1>
  {{greeting}}
  <input type="button" value="Click" />
</template>
```

We won't get into the details behind templates just yet, but this basic example should be straightforward. If we open up the browser on an already-started application on `http://localhost:3000`, we can see that the data got loaded into the template. When we click on the button, a `console.log("You pressed the button")` function is called, and the message should be displayed in the console. Note that this should be the console of the browser, not the server console, as that part is set to run on the client side.

The part of the code that deals with sensitive data, such as tokens or passwords should be only part of the server, and this can be done easily by placing that code in a folder named `server`. When the server is in the production mode, CSS files and JavaScript are served to the client, packed and bundled. While development, they are sent individually to make debugging simpler.

You may have noticed that the HTML file that got served to the client is a bit different and larger than the one we have in our application folder. This is because Meteor scans the HTML files for top-level elements `<head>`, `<body>`, and `<template>`. The `template` sections are converted into JavaScript functions that can be called from the `Template.*` namespace. As for the `<head>` and `<body>` elements, they get joined together separately, and the additional parts, such as the DOCTYPE and CSS, are included for us automatically.

There's more...

If we need Meteor to serve some static files such as `icons`, `images`, `pdf`'s, or, for example, `robots.txt`, we use the `public` directory for that purpose. The root of the application is the root of the `public` folder; for example, if we have a file called `meme.png`, it will be accessible via `http://localhost:3000/meme.png`.

The following is a simple directory structure:

```
`-- simple
    |-- public
    |   `-- meme.png
    |-- simple.css
    |-- simple.html
    `-- simple.js
```

Reactive programming and data in Meteor.js

Meteor uses NoSQL document-oriented storage and it comes by default with Mongo DB. The name comes form the word "humongous", meaning extremely large. The database is part of a NoSQL database family, meaning, it does not store the data as traditional relational databases. Mongo DB persists the date in a JSON-like document format, making the integration with JavaScript-based frameworks a lot easier. In this recipe, we are going to see how to use the database from Meteor, and how data access is orchestrated.

Getting ready

There is an `icon.png` image in the example files; besides that, only Meteor is needed to be installed on your machine and to have an open command line.

How to do it...

1. First we can start by creating the application named `movies` from the command line:

   ```
   >meteor create movies
   ```

   To simplify the generated structure, we will create two folders: one called `server` and another called `client`. The `movies.css`, `movies.js`, and `movies.html` files can be placed in the `client` directory, as we will putting client-related code there.

2. In the `server` directory, we create a file called `bootstrap.js` that will initialize the database with the few objects that we will define:

   ```javascript
   Meteor.startup(function () {
     if (Movies.find().count() === 0) {
       var data = [
         {
           name: "North by northwest",
           score: "9.9"
         },
         {
           name: "Gone with the wind",
   ```

```
      score:"8.3"
    },
    {
      name: "1984",
      score: "9.9"
    }
  ];

  var timestamp = (new Date()).getTime();
  for (var i = 0; i < data.length; i++) {
    var itemId = Movies.insert({
      name: data[i].name,
      score: data[i].score,
      time: timestamp
    });
  }
}
});
```

3. The first thing you might be wondering is, what is this `Movies` object? It is a collection that we will define in a different file that can be called `publish.js`, as in it we are going to publish the collection from the server. This file will include the following:

```
Movies = new Meteor.Collection("movies");
Meteor.publish('movies', function () {
  return Movies.find();
});
```

4. As for the client side, we have the generated files, so we start creating a simple HTML and a handlebar template to go with it. Inside the template, we will just iterate over Movies and print out a list of elements with the movie name and score. Additionally, in the template, we place button that will contain reference to an image:

```
<body>
  <div id="main">
      {{> movies}}
  </div>
</body>

<template name="movies">
  <h3>List of favorite movies</h3>
  <div id="lists">
    <div>
      <ul>
        {{#each movies}}
          <li><b>{{name}}</b>  {{score}}<li/>
```

```
          {{/each}}
        </ul>
        <button>
          <img src="icon.png" width="30px" height="30px" />
        </button>
      </div>
    </div>
</template>
```

In order to make the `icon.png` image available as a static file, we need to create a folder named `public` and place the image there. This follows the principle of *convention over configuration*, and there is no real need why you should not follow it, at least most of the time.

5. As for the client side, in the previously generated `movies.js` file, we should automatically subscribe to the `servers` collection of movies. Also, we will add a functionality to fill the `movies` variable and add an event also for the button that will trigger a save of a random new movie:

```
// Define mongo style collections to match server/publish.js.
Movies = new Meteor.Collection("movies");

// Always be subscribed to the movies list.
Meteor.autorun(function () {
    Meteor.subscribe('movies');
});

// fill the movies variable with data from the collection sorted
by name
Template.movies.movies = function () {
  return Movies.find({}, {sort: {name: 1}});
};

// on click we insert a random movie
Template.movies.events({
  'click button': function(){
    Movies.insert({
      name: "random awesome movie",
      score: Math.random() * 10
    });
  }
});
```

6. Now everything should be working. After starting the application with `meteor`, we can access it in the browser on the default port `http://localhost:3000/`. If we want to change the port on which the application runs, for example on port `3333`, we can use the following command:

```
meteor --port 3333
```

How it works...

We can first start with the data, if we have the server running, we can open up another console, where we can access the same directory. Then, after opening the same folder in the console, we run the following command:

```
meteor mongo

MongoDB shell version: 2.2.3

connecting to: 127.0.0.1:3002/meteor
```

That opens up a simple console on which we can query our database. Mongo stores the data as collections, and in order to get the names of all of our available movies, we can use the following command:

```
> db.getCollectionNames()

[ "movies", "system.indexes" ]
```

The `movies` collection is the one we defined in our `bootstrap.js` initialization; as for `system.indexes`, it is a collection contains all the indexes of the database. To manipulate data with this collection, we can use `ensureIndex()` and `dropIndex()`.

In the console, we can assign the following variables:

```
> var x = db.getCollection("movies");

> x

meteor.movies
```

Collections can be queried with `find()`; if we try to call it without arguments, it returns all the elements:

```
> x.find();

{ "name" : "North by northwest", "score" : "9.9", "time" : 1360630048083,
"_id" : "bc8f1a7a-71bd-49a9-b6d9-ed0d782db89d" }

{ "name" : "Gone with the wind", "score" : "8.3", "time" : 1360630048083,
"_id" : "1d7f1c43-3108-4cc5-8fbf-fc8fa10ef6e2" }

{ "name" : "1984", "score" : "9.9", "time" : 1360630048083, "_id" :
"08633d22-aa0b-454f-a6d8-aa2aaad2fbb1" }

...
```

The data is basic JSON, making it easy to manipulate with JavaScript. If you take a look at the objects, you can notice the `"_id" : "08633d22-aa0b-454f-a6d8-aa2aaad2fbb1"` key-value pair. This is a unique key generated by Mongo and we use it to reference and manipulate that object, commonly referred to as **document**.

If we wanted to delete the record with an ID of `beef20a3-c66d-474b-af32-aa3e6503f0de`, we can use the following command:

```
> db.movies.remove({"_id":"beef20a3-c66d-474b-af32-aa3e6503f0de"});
```

After that, we can call `db.movies.find()` to see to notice that one is now missing. There are plenty of other commands used for data manipulation, but most of them are intuitive, and you can easily guess by their names. As a quick reminder and a learning tool, there is a `help` function that can be called:

```
>help
```

```
>db.help()
```

These two bring up a list of commands and a short explanation of what each does. You should not get overwhelmed by the number of commands, as we will not use most of them, but it still makes a good reference.

> For a more detailed tutorial on MongoDB commands, visit `http://mongodb.org` and click on **TRY IT OUT** to try the online shell. There are tones of resources for NoSQL on the Web, but one great introduction done by *Martin Flower* is available at `http://www.youtube.com/watch?v=qI_g07C_Q5I`.

If we open a browser, we may notice that on every click on the Random button, a new record is added instantly. This looks extremely fast and it is not just because the server is running locally. Every time a client issues a write to the server, it instantly updates the local cache without response from the server if the write went successful. When the server receives the request and accepts the update, then the client does not have to do anything on the screen. This should happen most of the time and it saves the round trip waiting time, making the screen more responsive. On the other hand, if the server rejects the update, the client's cache gets updated with the correct result.

In Meteor, the same API is used for the client and the server in order to access the database. Emphasis is given to reducing the time for round trips to the server for every design decision in the framework. Requests and responses, as well as message invalidation, are orchestrated to do this.

We used `autorun` to automatically get updates from the server in our `movies.js`:

```
Meteor.autorun(function () {
    Meteor.subscribe('movies');
});
```

The block of code in the `autorun` function is a so-called **reactive context**, enabling us to write code in an imperative style, but get a reactive behavior.

Reactive programming is one of the programming paradigms that are oriented around propagation of change. In imperative programming, if we have an expression such as $z = x + y$, this means that the result of the evaluation of $x + y$ will be assigned to z as expected. For example, if we have $x = 42$ and $y = 13$, then $z = 42 + 13$ or $z = 55$. The values of x and y can be changed later, for example, they can be changed to $x=4$ and $y=4$, but this will not affect z in any way, it will still be 55.

The simplest example for this is a modern spreadsheet program, such as Microsoft Excel or Google docs spreadsheet. Spreadsheet cells commonly contain literal values such as number for example, or can contain formulas that have derived values from some other cells. In our cell C3 we could have the formula `"=A1+B1"` meaning when we change some of the values in A1 or B1, C3 will get autoupdated.

In MVC architecture, a simplification can be made using reactive programming, where we automatically propagate the changes from the view towards the model and back that can be very beneficial in real-time systems.

The use of reactive contexts saves us from writing a whole class of calls. In our example, we would first need to unsubscribe when something has changed and then again resubscribe to get the data back from the server. This reduces a substantial amount of code that could end up being error-prone and add more complexity in the maintenance phase.

> Besides `Meteor.autorun`, reactive context is applied in `Templates` and in the `Meteor.render` and `Meteor.renderList` functions.
>
> As for the data sources that can trigger changes, we can use database `collections` and `session` variables, and a few other functions related to authentication and authorization. You can find more details about it in the documentation of Meteor about reactivity at `http://docs.meteor.com/#reactivity`.

If you open up two different browsers side by side, you may notice that the same data is shown even if the sessions are different. In order to have user-specific data, we will create an example in the next recipe.

You might wish to send the entire collection to the client, but first think thoroughly if that is what the client actually needs. Often, it might be a lot wiser to send only certain fields rather than entire documents. In order to lower the network traffic, certain parts of the client can have subscription turned off and the documents for those parts will be removed from the local cache unless used in other active subscription.

There's more...

Because the data we used is stored in the database, if we changed the data there using some external application, it will also trigger changes to the client. In the next recipe, we will see how we can allow multiple users to have their own favorite list for each of them instead of a single global list.

Live HTML and user-specific data in Meteor.js

You may have noticed in the previous recipe that the data we used was global and not user-specific. In this recipe, we will see how we can create session data and take a deeper look into the templates as well as the data associated with them. In order to demonstrate this, we will create a small image-voting application, where the user will be prompted for the name, and after that they are given 50 points that they can spend for votes on the images.

Getting ready

To make the recipe simpler, we will serve the images statically from our `public` directory so you can download the sample images that are part of the example code or use your own ones.

How to do it...

1. We start as any other normal Meteor application:

    ```
    >meteor create gallery
    ```

2. Because we will use a little bit more code in this recipe, it makes sense to create a structure with a `public` folder for the static files, and the `server` and `client` folders for the server and client code respectively. After that, we can move the generated gallery files to the `client` folder and add the images to the `public` folder. The images, for simplicity, will be named `1.jpg`, `2.jpg`, `3.jpg`, and guess what, `4.jpg`. Then we proceed with creating a `bootstrap.js` file in the `server` folder:

    ```
    // if the database is empty fill it with data
    Meteor.startup(function () {
      //has some images
      if (Images.find().count() < 4) {
        var images = [
    ```

```
  {
    name: "Awesome Cat",
    url: "img/1.jpg",
    votes: "0"
  },{
    name:"Cool Cat",
    url: "img/2.jpg",
    votes: "0"
  },{
    name:"Mjauuu",
    url: "img/3.jpg",
    votes: "0"
  },{
    name:"The Cat",
    url: "img/4.jpg",
    votes: "0"
  }
];

for (var i = 0; i < images.length; i++) {
  Images.insert(images[i]);
}

Users.insert({
  name: "awesome user",
  pointsLeft: "30"
});
    }
  });
```

3. This will initialize the database with a simple user and add some data about the images, as well as add a condition that this should happen only when there are less than four images in the database.

> You may notice that we are using a `for` loop to insert the data, but since Version 2.2 of MongoDB, the `db.collection.insert()` function can accept an array of elements and do a bulk insert of them into the collection, but we are not using the method like that, as it will result in a slightly more complex structure, and we want to go with the simplest case. You can read more about the `db.collecton.insert()` on `http://docs.mongodb.org/manual/reference/method/db.collection.insert/`.

4. After this, we can proceed with the definition and the publishing of the collections, making the collections available to the client side:

```
// DB collection of movies
Images = new Meteor.Collection("images");

// DB collection of users
Users = new Meteor.Collection("users");

// Publish complete set of lists to all clients.
Meteor.publish('images', function () {
  return Images.find();
});

// Publish for users
Meteor.publish('users', function () {
  return Users.find();
});
```

5. Now we can continue with the template code in `gallery.html`:

```html
<body>
  <div class="box">
    {{> main}}
  </div>
  {{> footer}}
</body>

<template name="footer">
  <footer>
    {{footerText}}
  </footer>
</template>
```

6. The `main` template will check whether there is a user currently present. If present, it will display the voting, otherwise, it will display a simple form to enter a name:

```html
<template name="main">
  {{#if hasUserEnteredName}}
    {{> votes}}
    {{> gallery}}
  {{else}}
  <label>Please insert your name
    <input name="name">
    </input>
    <button class="name">start</button>
    </label>
  {{/if}}
</template>
```

7. The `votes` template will show how many votes are there left for the user, and the gallery will display the images together with the info about current number of votes, as well as add a button that will be used for voting:

```
<template name="votes">
  <h3>You have <i>{{numberOfVotes}}</i> votes left</h3>
</template>

<template name="gallery">
  <div>
    {{#each images}}
    <div class="item">
      <p>
        <b>Cat named:</b>{{name}}
        </p>
      <img src="{{url}}" />
      <p>
        Votes:
        <progress value="{{votes}}" max="500" />
        <output>{{votes}}</output>
      </p>
      <button class="vote">Vote for me</button>
    </div>
    {{/each}}
  </div>
</template>
```

8. We can start up the application and see if everything turned up as expected. If you open up the application on two browser sessions side by side, and enter two different names, you can notice that when we vote on the images, the number of votes gets updated instantly on the other browser session.

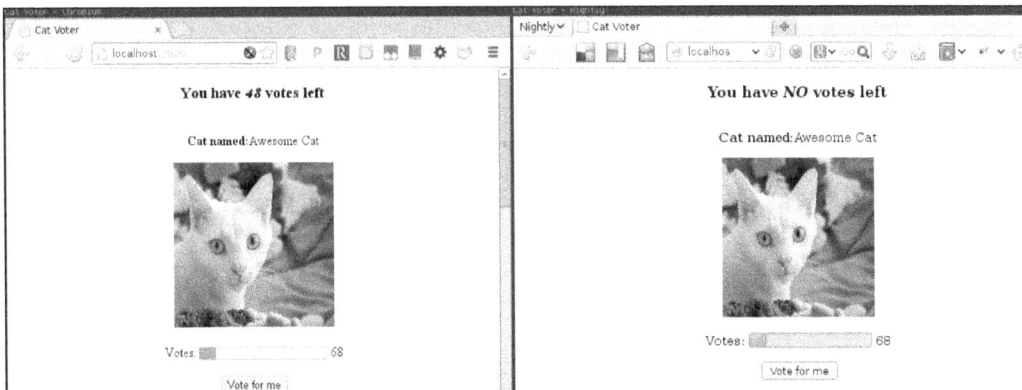

How it works...

The first thing you might want to see is what is the state in the database. While having the server up, you can start the `meteor mongo` console and list the collections with `db.getCollectionNames()`, where you should have the following result:

```
[ "images", "system.indexes", "users" ]
```

The collection names are the ones we defined in our `publish.js` file. As for the data contained in the database, we decided on having URL to the images in the `public` folder for the image collection, because that is simpler for this case.

> If you need to store or manipulate binary data such as images, you can do that in MongoDB, and it plays very well with Meteor. There we can use EJSON, where the E stands for extended. Basically, it supports all JSON types while adding additional Data via the JavaScript `Date()` object and Binary data via `Uint8Array`. You can also define your own custom datatypes and use the EJSON object similarly to the regulator JSON. There are a few other methods such as `EJSON.newBinary(size)` and `EJSON.addType(name,factory)`, and you can read more about them on `http://docs.meteor.com/#ejson`. There is also the option to configure your own already existing MongoDB instance. This is done by defining an environment variable before starting meteor:
>
> `MONGO_URL=mongodb://localhost:3317 meteor`
>
> This makes it convenient to have a same MongoDB server that is used by non-Meteor applications.

In the `gallery.js` file, in order to have some data in the client side, we used `Session` variables. This is actuality a global object that can be used on the client side to store any key-value pairs. Just like you are used to in other frameworks and languages, we have `Session.set("theKey", someValue)` that stores `someValue` for `theKey` and `Session.get("theKey")` is used to retrieve the data. As for initialization, there is the `Session.setDefault("theKey", initalValue)`, making it handy to avoid reinitialization of the variable every time a new version of your application is loaded.

> You can read more about the Session object in the Meteor specification at `http://docs.meteor.com/#session`.

As you have probably noticed so far, we can nest templates. This is a standard handlebar behavior, and in our case, we use it to simplify the view logic. In the real-life scenario, it not only makes more sense to separate only the parts that can be reused in some other sections of the application, but also at the same time, you don't want to have huge templates that make your code hard to read. In order to have events, we can use standard CSS selectors to add them to our template, so if we want to attach a callback on the `click` event of an element using the `.name` CSS class in the `main` template, we can use the following code:

```
Template.main.events({
    'click .name' : function () { ... }
});
```

In the event callback, we can access several objects that are of use to us. We used some of them in `Template.gallery.events`, where `onclick` callback accepts two arguments; we can see that in this object, and we have access to the related document. Having the data context of where the element was triggered allows easy manipulation of that section:

```
Template.gallery.events({
  'click .vote' : function(e,t) {
    //this object can be used to access elements
        }
});
```

The two arguments that are passed in the callback allow access to the event type as well as the `DOMElement` of the current target.

> More about how event maps and selectors are used as well as what else is accessible in the event callback can be found at `http://docs.meteor.com/#eventmaps`. You can also attach callbacks that would be called after the template is rendered, `http://docs.meteor.com/#template_rendered`. There is also an option to use other template engines instead of handlebars, such as Jade, for example, `http://docs.meteor.com/#templates`. This can be done as the reactive context for the templates is not dependent on the engine; you can even construct the HTML manually by appending string and it will still work.

In the `main` template besides `Users.insert`, we used the `db.collection.findOne` function that returns the first object that is found. This is done by matching the query that we specify with the database and retrieving the first result in natural order if found.

> More detailed explanation of `findOne` is available in the MongoDB documentation at `http://docs.mongodb.org/manual/reference/method/db.collection.findOne/`.

As for the update of the elements, the collection accepts two arguments, first being the selection query where, for example in `voteForImage`, we used the MongoDB-generated `_id` for matching the element, and the second is the new update using the `$set` modifier to update the `pointsLeft` property of the selected documents:

```
Users.update(
    {_id:currentUser._id},
    {$set:{pointsLeft:currentUser.pointsLeft}}
);
```

> There are several different update modifiers that can be used, and you can read about them in great detail in the documentation, but to get you up to speed with the basics,, you can use some of the reference cards provided by 10gen, the company behind MongoDB. More details can be found at `http://www.10gen.com/reference`.

In our case, we could have used the `$inc` modifier that increments the value we want for a given amount, but for simplicity, we picked the more general `$set` modifier. Also, one other additional improvement that can be done is to move the collection declarations, such as `Images = new Meteor.Collection('images')`, into a common file for the server and the client that is not in the respective folders so that we can reduce the code duplication.

There's more...

At some point of time, you may want to have some kind of timer based on the standard JavaScript `setTimeout` or `setInterval` functions. You will get an error if you try to do so, but the same functionality is provided by `Meteor.setTimeout` and `Meteor.setInterval` functions (`http://docs.meteor.com/#timers`).

When it comes to the view, you may have seen so far that it is entirely handled with JavaScript. This is one of the problems with Meteor, because the content generated like this is hard to get indexed by search engines such as Google. In order to help you out with this problem, there is a package called **spiderable** (`http://docs.meteor.com/#spiderable`) that can be used as a temporary fix.

Security mechanisms in Meteor.js

There has been a lot of controversy around the security in Meteor. Database everywhere does not scream security. We are using the same API for the client- and server-side code, and it does not take a genius to tell that we can also delete collections. After playing around for a while with the JavaScript console, we could easily delete all the Users in our previous example. You can always roll your own implementation for the security; for example, you can override the default server method handlers, making the Users and Images collections accessible from the client:

```
Meteor.startup(function () {
  var collection = ['Users', 'Images'];
  var redefine = ['insert', 'update', 'remove'];
  for (var i = 0; i < collection.length; i++) {
    for (var j = 0; j < redefine.length; i++){
      Meteor.default_server.method_handlers['/' + collection[i] + '/'
+ redefine[j]] = function() {
        console.log('someone is hacking you, oh no !!! Too bad for
him...');
      };
    }
  }
});
```

In this recipe, we will take a look at what is the Meteor's way of securing the applications, and some of the mechanisms for authentication and authorization. To do this, we will create a simple list-entering application.

Getting ready

There are no special preparations required for this recipe; you only need command line and an installed version of Meteor.

How to do it...

Let's get started with it.

1. Create an application named `secure` using `meteor create secure`. In the generated `secure.html` file, we will define a small template that will contain an input element, a button, and a list of already available list entries:

    ```
    <body>
      {{> list}}
    </body>

    <template name="list">
      <h1>This is my awesome list</h1>
      <input placeholder="enter awesomeness"> </input>
      <button>Add</button>
      <ul>
        {{#each items}}
          <li>{{text}} </li>
        {{/each}}
      </ul>
    </template>
    ```

2. The accompanied code in `secure.js` will initialize one element of the list and add the date for the rendering of the templates:

    ```
    Notes = new Meteor.Collection("Notes");

    if (Meteor.isClient) {
      Template.list.items = function () {
        return Notes.find();
      };

      Template.list.events({
        'click button' : function () {
          Notes.insert({
            text: $('input').val()
          });
        }
      });
    }

    if (Meteor.isServer) {
      Meteor.startup(function () {
        //initialize
        if(Notes.find().count() < 1){
    ```

```
      Notes.insert({
        text: "awesomeness"
      });
    }
  });
}
```

3. Start the application and play around with it to check if it is working. If you open up the browser's console at this point, we can directly access `Notes.remove()`, and this is one of the things that we usually want to forbid. We can remove one of the default smart packages that is part of the generated application with the following command:

   `meteor remove insecure`

4. The same thing can be achieved by manually editing `.meteor/packages`. This will make our application "secure", even too much secure, if there is such a thing.

5. Now if we try to toy with the browser's console, we'll get the following message:

   `insert failed: Access denied`

   The same message appears if we just click on the **Add** button that previously worked. This is because all the requests to the DB are now treated as anonymous, and we only get what is published from the server.

6. We can always roll our own authentication, but there is a great one built in; to add it in our project, we can use the following code:

   `> meteor add accounts-base`

   `accounts-base: A user account system`

   `> meteor add accounts-password`

   `accounts-password: Password support for accounts.`

   `> meteor add email`

   `email: Send email messages`

   `>  meteor add accounts-ui`

   `accounts-ui: Simple templates to add login widgets to an app.`

7. As previously mentioned, we can add these packages directly in our `packages` file; it is a good idea to check often what you have there in the example applications you try out so that you won't be surprised.

> A variety of packages and third-party libraries extend the core Meteor functionality. There are packages for D3, underscore, backbone, and plenty more added each day. Those and some basic supporting logic can be found at `http://docs.meteor.com/#packages`. There is also a way to create your own extension and common logic for your applications.

8. The packages we included are a set of helpers that make the authentication user management logic automatic. Accounts-UI even enable us to have great user interface to log in with negligible effort. So what efforts do we need to make to enable it? First, we'll add a small block of code in the place where we what the login UI to appear:

```
<div id="login">
    {{loginButtons align="right"}}
</div>
```

9. Also we need to configure the type of login we want, so in our case, we use a simple username and password type, where optionally an e-mail can be entered. We add this config in the `secure.js` file:

```
Accounts.ui.config({
    passwordSignupFields: 'USERNAME_AND_OPTIONAL_EMAIL'
});
```

10. One other thing you might want to add is a simple CSS style to position the login box:

After a simple signup and login to the account, we should notice a user link with our username. We could use this in order to sign out. As you can notice, this was as effortless as it gets.

There are plenty of other configuration options for the Accounts-UI, as well as extensions for connecting with Twitter, Facebook, Google, and GitHub accounts. More information can be found on `http://docs.meteor.com/#accounts_ui_config`, and the package documentation can be found at `http://docs.meteor.com/#accountsui`. Also, you can use features such as sending a verification e-mail or confirmation.

How it works...

After login, if we try to add text using our button, we will notice that we still don't have access, as our user is not authorized to do inserts. To allow inserts for specific users, use the following code:

```
Notes.allow({
    insert: function (userId, doc) {
      console.log(userId);
      console.log(doc);
      //do the check for the permission and return true if allowed
      return true;
    }
});
```

In this insert callback, we can allow or deny access to the user with `userId` for the given document. For our case, the document is the `Notes` object that we are trying to insert and the `userId` is the ID of the currently logged user. Besides `collection.allow`, there is also its counterpart `collection.deny` that we can use to forbid access for certain methods even if there is an `allow` rule.

Now, it is very easy to create an advanced authorization system where we specify access rights programmatically. There are programmers who argue that this causes a lot of overhead, and it might be the case for certain applications, but for most of them, it should be very simple to set up access rights like this.

In general, we should never, ever trust data that is coming from the client. Access should only be given to the parts that they must use and the input should be filtered. Having credit card data sent to the client is an easy way to destroy your business. Just because Meteor does so many things for us, that does not mean that we should forget about other common practices, such as data validation.

You might be wondering where the user data, which we used for signup, is stored. If we access the Mongo console with `meteor mongo`, there is a `users` collection that should contain something like the following:

```
{
  "createdAt": 1362434550460,
  "services": {
    "password": {
      "srp": {
        "identity": "bE9uYyziWxM2soGem",
        "salt": "FDEduAsvpf5ZJCWea",
```

```
        "verifier": "11a2fa4139c8283db1ce61e5f5fa7bf875da27a9b8ec195
    baae49cd69c7f3ea48e1c1db471e1bc6aa1a9894a0633f44098717e0c6af367dcd39f
    964d63f4fd5346f3b314bd897b76d3f31aa8aeb37030e5fef099b77efb594ad07103
    6ec31fb6a3016f0c6cc43605469f798e20fc5b005e982e579014aef7742aac3
    bc5792271"
        }
      },
      "resume": {
        "loginTokens": [
          {
            "token": "PDbpT6jtKcdvZMurr",
            "when": 1362434550460
          }
        ]
      }
    },
    "username": "mite",
    "emails": [
      {
        "address": "mitemitereski@gmail.com",
        "verified": false
      }
    ],
    "_id": "QuZEe4uSPK6MfM5PQ"
}
```

As you can notice, it's more or less a standard data of what you might expect to be stored in the database. The passwords are stored hashed with salting to prevent some common attacks.

And that is it; we have a very simple yet secure application. The data of the list is of course not user-specific but that could be easily extended by adding an owner field of each of the created documents.

There's more...

One thing you should accept is that Meteor is still not completely finished. There are a lot of changes being done with every version until it gets fully stable. Most of the stuff that the users requested is being added, as well as other significant architecture improvements are being implemented, so you need to update parts of the code with every version.

One great resource for information are the example apps; you can list them by calling example apps using the `meteor create –list` command; as for getting the code again, you can use `meteor create -example nameofexample`.

When it comes down to deployment, we can freely use the server that is provided as our own, but there is an option to have it deployed on `www.meteor.com`. This is a service provided by a startup company behind this fun framework. The deployment there is just one command:

```
>meteor deploy myapp.meteor.com
```

More information about the cloud solution can be found at `http://docs.meteor.com/#meteordeploy`.

There is also the option to generate a fully contained Node.js application from our Meteor app and use some other cloud service. This can be done using the following command:

```
>meteor bundle packed.tgz
```

As for the running of the unpacked file use the following command:

```
> PORT=3000 MONGO_URL=mongodb://localhost:2222/myapp node main.js
```

This is possible as Meteor, behind the scenes, is a Node.js framework with different kind of packaging.

11
Data Storage

This chapter covers the following recipes:

- ▸ Data URI
- ▸ Session and local storage
- ▸ Reading data from files
- ▸ Using IndexedDB
- ▸ Limits of the storage and how to ask for more
- ▸ Manipulating the browser history

Introduction

When we talk about storage, most of the developers think about storing data on the server on some database. HTML5 really makes a leap forward on what can be passed around and saved to the client side. Whether is for some temporary use, caching, or full offline usage of entire apps, client-side storage is becoming more and more common.

All of these great features that enable us to store data at the client side making the applications ultimately faster, more usable and reachable. Even in cloud-based solutions we still need some local data that will make the user experience nicer.

The chapter covers some of the features that are related to HTML5 and are about data storage.

Data URI

We have already used on several occasions Data **URI** (**Uniform resource identifier**) throughout this book, but never got into details on what can we use it for as well as what are the limitations. Data URI are often referred to as Data **URL** (**Uniform Resource Locator**) though technically speaking they don't actually locate anything from a remote site.

In this example, we will use different media types and check the size constraints.

Getting ready

We will only need browser and some sample text files for this example. The files can be downloaded as part of the `files` folder in the example files.

How to do it...

In order to see some of the options available we will create a simple HTML file with few different use scenarios:

1. The `head` section will include the `example.css` file:

   ```
   <head>
   <title>Data URI example</title>
   <link rel="stylesheet" type="text/css" href="example.css">
   </head>
   ```

2. In the `body` section we add a `div` element that will serve as a container for the CSS image Data URI:

   ```
   <div id="someImage">
   CSS image
   </div>
   ```

3. By using Data URI we can create a simple editor that will be opened by clicking on a link:

   ```
   <a href="data:text/html,<body contenteditable>write here">open editor</a>
   ```

4. base64 is optional and character set can be used:

   ```
   <a href="data:text/plain;charset=utf-8,▨▨▨▨▨▨▨▨▨▨▨▨%20▨▨%20▨▨%20
   ▨▨▨▨▨▨%20▨▨▨▨▨">this is some UTF-8 text </a>
   ```

5. Data URI can be a raw SVG:

```
<p>Image tag </p>
<imgsrc='data:image/svg+xml,<svgxmlns="http://www.w3.org/2000/
svg" version="1.1"><circle cx="100" cy="50" r="40" stroke="black"
stroke-width="1" fill="red" /></svg>' />
```

6. The accompanying CSS code with Data URI is used to represent `background-image`:

```
img {
   width: 300px;
   height: 110px;
}


#someImage {
   background-image : url('data:image/svg+xml,<svgxmlns="http://
www.w3.org/2000/svg" version="1.1"><path d="M 100,100
l150,0a150,150 0 0,0 -37,-97 z" fill="green" stroke="black"
stroke-width="2" stroke-linejoin="round" /></svg>');
}
```

This will display two images and links to simple editor and a small text file:

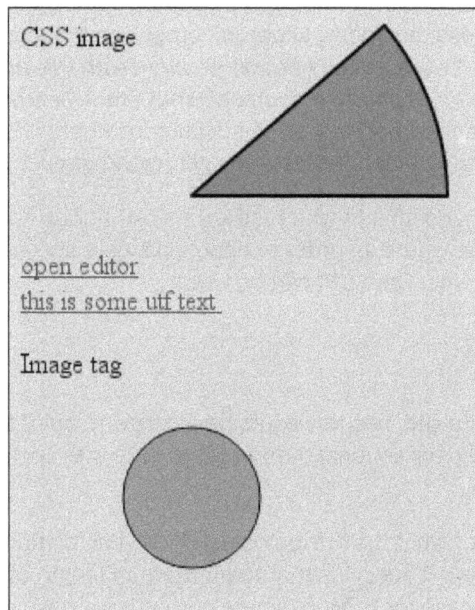

How it works...

One common misconception is that Data URI can be used only to represent images. As we have seen in our example this is not the case. Strictly speaking, Data URI is not an HTML5 feature but included in RFC-2397 (`http://tools.ietf.org/html/rfc2397`), specified in 1998 with the original proposal of the idea in 1995. The idea behind it is to have an embeddable data directly inline. The URI form is specified as:

```
data:[<mediatype>][;base64],<data>
```

The `mediatype` attribute is Internet media type or its older name is MIME. In case we don't specify it, it defaults to `text/plain;charset=US-ASCII`.

Besides being cool and different why should we use Data URI?

One good reason is to derive data from the currently displayed document. For example, we could create an image from a `canvas` element or have a CSV file generated from the current table.

Another reason is speed of loading a web page. This is contradictory, since Data URI often is base64 encoded and this increases the size of the document to 1/3rd. The principle behind the speed up is the reduction in the number of requests. This makes sense for transfer of small files that should be less than a few kilobytes, otherwise the gain from not making another request is small if it even exists. Another problem with this approach is that we are losing the individual cache for separate resources. What otherwise would be a separately cached file, now has the same properties as the document where it is embedded. If that document changes often, the embedded data will get reloaded each time.

The other use cases are environments with restrictions on various resources. E-mail is an example of this kind of case where, in order to enable a single document experience without having images as attachments, Data URI can be used.

There's more...

In some applications of Data URI, security could be a concern, but if the client app in most of the browsers follow the specifications, then only the data with `mediatype` allowed will be handled.

There are also size limits for what the attributes in HTML5 can contain. HTML 4 has the `ATTSPLEN` restrictions where it specifies that the maximum length of the attributes is 65536 characters. This is not the case for HTML5, where currently we have different state on each browser version. For Firefox 3.x it was 600 KB, for Chrome 19 it was 2 MB, and IE 8 has a limit of 32 KB. It is safe to say that it makes sense only for smaller resources.

Session and local storage

Cookies are a common way to save state from our application at the client side. This might be some checkboxes that were selected or some kind of temporary data, for example, current flow in a wizard app or even a session identifier.

This is a proven method for quite some time, but there are a few use cases where it is just uncomfortable to create cookies and they impose certain limits and overhead that can be avoided.

Session and local storage solve some of the issues with cookies and enable a simple storage of data on the client. In this recipe we will create a simple form that will take advantage of the HTML5 storage API.

Getting ready

In this recipe we will use several images that can be retrieved from the `images` folder or you can use your own selection. Additionally since we will use a simulated response from the REST API of a JSON object we need to start a local HTTP server that will serve our static files.

How to do it...

We can start off by creating a form that will have a dog selection and an area to leave comments. When we click on a button in the form, an image will be displayed of the selected dog. In addition to that, we shall have an output field for the number of visits made by the current user:

1. We link a simple CSS class in the `head` section:

    ```
    <meta charset="utf-8">
    <title>Session and storage</title>
    <link rel="stylesheet" type="text/css" href="example.css" />
    ```

2. The form will contain the following radio buttons and a text area:

    ```
    <form id="dogPicker">
    <fieldset>
    <legend>Pick a dog</legend>
    <div id="imageList"></div>
    <p>The best is:</p>
    <p>
    <input id="dog1" type="radio" name="dog" value="dog1" />
    <label for="dog1">small dog</label>

    <input id="dog2" type="radio" name="dog" value="dog2" />
    ```

```
<label for="dog2">doggy</label>

<input id="dog3" type="radio" name="dog" value="dog3" />
<label for="dog3">other dog</label>
</p>
</fieldset>

<label for="comment">Leave a comment</label>
<textarea id="comment" name="comment" ></textarea>
<button id="send" type="button">Pick</button>
</form>
```

3. We add a counter for the number of visits as follows:

```
<p>
        You have opened this page <output id="counter">0</output>
times
</p>
```

4. Also a simple `div` element as a placeholder for the selected dog image and the dependency to jQuery, and include the `example.js` file that we will write later on:

```
<div id="selectedImage"></div>
<script src="//cdnjs.cloudflare.com/ajax/libs/jquery/1.8.3/jquery.
min.js"></script>
<script src="example.js" ></script>
```

5. For the `example.js` file we create a function that will store the comment in the session on clicking on a button. If the data is not available a request to the `"dogs. json"` variable will be made:

```
$(function() {
  $('#send').click(function() {
vardogId = $("#dogPicker :radio:checked").val();
var comment = $('#comment').val();
    //different ways to set data
sessionStorage.comment = comment;
    // if no data available do AJAX call
    if (localStorage.dogData) {
showSelectedImage(dogId);
    } else {
      $.ajax({
url: "dogs.json",
      }).done(function(data){
localStorage.dogData = JSON.stringify(data);
showSelectedImage(dogId);
      });
    }
  });
```

> With #dogPicker :radio:checked, we select all the checked input radio subelements of the element with ID dogPicker.

6. Since the data for the comment is stored in the session, upon clicking on that we can have a way of loading it for the next time:

```
if (sessionStorage.comment) {
    $('#comment').val(sessionStorage.comment);
}
```

7. But using localStorage we can increment the viewCount variable or else initialize it for the first time:

```
if (localStorage.viewCount) {
localStorage.viewCount++;
    $('#counter').val(localStorage.viewCount);
} else {
localStorage.viewCount = 1;
}
```

8. The showSelectedImages method goes through each of the dog object, in the list we have in localStorage and creates an image element with the selected file:

```
function showSelectedImage(dogId){
vardogList = JSON.parse(localStorage.dogData);
vardogFile;
    $.each(dogList.dogs, function(i,e){
        if(e.id === dogId){
dogFile = e.file;
        };
    });
        $('#selectedImage').html("<imgsrc='images/" + dogFile +
"'></img>");
    }
```

If we select a radio button and click on the it, an image of a dog should be displayed, if we try to reload that cache then (*Ctrl + F5*) in most browsers the comment data will still remain there. If we open the same URL it in another tab then the comment should not be there, meaning that the session is tied to a single browser window or a tab. On the other hand the counter should increment each time and no additional requests are done for the dogs.json file.

How it works...

Both `sessionStorage` and `localStorage` share the common `Storage` interface, and they are defined as part of `http://www.w3.org/TR/webstorage/`. We can use the dot notation to read or write to the storage, for example `storage.key = someValue` and `someValue = storage.key`. The longer form is to access data using method calls, `storage.setItem(key, value)` and `storage.getItem(key)`.

Tne restriction we have for the key and values here is that is that they need to be "strings". In our example, we needed to store JSON, so in order to make it compatible for values, we used `JSON.stringify` and `JSON.parse`. There is also a method `storage.removeItem(key)` to delete an item, or to clear the entire storage with `storage.clear()`.

`sessionStorage` is an object that can be used for storing information that last for the duration of a browser's session, this is where the name originates. Information is retained even after reload occurred making it a powerful alternative to session cookies. The context of which the items stored are valid is the current website domain for the duration of the session of the currently opened tab. For example, if we store an item on domain `http://example.com/1.html`, it will be accessible at `http://example.com/2.html` or any other page of the same domain.

`LocalStorage`, on the other hand, is a persistent storage, and unlike `sessionStorage`, it applies even after the end of session. This is similar to the behavior of standard cookies, but unlike them which can hold very limited amount of data. `localStorage` comes with 5 MB by default on most of the browsers and 10 MB on IE. You need to keep in mind that we are storing the data as strings rather than their original form, for example, integers or floats, so the final representation that will be stored will be larger. If we happen to overcome the size limit of our storage, then an exception with the `QUOTA_EXCEEDED_ERR` error message will be thrown.

In our code, we used `localStorage` to cache a JSON resource, giving us a full control of invalidation. Also, we created a simple counter for the number of visits by a given user.

The obvious isolation for which separate storage exists is the combination of `hostname` and `port`. Less common knowledge is the isolation of the web storage depending on the tuple of `scheme/host/port`. Scheme contains the subdomain and protocol. So, if a page has a mixed type of resources loaded with `https` and `http`, you might not get so obvious results. Having mixed resources similar to that is not a good security practice, but it often happens nonetheless. In either case, no sensitive data should be stored in local or session storage.

Another case is the private/incognito mode that most of the browsers nowadays have. While the page is opened in that mode, a new temporary database for those values will be used. Everything that will be stored while in this mode will only be part of that session.

There's more...

Local Storage uses an synchronous API that runs on the main UI thread in the browser. Because of that, there is a very small possibility that a race condition can happen if we have the same site opened on multiple, different windows. This is not a real problem for most of the use cases. For clearing data from the client side, we can always call `storage.clear()`, but most browsers now have developer tools that ease the manipulation:

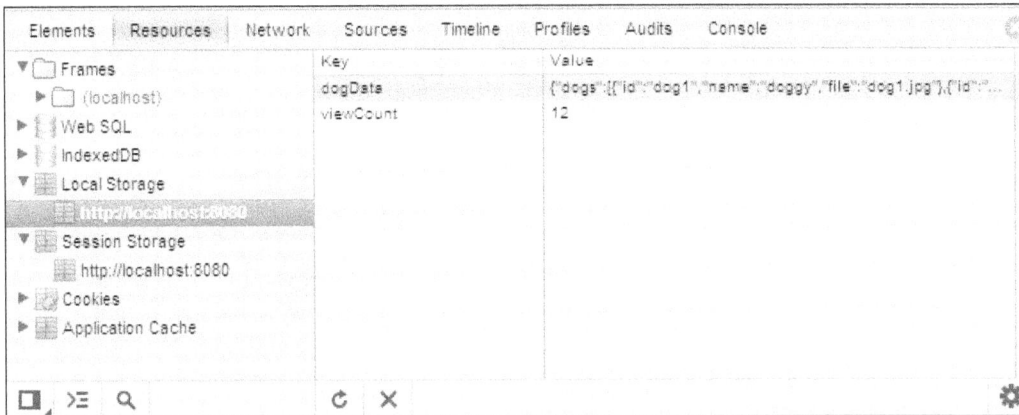

When it comes to polyfills there are plenty of them available, for example `https://code.google.com/p/sessionstorage/` or `https://gist.github.com/remy/350433`. You might be wondering how they work, because storage is a new feature that is added to the browsers. Most of them use cookies to store data, so they are usually limited to 2 KB, the maximum size of cookie. Others use the IE userData(`http://msdn.microsoft.com/en-us/library/ms531424%28VS.85%29.aspx`) object to enable its usage on an older version of IE. There are also libraries, for example, `http://www.jstorage.info/` that provide the same interface for multiple browser versions. Also, there is `Persists.js` that enables multiple different fallback solutions: flash – Flash 8 persistent storage, gears – Google gears-based persistent storage, localstorage – HTML5 draft storage, whatwg_db – HTML5 draft database storage, globalstorage – HTML5 draft storage (now obsolete), IE – Internet Explorer user data behaviors, and cookie – Cookie-based persistent storage.

> There is also a custom object-based fallback that can be created to enable `localStorage` on older browsers. More info on MDN can be found at `https://developer.mozilla.org/en-US/docs/DOM/Storage#Compatibility`.

`globalStorage` is implemented in several versions of Firefox, but because there was a lot of confusion related to the implementations, it has been removed from Firefox 13, as well as the specification for Web storage.

When it comes to security, it is never a good idea to have sensitive data at the client side storage. If there is an XSS vulnerability in your site then the storage can be read. It does not make much sense to encrypt the data with server side-based key, since that will make us dependent on the server data. There is also a possible DNS spoofing attack that can happen on non-TLS sites. If the domain is spoofed the browser will not be able to tell if the data is accessed from a "wrong" site.

A lot of criticism has been directed towards Web storage mostly due to user tracking. If we have the same advertiser in several different sites then he can easily track the user visits in those sites. This make the users a lot less anonymous and an easy target. There are several proposed solution to fix this problem, for example, having restrictions for third-party `iframes` and blacklisting of domains that create such data but none of them fix the problem fully at the moment.

Reading data from files

We have already used file input to read some of the data, but never went into details about file reading and the objects that are available to us. In this recipe, we will create a simple file reader using input file that will act as a mini demonstration of some of the options provided in the File API: Directories and System, `http://www.w3.org/TR/file-system-api/`.

How to do it...

We will create an HTML file containing a file input control and a progress output for the state of the upload:

1. We create the controls and a few output placeholders:

```
<body>
<p>
<progress id="progress" value="0" max="100"></progress>
<output id="percent" for="progress">0</output>
</p>
<p>
<div id="fileInfo"></div>
</p>
<input type="file" id="file" value="Choose text file">
<button type="button" id="abort">Abort</button>
<button type="button" id="slice">Read 5 bytes</button>
<div id="state"></div>
<br />
<label>
        Contents:
<div id="content"></div>
</label>
```

2. Add dependencies to jQuery and our `example.js`:

```
<script src="http://ajax.googleapis.com/ajax/libs/jquery/1.8.2/
jquery.min.js"></script>
<script type="text/javascript" src="example.js"></script>
```

3. We can proceed to the creation of the `example.js` file; here we attach an event handler on the `abort` button and use a `FileReader` object:

```
$(function() {

varfr = new FileReader();

  $('#abort').click(function(){
fr.abort();
console.log('aborting file change');
  });
```

4. From the selected file input, we will iterate over the uploaded files with our current configuration item, and add event handles for some of the common events:

```
$('#file').on('change', function(e) {
    for (var i = 0; i <this.files.length; i++) {
var f = this.files[i];
fr = new FileReader();

fr.onerror = function (e) {
        $('#state').append('error happened<br />').append(e).
append('\n');
    }

fr.onprogress = function (e) {
var percent = (e.loaded * 100 / e.total).toFixed(1);
        $('#progress').attr('max', e.total).attr('value',
e.loaded);
        $('#percent').val(percent + ' %');
    }
fr.onabort = function() {
        $('#state').append('aborted<br />');
    }

fr.onloadstart = function (e) {
        $('#state').append('started loading<br />');
    }

    if (f.type&& (f.type.match('image/.+')) || (f.type.
match('video/.+'))) {
```

```
fr.readAsDataURL(f);
        } else if (f.type.match('text/.+')) {
fr.readAsText(f);
        } else {
          $('#state').append('unknown type of file loaded, reading
first 30 bytes <br />');
        }


fr.onload = function(e) {
        $('#state').append('finished reading <br />');
appendContents(f,e);
      }
      $('#fileInfo').html(getMetaData(f));
    }
  });
```

5. The getMetaData function will read the available metadata form the file object
    and create a simple HTML representation:

```
function getMetaData(file){
var text = "<b>file: </b>" + file.name + " <br />";
    text += "<b>size: </b>" + file.size + " <br />";
    text += "<b>type: </b>" + file.type + " <br />";
    text += "<b>last modified: </b>" + file.lastModifiedDate.
toString() + " <br />";
    return text;
  }
```

> You can read more about the File interface in W3C File API
> specification at http://www.w3.org/TR/FileAPI/#dfn-file.

6. By reading the file type, we can also determine what will be the output. In our case,
    if we have file, that is, image we append the data as src on a img tag, on the other
    hand for other file types, we just print the text representation:

```
function appendContents(f,e) {
    if (f.type&&f.type.match('image/.+')){
      $("<img />").attr('src', e.target.result).
appendTo("#content");
    } else {
      $("<pre />").text(e.target.result).appendTo("#content");
    }
  }
```

7. There is also another way to read the files list in file input by accessing the property files. The `slice` button will only read the first 15 bytes from the file:

```
$('#slice').click(function(){
varfileList = $('#file').prop('files');
    $.each(fileList, function(i,file) {
fr = new FileReader();
var blob = file.slice(0, 15);
fr.readAsBinaryString(blob);
fr.onload = function(e) {
        $("<pre />").text(e.target.result).appendTo("#content");
      }
    });
  });
});
```

At this point we should have a running site where once we upload a file, the file will be read and displayed. In order to see the progress events you can try out with a large file, because otherwise it could be run in an instant. As for the `slice` button it is best if you try it out with a simple `.txt` file so that you can see the contents.

How it works...

The main idea behind these specifications is to enable fully-featured API for handing the file system at the client side. One unfortunate thing about the current state of matter is that only Chrome has implemented most of the features from the Filesystem and FileWriter API, while the others support the FileReader and File API. That is why we decided on having a working example that is supported in all of the major browsers and uses the features that are most common.

For reading and simple manipulation, we use `FileList` that contains the `File` objects that can be read with `FileReader`. HTML5 defines a files property on a `<input type="file">` control that can be accessed using jQuery (`$('#file').prop('files')`) or directly from the selected HTML element like we did in case of `this.files.length`. This property is actually an array-like object called `FileList` that contains the `File` objects. The `FileList` instance has a method, `item(index)`, and an attribute `length`. Each item is a `File` object, an interface that extends a `Blob`, immutable raw binary data. The File is a representation and has the following attributes:

- ▸ `name`: This attribute represents the name of the file.
- ▸ `lastModifiedDate`: This attribute represents the last modified date of the file. If this is not available to the browser, then the current date and time are set as the `Date` object.

But besides them, there are also the ones that come from the `Blob` interface, which are as follows:

- ▶ `size`: This attribute represents the size of the file in bytes

- ▶ `type`: The MIME type. This metadata can be read directly as we did in our `getMetaData` function. The metadata can be used in various different ways, for example in our case depending on the type of file we are matching the images `f.type&&f.type.match('image/.+')`, and then displaying a `img` tag or text otherwise.

The `Blob` type also contains the definition of the `slice` method and since `File` extends `Blob` it can also be used there. The `slice(start, end, contentType)` method returns a new object with the new `contentType` attribute being sliced, the new file will have the slice from the original.

> In older browser versions, for example, Firefox version less than 12 and Chrome version less than 21 you needed to use a prefixed version of the `slice` method. For Chrome it was `File.webkitSlice()` and for Firefox, `File.mozSlice()`. The `Blob` object can also be created from a byte array.

The `FileReader` object is the actually object that does the reading of the data contained in a file, since by itself the `File` object is just a reference to the real data. In `FileReader` there are methods for reading from `Blob`, which are as follows:

- ▶ `void readAsArrayBuffer(blob)`: This method reads the file as a binary array

- ▶ `void readAsText(blog, optionalEncoding)`: This method reads the file as text where the optional string name of the encoding can be added to designate the one that should be used. If the encoding is omitted, then the encoding is picked automatically using the encoding determination algorithm, as defined in the specification which should be sufficient in most cases.

- ▶ `void readAsDataUrl(blob)`: This method creates a data URL from the given file

You may notice that the methods don't actually return the read data. This is because the `FileReader` object is reading data asynchronously, so a callback will be run once the data is read. There is also an `abort` method that can stop the reading of a file once called, this is the method we call upon clicking the `abort` button in our example.

Event handlers that can be attached to a file reader that could get triggered on certain cases. In our example, we only print the state of the file reader. The following events can be handled:

- ▸ `onabort`: This event gets triggered once the reading operation is aborted.

- ▸ `onerror`: This event is called when an error happens. This is the one we often want to handle it or at least know when it happened even though the handler is optional. The errors can happen for various different reasons, and our handler can accept an argument to check the `FileError` error code. For example, the handler could do the following:

```
fr.onerror = function (err){
  switch(err.code){
    case FileError.ENCODING_ERR:
      // handle encoding error
      break;
    case FileError.SYNTAX_ERR:
      // handle invalid line ending
      break;
    case FileError.ABORT_ERR:
    // handle abort error
    break;
    default :
    //handle all other errors , or unknown one
    break;
  }
}
```

The `FileError` object contains the corresponding error that has happened, but we handle only some of these cases for a given scenario.

- ▸ onload – This event is the one that gets called once the read, operation is successfully completed. The handler accepts and progresses an event from where we can read the data:

```
fr.onload = function (e){
    // e.target.result contains the data from the file.
}
```

- ▸ `onloadstart`: This method is called at the very beginning of the reading process.

- ▸ `onloadend`: This method is called when we have successful read but also even if an error has happened, making it a good candidate for clearing up the resources that we don't need.

▶ `onprogress`: This method is called periodically while we are reading the data. In the progress handler, we can read several properties that are of use to us for making an update on a `progress` element. We can read the total amount of bytes for that file that is read, meaning that we can simply calculate the percentage of data:

```
fr.onprogress = function (e) {

var percent = (e.loaded * 100 / e.total).toFixed(1);

        $('#progress').attr('max', e.total).attr('value',
e.loaded);

        $('#percent').val(percent + ' %');

    }
```

In most use cases, `onload` and `onerror` are sufficient, but we may need to show a visual display to the user or notify him or her of the reading state.

For checking if the functionality we used is supported by a browser we can use:

```
if (window.File&&window.FileReader&&window.FileList&&window.Blob) {
    // has support for File API
}
```

There's more...

For more advanced logic and writing to files, there is `FileWriter`, `DirectoryReader`, `FileEntry`, `DirectoryEntry`, `LocalFileSystem`, and so on. The issue with this is that at the time of this writing only Chrome has support for them.

To request a sandboxed filesystem, we make a call to `window.requestFileSystem(type, size, successCallback, errorCallback)` that is a part of the FileSystem API. The sandbox means that this filesystem is separate from the one of the user, so you can't really write anywhere you wish to do so.

The filesystem has been prefixed since Chrome 12 and the current version of Chrome 25 are still using that version. A simple request for filesystem would be:

```
window.webkitRequestFileSystem(
window.TEMPORARY,
  2*1024*1024,
  function (fs){
console.log("Successfully opened file system " + fs.name);
  });
```

The files in the sandboxed environment are represented with `FileEntry`, and the directories with `DirectoryEntry`.

Once we have successfully opened the filesystem, we can read the `FileEntries`:

```
function (fs){
fs.root.getFile(
    "awesome.txt",
     { create : true },
     function (fileEntry) {
console.log(fileEntry.isDirectory); // false
console.log(fileEntry.fullPath); // '/awesome.txt'
    }
   );
}
```

This `fs.root` call is a reference to the root of the filesystem, as for the `fileEntry` parameter there are a lot of methods that can be used for moving the file, deleting the file, converting it to a URL, copying, and all the other functionality you might expect from a filesystem. The URLs are relative for the given sandboxed filesystem so we can expect to have something similar to `/docs/books/dragon/` for the `root` directory for that specific sandboxed file system.

Erick Bidelman, one of the programmers behind the FileSystem API has implemented great wrapper of the functionality that uses well known UNIX commands such as `cp`, `mv`, `ls`. The lib is called `filer.js`, `https://github.com/ebidel/filer.js`. He also has polyfill for FileSystem API called `ibd.filesystem.js`, (`https://github.com/ebidel/idb.filesystem.js`), that uses IndexedDB to simulate the functionality in other browsers.

There is also a synchronous version of the API where we call it using `webkitRequestFileSystemSync`. The reason why we would want to use synchronous reading is Web workers, where it makes sense, since we are not blocking the main application like that.

There are several use cases mentioned in the specification, so a summarized version of these use cases would be as follows:

▶ Persistent uploader is a way to upload a file to the server one chunk at a time, so that when we have a server or browser failure it can continue with the last chunk that the server received, rather than reuploading the whole file all over again.

▶ Game or a rich media application where the resources are downloaded as tarballs and are expanded locally, the same resources could be prefetched having only one request instead of many small requests, which can reduce the lookup times.

▶ The files that will get created by applications such as offline video, audio or any other type of binary file viewer, and editor can be saved in local system for further processing.

Using IndexedDB

Besides local and session storage, IndexedDB also provides us with a way to store user data in the browser. IndexedDB is more advanced than local storage: it allows us to store data in object stores and supports indexing the data.

In this recipe, we're going to create a simple todo list app which stores its data in IndexedDB. We're going to use the Angular framework covered in *Chapter 10, Data Binding Frameworks* to simplify our code. We're going to find out if IndexedDB is a better choice for larger, more complicated data models with more complex search and retrieval needs.

The todo list application will support current and archived items and will allow filtering the items by date.

How to do it...

Let's write the code:

1. Create `index.html`. To simplify our application code, we're going to use `angular.js` templates. Our template will contain the following elements:

    ❑ A select to pick between current and archived todos

    ❑ A date range filter using HTML5 date components

    ❑ A todo list with a checkbox and age for each item

    ❑ A form to add a new item

    ❑ An archive button for current items that are done

```html
<!doctype html>
<html ng-app="todo">
<head>
<script src="https://ajax.googleapis.com/ajax/libs/
angularjs/1.0.5/angular.min.js"></script>
<script src="example.js"></script>
<script src="service.js"></script>
<meta charset="utf8">
<style type="text/css">
        .todo-text {
            display: inline-block;
            width: 340px;
vertical-align:top;
        }
</style>
</head>
<body>
```

```
<div ng-controller="TodoController">
<select ng-model="archive">
<option value="0">Current</option>
<option value="1">Archived</option>
</select>
        From: <input type="date" ng-model="from">
        To: <input type="date" ng-model="to">
<ul>
<li ng-repeat="todo in todos | filter:{archived:archive}">
<input type="checkbox" ng-model="todo.done"
ng-disabled="todo.archived"
ng-click="updateItem(todo)">
<span class="todo-text">{{todo.text}}</span>
<span class="todo-age">{{todo.date | age}}</span>
</li>
</ul>
<form ng-submit="addItem()">
<input ng-model="text">
<input type="submit" value="Add">
</form>
<input type="button" ng-click="archiveDone()"
            value="Archive done">
<div ng-show="svc.error">{{svc.error}}</div>
</div>
</body>
</html>
```

2. Create example.js, which will define the controller that sets up and manipulates the scope of the template in index.html and defines the age filter for dates:

```
var app = angular.module('todo', []);

app.filter('age', function() {
    return function(timestamp) {
var s = (Date.now() - timestamp) / 1000 / 3600;
        if (s < 1) return "now";
        if (s < 24) return s.toFixed(0) + 'h';
        if (s < 24*7) return (s / 24).toFixed(0) + 'd';
        return (s /24/7).toFixed(0) + 'w';
    };
});
var DAY = 1000*3600*24;

function TodoController($scope, DBTodo) {
    $scope.svc = DBTodo.data;
```

```
        $scope.archive = 0;
        $scope.from = new Date(Date.now() - 3*DAY)
            .toISOString().substr(0, 10);
        $scope.to = new Date(Date.now() + 1*DAY)
            .toISOString().substr(0, 10);
        $scope.todos = [];

        function updateItems() {
DBTodo.getItems(
                new Date($scope.from).getTime(),
                new Date($scope.to).getTime(),
                function(err, items) {
                    $scope.todos = items;
                });
        };
        $scope.addItem = function() {
DBTodo.addItem({
                date: Date.now(),
                text: $scope.text,
                archived: 0,
                done: false
            }, function() {
                $scope.text = "";
updateItems();
            });
        };
        $scope.updateItem = function(item) {
DBTodo.updateItem(item);
        };
        $scope.archiveDone = function(item) {
DBTodo.archive(updateItems);
        };
        $scope.$watch('from',updateItems);
        $scope.$watch('to', updateItems);
}
```

3. Define the `DBTodo` service required by the controller in `service.js`:

```
angular.module('todo').factory('DBTodo', function($rootScope) {
```

First, we need to remove the prefix from the global definitions:

```
window.indexedDB = window.indexedDB || window.mozIndexedDB ||
window.webkitIndexedDB || window.msIndexedDB;
window.IDBTransaction = window.IDBTransaction ||
window.webkitIDBTransaction || window.msIDBTransaction;
```

```
window.IDBKeyRange = window.IDBKeyRange ||
window.webkitIDBKeyRange || window.msIDBKeyRange;

var self = {}, db = null;
self.data = {error: null};
```

Our initialization function opens the database and specifies the requested version. When the database doesn't exist, the onupgradeneeded function is called, and we can use it to create our object store and indices. We also populate the database with some randomly generated items:

```
    function initialize(done) {

varreq = window.indexedDB.open("todos", "1");
varneedsPopulate = false;
req.onupgradeneeded = function(e) {
db = e.currentTarget.result;
varos = db.createObjectStore(
                "todos", {autoIncrement: true});
os.createIndex(
                "date", "date", {unique: false});
os.createIndex(
                "archived", "archived", {unique: false});
needsPopulate = true;
        }
req.onsuccess = function(e) {
db = this.result;
            if (needsPopulate) populate(done);
            else done();
        };
req.onerror = function(e) {
self.data.error = e.target.error;
        };
    }


Random item generator
    function pickRandomText(k) {
var texts = ["Buy groceries",
            "Clean the car",
            "Mow the lawn",
            "Wash the dishes",
            "Clean the room",
            "Do some repairs"],
            selected = texts[(Math.random() * texts.length)
                .toFixed(0)];
            return selected + " " + k;
    }
```

This function populates the database with 50 random items that are spread within 25 days:

```
     function populate(done) {
var now = Date.now();
var t = db.transaction('todos', 'readwrite');
t.oncomplete = done;

vartbl = t.objectStore('todos');
var N = 50;
        for (var k = N; k > 0; --k) {
tbl.add({
            text: pickRandomText(k),
            date: Date.now() - (k / 2) * DAY,
            archived: k > 5 ? 1 : 0,
            done: (k > 5 || Math.random() < 0.5)
        });
    }
}
```

`withDB` is a helper function that makes sure the database is initialized before executing the specified function:

```
     function withDB(fn) {
        return function() {
varargs = arguments, self = this;
            if (!db) initialize(function() {
fn.apply(self, args);
            });
            else fn.apply(self, args);
        };
    }
```

`withScope` is a helper function that creates a function which is called within `$rootScope.$apply` to indicate an update of angular scope objects:

```
     function withScope(fn) {
        return function() {
varargs = arguments, self = this;
            $rootScope.$apply(function() {
fn.apply(self, args);
            });
        };
    }
```

Finally, `getItems`, `updateItem`, `archive`, and `addItem` are the public API of the DBTodo service:

```
self.getItems = withDB(function(from, to, cb) {
var list = [];
var index = db.transaction('todos')
          .objectStore('todos').index('date');
varreq = index.openCursor(IDBKeyRange.bound(from, to, true,
true));
req.onsuccess = function(e) {
var cursor = e.target.result;
          if (!cursor)
              return withScope(function() {
cb(null, list);
              })();
list.push(cursor.value);
cursor.continue();
      };
  });

self.updateItem = withDB(function(item, done) {
var t = db.transaction('todos', 'readwrite'),
          ix = t.objectStore('todos').index('date'),
req = ix.openCursor(IDBKeyRange.only(item.date));
t.oncomplete = done &&withScope(done);
req.onsuccess = function(e) {
var cursor = e.target.result;
          if (cursor) cursor.update(item);
      };
  });

self.archive = withDB(function(done) {
var current = IDBKeyRange.only(0);
var t = db.transaction('todos', 'readwrite'),
req = t.objectStore('todos')
          .index("archived")
          .openCursor(current);

t.oncomplete = withScope(done);

req.onsuccess = function(e) {
var cursor = e.target.result;
          if (!cursor) return;
          if (cursor.value.done) {
cursor.value.archived = 1;
```

```
        cursor.update(cursor.value);
                    }
    cursor.continue();
            };

        });

    self.addItem = withDB(function(item, done) {
    var t = db.transaction('todos', 'readwrite'),
    os = t.objectStore('todos');
    t.oncomplete = withScope(done);
    os.add(item);
        });

        return self;
    });
```

4. Open `index.html` in a browser that supports IndexedDB and date inputs (for example, Google Chrome).

How it works...

Compared to the average JavaScript API, the IndexedDB API is quite verbose. IndexedDB uses DOM events to signal the completion of an asynchronous task. Most API calls return a request object. To get the results, we need to attach event listeners to this object.

For example, opening the database results with a request object. We can attach three event listeners to this object:

- ► `onsuccess`: This is called when the database has been successfully opened

- ► `onerror`: This is called when there is an error

- ► `onupgradeneeded`: This is called when the database is not the specified version or doesn't exist yet

An IndexedDB database is an object-oriented database that contains one or more object stores.

Object stores have a primary key index. The primary key is autogenerated in our example, but we can also specify an exiting property to serve as the primary key.

Every object store may have one or more indexes. Indexes can be added by specifying the path of the property that should be indexed – in our case, we define two indexes for our `todos` store on the date and archived fields.

All queries to the database are performed within transactions. When creating a transaction, we define the object store that will be used in the transaction. Like requests, transactions also have event listeners:

- `oncomplete`: This is called when the transaction is complete
- `onerror`: This is called if an error occured
- `onabort`: This is called if a transaction was aborted

Within the transaction we can access the object store by calling `transaction.objectStore('name')`. All operations on this object store will be done inside the transaction.

The object store supports multiple methods to add, get, and delete items, as well as means to access the indexes. To add items we use the `add` method. To access items we need to show or update, we use the index by calling `objectStore.index('name')`.

The index provides a subset of the object store API used to retreive data, such as `get`, `count`, and `openCursor`.

To update an item or fetch multiple items, we use the `openCursor` method. It returns a `request` to which we can attach an `onsuccess` listener. This listener will be called for every item accessed by the cursor. The `cursor` can be accessed via `request.result`.

When we're done with the visited item, we can call `cursor.continue` to advance to the next item. The `onsuccess` listener will be called again, this time with the cursor pointing to the next item.

We can restrict the cursor by specifying a key range to visit, as well as the direction (ascending or descending). A key range can be generated with the `IDBKeyRange` methods:

- `upperBound`: This method is used to specify an upper bound range
- `lowerBound`: This method is used to specify a lower bound range
- `bound`: This method is used to specify both upper and lower bound range
- `only`: This method is used to specify a range that includes only one key.

Besides specifying the bounds, `upperBound`, `lowerBound`, and `bound`, they also support additional Boolean parameters which allow us to specify if the bounds are inclusive.

To sum it all up, when implementing our `getItems` method to fetch all the items between the specified dates, we need to:

- Open a transaction to the todos object store
- Open the todos object store from the transaction
- Open the `date` index from the object store

- ▶ Create a `IDBKeyRange` bound specifying the first date as the lower bound and the second date as the upper bound (and two true parameters indicating that the bounds are inclusive)
- ▶ Open a cursor from the `date` index using the created key range
- ▶ Use the cursor request to iterate through all the items and add them into an array
- ▶ Use the transaction `oncomplete` handler to call the callback function with the list when all the items are added

There's more...

The IndexedDB API is very verbose and low-level. It is not meant to be used directly by web applications; instead, it's meant to provide means to write more high-level database implementations on top of it.

But more than that, IndexedDB doesn't support some fundamental features we've come to accept as standard in real databases:

- ▶ There are no compound indexes, which means we can't write efficient queries that bound multiple properties of the object.
- ▶ If we wish to order the items in an order different than the one that the index key provides, we will have to fill an array and sort the result manually.
- ▶ There are no joins, which means that we would need to write the code to join two object stores and pick the most appropriate indexes to minimize the workload by hand.

As a result, we cannot recommend using the IndexedDB API until it matures, or other more complete and less verbose database implementations are written on top of it.

> Check out PouchDB (`http://pouchdb.com/`) for a more complete solution, or `db.js` (`http://aaronpowell.github.com/db.js/`) for a more succinct API.

Limits of the storage and how to ask for more

So far we have seen several different ways to have storage and access it at the client side. All these ways gives us the option to store large amounts of data at the client side. The question arises how come there are no hacks out there that fills up the storage of all the devices?

We will see why this is not happening everywhere, at least not without some browser vulnerability. To do this, we shall create a simple case where we will store data to the browser using `localStorage`, as long as we are allowed by the user agent.

How to do it...

1. We can start by creating a file called `example.js`, there we will generate data with size of `1 k` and size of `100 k`. The data for 1k can be generated by creating an array of `1025` elements, which we will join with the letter `"a"`, resulting in `1024` character string of `"a"`'S:

```
var testing = (function (me) {
me.data1k =   new Array(1025).join("a"); // about 1k
me.data100k = new Array((1024*100)+1).join("b");// about 100k
```

2. Following that we will create a simple function that will accept number of entries and data for each of them:

```
me.run = function (max, data) {
var el = document.getElementById('status');
el.setAttribute('max', max);
    try {
       for (i = 0; i < max; i++) {
console.log(i);
el.setAttribute('value', 1+i);
localStorage.setItem(i, data);
       }
       } catch (err) {
maxReached(i, err);
       }
}
```

The maxReached function will display the last entry that was successfully stored:

```
   function maxReached(i, err) {
console.log("max reached");
console.log(err);
var div = document.getElementById('max');
div.innerHTML = "Reached max " + i + " entry";
   }
```

3. We will also add a function that will clear the entire `localStorage` object:

```
me.clear = function() {
var progress = document.getElementById('status');
progress.setAttribute('value','0');
localStorage.clear();
console.log("removed all data from localStorage");
   }
```

4. After having this we can create an HTML file, where we will have a few buttons, one for clearing all the data and others for filling the storage up with generated data:

```
<body>
<progress id="status" value="0" max="100"></progress>
<div id="max">have not reached max</div>
<button type="button" onclick="testing.clear()" >clear</button>
<button type="button" onclick="testing.run(100,testing.data1k)"
>100 entries 1K</button>
<button type="button" onclick="testing.run(500,testing.data100k)"
>500 entries 100K</button>
<script src="example.js"></script>
</body>
```

How it works...

Storage limitations as well as the behavior depend on the browser. The specification itself says that user agents should limit the total amount of space allowed for storage area. Additionally they should grant the same amount of storage for each subdomain (for example, a.example.com, b.example.com, and so on). There is also an option to prompt the user to request more storage; unfortunately, this is only currently done by Opera.

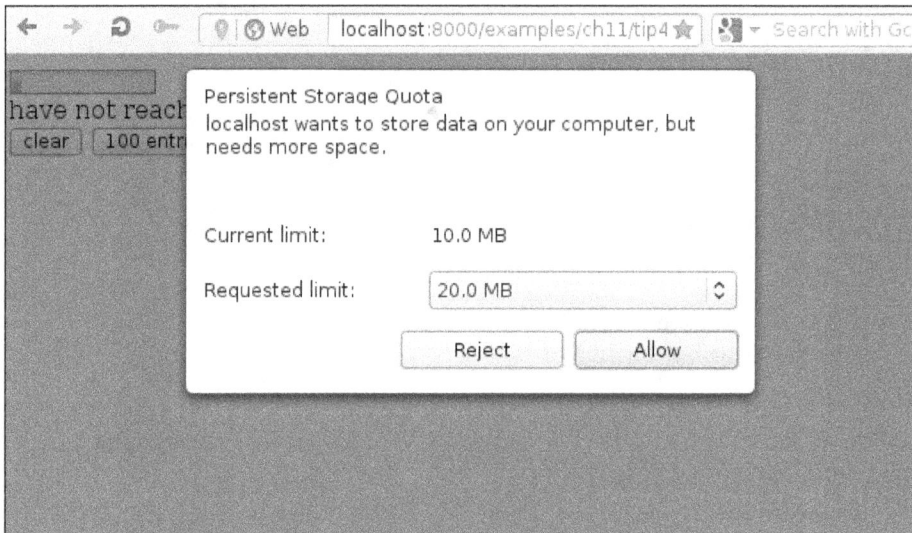

There is a configurable property in Firefox called dom.storage.default_quota that can be found in about:config, but you can't really expect the user to set an increased value manually there. For IndexDB, there are no limitations on the storage size but the initial quota is set to 50 MB.

There's more...

If we are talking about limitations in HTML5 Filesystem API, we have several storage type definitions.

Temporary storage is the basic one, so we do not need special permissions to obtain it; making it a good pick for caching. Chrome currently has a temporary pool of 1 GB and there are plans for IndexedDB and WebSQL to become part of the same pool. For temporary storage there are no guarantees for persistence, so it can be removed at any time.

> More on WebSQL can be found on W3C, although the specification is no longer developed or maintained `http://www.w3.org/TR/webdatabase/`.

Persistent storage on the other hand is well persistent. Data remains there after restart, and it is there until manually deleted by the user or our application. When we do a request file system call, the browser will prompt us for permission and if we spend that we will get `QUOTA_EXCEEDE_ERR`.

There is also a storage that is of type unlimited, but that is Chrome-specific, and intended to be used from extensions and Chrome apps.

Some efforts have been taken to standardize the way storage is requested, so the Quota API specification, `http://www.w3.org/TR/quota-api/`, was created for the purpose. The specification itself defines an API to manage the usage and availability of local storage resources for various persistent API's.

There is a `StorageQuota` interface where the process of getting more `PERSISTENT` data is described. A prefixed version of the implementation is available in Chrome:

```
window.webkitStorageInfo.requestQuota(PERSISTENT, 10*1024*1024,
function(bytes){
console.log(bytes);
}, function (error){
console.log(error);
});
```

By calling the method, a prompt will appear to the user to ask for permission.

Manipulating the browser history

History API allows you to manipulate the browser history using JavaScript. Some of the manipulations were available in the user agents for a long time. A new feature is an option to add new entries in the history, change the URL show in the location bar, and so on.

This means that we can create a single page app that will respect the REST way. The pages now can have unique identifier that will lead directly to certain view with specific state without doing page reloads or some client-side hacks.

Getting ready

In this recipe, we will use few images, so you can pick your own selection or use the ones provided in the example files located under the `img/` folder. The images will also be served in `img/` for our web page, so you should have the HTTP server running.

How to do it...

Let's get started:

1. We create the HTML code for a cat viewer:

```
<div>
<nav>
<ul>
<li><div data-id="0" data-url="/mycat.html">A cat</div></li>
<li><div data-id="1" data-url="/awesome.html">Some cat</div></li>
<li><div data-id="2" data-url="/somecat.html">The cat</div></li>
</ul>
</nav>
<div id="image">
</div>
</div>
```

2. We include a dependency to jQuery and our script, `example.js`:

```
<script src="http://ajax.googleapis.com/ajax/libs/jquery/1.8.2/
jquery.min.js"></script>
<script src="example.js"></script>
```

3. Optionally we can add some very basic style to make the behavior of the div elements more like links, although in the general case we could also use `<a>` elements but it's not always the best idea to override the click behavior on anchors. The style could be something similar to the following:

```
<style>
nav div {
text-decoration:underline;
    cursor: pointer;
  }
</style>
```

4. As for the `example.js` file we have a small JSON like structure called `catson` that describes our data:

```
varcatson = [
  {
  "name":"Awesome cat",
  "url":"1.jpg"
  },
  {
  "name":"Crazy cat",
  "url":"2.jpg"
  },
  {
  "name":"Great cat",
  "url":"3.jpg"
  }
];
```

5. When the document is loaded, we check for the support of the history API in the current user agent:

```
$(document).ready( function() {
  function hasSupportForHistory() {
    return window.history&&history.pushState;
  }

  if ( !hasSupportForHistory() ) {
     $('body').text('Browser does not have support for History fall
backing');
    return;
  }
```

6. Following this we add an on-click handler for our navigation elements:

```
$("nav div").click( function(e) {
console.log('clicking');

var title = $(this).text(),
url = document.URL.substring(0, document.URL.lastIndexOf('/')) +
$(this).data('url'),
        id = $(this).data('id'),
img = '<imgsrc="img/'+ catson[id].url +'" />',
        text = '<h1>'+catson[id].name+'</h1>';

    // change the displayed url
history.pushState(null, title, url);
    $('#image').html(text + img);
    // stop default propagation of event
e.preventDefault();
    })
```

At this point you should have a running example, where if you click around, you will notice that the browser URL gets changed but we rely on having only one page.

If you do a refresh on some of the other URL's that are generated, you should get a message similar to:

Error code 404.

Message: File not found.

Error code explanation: 404 = Nothing matches the given URI.

This is because we are only simulating the web page, while the page itself does not exist.

How it works...

The idea behind the History API is simple. It's an object that allows us to manipulate browser history through the `window.history` object.

If we want to go one page back we simply call:

```
window.history.back();
```

Or to go to the next page:

```
window.history.forward();
```

There is also a more general method that allows us to go + or – n pages in the history, for example to go three pages back we call:

```
window.history.go(-3);
```

The most interesting of all of these methods that come with this API are probably the `pushState(state, title, url)` and `replaceState(state, title, url)`. The first one we used in our example adds a URL to the history stack with the given state object. To be completely conformist with the rules we should have used the first argument of the method which is the state object that represents the current document state. In our case this would have been one cat object for the `catison` list.

Similarly as the `pushState`, the `replaceState` methods are updated rather than adding a new state on the history stack with the same arguments.

The state object itself is reachable under the `history.state` variable, similar to the `history.state` variable there is also a `history.length` variable for the size of the current stack. The `history.state` variable can be used to store data for the given segment, making it yet another option for storing data in the browser.

> You can read more about History API on the live specification on WHATWG: `http://www.whatwg.org/specs/web-apps/current-work/multipage/history.html`.

The first thing you need to consider is making a clever routing so that you will not have broken and non-existent URL's. This means that we might need some work at the server side so that the state of the URL will be available for rendering. The main goal is to improve usability and not to overuse the cool new features, so be careful where you really need this functionality.

For older browsers there is a great polyfill called `history.js`, (`https://github.com/browserstate/history.js`) that additionally adds few other nice features for development.

There is also a library called `Path.js`, that uses History API for advanced routing, but also abuses `hashbangs` (#) to achieve nice functionality.

While we are talking about complete abuse, there is a whole game written that uses `history.replaceState` to make the URL bar a screen. The game is called Abaroids and can be found at `http://www.thegillowfamily.co.uk/`.

12
Multimedia

In this chapter we will cover the following recipes:

- ▸ Playing audio files
- ▸ Playing video files
- ▸ Customizing controls for media elements
- ▸ Adding text to your video
- ▸ Embedding multimedia
- ▸ Converting text to speech using HTML5 audio

Introduction

HTML5 adds two elements audio and video, which provide a functionality that was previously done with use of add-ons to the browsers. In most of the cases, we find players that are Flash-based but that is lately being changed. Most of the browsers now have a good support for the basic HTML5 media element related functionality.

Customization options for the player were very limited and vendor specific. Most of the sites had and some still have their own custom players that were done in Flash, since it was the best way to do the job.

Flash by itself is not going to disappear all of a sudden, but having alternative that uses open standards always makes a compelling case on why not to use it. The same is happening in the web game industry, HTML5 is taking over Flash-based games market each day.

Playing audio files

The audio element enables a simple way to play audio files in the browser. Adoption of this element had many controversial discussions mostly due to the lack of common grounds for a format. Initially Ogg Vorbis (http://www.vorbis.com/) was the format suggested in the W3C specification.

> Up-to-date information on browser support for different formats can be found on www.caniuse.com.

In this recipe, we will take a look at the element and some of the basic attributes that can be applied on it.

Getting ready

In order to play an audio we need an actual audio file. You can pick one on your own or use the one that comes with the example. The file will be served from the music folder. We will use Mozart—Clarinet Concerto in A K. 622, II. Adagio by Jason Weinberger & the WCFSO available at the free music archive http://freemusicarchive.org/music/Jason_Weinberger__the_WCFSO/Jason_Weinberger__the_Waterloo-Cedar_Falls_Symphony_Orchestra/.

The file is of type .mp3, but for the purpose of this example, we also need a .ogg file. There are plenty of converters available both online and offline so we can use http://media.io for example. There is also a converted song.ogg file available in the example files if you don't want to go through the hassle.

How to do it...

We will create a HTML file that will contain an audio player:

1. The body section will contain the following:

```
<p>
  <audio id="mulipleSrc" controls preload loop>
     Audio not supported
  <source src="music/Jason_Weinberger__the_WCFSO_
-_04_-_Mozart_-_Clarinet_Concerto_in_A_K_622_II_Adagio.mp3"
 type="audio/mpeg" />
  <source src="music/song.ogg" type="audio/ogg" />
 <a href="music/song.ogg">download file </a>
  </audio>
 <p>
```

2. A small text for attribution:

```
    Mozart - Clarinet Concerto in A K. 622, II. Adagio by <a
href="http://freemusicarchive.org/music/Jason_Weinberger__
the_WCFSO/Jason_Weinberger__the_Waterloo-Cedar_Falls_Symphony_
Orchestra/">Jason Weinberger</a> & the WCFSO is licensed under a
Creative Commons Attribution License.
    </p>
```

And that is it, you should have an audio player accessible in your browser.

How it works...

The old way was to use `<object>` and `<embed>` with a lot of player specific parameters passed to the embedded `.swf` file, looking something like the following code:

```
<object data="somePlayer.swf">
  <param name="quality" value="medium">
</object>
```

The new way is fairly simple, we can add an audio element with the `src` attribute specified:

```
<audio src="myFile.ogg" autoplay>
  Some fallback HTML code
</audio>
```

This will automatically play a file on the page without giving options to the user about stopping the music. In order to have a player rendered by the user agent we add the attribute controls. One other limitation we impose by setting the `src` attribute is that only that file will be played. You might be wondering why we would need multiple sources but the reasoning is simple. With the current state some browsers support certain format but others do not. If we want to have support in all modern browsers then we supply the option to have multiple sources.

> At the time of writing this was the rough state of the browser format support using Windows as operating system.

Browser/Feature	WAV	Opus	Ogg	MP3	ACC
Firefox 20	Yes	Yes	Yes	No	No
Chrome 26	Yes	Yes	Yes	Yes	Yes
IE 9	No	No	No	Yes	Yes
Opera	Yes	No	Yes	No	No

> Beside the standard web sites that provide browser support stats you can also use a test suite done by SoundCloud to check individual features at `http://areweplayingyet.org/` or the source on `https://github.com/soundcloud/areweplayingyet`.

The source element provides us to specify multiple alternative resources for any media element. By itself it has no meaning so it should be part of some media tag. We can have multiple source elements that have different `src`, type, and media attributes. For example, we could have the following element:

```
<source src='audio.oga' type='audio/ogg; codecs=flac'>
```

In case you are not sure that any of the source you have provided can be used in the users browsers, you can attach `onerror` event listener on the `source` element. This handler could serve to execute a fallback.

There are few other attributes that can be used on a media elements. Besides the global attributes the media specified ones are:

- The `autoplay` attribute: It is a Boolean value attribute that defines if browser should start playing the instant it has a big enough portion of the media file. The default state for this element is to be missing, meaning that we don't have auto play by default.

- The `preload` attribute: It gives a hint to the browsers that the source file should be downloaded even if the user has not yet click on play. The idea here is that we expect at some point in the future that the file will be played, being synonymous with setting the value to `auto`. The value can be also set to `none` which hints that the browsers should hold on preloading since we don't expect the user to press the play button. There is also the option to have the value of metadata, which would mean only to load the metadata of the media file, like the length for example.

- The `muted` attribute: It is also a Boolean-based attribute the has default value of false meaning there will be sound.

- The `loop` attribute: It sets the audio to beginning once finished.

- The `controls` attribute: It simply adds player controls.

- The `mediagroup` attribute: It is used to group multiple media elements, for example, if we want to have same controls for two elements we can set them to use the same media group.

- The `crossorigin` attribute: It can be specified to restrict the src attributes to conform with **Cross Origin Resource Sharing** (**CORS**).

Most of the other customization's and access from JavaScript will be part of the following recipes. If we use the element without the controls attribute set it is a good idea to set the CSS for the audio element to `display:none` in order to ensure it will not take page space.

Playing video files

In order to add native support for videos in the browsers, HTML5 introduced the video element. This is very similar to an audio element, and the same attributes apply since they both share common interface. There are few other attributes that are available only for the video element. Also the codecs for the source are mostly different, for video we have H.264/MPEG-4, VP8, VP9, and Theora.

In this recipe we will see how to use the built-in player by creating a simple page.

> HTML5 specification on media elements can be found at
> `http://www.whatwg.org/specs/web-apps/current-work/multipage/the-video-element.html`.

Getting ready

We need a video file to play with our player, so you can pick one on your own. We have picked to use one of the videos available at `http://archive.org/details/animationandcartoons`.

The video is called "Boogie Woogie Bugle Boy" by "Walter Lantz Productions" and in 1941 it was nominated for Oscar.

> Archive.org also known as Internet Archive is a non-profit digital library with a mission of "universal access to all knowledge". Beside being a book library it also hosts a variety of multimedia. One of the more famous sub projects is the wayback machine, `http://archive.org/web/web.php`, an archive of snapshots from states of a website in the past. There is also a sub project called `nasaimages.org` intended co make images and video from NASA closer to the public. The amount of data available at Internet archive is enormous making it a great source of information.

Additionally, we will use a poster image that will be shown before the video starts; the image is titled `poster.png`, and is part of the example source, but you may use any image you like.

How to do it...

We create a simple HTML that will contain the video element and have a source to our video:

1. The body section will contain the following code:

```
<p>
    <video width="640" height="360" poster="poster.png" controls
preload loop>
        Video not supported <a href="http://archive.org/
download/WalterLantz-BoogieWoogieBugleBoy1941/WalterLantz-
BoogieWoogieBugleBoy1941.ogv"> download </a> instead
        <source src="http://archive.org/download/WalterLantz-
BoogieWoogieBugleBoy1941/WalterLantz-BoogieWoogieBugleBoy1941.ogv"
type="video/ogg" />
    </video>
```

2. And the attribution will contain the following code:

```
<p>
Video is part of animation shorts on <a href="http://archive.
org/details/more_animation"> archive.org</a>. The video
is titled : Walter Lantz - Boogie Woogie Bugle Boy
</p>
```

After opening this we should have a running video player like the following screenshot:

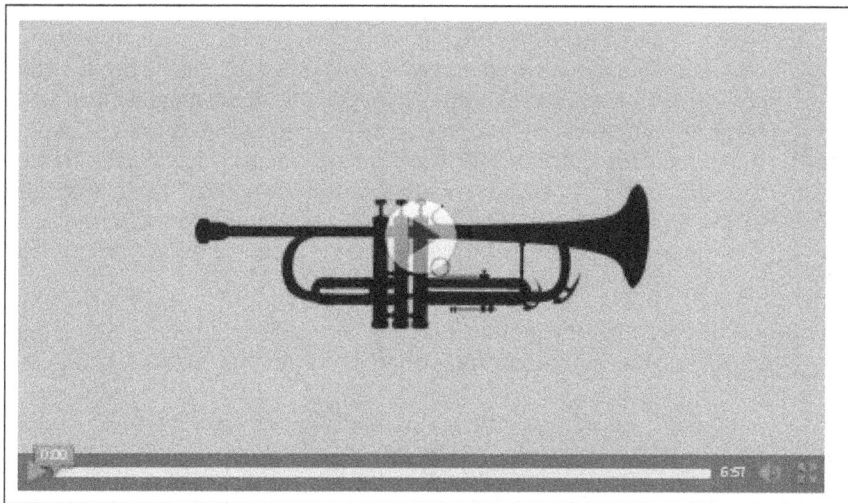

How it works...

The video element is very similar to an audio element and all the attributes from audio apply on a video element. The video specific attributes are:

▶ `Width` and `height`: They represent the width and height of the element. To control will re-size the video to fit into the size specified. The actual size of the video depends on the file being played.

▶ `poster`: It is an attribute that enables us to provide a static image to display on the video element until the user decide to play the video.

By adding various combination of attributes to the video, we can make the user experience much better; in our code example the video will get centered since the width and height attributes do not match the real width and height of the video.

If we want to play specific range of the video there is a built-in support for that as well. For example we may want to play our video from the 30th second to the 40th second. To do this in the URL of the `src` attributes, we append a hash (#) followed by the fragment definition as in the following code:

```
<source src="myvideo.ogv#t=30,40" />
```

The generic definition is as follows:

```
#t=[starttime],[endtime]
```

Variables `starttime` and `endtime` are optional, and can have a number that specifies the number of seconds from the start or have `hours:minutes:seconds`.

If we want to play from the 80th second until the end of the video, the source will be as follows:

```
<source src="myvideo.ogv#t=80" />
```

Videos are often served encoded in some lossy compressed format since they are very large to be transmitted as raw format.

> You can read more about lossy compression on the following link `https://en.wikipedia.org/wiki/Lossy_compression`. The main idea is that the size of the original video is significantly reduced by sacrificing certain level of information and quality.

Microsoft and Apple have license to use H.264, or more commonly known by the extension `.mp4` or `.m4v`. The codec has may different versions and combinations, additionally it is supported by YouTube and iTunes making it a very popular choice. Firefox and Chrome had plans to drop support for it since the format is proprietary and certain royalties must be paid, making it a very controversial choice. Firefox is planned to support the codec in the future but only when a third-party decoder is available.

> More on H.264 can be found on `http://en.wikipedia.org/wiki/H.264/MPEG-4_AVC`.

Ogg Theora comes from `Xiph.org`, the organization that provided the `.ogg` container and the Vorbis audio codec we used in the audio element recipe, among other contributions. This is supported by Firefox, Opera, and Chrome, but not on IE and Safari, at least not by default.

> More on Ogg Theora can be found on `http://www.theora.org/`.

WebM is supports Vorbis as audio codec and VP8 as video. VP8 is a codec developed by a company called On2 that got bought by Google. Additionally there is WebM is supported by Chrome, Opera, and Firefox natively, as for IE and Safari the user is required to download additional plugin.

> More on WebM, the format, tools, and documentation sounding it can be found on `http://www.webmproject.org/`.

There's more...

Having multiple source is good but not always an option. We also want to have a fallback for older browsers and to do that we must depend on a plugin.

If you referencing a video from third-party pay site such as YouTube or Vimeo, you can simply place an `iframe` of the embedded player:

```
<iframe width="420" height="345"
  src="http://www.youtube.com/embed/WEbzZP-_Ssc">

</iframe>
```

There are also server JavaScript libraries that make the fallback process simple. One of them is `http://mediaelementjs.com/`.

The installation is simple since we only include the `.js` and `.css` files as dependencies as in the following code:

```
<code><script src="jquery.js"></script>

  <script src="mediaelement-and-player.min.js"></script>

  <link rel="stylesheet" href="mediaelementplayer.css" />

</code>
```

As for the player fallback player:

```
<video src="myvideo.ogv" />
  <!-- other sources -->
  <object width="320" height="240" type="application/x-shockwave-
flash" data="flashmediaelement.swf">
    <param name="movie" value="flashmediaelement.swf" />
    <param name="flashvars" value="controls=true&file=myvideo.mp4" />
    <img src="myvideo.jpg" width="320" height="240" title="No video
playback capabilities" />
  </object>
</video>
```

The fallback player is just one of the many features that come with `mediaelement.js`; there are lot of options for mobile browsers as well as lot of simplification for the API.

> If you are interested into more details on possible conversion tool or the politics behind the codecs as well as detailed explanation of them, take a look at Mark Pilgram's book *Dive into HTML5*, it is available at `http://fortuito.us/diveintohtml5/video.html`.
>
> There is also an interesting article titled "Video for everybody" on the topic of enabling video support on different browsers, `http://camendesign.com/code/video_for_everybody`.

Customizing controls for media elements

Media elements, currently video and audio, can be controlled using JavaScript since the elements theme self contain useful methods and attributes. In this recipe, we will go through some of the most basic functionality and methods that can be applied on elements that have the `HTMLMediaElement` interface.

> Specification on the HTML5 media element can be found at `http://www.w3.org/TR/html5/embedded-content-0.html#htmlmediaelement`.

Getting ready

In this recipe we will also need a video file, so we can use the same one from the previous recipe.

How to do it...

We start by creating a JavaScript controller that will have very rudimentary functionality of a media player.

1. Our controller methods will accept a selector for a command and execute the command, we need the following:

```javascript
var videoController = (function () {
  var my = {};
  function findElement(selector){
   var result = document.querySelector(selector);
   if (!result) {
    throw "element " + selector + " not found ";
   }
   return result;
  }

  function updatePlaybackRate(el, speed) {
   el.playbackRate += speed;
  }

  function updateVolume(el, amount) {
   el.volume += amount;
  }

  my.play = function(video) {
   var el = findElement(video);
   el.play();
  }

  my.pause = function(video) {
   var el = findElement(video);
   el.pause();
  }

  my.toggleMute = function(video) {
   var el = findElement(video);
     el.muted = !el.muted;
```

```
  }

 my.increasePlaybackRate = function(video, speed) {
  var el = findElement(video);
  updatePlaybackRate(el, speed);
 }

 my.decreasePlaybackRate = function(video, speed) {
  var el = findElement(video);
  updatePlaybackRate(el, -speed);
 }

 my.increaseVolume = function(video, amount) {
  var el = findElement(video);
  updateVolume(el, amount)
 }
 return my;
}());
```

Now in a simple scenario we probably could just use the standard methods without adding another layer, but the idea here is that we can extend the functionally as we see fit since we have accessible element from JavaScript.

2. For the HTML we shall have a similar version to the one in the playing videos recipe. We will have a few buttons that will use our video controller and additionally add a simple style. Let's add the following to the head section:

```
<head>
  <title>Video custom controls</title>
  <style>
    video {
      box-shadow: 0 0 10px #11b;
    }
  </style>
</head>
```

3. The body part will contain the control buttons:

```
<p>
    <video id="theVideo" width="640" height="480"
poster="poster.png" preload loop>
        Video playback not supported <a href="http://archive.
org/download/WalterLantz-BoogieWoogieBugleBoy1941/WalterLantz-
BoogieWoogieBugleBoy1941.ogv"> download </a>
      <source src="http://archive.org/download/WalterLantz-
BoogieWoogieBugleBoy1941/WalterLantz-BoogieWoogieBugleBoy1941.ogv"
type="video/ogg" />
```

```
        </video>
      </body>
      <p>
      The Dashboard: <br/>
        <button onclick="videoController.play('#theVideo')">Play</
button>
        <button onclick="videoController.pause('#theVideo')">Pause</
button>
        <button onclick="videoController.increasePlaybackRate('#theV
ideo',0.1)">Speed++</button>
        <button onclick="videoController.decreasePlaybackRate('#theV
ideo',0.1)">Speed-- </button>
        <button onclick="videoController.decreaseVolume('#theVideo',
0.2) ">Vol-</button>
        <button onclick="videoController.increaseVolume('#theVideo',
0.2) ">Vol+</button>
        <button onclick="videoController.
toggleMute('#theVideo')">Toggle Mute</button>
      <p>
      Video is part of animation shorts on <a href="http://archive.
org/details/more_animation"> archive.org</a>. The video
      is titled : Walter Lantz - Boogie Woogie Bugle Boy
      </p>
```

4. And we add the dependencies to our `example.js` file.

```
<script src="example.js"> </script>
```

After that we should have a fully running video player.

How it works...

With JavaScript we can access and manipulate the attributes of any media element. This option enable us to do many different types of customization on the standard elements. Most of these properties are defined in `HTMLMediaElement`; there we can read and write to the `currentTime`, `playbackRate`, `volume`, `muted`, `defaultMuted`, and so on.

> For a more comprehensive list `HTMLMediaElement` attributes and what is read only please refer to the specification available at `http://www.w3.org/TR/html5/embedded-content-0.html#media-elements`.

By changing attributes we can make custom players but also various different visual updates. There are large amount of different events that get trigger by media elements. On the events we can attach event listeners and make updates depending on the state change. The following events get triggered: `loadstart`, `abort`, `canplay`, `canplaythrough`, `durationchange`, `emptied`, `ended`, `error`, `loadeddata`, `loadedmetadata`, `pause`, `play`, `playing`, `progress`, `ratechange`, `seeked`, `seeking`, `stalled`, `suspend`, `timeupdate`, `volumechange`, and `waiting`.

> The name of the events are self-explanatory, if you are interested into more details about a specific event you can read up what they are intended for, in the documentation at `http://www.w3.org/TR/html5/embedded-content-0.html#mediaevents`.

In our example we could add a listener to the rate speed that will display the current rate:

```
my.displayRate = function (video, output) {
  var vid = findElement(video),
      out = findElement(output);

  vid.addEventListener('ratechange', function(e) {
    console.log(e);
    out.innerHTML = 'Speed x' + this.playbackRate;
  }, false);
}
```

And then add an output element in the HTML with a call to our newly added method:

```
<output id="speed"></output>
<script>
  videoController.displayRate("#theVideo","#speed");
</script>
```

Now the first time the video is played the rate change event get's triggered and the rate is set to `1`. Every consecutive rate change will trigger the same event.

> W3C has a a great demo on events triggered by media elements at `http://www.w3.org/2010/05/video/mediaevents.html`.

One other interesting thing to note here is that `<audio>` element can be used on video files as well, but only the audio stream from the files will be played.

Adding text to your video

When displaying multilingual videos we often want to provide text for persons who speak other languages. This is a common practice for many conference talks as well as plenty of movies and TV shows. In order to enable external text track resources in the video the WebVTT (`http://dev.w3.org/html5/webvtt/`) standard was created.

Getting ready

For simplicity, we will use the same video together with the poster images, same as we used in the other examples. As for the other files we will create them ourselves. You can also pick other video on your own since the video itself will not be all that relevant.

How to do it...

We start with the HTML, where we include the video element and additionally add track elements as well as simple `example.js`. Perform the following steps:

1. In the body element we include :

```
<p>
    <video width="640" height="360" poster="poster.png" controls
preload loop>
    Video playback not supported <a href="http://archive.org/
download/WalterLantz-BoogieWoogieBugleBoy1941/WalterLantz-
BoogieWoogieBugleBoy1941.ogv"> download</a> instead
        <source
        src="http://archive.org/download/WalterLantz-
BoogieWoogieBugleBoy1941/WalterLantz-BoogieWoogieBugleBoy1941.ogv"
type="video/ogg" />
        <track src="video.vtt" kind="subtitles" srclang="en"
label="English" default />
        <track src="karaoke.vtt" kind="captions" srclang="gb"
label="Other" />
    </video>
    <p>
    Video is part of animation shorts on <a href="http://archive.
org/details/more_animation"> archive.org</a>. The video
    is titled : Walter Lantz - Boogie Woogie Bugle Boy
    </p>
    <script src="example.js"></script>
```

2. The JavaScript will only log the objects available to our video element. The idea here is to show that tracks can be accessed and manipulated by code. The script will contain the following:

```
(function(){
  var video = document.getElementById('theVideo'),
      textTracks = video.textTracks;

  for(var i=0; i < textTracks.length; i++){
   console.log(textTracks[i]);
   }
}())
```

3. As for the `.vtt` flies that we included for the tracks we will create them manually. The file `video.vtt` will contain the following:

```
WEBVTT

1
00:00:01.000 --> 00:00:13.000
this is the video introduction

2
00:00:15.000 --> 00:00:40.000
There is also some awesome info in
multiple lines.
Why you ask?
Why not ...

3
00:00:42.000 --> 00:01:40.000
We can use <b>HTML</b> as well
<i> Why not?</i>

4
00:01:42.000 --> 00:02:40.000
{
"name": "Some JSON data",
"other": "it should be good for meta data"
}

5
00:02:41.000 --> 00:03:40.000 vertical:lr
text can be vertical

6
```

```
00:03:42.000 --> 00:04:40.000 align:start size:50%
text can have different size relative to frame
```

4. As for `karaoke.vtt` it will contain the following code:

```
WEBVTT

1
00:00:01.000 --> 00:00:10.000
This is some karaoke style  <00:00:01.000>And more <00:00:03.000>
even more  <00:00:07.000>
```

After running the example we should have subtitles at the given ranges.

> If you construct the WebVTT file manually you can notice that it is easy to make a mistake. There is good validator available at `http://quuz.org/webvtt/` with the source code on `https://github.com/annevk/webvtt`.

How it works...

Video has been available for quite some time now but adding subtitles was not an option. The track element enables us in a standard way to add information to our video. Tracks are not just used for subtitles, but can also be used for other kinds of timed cues.

> The general definition for the word *cue* is that it represents a thing said or done that serves as a signal to an actor or other performer to enter or to begin their speech or performance.

Cues can contain other data formats like JSON, XML, or CSV. In our example we included a small JSON data snippet. This data can be useful in many different ways since it connected with a given portion of time, but subtitles are not the real use of it.

The track element can contain the following values for its `kind` attribute:

▶ **subtitles**: It is the transcription or translation for a given language.

▶ **captions**: It is very similar to subtitles but it may also include sound effects or other audio. The main intention of this type is use for cases where the audio is not available.

▶ **descriptions**: It is a text description of the video meant for use where the visual part is not available. For example, it can provide description for users who are blind or unable to follow the screen.

▶ **chapters**: This track can contain chapter titles for given periods.

▶ **metadata**: This is a track is very useful for storing meta data that can latter be used by a script.

Besides the kind attribute there is also the `src` attribute that is mandatory and shows the URL of the track source. The track element can also contain `srclang` containing the language tag of the timed track.

> The language tax often has two-letter unique key for representation of the specific language. For more details you can take a look at `http://tools.ietf.org/html/bcp47`.

There is also the attribute `default`, where if present on a track that is the track that will be shown by default.

Also we can use the `label` attribute that can have free text value specifying a unique label for the element.

> One clever use of the track element can be found on : `http://www.samdutton.net/mapTrack/`.

The WebVTT standard defines that the file needs to start with the string "WEBVTT". Following that we have the cue definitions, zero or more such elements.

Each cue element has the following form :

```
[idstring]
[hh:]mm:ss.ttt --> [hh:]mm:ss.ttt [cue settings]
  Text string
```

The `idstring` is an optional element but it is good idea to have it specified if we need to access the cue using a script. As for the `timestamp` we have a standard format where the hours are optional. The second `timestamp` must be greater than first one.

Text string is allowed to contain simple HTML formatting like <b>, <i>, and <u> elements. There is an option to add a <c> element that can be used for adding a CSS class for portions of the text, for example `<c.className>styled text </c>`. There is also an option to add a so called voice label `<v someLabel> the awesome text </v>`.

The cue settings are optional as well and are appended after the time range. In this setting we can pick whether the text is shown horizontally of vertically. The settings are case sensitive so they must be in lowercase as shown in the examples. The following settings can be applied:

▸ **vertical**: It is used with values `vertical:rl` where the `rl` stands for writing right to left and `vertical:lr` for left to right.

- ► **line**: This setting specifies where the text will be shown vertically or in the case where we have already used vertical, it specifies the horizontal position. The value is specified with percentage or a number where the positive value means top and negative bottom. For example, `line:0` and `line:0%` indicate top and `line:-1%` or `line:100%` indicate bottom.

- ► **position**: It is a setting that specifies where the text will be shown horizontally, or if we have vertical property set it specifies where the text is shown vertically. It should have value between 0 to 100 percent. For example, it can be `position:100%` meaning right.

- ► **size**: It specifies the width/height of the text area in percentage depending on the additional vertical setting. For example, `size:100%` means the text area will be shown.

- ► **align**: It is a property that sets the aligning of text within the space of the area defined by the size setting. It can have the following values `align:start`, `align:middle`, and `align:end`.

In the text string we can also add more detailed order of appearance of given words, in a sort of karaoke style. For example, see the following:

```
This is some karaoke style  <00:00:02.000>And more <00:00:03.000>
```

It states that before the 2 seconds we have some text and the active cue `And more` is between 2 to 3 seconds.

One other thing to note about the text string is that the it cannot contain the string `-->` string, ampersand `&` or the less than character `<` since they are reserved. But no worries there we can always used the escaped version, for example `&amp;` for ampersand.

These restrictions do not apply if we use the file for metadata track.

There's more...

We also have the option to style the text using CSS. As previously mentioned VTT files can contain tracks with `<c.someClass>` for a more fine-grained styling but in the general case we want to apply the style on the entire track. Applying style for all the cues can be done:

```
::cue  {
        color: black;
        text-transform: lowercase;
        font-family: "Comic Sans";
}
```

But you may alienate the users by making their subtitles in comic sans.

There are also selectors for the past cues `::cue:past{}` and `::cue:future{}` that can be useful for making a karaoke-like rendering. We also can use the `::cue(selector)` pseudo selector to target a node matching some criteria.

Not all of the feature are fully available in the modern browsers, most compliment at the time of writing is Chrome so for the others it is a good idea to use a polyfill. One such library is `http://captionatorjs.com/` that adds support to all the modern browsers. Besides adding support for the WebVTT it also supports formats like `.sub`, `.srt` and YouTube's `.sbv`.

There is also one other format that was developed for the video tracks. The name is **Timed Text Markup Language** (**TTML**) 1.0 `http://www.w3.org/TR/ttaf1-dfxp/` and it is only supported by IE without having any plans to get support in other browsers at the time of writing. The standard is more complex and it is based on XML but as such it is lot more verbose.

Embedding multimedia

Media element can cooperate and be combined with other elements. Various CSS properties can be applied to the elements and there are options to combine video with SVG. We can embed video in canvas element and apply processing on the rendered images.

In this recipe we will create a simple case where we embed a video inside canvas.

Getting ready

In this recipe we will need a video for our video element and an additional requirement is that the video has Cross-Origin Resource Sharing support or is located on our local server. The simplest way to make sure of this is to have a video with our locally running server.

> There are many videos with different formats available from NASA and ESA at `http://www.spacetelescope.org/videos/astro_bw/`.

How to do it...

We will render a video on a canvas element by performing following steps:

1. First start with the HTML file where we add a video element and a canvas:

```
<video id="myVideo" width="640" height="360" poster="poster.
png" controls preload>
    Video not supported
  <source src="video.mp4" type="video/mp4" />
</video>
  <canvas id="myCanvas" width="640" height="360"> </canvas>
  <button id="start">start showing canvas </button>
<script src="example.js"> </script>
```

2. Our example of JavaScript code will attach event handler that will start rendering a gray-scaled version of the video on a canvas element:

```javascript
(function () {
  var button = document.getElementById('start'),
      video = document.getElementById('myVideo'),
      canvas = document.getElementById('myCanvas');

  button.addEventListener("click", function() {
    console.log('started drawing video');
    drawVideo();
  },false);

  function drawVideo(){
   var context = canvas.getContext('2d');
   // 0,0 means to right corner
  context.drawImage(video, 0, 0);
   var pixels = context.getImageData(0,0,640,480);
   pixels = toGrayScale(pixels);
   context.putImageData(pixels,0,0);
   // re-draw
   setTimeout(drawVideo,10);
  }

  function toGrayScale(pixels) {
    var d = pixels.data;
    for (var i=0; i<d.length; i+=4) {
      var r = d[i],
          g = d[i+1],
          b = d[i+2],
          v = 0.2126*r + 0.7152*g + 0.0722*b;
      d[i] = d[i+1] = d[i+2] = v
    }
    return pixels;
  };
}())
```

We should have a running example. One additional note here is that our original video should be in color in order to notice the difference.

How it works...

The video element should be clear by this point as for the canvas, we will start with the restrictions. Drawing an image on canvas has a CORS restriction. This security constrain actually makes sense since we are reading data from the image and executing code depending on that. This could be exploited by some malicious source so for that reason the constraints are added.

Using the `canvas.getContext('2d')` we get a drawing context where we can draw the current image from our video element. Upon drawing the image we can modify the individual pixels. This gives us the option to create filters on our video.

For our example we create a simple grayscale filter. The filter function `toGrayScale` iterates over the pixel data and since every three values represent the color for a pixel in RGB, we read their data and create an adjusted value:

```
v = 0.2126*r + 0.7152*g + 0.0722*b;
```

Following this we apply the adjusted value to all of the three values. The magic number are picked so that they would compensate for the red and blue values since the average human eye is bad at seeing them. We could have used the average value of the three values here with similar results.

> If you are interested into other filters there is a great article on the subject on `http://www.html5rocks.com/en/tutorials/canvas/imagefilters/` where the filters apply on a image but the same rules apply on videos as well.

There's more...

One other interesting demo worth looking at is the Cube-like video player, `http://html5playbook.appspot.com/#Cube`, that uses variety of different ways to create cool effects.

If you are interested in processing and synthesizing audio in an HTML5 application there is a new high-level API at `http://www.w3.org/TR/webaudio/` that enables just that.

Converting text to speech using HTML5 audio

If we were to build a web-based navigation applications today, most of the components would already be available. There are Google maps or open street map components to display maps, as well as API services that provide driving directions.

But what about voice-based navigation guidance? Wouldn't that require another API service that converts text to speech?

Thanks to HTML5 audio and Emscripten (a C to JavaScript compiler), we can now use a free text-to-speech engine called espeak that works fully in the browser.

In this example we're going to use espeak to generate text entered by the user on a simple page. Most of the work will consist of preparations—we will need to set up `espeak.js`.

Getting ready

We need to download the speak.js from (`http://github.com/html5-ds-book/speak-js`). Click on the download zip button and download the archive to a newly created folder. Extract the archive in that folder—it should create a sub folder called `speak-js-master`.

How to do it...

Perform the following steps:

1. Create the page `index.html` containing a text input field and a `Speak` button:

```
<!doctype html>
<html>
  <head>
    <script src="http://ajax.googleapis.com/ajax/libs/
jquery/1.8.2/jquery.min.js"></script>
    <script src="speak-js-master/speakClient.js"></script>
    <script src="example.js"></script>
    <meta charset="utf8">
  </head>
  <body>
    <div id="audio"></div>
    <input type="text" id="text" value="" placeholder="Enter text
here">
    <button id="speak">Speak</button>
  </body>
</html>
```

2. Create `example.js` and add an on click action to the button:

```
$(function() {
    $("#speak").on('click', function(){
        speak($("#text").val());
    });
});
```

3. From the command line, install `http-server` if not already installed then start the server:

```
npm install -g http-server
http-server
```

4. Open `http://localhost:8080` in your browser and test the demo.

How it works...

The engine that converts the text to speech is eSpeak (`http://espeak.sourceforge.net/`). This engine is written in C, however, the only language natively supported by browsers is JavaScript. How can we use this engine in the browser?

Emscripten is a compiler designed to work around this limitation. It takes LLVM bytecode generated by a LLVM compiler from C or C++ source code and converts it to JavaScript. Emscripen utilizes a lot of modern JavaScript features such as typed arrays, and relies on the great performance of modern optimizing JavaScript JIT compilers.

To avoid blocking the browser, the speech generator is invoked from a web worker created in `speakClient.js`. The generated WAV data is passed back by the worker, converted to base64 encoding and passed as a data URL to a newly created audio element. This element in turn is appended to the #audio element on the page and playback is activated by calling the `play` method.

There's more..

Espeak is licensed under the GNU GPL v3 license. As such, it might not be suitable for proprietary projects.

More information about Emscripten can be found on the Emscripten wiki at `https://github.com/kripken/emscripten/wiki`.

A

Installing Node.js and Using npm

Introduction

Node.js is an event-driven platform built on top of V8, the JavaScript engine of Google Chrome. The platform implements fully non-blocking I/O for V8, and is mainly used for building real-time I/O-intensive web applications.

The Node.js installer provides the following two main components:

- ▶ the node binary, which can be used to run the JavaScript files written for the platform
- ▶ the node package manager **npm**, which can be used to install the node libraries and tools written by the node community

Installing Node.js

The Node.js installers and distributers can be found on its official website `http://nodejs.org/`. The installation procedure differs, depending on the operating system.

On Windows, two MSI based installers are provided at `http://nodejs.org/download/`, one for a 32-bit OS, and another for a 64-bit. To install Node.js on Windows, simply download and execute the installer.

For Mac OS X, a `pkg` installer is available at the same location; downloading and running the PKG file will allow you to install Node.js with the Apple installer.

On Linux, the installation procedure depends on the distribution. Instructions for many popular distributions are available on the node wiki at `https://github.com/joyent/node/wiki/Installing-Node.js-via-package-manager`.

Using npm

The node package manager npm comes with the Node.js installer. npm is used for the command line; to use it, we will need to run a terminal program (a command prompt).

On Windows, we can use the basic `cmd.exe`, or alternatively, we can download and install Console from `http://sourceforge.net/projects/console/`.

On Mac OS X, `Terminal.app` can be used to run commands.

On Linux, use your favorite terminal. The default on Ubuntu Linux is the gnome terminal.

Open the terminal and type: `npm`. This command runs npm without any parameters. As a result, npm will print a general usage overview listing the available subcommands.

Installing a local package

Let's create an empty directory for our project named `test`, navigate to that directory, and install the `underscore` library there, using npm. Run the following commands:

```
mkdir test
```

```
cd test
```

```
npm install underscore
```

The last command will tell npm to run the `install` subcommand with the argument `underscore`, which in turn will install the package underscore locally. npm will output some progress information as it downloads and installs the package.

When installing a package locally, npm creates a subdirectory in the current directory named `node_modules`. Inside that directory, it creates another directory for the installed package. In this case, the underscore package will be placed inside the `underscore` directory.

Installing a global package

Some npm packages are designed to be installed globally. Global packages add new functionality to the operating system. For example, the coffee-script package can be installed globally, which will cause the command `coffee` to become available on our system.

To install global packages we use the -g switch. Have a look at the following example:

```
npm install -g coffee-script
```

On some systems it's necessary to request the administrative privilege to run this program. You can do that by using the `sudo` command:

```
sudo npm install -g coffee-script
```

npm will download and install coffee-script along with all its dependencies. After the process is complete, we can start using the command `coffee`, which is now available on our system. We can now run coffee-script code. Lets say we want to run a simple hello-world script written in-line; we can use the `-e` switch for that. Have a look at the following example:

```
coffee -e "echo 'Hello world'"
```

To learn more in the global package about npm subcommands, we can use npm's help subcommand. For example, to learn more about the `install` subcommand, run the following command:

```
npm help install
```

More information about the latest version of npm can be found on the official npm documentation at `https://npmjs.org/doc/`.

B
Community and Resources

WHATWG

In 2004, the WHAT Working Group was formed with members from Mozilla, Apple, and Opera. The more commonly used name **WHATWG** stands for Web Hypertext Application Technology Working Group. The groups main goal was to enable the evolution and development of HTML. Slow development of HTML by **W3C** was also a reason for the group formation.

The focus of the group is the HTML standard, which also includes web storage, web sockets, web workers, and server-side events. There were other standards as well that were developed and discussed in the past. The editor of the specification is Ian "Hixie" Hickson (`http://www.hixie.ch/`).

We often referred to the WHATWG specification throughout the book, and it is the most up-to-date document, because it is a living standard. This means that the standard is continuously updated as requests for change arrive from the community. On the other hand, the specification does not simply break in backwards-incompatible ways.

More on the organization can be found from `http://www.whatwg.org/`.

There is also a developer oriented specification available at `http://developers.whatwg.org/`.

World Wide Web Consortium

This organization also known as W3C is the main international web standards producer. It was founded in 1994, and lead by Tim Berners-Lee, having a full-time staff that works and coordinates the various specifications.

The consortium is governed by its members, `http://www.w3.org/Consortium/Member/List`, including non-profit organizations, companies, as well as individuals. You must be a member to access this site. Anyone can become a member as long as his/her application is approved by W3C. Additionally, each member pays fee adjusted for the country's income.

There has been some criticism regarding the membership base, because it is mostly composed of companies, who can afford to pay and spend considerable amount of money on meetings and travel.

In 2006, W3C announced that it will work with WHATWG and stop developing the XHTML standard that never fully took-off. Currently, the two groups have different goals. WHATWG is more focused in what browsers should aim for, on the other hand, W3C has specific snapshots of the living standard making them diverge. Hixie, the editor of WHATWG, sends the feedback to both the groups. For more information on how the two specifications differ see the following URL:

`http://www.whatwg.org/specs/web-apps/current-work/multipage/introduction.html#how-do-the-whatwg-and-w3c-specifications-differ?`.

And the official website for W3C is `http://www.w3.org/`.

Other resources

Mozilla Developer Network (MDN), `http://developer.mozilla.org`) provides a large amount of data regarding web development. There are topics such as HTML, JavaScript, CSS, DOM, AJAX, SVG, WebGL, and plenty more. Some of the information may be Firefox specific but most of them are not. Kuma, the platform that powers MDN is available on GitHub, `https://github.com/mozilla/kuma`. Besides that there are many other ways to contribute towards the improvement of the documentation, see more on `https://developer.mozilla.org/en-US/docs/Project:About#About_MDN`. At the time of writing, MDN is the most comprehensive and the simplest documentation for everyday web development.

HTML5 rocks (`http://www.html5rocks.com`) is a great resource for tutorials and articles. The project is run by Google and most of the Chrome team, but there are many other nongooglers joining in. Some of the tutorials are using a lot of Chrome specifics, but they are still one of the best articles out there. The project is available as GitHub repository on `https://github.com/html5rocks`.

Dive into HTML5 (`http://diveintohtml5.info/`) by Mark Pilgrim is one of the cult books that is funny and provides great starting point.

HTML5 test (`http://html5test.com/`) gives a score of your browser, and offers comparison between different major browsers.

More detailed information on support across browsers is available on quirks mode `http://www.quirksmode.org/compatibility.html`.

Index

L

label attribute 439
label property 57
latin-name value 141
latin-prose value 142
latin value 141
layouts
  using, in Jade 339-343
Leaflet library 151
LED scoreboard
  creating, web fonts used 88-93
line chart
  about 50
  creating 50-52
line setting 440
lines property 60
liszt:updated event 190
local storage
  about 393-397
  limits 414-417
loop attribute 426
lowerBound method 413

M

map
  marked location, showing 69,70
  used, for geographic location
      input 192-194, 197
  with path, displaying 71-73
Markdown
  about 44
  rendering 44, 45
Math
  displaying 24-27
Mathematical Markup Language. *See*
      MathML
MathML 25
media elements controls
  customizing 431-434
  working 435
mediagroup attribute 426
mediatype attribute 392
Mercator projection 128
Meteor.js
  application, structuring 364-367
  live HTML 374-380

reactive programming 368-373
  security mechanisms 381-387
  user-specific data 374-380
metric measurements
  displaying 12-19
minLength attribute 183
mixins
  using, in Jade 336-339
Moment.js 22
motion chart
  creating 96-100
move() function 127, 128
move() method 126
Mozilla Developer Network (MDN) 452
multimedia
  embedding 441-443
multiple-choice filters
  creating 36, 37
  working 38
multiple-choice select lists
  using 149-151
multiple selection list
  creating 190-192
muted attribute 426

N

ng attributes 348
Node.js
  installing 447
  used, for creating SSL connection 293-296
Nominatim 193
npm
  about 447
  global package, installing 448, 449
  local package, installing 448
  using 448
Number.prototype.toFixed() function 9
numbers
  padding 10-12
  rounding 8-10
  validating, by range 205-207
numeric value 142

O

object
  rendering, EJS used 312-314

[PACKT]
PUBLISHING

Thank you for buying
HTML5 Data and Service Cookbook

About Packt Publishing

Packt, pronounced 'packed', published its first book "*Mastering phpMyAdmin for Effective MySQL Management*" in April 2004 and subsequently continued to specialize in publishing highly focused books on specific technologies and solutions.

Our books and publications share the experiences of your fellow IT professionals in adapting and customizing today's systems, applications, and frameworks. Our solution based books give you the knowledge and power to customize the software and technologies you're using to get the job done. Packt books are more specific and less general than the IT books you have seen in the past. Our unique business model allows us to bring you more focused information, giving you more of what you need to know, and less of what you don't.

Packt is a modern, yet unique publishing company, which focuses on producing quality, cutting-edge books for communities of developers, administrators, and newbies alike. For more information, please visit our website: www.packtpub.com.

Writing for Packt

We welcome all inquiries from people who are interested in authoring. Book proposals should be sent to author@packtpub.com. If your book idea is still at an early stage and you would like to discuss it first before writing a formal book proposal, contact us; one of our commissioning editors will get in touch with you.

We're not just looking for published authors; if you have strong technical skills but no writing experience, our experienced editors can help you develop a writing career, or simply get some additional reward for your expertise.

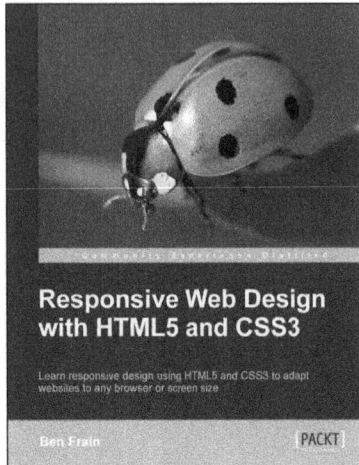

Responsive Web Design with HTML5 and CSS3

ISBN: 978-1-84969-318-9   Paperback: 324 pages

Learn responsive design using HTML5 and CSS3 to adapt websites to any browser or screen size

1. Everything needed to code websites in HTML5 and CSS3 that are responsive to every device or screen size

2. Learn the main new features of HTML5 and use CSS3's stunning new capabilities including animations, transitions and transformations

3. Real world examples show how to progressively enhance a responsive design while providing fall backs for older browsers

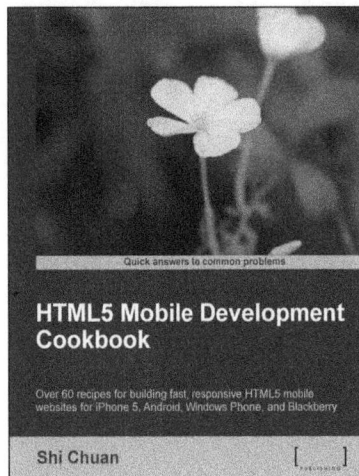

HTML5 Mobile Development Cookbook

ISBN: 978-1-84969-196-3   Paperback: 254 pages

Over 60 recipes for building fast, responsive HTML5 mobile websites for iPhone 5, Android, Windows Phone, and Blackberry

1. Solve your cross platform development issues by implementing device and content adaptation recipes

2. Maximum action, minimum theory allowing you to dive straight into HTML5 mobile web development

3. Incorporate HTML5-rich media and geo-location into your mobile websites

Please check **www.PacktPub.com** for information on our titles

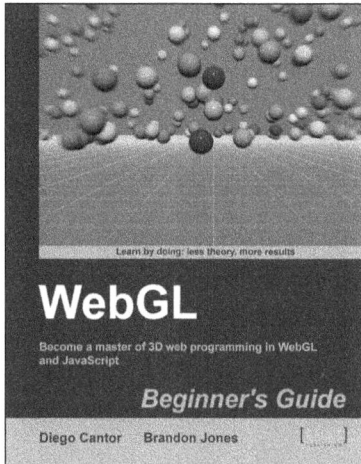

WebGL Beginner's Guide

ISBN: 978-1-84969-172-7   Paperback: 376 pages

Become a member of 3D web programming in WebGL and JavaScript

1. Dive headfirst into 3D web application development using WebGL and JavaScript.

2. Each chapter is loaded with code examples and exercises that allow the reader to quickly learn the various concepts associated with 3D web development

3. The only software that the reader needs to run the examples is an HTML5 enabled modern web browser. No additional tools needed.

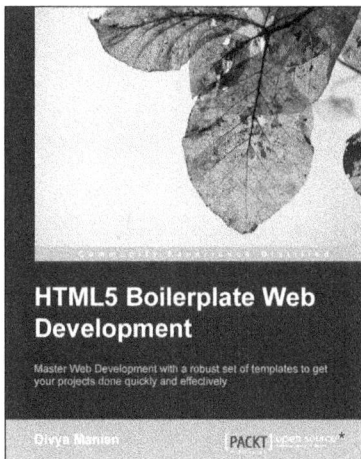

HTML5 Boilerplate Web Development

ISBN: 978-1-84951-850-5   Paperback: 174 pages

Master Web Development with a robust set of templates to get your projects done quickly and effectively

1. Master HTML5 Boilerplate as starting templates for future projects

2. Learn how to optimize your workflow with HTML5 Boilerplate templates and set up servers optimized for performance

3. Learn to feature-detect and serve appropriate styles and scripts across browser types

Please check **www.PacktPub.com** for information on our titles